Not So Easy, Lads

Wearing the Red Coat 1786–1797

Vivien Roworth

Helion & Company

Honouring
Mary Osborn Roworth Dolman
Emma Roworth Wood
Mary Jordinson Roworth

For my own particular company: Don, Gavin, Mark and Ben

Helion & Company Limited
Unit 8 Amherst Business Centre
Budbrooke Road
Warwick
CV34 5WE
England
Tel. 01926 499619
Email: info@helion.co.uk
Website: www.helion.co.uk
Twitter: @helionbooks
Visit our blog at http://blog.helion.co.uk/

Published by Helion & Company 2023
Designed and typeset by Mach 3 Solutions (www.mach3solutions.co.uk)
Cover designed by Paul Hewitt, Battlefield Design (www.battlefield-design.co.uk)

Text © Vivien Roworth 2023
Cover: Serjeant Major William Roworth, 44th Foot, ca 1795, by Alix Baker (Author's Collection) Background, engraving after Langendyck; retreating army moving through winter landscape (Anne S.K. Brown Military Collection)
Illustrations © as individually credited
Maps by George Anderson © Helion & Company 2023 unless otherwise credited

Every reasonable effort has been made to trace copyright holders and to obtain their permission for the use of copyright material. The author and publisher apologise for any errors or omissions in this work, and would be grateful if notified of any corrections that should be incorporated in future reprints or editions of this book.

ISBN 978-1-915113-86-3

British Library Cataloguing-in-Publication Data.
A catalogue record for this book is available from the British Library.

All rights reserved. No part of this publication may be reproduced, stored in a retrieval system, or transmitted, in any form, or by any means, electronic, mechanical, photocopying, recording or otherwise, without the express written consent of Helion & Company Limited.

For details of other military history titles published by Helion & Company Limited, contact the above address, or visit our website: http://www.helion.co.uk

We always welcome receiving book proposals from prospective authors.

Contents

Preface		iv
Acknowledgements		ix
1	Going For a Soldier: Filling up the Holes	11
2	Men, Miscreants and Marriage: The Military Mindset	36
3	Smallpox to Smuggling: Leeds to the Isle of Man	57
4	The Land of the Irish: Home of Hostilities	73
5	Laxity, Lawlessness and Loathing: Allies or Enemies?	94
6	The Battle of Boxtel: 14–15 September 1794	109
7	Indeed a Hostile Shore: Sint Andries and Nijmegen	117
8	Winter Retreat: 1794–1795	135
9	From Bremen to Nursling	148
10	Tragedy in the Channel: Like Nothing in the World	165
11	Attacking the Atlantic: It Makes My Blood Run Cold	180
12	Late Arrivals: The Waiting Game	191
13	St Lucie: La Fidèle	199
14	Brigands and Bushfighters: April 1796	210
15	The Taking of Morne Fortuné: Thank God for the 27th!	226
16	Governor and Guerrillas: The Reluctant Ruler June 1796 – July 1797	233
17	Yellow Jack: One Has Not a Man Fit for Duty	248
18	Redcoats All: Resolution and Reckoning – The Regiments and the Men	259
19	Those Who Remained: The Long View	271
Bibliography		278

Preface

When considering the British soldier of the last three and a half centuries, perhaps the image which comes to mind is his bright red coat. For the British public, at least, there must be very few who are not familiar with it, still in use today as a showcase on days of pomp and parade. In fact, watching the occasional scarlet-faced soldier faint in the ceremonial ranks of royal occasions on a hot summer's day (his famous bearskin contributing to the overheating but conveniently taking most of the damage to his head) brings to mind the difficulties of other days, not so very far in the past when the British soldier's duty was to fight, in that famous red coat, often at intense extremes of temperature. The red coat was all that was between him and a tropical furnace or death by exposure in the depths of winter. In neither case did it answer the need, but both of these parameters are to be met with here, in the military experience of a young soldier in the British Army of King George III.

William Roworth spent barely 11 years in the service of his king and country, yet the events in which he was involved open a window on the particular services it was his lot to experience, together with the officers and men of his regiment, the 44th (East Essex) Regiment of Foot. The exigencies of Roworth's daily life were the same for thousands, during that specific period of British Army history when 'the scum of the earth' were famously supposed to fill its ranks and indeed a fair few probably did. Roworth highlights events on his own journey for all those, of whatever rank or status, who were wearing the 'red coat', the sight of which by the populace might, according to circumstances, cause in turn relief and delight, or fear and hatred. Yet there they all were, mostly by choice, so what affected one to some extent affected them all simultaneously because of, or in spite of, the notoriety and symbolism of that bright red cloth, which had its last combat outing on 30 December 1885, when British troops fought Sudanese rebels.

Roworth shed light on his own service to the King through letters written home to his wife, Mary, over a period of just two and a half years, when he served in two very different and difficult arenas abroad. However, research into his life in the British Army as a whole, conveniently divides into four distinct stages, the first of which covers his experience from enlisting in 1786 to his first duties abroad; the second, his service in the Low Countries and his return to England; the third, the months leading up to and including the voyage to the West Indies to retake St Lucia; and finally, service under the command of Sir Ralph Abercromby and Sir John Moore, leading to Roworth's own death from yellow fever in 1797 aged 32.

His letters were intended only for his wife's eyes, but the fact that they were kept by his family for some 150 years before being placed for safe keeping in Nottinghamshire Archives must have pointed towards some presumed value of their content. William Roworth wrote in some detail about the thoughts, feelings and difficulties which must have plagued all but the hardiest young men. His words provide a route map through a life shared by his fellow soldiers, both rank and file and officers, and open up other vistas which have brought further insights into that particularly malign term 'the scum of the earth', which has exercised minds ever since it was written.[1] Although we follow the route map of Roworth's service, this book is essentially about soldiers as individual men, comrades and participants, how the army treated them and how they treated the army, warts and all. Soldiers were then, as they are today, quite capable of upsetting the military apple-cart and giving their officers the mother of all migraines. Soldiers do not live in a vacuum, but they do live in specialist territory. In the eighteenth century their close community was ruled with the uncertain weathervane of the War Office, the meddling fingers of politicians, the qualities of the Commander-in-Chief and the vagaries of their own military hierarchy. For reasons discussed within these pages, public perception of the military swung between revulsion and adulation or – depending on circumstances – from saviours to villains.

It is hoped that Roworth's experiences add a little more light and shade to the last decade of the eighteenth century. No doubt there are still some soldier memoirs and letters left to come to light, but they are becoming fewer and all are equally as precious as those which went before, however small the enlightenment they have to offer.

In the text, the reader will find that some terms or ranks are retained in the spellings of the time so that when Roworth received his step up from corporal, he became a serjeant, not a modern sergeant. This spelling has been retained as it was correct for the time; therefore, it is the spelling he used and recognised. Roworth's name is as he spelled it, not as it was often spelled in the muster rolls with an 'a' in the second syllable. Apart from Roworth's consistency when spelling his own name, the rest of his spelling could be somewhat haphazard and bizarre, as was often typical of the time, so it has been tidied up for reasons of fluency (and to prevent reader hysteria when encountering a word or two which now have quite different meanings). The grammar has been virtually untouched and the erratic capital letters remain. Both leave a flavour of his own life and times.

There are certain military personalities and events Roworth comments upon very little or not at all, but because these men were known to him, however peripherally, they are included. Their decisions and opinions are important to the stage upon which they all played. As Roworth learned,

---

1   See, Dr Zack White, 'Did the Duke of Wellington really call his troops the "scum of the Earth"?', *History Extra*, <https://www.historyextra.com/period/georgian/did-the-duke-of-wellington-really-call-his-troops-the-scum-of-the-earth/>, accessed July 2023.

major players on his personal stage would often come hand-in-hand with major repercussions – to family life included.

I make no apologies for relying heavily on a number of books for source material, in particular, for trawling Edwina Boult's indisputably excellent and major work *Christian's Fleet* for the harrowing details of the storms in the Channel in November 1795 and their subsequent consequences to both navy and army. I rely heavily on books which could almost be called 'the collected Diaries of Sir John Moore', viz., those edited by Major General Sir J.F. Maurice, James Carrick Moore, Beatrice Lady Brownrigg and Henry Hegart Breen. All form the bedrock of information mined from within their pages (Maurice more than the others), not least to throw some light on the thinking, the actions and their consequences, of Sir John Moore himself. He is frequently to be found marching across the hot and topographically challenging West Indian stage, because that is what he did (for good or ill) to himself or to those around him. For the subject of the nursery rhyme 'The Grand Old Duke of York' substitute Sir John Moore. In St Lucia he made life very difficult for many of his men who apparently did likewise in his personal estimation (as will be seen), albeit that they were virtually dropping dead at his feet. For all other things military, there are the memoirs, diaries, letters and narratives of young redcoats who recorded their own stories, reasoning and feelings, both good and bad, before and during 'Pitt's Reign of Alarm, the 1790s', as Kenneth Johnston referred to that decade.[2] Also, many books of considered comment and opinion have enabled me to delve into lives and times more thoroughly (including the all-important social history), while those muster rolls and monthly returns, some of which (on first sight) have had battles of their own, have been – of their nature – invaluable. There is little written record of the duties of the 44th Regiment at this time, so that the descriptions available from other brother regiments must sometimes serve as a blanket for all.

No apologies are made for mining contemporary newspapers, both national and local. The latter are particularly helpful for dates, comment and for following the minutiae of the military set out for local consumption. On a larger scale, it was a practice at the time to publicly print the letters of army officers, campaign bulletins and particularly official eyewitness statements to keep the populace informed and to fill column inches, even to the doings of the king's messengers. What was news then, can add to our enjoyment as well as our enlightenment now.

The appellation of the various regiments' titles is not held rigidly. For example, the full name of the 44th (East Essex) Regiment of Foot, acquired in 1782, is obviously cumbersome yet in times of solemnity or importance may be referred to as such; 'regiment' itself is the oldest of these terms, meaning to organise or excessively control; to differentiate those on horseback from those on foot, the latter were first known as infantry, which was changed to 'Foot' in the mid-eighteenth century until 1882; the number of the regiment (44th) is often used more colloquially as the soldiers would have used it to

---

2   K.R. Johnson, *Unusual Suspects; Pitt's Reign of Alarm and the Lost Generation of the 1790s* (Oxford: Oxford University Press, 2013).

discriminate one from another; the county name (East Essex), is used less often, again for more formal discriminatory purposes. In this book, the regiments are introduced by their full title and thereafter, by the number, occasionally to be followed by 'Foot' 'Rifles' 'Hussars' 'Dragoons', etc., again to recognise a distinction.

The joys of reading the words of people long gone are immense, and who could possibly dare to paraphrase or alter much of the original? We were not there – we do not know – we did not see. Therefore, you will find that (where appropriate) the actual words from the past, spoken or written, will be there to savour – just occasionally at length. We can listen to the voices in their own accents – after all, received pronunciation was only adopted around 1869. Personally, I find much delight is to be had absorbing the language of contemporary documents, which become not only a window of their time, but by 'listening' to the spelling, can give clues to the actual dialect. My prime example here is Roworth's own reference to a man he calls John Mortial. No John Mortial to be found. Possibly Roworth had not seen the word written down. But it is no great jump to get to the word 'martial' – he was likely to have seen the spelling of that. Bullseye! We have the name John Marshall who, although only mentioned once, was an acquaintance of Roworth at home and to whom he wished to be remembered. That spelling also provides a clue as to William's accent when he changes the 'ar sound' into 'or'. It may be useful to know here that he was a Cheshire man, born and bred, who often spelled his written words as he pronounced them. Dialect speakers in Cheshire dropped their aitches, and so Roworth spelled and spoke his 'ertford, 'ereford and 'ampshire. The spelling of place names has proved somewhat illusory too. At the time there were often multiple spellings, e.g., was it Nimegen, Nijmegen, Nimeguen or Nimmegen? I have used Nijmegen. With Sint Andries, the name was different with each allied language, thus St Andrew, St André, Sint Andries, etc., but here it remains with the Dutch spelling.

Considerable emphasis has been placed on the third section, most of which was played out on salt water. It was not just the navy nor the seamen on transports who endured the horrendous and extended voyage to the West Indies, but the thousands of soldiers who suffered with them. Many of the troops were trapped on the transports from mid-October 1795 until the last week of April 1796, not only on ships that moved at the slightest encouragement but with the men living cheek by jowl like sardines. The voyage was where much of Roworth's distress and difficulties were played out in his letters. As a serjeant major, he had more responsibilities to the regiment, but as a man he shared the same fears, distress and illness as the rest of the redcoats.

Finally, on to the disaster area that was to be the island of St Lucia, with its own unique discomforts and dangers. There have been multiple tales of disease in the Windward and Leeward Islands. The period covered here was to be one of the worst. Rumour and tales of the devastation of life were undeniable while the forests of St Lucia held the unseen but often very effective enemy. As with the war in Flanders, the result of the investment boiled down to numbers.

For all those soldiers of the 44th, 27th, 31st, 48th and the 55th Regiments doing their duty in Flanders and the West Indies, life would never be the same, so march in their shoes for the duration while British soldiers were laid waste – yet again.

There is an ancient Chinese curse: May you live in interesting times. For many thousands of redcoats, these were to be their 'interesting times'. The curse prevailed.

Acknowledgements

Historians, both professional and amateur, have been unstinting in sharing their expertise, enthusiasm and knowledge, all of which has enabled me to write this book. My enduring thanks go to all of the following for their input, great or small.

Archives, Museums and Universities

Ayrshire Archives; Black Watch Museum and Archives; Cork Archives; Durham University; East Essex Regiment Museum, Chelmsford; Exeter Cathedral; Ilfracombe Museum; National Army Museum; Inniskilling Museum; Manx National Heritage; National Archives Ireland; National Library, Scotland; National Library, Ireland; National Portrait Gallery; Northampton Record Office; Nottingham Archives; Nottingham University Library; The National Archives, Kew; Wellcome Collection, London.

England

Alix Baker; Mark Adkins; Reginald Beer; Paul Blake; Edwina Boult; Geoff Buchan; Mandy Caine; Sheila Cawes; Sarah Christian; Alan Crewe; Len Davenport; Carole Divall; David Druett; Sophie Dupre; Rachel Farrand; Charles Foster; Simon Fowler; Gwyneth Gale; Gary Hepburn; Ian Hook; Robert Jarvis; Ellie Jones; Claire Keane; Robert Latter; Laura Latter; Elizabeth Lawton; Annie Makepeace; Alastair Massie; Margaret Maun; Lyn McCulloch; Sylvia Milne; Judith Mitchell; Judith Moore; Keith Oseman; Claire Parvin; Sue Rimmington; Joseph. T. Robinson; Martin Rogers; N.A.M Rodger; Ian Ross; John Spencer; Paul Ternent; Ben Townsend; Tania West; Michael Yates.

Scotland

Sally Harrower; Tommy Smyth.

Ireland

Larry Breen; William Fraher; Brian McGee; the late Gregory O'Connor; Kim Smyth; Claire Stack; Julian Walton.

Isle of Man

Frances Coakley; Alison Crellin; John Christian; Jo Davies; Charles Guard; Mike Hoy; Sue Nicols; Jennie Richardson; Matthew Richardson; Martin Shimmin; Jane Subachus; Paul Weatherall; the late Major Charles Wilson; Lady Eva Wilson; Derek Winterbottom.

Europe

Paul Cretier; Hilde Laenen; Rainer Rauhut.

St Lucia

Roger Graveson; Beverley Lansiquot; Catherine Octave-Isaac; Deidre and Gregor Williams - my St Lucian mentors and supporters.

Especial thanks to: Garry David Wills for clarifying Roworth's own battle of Boxtel for me and to my illustrators Alix Baker and Jo Davies, for applying their own particular skills to *Not So Easy, Lads*. Thank you to all at Helion for their ministrations and particularly to Andrew Bamford who has given me the opportunity to add William Roworth's words, as an eighteenth-century soldier, to the ever-expanding military story; finally, thanks go to Rob Griffith, my patient answerer of all questions, however trivial or imbecilic, for his long-suffering kindness and for teaching me 'what not to do'.

My loving thanks to my supportive and encouraging sons, Gavin, Mark and Ben for keeping my nose to the proverbial grindstone and cheering me on from the wings – constantly. Finally, a huge debt of gratitude to my husband, Don, for his many hours of proof-reading, picture enabling and photography (also general household factotum) at all stages of incubation of this particular 'baby' which has taken some 40-odd years finally to hatch. Thank you all.

1

Going For a Soldier: Filling up the Holes

Until the two world wars of the twentieth century, history had rarely been kind to the British soldier. Indeed, the second half of the long eighteenth century was said to be one of the lowest periods in his history due to the incompetence of officers and poor calibre of the rank and file. With the signing of the Treaty of Paris in 1763, an end was brought to the Seven Years War in Europe and America and to the Third Carnatic War in India. Once victory in its multiple wars had been claimed or surrendered by the British government, its ministers, who played a major part in military decisions, appear to have relapsed into their usual myopic state regarding the condition of their army. Standing armies were never popular in Britain, often looked upon as dangerous, with successive governments preferring to remove any possibility of insurrection from their military. The fewer potential rebels, the better. The populace did not approve of a standing army either, regarding them as too many men with too little to do – and that spelt trouble.

Right up to and including the present day, successive policies by the British Government appear to have focused on cutting back on their spending after military conflict. This included paring down their forces to the minimum and leaving only a small standing army to deal with primarily internal conflicts or peace-keeping duties abroad. At the first sniff of war, the initiators (or the inheritors) of this ill-thought-out practice were induced to make a smart about-face. This provided an immediate impetus to the collective mind of the eighteenth-century military and its government, viz., the insatiable demand to provide fighting men at almost a moment's notice.

The Royal Navy was forever propped up by its somewhat pernicious and archaic, though relatively effective system of pressing potential sailors (a form of legal kidnapping). The key to supplying deficiencies in Britain's army was by way of three even less reliable routes – volunteering, recruitment, and enlistment – each one dependent on the other two.

In fact, the British Army had always been made up of volunteers. It would remain so until the two world wars of the twentieth century when necessity persuaded the government finally to succumb to conscription, previously only dabbled with a couple of times in earlier centuries. At the end of the second decade of the twenty-first century, some countries, albeit in the minority – for example Russia, Israel, and Egypt – continue conscription to fill their massive standing armies. North Korea conscripts every able man for 10 years' service and every able woman for seven. It is still the case that the British Army continues to rely on volunteers for the strength of its fighting force.

But, in eighteenth-century Britain, at the first sign of war, the pressure was on the regiments to attract likely volunteers to sign up and enlist into the army's man-hungry ranks. Although the army serjeant, with his recruiting party, could recruit all he liked, he would return to barracks empty-handed unless young men stepped up and volunteered their lives for king and country. In fact, there were as many reasons for young men to volunteer in the British Army as there were soldiers. We learn of those from that significant minority of non-commissioned officers and private men who put pen to paper to record their various experiences.

After the end of the Napoleonic Wars, when more people could read and write (at least, more than in previous centuries) and had access to a modicum of education, there was a flurry of military publications under an umbrella of different guises. These were unveiled for the greedy appetite of the general public (which was no different then than now) and were lapped up through accounts of expedition and battle – the 'why' and the 'how' equally as important to their readers as the 'where' and the 'who'. There was also a genuine interest in the workings of the army by a public whose perceptions could be clouded by previous experience of the military. These insights were, perhaps, a response to the wickedly perceptive and satirical military cartoons of Gillray and Rowlandson; or a close and personal encounter with a drunken soldier on the city streets; or the billeting of soldiers who ate and drank the (often struggling) household dry, or even learned the hard way as a food-hungry rioter facing a soldier with a Brown Bess in his hands.

To explore the reasons, even attractions, of 'going for a soldier' in the eighteenth century requires a brief look at the three sides of a kind of military triangle – volunteering, recruiting and enlisting – through the eyes of young men who, for their own personal reasons, gave up their freedom as members of their community voluntarily. One day they might have been apprentices, labourers, shoemakers or servants and the next found themselves in barracks, gazing down at the amazing scarlet coats upon their persons.

Perhaps the easiest way to accomplish this is to take a look at the accounts of those men who recorded the happenings, the personal milestones, the past they had left behind them, bearing in mind that they were just a very few of the many thousands of men who left no trace of their military lives at all – except for a name on a muster roll. To those few we owe a great deal. Yet because they are so few, they cannot be taken as statistically significant, but their accounts provide some insight and can even provoke empathy from the observer. A very similar analysis may be found in David Clammer's, 'A Disposition to Wander: Reasons for Enlisting in the British Army during the Napoleonic Wars'.[1]

---

1   David Clammer, 'A Disposition to Wander: Reasons for Enlisting in the British Army during the Napoleonic Wars', *Journal of the Society for Army Historical Research*, vol.100, Summer 2022, pp.98–106.

By the end of the first two decades of the nineteenth century, the trickle of accounts, journals and diaries had turned into a minor flood, arguably starting with a not-so-impartial *Impartial Journal* published by Corporal Robert Brown of the 2nd Foot Guards, the Coldstream Guards. It was published in 1795, at the end of the War of the First Coalition on the Continent against revolutionary France. Brown had already been promoted through the ranks to serjeant, but had been demoted to private (for reasons unknown) and was working his way back up again, which he did successfully. His powers of observation, description and comment set the imagination of the collective public alight. So much so that after the world-defining Battle of Waterloo in 1815, memoirs and journals, diaries and narratives of both commissioned and non-commissioned officers, rank and file, from those who survived and had a tale to tell (and who did not?), began to fill the shelves of those avid readers who could afford them. It was from these that individual reasons for volunteering and enlisting were caught in the varied voices of men whose allegiance was to king and country.

So why volunteer in the first place? Of the 40 or so accounts considered here, the largest group constituted discontented and restless spirits, from whom there were 12 accounts. For some it had been quite a journey of body and mind to reach even the point of decision. One, John Green, a Nottingham lad born in 1790, was apprenticed aged 13 to a carpet manufacturer from whom he walked away after three years (of his seven-year apprenticeship), joining the privateer *Anne* for three months. Next, a walk of nearly 200 miles from Elkington in Lincolnshire, via the scenic route, touching Horncastle, Lincoln, and Doncaster to Leeds, where followed two more fleeting (and failed) attempts at carpet-making. By this time, 'bent on being a soldier', he enlisted in the 68th (Durham) Regiment of Foot on 24 October 1806.[2] Army life suited him very well until he was wounded in Portugal with a ball lodged near his heart. He made it back to Britain and was discharged with a pension at the Royal Hospital, Kilmainham, on 31 December 1814, thereby missing, arguably, the most famous land battle of them all.

An anonymous soldier of the 68th who volunteered in April 1758, declared himself to be 'of a rambling disposition' in his journal.[3] As did William Green, a serjeant of the 95th Rifles, while Benjamin Miller, another serjeant, 4th Battalion of the Royal Regiment of Artillery, was of a 'roving disposition'.[4] John Stevenson of the 3rd (Scots) Guards successfully walked out of his building apprenticeship after four years (never to return) and volunteered on 3 June 1793.[5] Of the seven remaining discontented young

---

2 John Green, *Vicissitudes of a Soldier's Life. Or, a Series of Occurrences From 1806 to 1815* (Louth: Jackson, 1827), pp.1–11.

3 Anon., *A soldier's journal, containing a particular description of the several descents on the coast of France last war; with an entertaining account of the islands of Guadeloupe, Dominique and also the isles of Wight and Jersey* (London: E. and C. Dilley, 1770), p.2.

4 Benjamin Miller, *The Adventures of Serjeant Benjamin Miller Whilst Serving in the 4th Battalion of the Royal Regiment of Artillery 1796–1815* (Uckfield: Naval & Military Press, 2009), p.4.

5 Gareth Glover (ed.), *The Third (Scots) Guards in Time of War: The Memoirs of Sergeant John Stevenson, 1793–1814* (Huntingdon: Ken Trotman Books, 2019), p.7.

men, James Hale volunteered into the Royal North Gloucestershire Militia, enlisting on 4 August 1803, five years after the militia had been put on a formal footing and men were balloted for duty in the home service. Hale spent four years on duty at various barracks and camps. He kept his journal so religiously that every march was documented in exact detail of place and time, for example, the following, one of many:

> On the 1st of April [1807], we commenced our route, and marched to Wells; the 2d, to Somerton; the 3d, we halted; the 4th, to Taunton; the 5th, we halted, being Sunday, and attended divine service; the 6th to Tiverton; the 7th, to Crediton; the 8th, to Oakhampton [sic]; the 9th we halted; the 10th to Tavistock; and the 11th, to Plymouth, and took up our quarters in Stonehouse Barracks … I was then got quite tired of rambling about England … I volunteered my service on 23 August, 1807, to serve seven years in his Majesty's 9th or Britannia Regiment of Foot.[6]

As a member of the militia, Hale was an example of the use the government made of their partial mobilisation of the British home force – get them in and hope they like it enough to volunteer for the regular army. He had received five guineas for joining the militia and then 10 guineas for transferring to the regulars.

In Manchester, 22-year-old William Roworth volunteered on 2 February 1786 into the 44th (East Essex) Regiment of Foot.[7] His were somewhat unusual circumstances. William Roworth Senior worked in the household of minor aristocracy – that of the Honourable Booth Grey, MP for Leicester and the second son of the Earl of Stamford. It is not known if William followed his father, as there is no written evidence in his letters, but as the eldest son, he might well have been persuaded to start out as a servant. Or perchance his literacy may have influenced him.

Perhaps surprisingly for the time, four young men quoted their avid obsession with reading as the spur to their reasons to volunteer. John Spencer Cooper, 7th Fusiliers, read of wars and battles; Joseph Donaldson, 94th Foot, was a very early reader, as was an anonymous soldier of the 92nd Gordon Highlanders, who 'pretty early learned to read … I became exceedingly fond of it, even indeed to excess'.[8] William Brown, 45th Foot, was particularly florid regarding the part reading played in his decision to volunteer:

> With them I was truly delighted, and fondly anticipated that the time would come, when, instead of reading of foreign countries, I would see for myself the various empires, kingdoms and states of which the world was composed, with the diversity of man and manners in each. Thus were false and fatal ideas instilled into my mind, the consequence of which was discontentment, and a violent desire for traveling [sic].[9]

---

6   James Hale, *Journal of James Hale, Late Sergeant in the Ninth Regt of Foot. 1826.* (Uckfield: Naval & Military Press, 2015), p.5.
7   The National Archives (TNA): WO 12/5638: Muster Roll for 25 December 1785 to 24 June 1786.
8   Anon, *Narrative of a Private Foot Soldier in His Majesty's 92nd Regiment of Foot* (Uckfield: Naval & Military Press, 2015), p.5.
9   William Brown, *The Autobiography, or Narrative of a Soldier: The Peninsular War Memories of William Brown of the 45th Foot* (Solihull: Helion, 2017), pp.18–19.

GOING FOR A SOLDIER: FILLING UP THE HOLES

By volunteering for the British Army, his wish was certainly fulfilled, on all counts.

Once in the army, substituting one man for another was quite legitimate and indeed was one of the army regulations. Alexander Andrew, 21, another Scot from Inverkeithny in Banff, went as a substitute into the 44th Regiment in 1772 to replace his own brother, William.[10] The reason for this is not known, but William Andrew was discharged from his regiment on Monday, 14 September 1772, while Alexander, his brother, was 'entertained' the following day. This was a good decision on Andrew's part, for he was retained as a servant by Lieutenant Colonel James Agnew and accompanied him to America in 1775 to help bring the rebellion to heel. To be chosen as a servant to his commanding officer spoke well of Alexander Andrew. To fulfil the requirements, he would have to be a capable soldier and quick to learn, clean and neat in his habits, of an obedient nature towards his superior and willing to be by his side on the field of battle.

This he did and (although wounded himself) was by his officer's side when Lieutenant Colonel Agnew was mortally wounded at the Battle of Germantown, near Philadelphia, on 4 October 1777. Andrew, together with others, brought James Agnew back to his tent, did what he could for his officer's wounds and was with him when he died. He was then subsumed by the army as a private again, though two months later, he was promoted to corporal on 15 December 1777, having been in the service for just over five years, then to serjeant after a further 10 months, on 25 October 1778. He returned to Britain with his regiment, the 44th, eight years later, in the September of 1786. They disembarked from their transports at Portsmouth, hardened long-service soldiers, after a gruelling 10-year stint of duty in America and Canada – Andrew amongst them. The regiment had suffered from depleted numbers lost to both illness and battle, as will be seen from their first review below. More is to be learned of Alexander Andrew from Don Hagist's book *British Soldiers, American War*.[11]

Substitution, which often walked hand in hand with bounty, could be critical in decisions where hunger was involved. Samuel Harrison hired himself out twice as a substitute. When money, work or hunger was paramount, substitution could help a man who was on short commons. At the age of 15, in December 1795, Samuel was paid nine guineas to replace a man in the 1st West York Militia, in which he served until the peace in 1802. A year later, when hostilities broke out again, he entered the 2nd West Yorkshire Militia as a substitute for payment of £11.[12] The life must have suited him, for he then volunteered into the 43rd Foot in 1807.

Schoolmaster John MacDonald, who played the bagpipes as an initial interest, enlisted in the North Fencibles in June 1778 at the relatively old age of 26. He seems not to have been given a bounty but signed up for a shilling

---

10 Don H. Hagist, *British Soldiers American War: Voices of the American Revolution* (Yardley: Westholme Publishing, 2014), p.224.
11 Hagist, *British Soldiers*, pp.226–235.
12 Gareth Glover (ed.), *The Peninsular War Journal Samuel Harrison of the 43rd (Monmouthshire Regiment of Foot, 1796–1812* (Huntingdon: Ken Trotman Publishing, 2017), p.5.

per day and the title of pipe-major. The pipes being always a draw, his party appears to have done quite well at recruiting, for '103 privates marched from their different rendezvous to the Meikle Ferry'. By April 1779, Macdonald had enlisted into the 73rd Foot and was both pipe-major to the Colonel's company, the recipient of 20 guineas of bounty money, plus back-pay of some several weeks at the statutory daily shilling.[13] What perks a musical skill could bring.

It was Robert Butler's skill with the fife which opened doors for him. He substituted and received £22 for his pains in 1804. Some weeks into his army life he was offered (literally within a few hours) the rank and pay of a serjeant and position of fife-major in the second battalion of the 1st (the Royal) Regiment of Foot. Truly he must have been an accomplished fife player.

In spite of the young men above and their multiple reasons for giving their lives to the service of 'King and Country' it remains likely that the majority of recruits enlisted with the army because they were hungry and impoverished, which Richard Holmes noted as 'the compulsion of destitution'.[14] There were periods in the long eighteenth century when famine, unemployment, or stringent and proscriptive laws lay weightily across the land, preventing the common man from feeding his family – let alone prospering. These invidious and heavy handcuffs applied themselves to many of the lower – and working – classes, as instanced by Serjeant Thomas Jackson, Coldstream Guards, from the metal-working town of Walsall in Staffordshire. He and his four brothers had been educated as children and then taught the family trade of buckle-making. After a short peace commencing 25 March 1802, war was declared again just a year later, on 18 May 1803, with his father 'always grieving' and his mother 'always weeping' Jackson wrote, 'Trade … stagnated, and nothing but starvation was looked for by the working classes.'[15] To alleviate his parents' distress, Jackson made the decision to exchange the strait-jacket of hunger for the uncertain embrace of the Staffordshire Militia. His bounty of £6, given him as a reward for substituting 'a drawn (or balloted) man', he was able to share with his father, simultaneously removing one hungry mouth from the family home.[16]

William Brown, on entering the Argyllshire Militia (believed to be in August 1807, when he would have been 19), presented himself as a substitute and was offered 30 guineas, but 'would not accept less than forty' and was successful in the attempt. The man for whom he substituted must have been both desperate to keep out of the military and relatively well-heeled.[17] While one of the more entrepreneurial volunteers was Charles O'Neil, an Irishman who, with his cousin, left home for Belfast, intent on joining the army and finding a recruiting officer to do so:

---

13 John Macdonald, *Autobiographical Journal of John Macdonald Schoolmaster and Soldier* (Edinburgh: Macleod, 1906), pp.34–40.
14 Richard Holmes, *Redcoat: The British Soldier in the Age of Horse and Musket* (London: Harper Collins, 2001), p.149
15 Thomas Jackson, *Narrative of the Eventful Life of Thomas Jackson Militiaman and Coldstream Sergeant, 1803–1815* (Solihull: Helion, 2018), p.16.
16 Jackson, *Coldstream Sergeant*, p.16.
17 Brown, *William Brown*, p.24.

> Near the centre of a small open place stood a covered cart, embellished with flaming handbills, giving a description of the success of the British troops on the peninsula. On its top stood a neatly dressed soldier, who was haranguing, with much earnestness, the motley group that surrounded him, and calling loudly for recruits to engage in such glorious service.[18]

Both O'Neil and his cousin signed up for life. 'Each of us then received from him eighteen guineas, and were sent to the barracks, as members of the 8th regiment of foot.' But, as O'Neil puts it, 'All is not gold that glitters.' He deserted – not once, but three times – garnishing 18 guineas on each occasion. After the 8th Foot in Belfast came the 64th Foot in Navan, then the Lowth Militia on the way to Dublin and finally, at Phoenix Park, in Dublin, 'where I volunteered from the Lowth Militia into the 28th regiment of foot for foreign service, and received eighteen guineas, as volunteer's pay, being the fourth time I received the same sum'.[19] In O'Neil's case, perhaps the guineas glittered after all.

The volunteer who received the least bounty – probably no more than a guinea and a half – was Roworth, when he volunteered for the 44th in Manchester. An appeal for volunteers was placed in the *Ipswich Journal* later that year detailing minutely the requirements of the regiment stating the above bounty. This advertisement can be found in John Burrows' *The Essex Regiment*.[20] If it was money Roworth was after, he could not have volunteered at a worse time. Like Jackson, Roworth enlisted during a peace in Europe. Only in times of war was the government ready to denude its pockets. But substitution and bounty, though attractive, was just one of the reasons for entry into the army. Starvation was another although Jackson seems to be among the few who openly admits to near starvation. Both Lieutenant John Shipp, 87th Foot, and Private Adam Reed, 47th Foot, spent time in their youth in their local workhouses and were unlikely to have arrived there with full stomachs – nor when they left.

Enlisting into the army was the one back-stop to a life of hardship where, at least in peacetime, a soldier could rely on two meals a day, small beer, pay (however irregular that might be) and somewhere to lay his head at night – be it in barracks, billet or camp, plus the camaraderie of the men who shared the vicissitudes of army life with him.

Benjamin Randell Harris, already in the 95th Rifles, commented from the perspective of those soldiers in the recruiting party who, 'worked hard in this business, and for three days and nights kept up the dance and the drunken riot. Every volunteer got ten guineas bounty. Two were kept back for necessaries, but the rest was spent in every sort of excess till all was gone'.[21]

---

18 Charles O'Neil, *The Military Adventures of Charles O'Neil Who was a Soldier in the Army of Lord Wellington During the Memorable Peninsular War and the Continental Campaigns from 1811 to 1815* (Worcester: Livermore, 1851), p.17.
19 O'Neil, *Military Adventures*, p.27.
20 J. Burrows, *The Essex Regiment, 1st Battalion (44th), 1714-1919* (Southend-on-Sea: Burrows & Sons, 1931).
21 Eileen Hathaway (ed.), *A Dorset Rifleman: The Recollections of Benjamin Harris* (Swanage: Shinglepicker, 1995), p. 135.

On the same occasion in 1809, he left perhaps what is the most evocative and well-known description of (in this case) his own recruiting serjeant major:

> [He] was quite a beau; he had a sling-belt to his sword like a field-officer, a tremendous green feather in his cap, a flaring sash, and his whistle and powder-flask were displayed. There was an officer's pelisse over one shoulder, and he had a double allowance of ribbons in his cap. I was as smart as I dared appear, with my rifle slung at my shoulder. In this guise we made as much of ourselves as if we had both been generals, and arm in arm we strutted up and down before their ranks, creating such a sensation that the militia-men cheered us until they were called to order by the officers.

Some young men decided early on that they needed to make their own way in life without interference from parents or peers. An anonymous soldier of the 43rd Foot was determined to 'walk alone', while William Nightingale, a bit of a rebel, endeavoured to conform to the discipline of his master (a stay-maker). The latter 'was kind and wages remunerative, but the restrictions of a pious family were too binding for so lax and dissipated a youth'. Nightingale himself owned up to being 'adept in insolence, self-will and drunkenness', but nevertheless entered the 84th Foot on 12 March 1794 and served until his discharge on 23 March 1819, 25 years later.[22]

John Shipp of the 87th Foot, Samuel Gallagher, Royal Regiment of Artillery and William Surtees, 95th Rifles, all fulfilled a life's dream to become a soldier, the latter declaring 'a great predilection for a military life'.[23] Shipp left for posterity probably one of the most entertaining memoirs. Having first enlisted into the 22nd Foot on 17 January 1797, aged 13 years, his was to be a meteoric rise through the ranks. In 1805 he was offered an ensigncy into the 6th Foot. A few weeks later, he was offered a lieutenancy into the 76th, both commissions dated March 1805. The same month he sold out of the army, which enabled him to pay off his debts. He promptly re-enlisted, as a private again, into the 26th Light Dragoons. In 1815 he was given an ensigncy in the 87th Foot by none other than Francis Rawdon, Lord Moira. Remaining in that regiment, gaining a lieutenancy on 5 July 1821, his service was very colourful and not without bravery. But he sold out of the regiment in 1825 under a cloud, stymied by his gambling. Notwithstanding, this amazing man who (by his own admission) as a child had been in the workhouse, then gained a post as an inspector in the Metropolitan Police and in 1833 became Master of the Liverpool Workhouse, dying in 1835 aged only 52. Strange that he should end up more or less where he began.[24]

Two young men fled into the army to escape the results of their own shortcomings – Daniel Nicol of the Gordon Highlanders was caught poaching

---

22 Joseph Parker, *A Soldier's Retrospect Being a Narrative of Events in the Life of William Nightingale, of Banbury, a Private in the Eighty-Fourth Regiment* (London: Thomas Nelson & Sons, 1854), pp.19–24.
23 William Surtees, *Surtees of the 95th (Rifles): A Soldier of the 95th (Rifles) in the Peninsular Campaign of the Napoleonic Wars* (Driffield: Leonaur Ltd, 2006), p.9.
24 John Shipp, *Memoirs of the Extraordinary Military Career of John Shipp – Late a Lieut. in His Majesty's 87th Regiment* (London: T. Fisher Unwin, 1890), p.222.

and promptly volunteered in order to dodge the upcoming court case.[25] He may well have been encouraged to do so by the family as the man on whose land he had been poaching was his grandfather's employer! In contrast, Thomas Playford appeared to have been a somewhat insular polymath, though not insular enough when, aged 15, he was hastened into the army by his parents for fathering a child with a local girl. Fortunately (morals aside), he was unusually tall at six feet two and just the right candidate for the Lifeguards.[26] One could claim that the Lifeguards saved him.

Ludwig Ebbecke lived in Luthorst in Lower Saxony and was a conscript. He is included here because his was an unusual story. He came from a military family and the time for conscription into the Hanoverian infantry was coming. Ebbecke wanted to become a cavalryman, as were his brothers. The day before the scheduled conscription, Ebbecke joined them in the 6th Dragoon Regiment. Later he, with one of his brothers, clandestinely made it to Britain and enlisted into the 2nd Hussars of the King's German Legion.[27]

It is unsurprising that Andrew, Butler, Green, Miller, and Roworth were all literate – for they were not alone in that. Only five of the 47 considered here were illiterate: Drummer Richard Bentinck of the 23rd; Corporal George Fox, 47th; Private Benjamin Harris, 95th; Serjeant William Lawrence, 40th; and Private William Nightingale, 84th. Each of these men had a scribe to record their oral memories in later life. Of these five, Serjeant Lawrence stood out, firstly, as he was the only serjeant and, secondly, because he managed to get through the whole of his military career without his lack of literacy ever being discovered – a considerable accomplishment in itself. This was far from the norm as the remaining 42 prove the rule, literacy being perceived as an important and necessary skill if a man had ambitions to become an officer, albeit non-commissioned. Of the 47 men concerned here, 18 (38 percent) worked their way up to serjeant.

The inimitable Serjeant William Lawrence, born in 1791 in Dorset to an agricultural family, progressed through his early life from scaring crows to working as a plough-boy, then moving on as an apprentice to a builder. Nine months of the latter was sufficient for him to discover his unsuitability. He enlisted into the 40th (2nd Somersetshire) Regiment of Foot sometime after his 14th birthday. The life must have suited him and to become the respected and reliable serjeant that he did was a huge accomplishment. After 17 years and seven months in total, he left the military, and he and his French wife ran a public house. Not bad for a little lad who started his working life scaring the birds in the grain fields of Dorset and who never learned to read.

Not one of all the men mentioned above who left memoirs, wrote letters, journals, narratives, vicissitudes, etc., admitted to entry through the guile

---

25   Daniel Nicol, *Sergeant Nicol: The Experiences of a Gordon Highlander During the Napoleonic Wars in Egypt, The Peninsular & France* (Driffield: Leonaur, 2007), p.13.

26   Gareth Glover (ed.), *A Lifeguardsman in Spain, France and at Waterloo: The Memoir of Sergeant-Major Thomas Playford 2nd Lifeguards 1810–1830* (Huntingdon: Ken Trotman Books 2006), pp.1–9.

27   Gareth Glover (ed.), *A Hussar Sergeant in the King's German Legion: The Memoirs of Cavalry Sergeant Ebbecke, 2nd Hussar Regiment King's German Legion, 1803–1815* (Huntingdon: Ken Trotman Books, 2017), pp.15–17.

of the serjeant-major and his recruiting party, although Benjamin Harris, already in the 66th Foot did admit to being beguiled by the uniform of the 95th Rifles and could not rest until he had joined their ranks.[28]

The personal accounts above portray clearly the multiple possibilities which induced young men to volunteer, and the incredible mix of young manhood received by the army in the late 1700s and early 1800s. Certainly, not all of the intake were candidates for Wellington's well-used umbrella phrase for his 'scum of the earth' army. Considering the potential of those volunteers demonstrated here – with their combined skills, from polymath to poacher, avid reader to adventurer, musician to memoirist, criminal to conscript – the one constant appears to be the desire to change their lives.

Once a young man expressed a wish to volunteer, the recruiting serjeant had to be aware of certain regulations and requirements when the time came for the former to enlist. For example, a recruitment advertisement for the 44th Regiment of Foot insisted that 'every candidate for the 44th must be sound, wind and limb, stout and well-made'.[29] Each recruit was allowed 24 hours after enlisting (and before signing his attestation papers) to change his mind and return his bounty. For most, of course, the money was a temptation too far and would be long gone before he wrote his signature or marked with a cross in front of a magistrate. Interestingly, some 83 per cent of the above candidates examined in this section did the former. After the Articles of War had been read to him and the surgeon had checked him for disease or abnormalities, he took his oath to the King.

From here, he was given his clothing and his necessaries, the former including 'a coat, waistcoat ... and breeches, a tricorne hat [to channel the rain away from the face], stockings, shoes and a couple of shirts'.[30] Any extras would have to be paid out of his subsistence of sixpence per day, which had to stretch as far as other necessaries, too. They were an important part of his daily life and comprised extra shirts, socks, a comb, and black ball to clean his shoes.

Fusilier John Cooper described his uniform, albeit with his tongue in his cheek, as 'like a child's doll in a toy-shop'. He claimed that:

> On his head he wore a cap covered with heel-ball, polished like a mirror. On the cap under a varnished rosette, stood a tuft of wool six inches long, neatly trimmed. This weighty cap, or rather helmet, had nothing attached to prevent its falling off. When it did, it took hours to repair the damage. All his hair, except for a little at the sides and front, was tightly bound round a piece of lead behind. The hair on the sides was rubbed round till matted, then greased and powdered with flour. The whiskers were greased, set up, and also powdered. About his neck he wore a stock of stiff leather four inches broad, well varnished. This thing was a real nuisance. Projecting two inches from his breast, he had a neatly crimped ruffle. On his shoulders there were two wings made of cloth and wool, neatly combed and trimmed. The wings were useful in keeping on the cross-belts. His jacket

---

28   Christopher Hibbert (ed.), *The Recollections of Rifleman Harris* (London: Leo Cooper Ltd, 1970), p.5.
29   *Ipswich Journal*, Saturday, 22 July 1786.
30   Stuart Reid, *British Redcoat 1740–1793* (Oxford: Osprey, 1996), p.7.

fitted far too tightly; his buttons were bright as silver; and the lace on his breast and cuffs were white as pipe-clay could make them.

His breeches were of white cloth, and reached a little below the knee; his long gaiters were black, and both breeches and gaiters were tight of course. To bring all parts of his dress and accoutrements into close contact, there were loops, loops, loops; loops to the gaiters; braces to the breeches; loops to the jacket; loops to the cross belts; loops to the wings, etc., etc. Should he try to reach the ground, it would have been fatal to some article of his set-off. Nothing could be contrived worse for real service.[31]

While the red coat may have looked very smart, it had the rather obvious disadvantage of being easy to see from a distance. An officer of the 60th Foot conducted some experiments in 1800 with rifle-armed troops firing at red, grey, and green targets and found that the red target received double the number of hits compared to the grey, with the green being between the two.[32] However, easy recognition of a body of troops from a distance was more important for line troops with the tactics of the day.

Among those transfixed by the scarlet coat were said to be women, who often had such drab lives, that to see a forest of redcoats and to hear their music and manly shouts livened the eyes and hearts with the excitement of what possibilities there might be. Holmes put this down to the 'seduction principle' of the design, while Henry Mayhew, sociologist and journalist spanning Georgian and (mainly) Victorian London, also 'thought that it was a major ingredient in soldiers' success with "dollymops" servant girls, nursemaids and shop girls … Nursemaids, in particular, were always ready to succumb to what he called "scarlet fever".'[33]

The advent of the red coat as uniform on a British soldier was possibly that from 'a contingent from Rye in 1461 which went to join the army of Warwick … dressed in red coats … was again seen in 1470 when a levy of men from Canterbury … were supplied with "jakettes" of red cloth costing three shillings a yard'.[34] From then red coats had been seen sporadically during the wars of the Tudors, briefly in Ireland during Elizabeth I's rule and then, perhaps surprisingly, taken up by Cromwell in England's Civil War. Early in the long eighteenth century, the design of the coat and its colour became standardised, but the linings were made of different colours, so that when the collars were turned down, the 'facings' would show up to designate specific regiments, again primarily for instant recognition within the British Army itself. Holmes records 'blue for the 1st Royal, sea green for the 2nd Queen's, buff for the 3rd' – hence the nickname the Buffs – and 'green of the 66th', etc. By 1768, all red-coated infantry regiments were recognisable

---

31 John S. Cooper, *Cooper: Experiences in the 7th (Royal) Fusiliers During the Peninsular Campaign of the Napoleonic Wars and the American Campaign to New Orleans* (Driffield: Leonaur, 2007), pp.131–132.
32 C. Hamilton Smith, 'Experiments on the Comparative Effect of Rifle and Musketry Fire on Different Colours', *Aide-Mémoire to the Military Sciences*, 1853, pp.257–259.
33 Holmes, *Redcoat*, p.191.
34 W.Y. Carman, *British Military Uniforms From Contemporary Pictures* (Feltham: Hamlyn, 1968), p.1.

by their facings and lace, for example, the 31st Regiment of Foot wore buff facings while the lace was 'White with Blue and Yellow worm, small Red stripe', and the 44th Regiment's facings were yellow, with lace of blue, yellow and black stripe.[35].

This uniform continued through the eighteenth and much of the nineteenth centuries, its final combat outing being 30 December 1895 in Sudan. From that time, the red coat has been in use for purely ceremonial purposes, which, even today, though no longer striking fear, evokes spectacle, ostentation, and a drama of its own, with the onlooker almost touching the past. Note the two great public events in Britain of the funeral of Queen Elizabeth II in 2022 and the subsequent coronation of King Charles III in 2023.

It is almost certain that most of the volunteers who donned the red coat for the first time would have stood straighter, taller and prouder. 'For king and country' stiffened the back and gave a purpose to life, as Thomas Jeremiah inferred when he stated in his account '… and proud I was when I found myself attired in His Majesty's royal livery'.[36]

Looked at through the eyes of the recruiting officer the main function of recruitment into the army then (as it is today) was to fill up the holes, even chasms on occasions, made by incursions into its manpower. Those incursions happened for a number of reasons, the most obvious in wartime – death, wounds received, or men missing; the latter primarily as prisoners of war, and deserters. As with all employments, military or otherwise, there was also wastage through retirement and perhaps the most insidious of all – disease.

Even peacetime would bring its own reasons for the holes in the ranks – discharge through sickness, accidental deaths, an execution for depredation or murder, desertion, and the discharge of old soldiers who were designated 'worn out'. So, there was a constant deficiency of men who would need replacing. The last two decades of the eighteenth century were no different to any other. British soldiers continued to die in America, as the War of Independence (in 1780) still had three of its eight years to run. Finding men to fill those gaps was an unremitting requirement and the British Army's recruiting parties endlessly essayed forth, week after week, month after month, into cities, towns, villages, and hamlets all over the country to entice as many young men as possible to volunteer for enlistment. In times of peace, an added drain on the army continued with the exigencies of disease in Britain's multiple overseas dominions.

In 1781, 20 years had passed since Campbell Dalrymple, Colonel of the 3rd Dragoons and Governor of Guadeloupe, published his essay in 1761, ostensibly focusing on the 'Raising, Arming, Cloathing and Discipline' of the private soldier, damning (not the volunteers) but those he believed to be the dross of the army, the men who filled the ranks, apparently forgetting that many of the latter were also volunteers.[37]

---

35 Carman, *Uniforms*, pp.95–96. From the Royal Warrant dated 19 December 1768.
36 Gareth Glover (ed.), *The Adventures of Private Jeremiah Thomas* (Huntingdon: Ken Trotman Publishing, 2008), p.7.
37 Campbell Dalrymple, *A Military Essay. Containing reflections on the raising, arming, cloathing, and discipline of the British infantry and cavalry; with proposals for the improvement of the*

> There are two ways of recruiting the British Army, the first and most eligible by volunteers, the last and worst by a press. By the first method, numbers of good men are enrolled, but the army is greatly obliged by levity, accident, and the dexterity of recruiting officers for them; by the second plan, the country gets clear of its banditti, and the ranks are filled up with the scum of every county, the refuse of mankind. They are marched loaded with vice, villainy, and chains, to their destined corps, where, when they arrive, they corrupt all they approach, and are whipt out, or desert in a month.[38]

The second of these methods he described was continued until a new Recruiting Act was passed in 1778 while a second followed in 1779.[39] Dalrymple's opinion of 'the first method' was very much as the volunteers (in the accounts above) portrayed themselves and their comrades. Those of the second method appear to refer to the felons, the corrupt, the convicts and 'the scum of every county'. Perhaps the Wellington had read Dalrymple's essay and coined part of that term as his own, though widening its scope from a mere county to the whole world, when (apocryphally) he first referred to the British soldier as 'scum of the earth' in 1800. The term 'scum of the earth' was in common usage from 1586, meaning (according to the *Oxford English Dictionary*), 'the offscourings of humanity; the lowest class of the population of a place or country'. Dalrymple may have taken it straight from 'The History of John Bull', by Jonathan Swift, first published in 1712, where the latter put words into that character's mouth: 'Scoundrels! Dogs! The Scum of the Earth!'[40] Whatever the derivation, that expression uttered by Wellington – has become etched in history as a great commander's miserable opinion of his (often) too equally miserable men. He wrote it, in a letter to Henry, Third Earl Bathurst, from Huarte, Spain, on 2 July 1813, following the looting of the French baggage after the Battle of Vittoria, 'we have in the service the scum of the Earth as common soldiers.'[41] After the triumph of Waterloo and throughout his life, Wellington had an overwhelming hold over much of British society, not unlike Winston Churchill in the twentieth century. The words of both these men were hung upon in much the same manner, as potential saviours of the nation. So, it is no surprise that certain phrases became ingrained in the nation's psyche, with Wellington's connotation.

Wellington and Dalrymple were (as are we all) products of certain times and mores. Both men were born into comfortable circumstances, and both entered the British Army through patronage and purchase. The damning phrases they used to describe the ordinary ranker, most of whom may never have seen the inside of a prison, (let alone arrived to greet the recruiting serjeant wearing chains), were most likely to have been conceived and nurtured by the inherent ideas of their ruling class – primarily moneyed nobility. This attitude

---

same (London: D. Wilson, 1761), pp.8–9.
38   Dalrymple, *A Military Essay*, p.18.
39   Recruiting Act 1778. 18 George III c. 53; Recruiting Act 1779 19 George III c. 10.
40   Jonathan Swift, *History of John Bull* (London: Midwinter & Tonson, 1750), p.71
41   Edward J. Coss, *All For the King's Shilling: The British Soldier under Wellington, 1808–1814* (Norman: University of Oklahoma Press, 2015), p.30.

was displayed by Dalrymple picking up on the words of Sir Walter Raleigh, who observed that 'there was in his day a midling [sic] sort of people, call'd yeomen, and their sons, who made excellent foot soldiers; but that species of people is now lost to the army.'[42] Dalrymple goes on to say: 'There are indeed severe laws to oppose the vicious disposition of young soldiers; but the most contracted brow of severity, armed with the awful cat of nine tails, can not reclaim every profligate, nor make a villain honest.'[43]

The damning judgements made by these two military leaders of men, but particularly by Wellington, of men who worshipped him, seem particularly harsh. He appears to make his uncomfortable accusations when the soldiers were either involved in stealing desperately needed food to survive (either eat or die – and some did die) or those occasions of his contempt when, after violent and bloody battles, such as the extended sieges of Ciudad Rodrigo, Badajoz or San Sebastian, the soldiers plundered the towns. At least in the case of the first two, Wellington himself gave his permission to the men who had just fought for him to do just that – and plunder they did, not just from the military enemy, but also the civilians through murder, rape and pillage. The revenge taken by the soldiers was horrific and cannot be contested. Fortunately, these occasions were not such regular occurrences as may be thought.

But were Wellington, Dalrymple and others correct in their assumption that the men involved were the dregs of society and predominantly convicts and vagrants?

To an extent, it would seem so, but certainly not sufficient to suffocate the rank and file with the blanket description of 'scum' or 'profligate villains'. Indeed, probably no more relevant than if that same description were employed to mirror the lower echelons of British society at the time. The true cause for all these accusations must surely be abject poverty and the struggles of the population to survive the famines and crippling laws of the eighteenth century. Edward Coss, in his book *All for the King's Shilling*, not only gives cogent and well-researched reasons for Wellington's perceptions of and relationships with the 'common soldier' but also looks carefully at the troops themselves and their reasons for enlisting. He points out that the accusations have been accepted as the truth because of the acquiescence of the status quo by subsequent historians with little or no re-examination of the facts to any depth.[44]

In May 1778, a Recruiting Act was passed to allow for a press for the military,[45] which provided for the 'levy and deliver[y] to the recruiting officers "all able-bodied idle, and disorderly Persons" who could not prove themselves to have a trade, together with "all Persons who should be convicted of running goods to the value of £40 or under in lieu of all legal penalties."'[46] So supposedly, it became a case of set a thief to catch a thief and then complain of the consequences.

---

42 Dalrymple, *Military Essay*, p.10.
43 Dalrymple, *Military Essay*, p.10.
44 Coss, *King's Shilling*, p.40.
45 Recruiting Act, 18 Geo. III, c.53.
46 Recruiting Act, 18 Geo. III, c.53.

For all these many hundreds, perhaps thousands, of criminals apparently let loose on an unsuspecting army, or at least a nucleus large enough to create the kind of military society believed to cause constant mayhem in the ranks, remarkably little evidence can be found. Actual data and statistics are relatively hard to find. Edward Curtis quotes from three examples, totalling 11 men in all. One concerns an Irish-American 'convicted of Orchard Robbing' (scrumping), probably through hunger and three who received the death sentence for stealing horses and sheep. Of the remaining seven, two were convicted of highway robbery, one each for shoplifting and burglary and two more 'being found at large', presumably having escaped from gaol.[47]

Even smugglers were also taken up when possible and given the choice of joining the army or navy, but understandably the majority gravitated towards the element most familiar to them. Conway found statistics for the resurgence of enlisting pardoned convicts from the beginning of the American War in 1775.[48] He shows that of the records available, 764 men in this category were enlisted in the six years up to and including 1781 – indicative of the need to boost numbers but averaging about 127 per year and a little more than one per regiment, so unlikely to make huge incursions of evil! Another reason for relatively few numbers of recruited convicts is that commissioned officers just did not want them. Conway points to three examples, specifically: 'Captain the Honourable George Napier of the 80th Foot held that the service was disgraced by the presence of criminals in the ranks'; that 'when Sir Stanier Porten, an Undersecretary of State, received an application for the pardon of several convicts, they remain a long time in the prisons, on the refusal of the officers to admit them into their corps'; similarly, that 'Captain Patrick Campbell of the 71st Foot ordered his recruiting sergeant not to enlist any vagrants into the company he was raising,' and had received an identical refusal from his own officers.[49]

In spite of certain regiments' delicacy, where convicts were concerned, there were certainly some attempts by magistrates to off-load convicts into the military and this can be seen from the 'Report of John William Rose, Recorder of London, on prisoners convicted at the Old Baily, (apart from those specified) and recommended to mercy as set against their names'.[50] It is dated 8 August 1795. Of the 27 men up before the magistrate, those relevant to the military were the two sent into the fencibles and 15 sent to the army specifically for service in the West Indies as soldiers. This is not to say that they were all accepted by the army, as we have seen in the previous paragraph. The remainder were listed under 'Not tried at the Old Baily', 'Unfit' or 'Transported'. But if this happened every week or even every month, then it appears that the judicial authorities were trying to off-load as many as possible.

---

47 Edward. E. Curtis, *British Army in the American Revolution* (Manchester: Cornerhouse Publications, 1998), pp.161–162.
48 Stephen Conway, 'The Recruitment of Criminals into the British Army, 1775–1781', *Bulletin of the Institute of Historical Research*, vol.58, no.137, May 1985, p.49.
49 Conway, '*Criminals*', pp.56–57.
50 TNA: HO 47/19/39: Report of John William Rose, Recorder of London, on prisoners convicted at the Old Bailey.

It was not only the justices, however, who thought that some of the prisoners at Newgate might make suitable candidates, as the following letter demonstrates, written by Major George Prevost of the 60th (Royal American) Regiment of Foot to Mr Evan Nepean at the Home Office in 1794:

> In the present scarcity of men to recruit His Majesty's Regiments I was led to visit Newgate & from Mr Kirby learnt that there was twelve or fifteen very proper subjects for soldiers. Men guilty of small offences & sentenced either imprisonment or a short transportation. Now, Sir, I take the liberty of troubling you to know whether His Majesty's pardon might be obtained for the above description of men on condition of their enlisting in the 60th Regt which may effectually take them out of the country & that Government of the expense.[51]

Receiving no quick reply to his letter, Prevost wrote again, stating that he 'has just been with the Keeper of Newgate and found that there is between thirty & forty prisoners who might make good soldiers'. Perhaps he reached a full company before he had a response! The current author did not discover the outcome. As Major Prevost would have been happy to assimilate them into his own regiment, it might have been successful. Newgate was one step up from the hulks. There were also prisoners individually offering themselves as soldiers. One such offer arrived at Sir Henry Dundas's office in a beautiful copperplate hand from a certain John Brown, who claimed to be imprisoned on board the notorious hulk *Prudentia*.[52]

Edward Coss collated data from 14 infantry, and four cavalry regiments, plus three artillery battalions into what he refers to as the British Soldier Compendium (BSC). He found that 40.59 percent of soldiers were recorded as being labourers in their former careers, of whom nearly half were Irish – reflecting the economic downturns, often to very specific years when enlistment in the army was preferable to hunger. The BSC noted, for example, the years 1800, 1806 and 1812 'in which such "crisis peaks" were prominent'.[53] Poor harvest years and a desperate economic situation together with lack of employment and the beginning of the Highland Clearances in Scotland cut swathes into the poor of the country in the late eighteenth century and intermittently thereafter.

Recruiting in war or peacetime could be a very hit-and-miss affair. John Green, 68th Foot (remembered for his dogged attempts to break into the carpet factory scene), related how at a time when, in 1811, the militia had been granted the freedom to volunteer for the regular army – the 68th had had no drafts from the militia whatsoever owing to rumours of immediate embarkation to the Peninsula. However, later in the year recruits came flooding in. Green claimed that men were coming from all over the north of England, Scotland and Ireland, that the regiment was receiving drafts

---

51   TNA: HO 42/30/77: Domestic Correspondence, Prevost to Nepean, 16 May 1794, p.197.
52   TNA: HO 42/30/60: Home Office, Domestic Correspondence, p.142.
53   Coss, *King's Shilling*, p.67.

GOING FOR A SOLDIER: FILLING UP THE HOLES

Hulks at Chatham, familiar to many volunteers, by Warren. (Author's Collection)

from the militia and that numbers were nearing the 850 mark, and more importantly, that the men were mostly between 18 and 30 years old.[54]

But at the first sniff of war, the government would send messages flying to all county lord lieutenants and their deputies. Initially, recruitment posters and newspaper advertisements would appear country-wide followed by recruiting parties consisting of '1 Commissioned-officer, 1 Sergeant, 1 Corporal, 1 drummer, and 2 private men'[55] who, in their best uniforms, would travel to cities, towns, villages and hamlets to entice as many young men as possible to enlist. War or no war, the recruiting parties were always a constant throughout the country and the recruiting serjeants knew their jobs – often far better than those commissioned officers accompanying them. The Recruiting Acts of 1778 and 1779 were the only occasions during the eighteenth century in which the government dabbled with army impressment. When that did not succeed, both acts were smartly repealed in 1780. By the end of the American War in 1783 and the army's return to Britain in the subsequent three years, from the public's point of view the condition and reputation of the soldiers appears to have been about as low as it could get. So Roworth seems to have volunteered at about the worst possible time, the beginning of a period of relative peace – all seven years of it, before the world stage exploded again, first, with the execution of the French King Louis XVI

---

54 Green, *Vicissitudes*, p.56.
55 Thomas Simes, *Military Guide for Young Officers* (Uckfield: Naval and Military Press, 2009), pp.205–210.

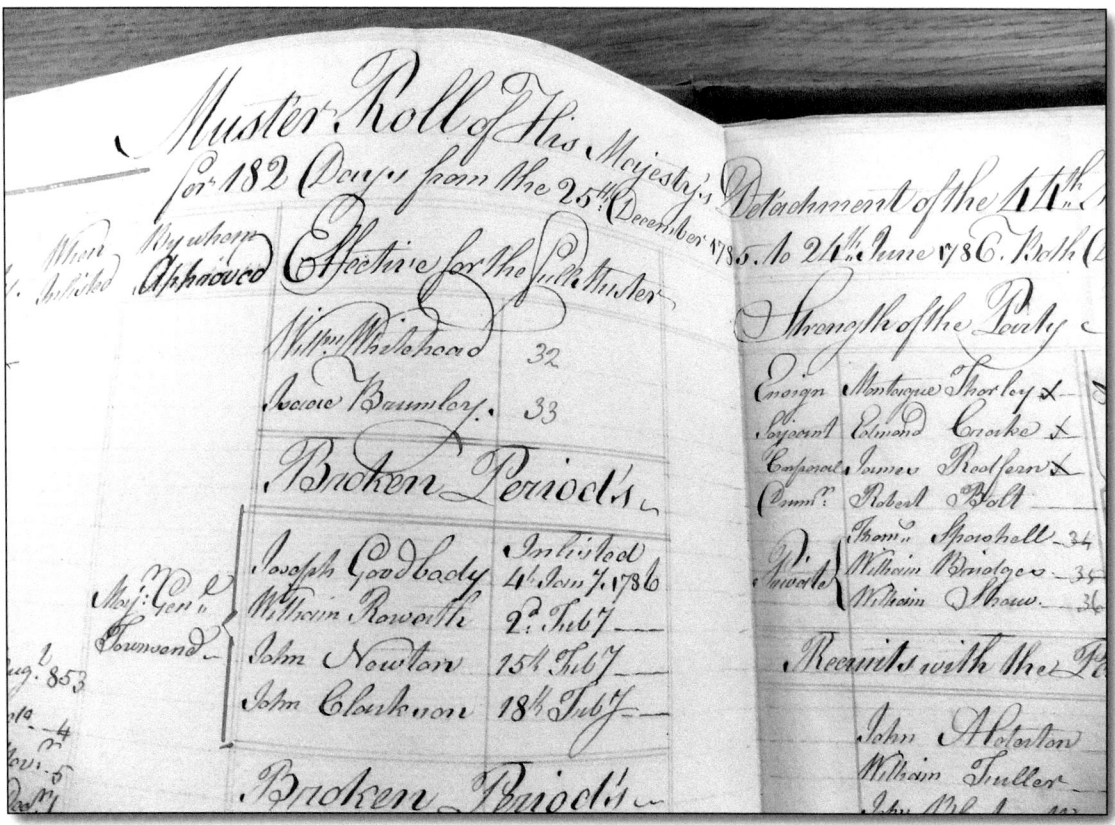

Roworth enlists at Manchester. Muster Roll record dated 25 December 1785 to 24 June 1786. (TNA: WO 12/5638)

in January 1793 and again at the entrance of Napoleon Bonaparte in 1796 when he fought his first major battle against Austria and won.

But during those seven years of peace that Roworth experienced, life in the British military jogged quietly on. All soldiers were recorded at least twice annually on a muster roll, which left a snapshot of the individual's career or time with the army. Roworth's name appears first on the 'Muster Roll of His Majesty's 44th Regiment of Foot for 182 Days from 25 December 1785 to 24 June 1786, with both days inclusive'.[56]

He came under the heading of 'broken periods', which accounts for soldiers who were not on the muster for the whole 182 days. His name was in a group of four volunteers – the others being Joseph Goodbody, who enlisted on 4 January 1786; John Newton on 15 February and John Clarkson on 18 February. All four were recorded together as having been recruited in Manchester by their recruiting officer, Lieutenant James Ogden, under the overall control of Major General Samuel Townsend, Inspector General of Recruiting.[57] They would have remained under Ogden's care in this select group with 10 others recruited at Manchester, before being escorted to Chatham.

---

56 TNA: WO 12/5638/1: Muster Roll for 25 December 1785 to 24 June 1786.
57 TNA: WO 65/36: Army List 1786.

Chatham dockyard entrance built 1720, with its reminder of service to the Crown. (Donald Roworth)

With his comrades, Roworth spent seven months in the military cradle of Chatham Army Barracks, where they learned their military disciplines of marching, drill and movements, how to care for their uniform, duties, and training with other young men from different regiments.

Recruits were sent to Chatham for their initial training if their parent regiment was still serving in abroad. The men were sent to the receiving house where they would have been inspected by the garrison surgeon, sworn their oath of allegiance, received their uniform, shown their quarters and 'commenced their drills and movements' on the country's most 'slanting parade ground' and where the soldiers slept two in a bed.[58]

Once this training was deemed sufficient, Clarkson, Goodbody, Newton and Roworth left Chatham and marched to Hilsea Barracks on Portsea Island to join their regiment, due home from America. Nine others were marked as 'Not Appointed' (though actually all deserted) and eight were rejected, making just over half of the original number recruited to join their regiment.

While Ogden was recruiting in Manchester, Ensign Montague Thorley, Serjeant Edmund Crake and Corporal James Redfern were doing the same in Colchester. These three men would become very familiar to Roworth during his time in the regiment.[59] Two had seen action in America; Crake was already a serjeant in Quebec by 1782 and Redfern a private at Paulus Hook, in 1780. Serjeant Crake's name appeared in print on Saturday, 22 July 1786, when the *Ipswich Journal* published a persuasive and flattering manifesto clothed in the guise of an advertisement for recruits:

VOLUNTEERS

The 44th (or East Essex) Regiment, commanded by Lieutenant General CHARLES RAINSFORD, which has so gloriously distinguished itself during the late troubles and the former war in America, returns to England this Autumn, 1786, and will want several to supply the places of those veterans who have deserved, and will be recommended, to be letter-men, at 1s. a day, and to the out-pension of Chelsea Hospital, for the rest of their lives. All clever young fellows of Suffolk, Norfolk, and Essex, who are free and able, and are ambitious of becoming Gentlemen, by bearing arms in the said honourable and redoubtable corps, are hereby invited to the Recruiting-Officer's Head-Quarters, Colchester, who promises they shall meet with every encouragement, to which merit and good behaviour can entitle them. Every candidate for the 44th must be sound, wind and limb, stout and well-made. Men, under the age of 25 years, must not be less than 5 feet 7 inches high; youths, under 18, 5 feet 5 inches; and very promising lads of 16 or 17, who have every appearance of growing will be accepted, tho' only 5 feet 4 inches and a ½: all are measured without their shoes. They will immediately enter into present pay, and, on joining their comrade recruits at Chatham barracks, near Rochester, in Kent, (where they are to remain until they shall march to the regiment on its landing and being fixed in quarters) they will immediately receive His Majesty's Royal Bounty of a Guinea and a Half, with complete clothing, arms and accoutrements.

---

58   Peter Kendall, *The Royal Engineers at Chatham 1750–2012* (Swindon: English Heritage, 2012), p.25.
59   TNA: WO 12/5638: Muster Roll for 25 December 1785 to 24 June 1786.

GOING FOR A SOLDIER: FILLING UP THE HOLES

Inside the originally white-washed military hospital at Chatham's Fort Amherst. (Donald Roworth)

The bringers of recruits are handsomely rewarded; but the officer rather wishes young fellows would come of their own accord, without such incumbrances; and that those who shall come from a distance, he will pay the outside passage to any of the Inns or public-houses in Colchester. Volunteers may also repair to Serjeant Crake at HADLEIGH; to Corporal Spashell, at the EIGHT-RINGERS, ST MILES'S, NORWICH; or to any of the non-commissioned officers, and soldiers of the party dispersed amongst the market towns near Colchester.

KING GEORGE and OLD ENGLAND for ever![60]

There were undoubtedly some 'free and able young men' who would have answered that particular call, but Roworth had already enlisted and was learning his drill and discipline at Chatham. At 22, he must have been at least five feet and seven inches to have passed the height stipulated. A fuller account of height regulations can be found in chapter three. Regulations could be relaxed a little in times of war as Brown of the 45th Foot, aged 19, discovered in 1809 when 'my height came to be ascertained I was found half an inch below the standard … A remedy, however, was found, by putting some pasteboard betwixt my feet and stockings, which made me just the thing'.[61]

The men of the 44th Foot were newly arrived from service in America and Canada, where they had been doing their duty throughout the War of Independence since June 1775. They had fought at the battles of Brooklyn, Brandywine, Germantown, and Monmouth and innumerable other skirmishes. But two incidents occurred during that time, which affected the whole regiment deeply. First, at the Battle of Germantown on 4 October 1777 when Brigadier General James Agnew of the 44th Foot lost his life. Then, two years later, while in convoy from New York to Quebec in September 1779, the *Empress* transport sank in a violent storm. Onboard were two and a half companies of the 44th (about 250 men) under Captain Twistleton Ridsdale.[62]

The remainder of the 44th arrived in Portsmouth on 13 September 1786 from America but stayed on board ship until Saturday 23 September, when they disembarked and immediately marched for Hilsea Barracks to spend the winter in rest and recuperation. The custom of retaining soldiers onboard ship for logistical purposes and to discourage desertion while in sight of land was always contentious with the soldiers themselves – understandably. As the 44th had been away for over a decade, those last 10 days – with home in sight and the pleasures of Portsmouth probably less than half a mile away – must have been particularly galling.

On the full muster roll covering the period from 25 June to 24 December 1786, Clarkson, Goodbody and Newton were present, but only Roworth and a William Chilvers were specifically referred to as having arrived at Portsea Island from Chatham on 29 September 1786.[63] When Roworth reached the Hilsea Lines, they would have been as familiar to him as the Chatham Lines,

---

60 *Ipswich Journal*, Saturday, 22 July 1786.
61 Brown, *William Brown*, p.24.
62 Burrows, *Essex Regiment*, pp.23–24.
63 TNA: WO 12/5638: Muster Roll for 25 June 1796 to 24 December 1786.

GOING FOR A SOLDIER: FILLING UP THE HOLES

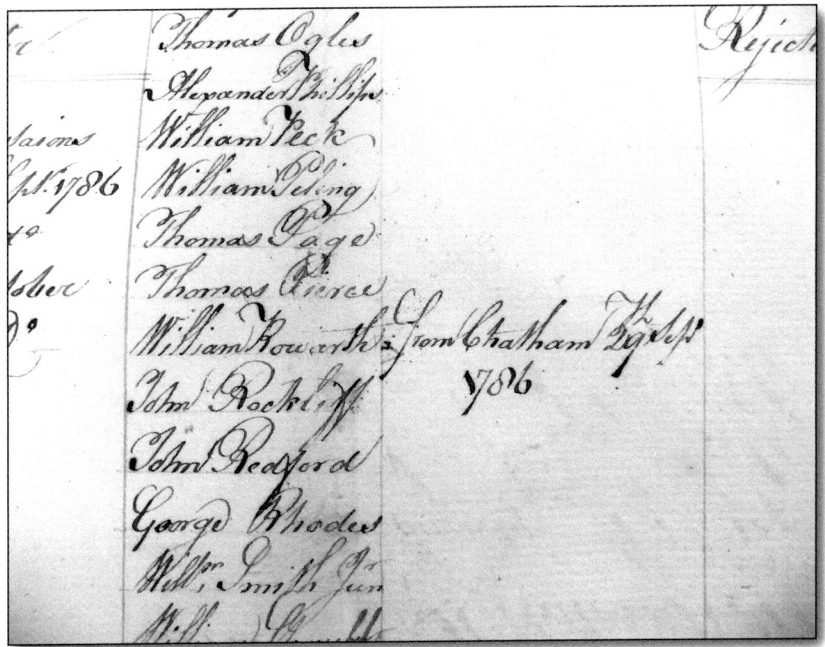

William Roworth marked on the Muster Roll on 29 September 1786 having arrived at Hilsea from Chatham. (TNA: WO 12/5638/1)

since both were had been designed by John Peter Desmaretz as landward-facing defences to repel any French attack from the interior. The Lines included magazines, storehouses and barracks for two battalions of soldiers at Hilsea Common, which could mean up to 2,000 men hypothetically, but the number of 1,000 per battalion was rarely achieved and then only in wartime, so it was probably fewer.[64]

Hilsea was where Roworth would get to know a good many of the men who were veterans from the war, at least by sight and reputation. Returning home to England was Alexander Andrew, servant to the deceased James Agnew and a serjeant since October 1778. He and Roworth would serve together as serjeants after Roworth's promotion, until Andrew's discharge in Ireland six years later. Another name mentioned by Roworth in his letters home during his service abroad (1794–1797) was Serjeant Samuel Fetherston, serving in Captain Richard Mark Dickens's company.[65] He suffered knee damage at the Battle of Brandywine, and his name crops up a number of times in the letters before his discharge from the service in February 1792. Another man mentioned with affection and respect was Quartermaster John Tuffie, head of an army family, which included his wife, Mary, and two sons, Samuel and William. Corporal Thomas Legge, who had been a serjeant as far back as 1780, but was reduced to private on 19 April 1781 – presumably for some misdemeanour – was still working his way back up to serjeant again when he and Roworth met up. These were just some of the men with whom Roworth would be making his new life and were to become lasting comrades.

---

64   'Hilsea Lines', *Welcome to Portsmouth*, <http://www.welcometoportsmouth.co.uk/hilsea%20lines.html>, accessed March 2022.
65   TNA: WO 121/13/305: Samuel Fetherston, discharge documents, 1792.

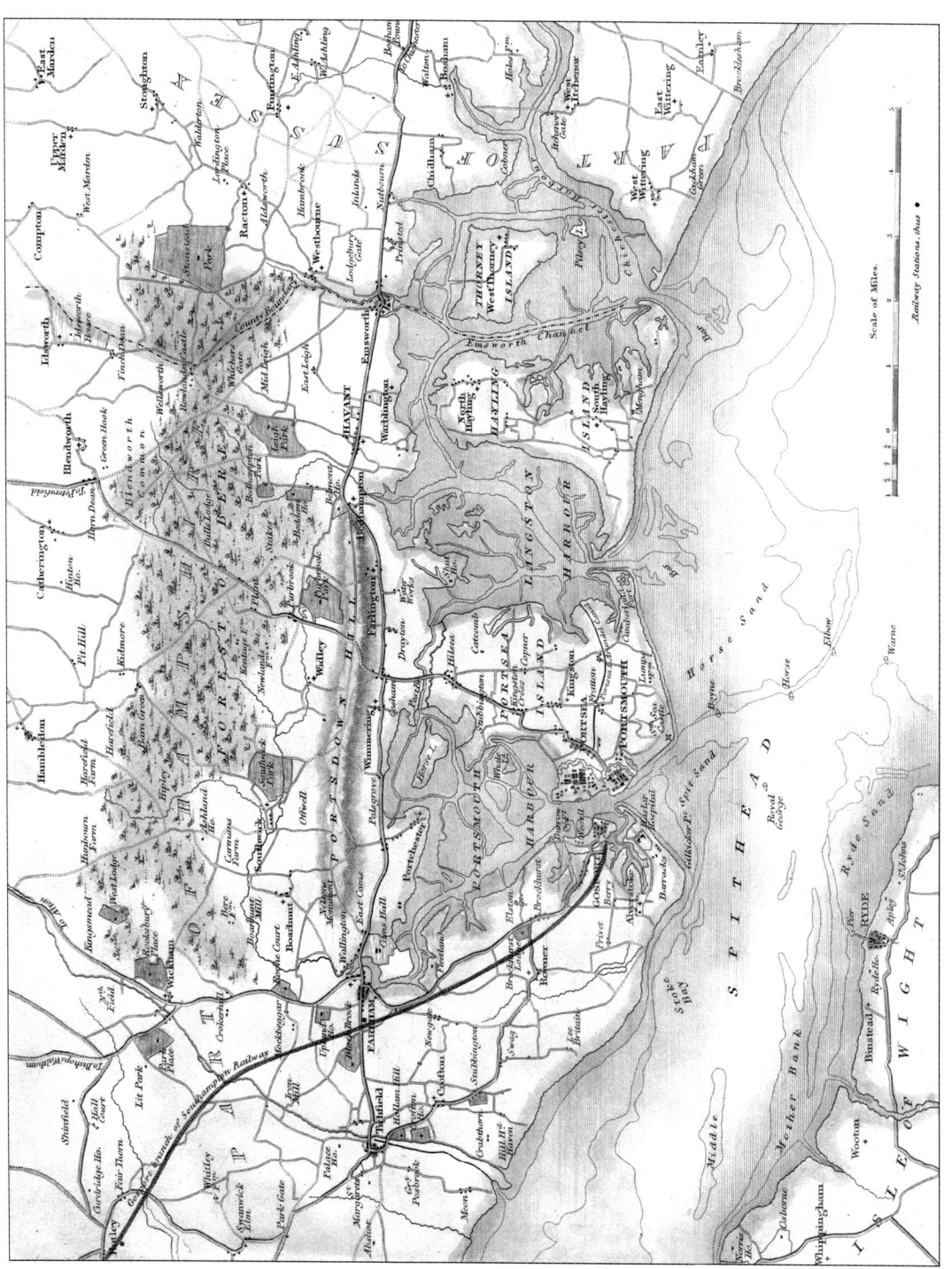

Portsmouth showing Portsea, Hilsea, Spithead and the Mother Bank. (Author's Collection)

The Gun Wharf at Portsmouth. (Author's Collection)

As with many others, Roworth was to prove a driven and ambitious man as the war-time letters to his wife attest. Still, before any promotion was considered feasible, he had to settle to army life at Hilsea and work hard to improve his chances, as would any ambitious soldier. The previous eight months in Chatham would have been a personal testing ground as to his intentions.

Bearing in mind that the young men considered in the section above stood out because they were able to record their own military histories, either by their own hands or by amanuenses, Richard Holmes believed that the vast majority were recruited by 'the entrancing rattle of the drum and the power of the spoken word, lavishly supported with drink … and the officer and serjeants [who] declaimed upon the unrivalled opportunities to be had by volunteering for the regiment'.[66] But had it always been so?

---

66   Holmes, *Redcoat*, pp.139–140.

2

Men, Miscreants and Marriage: The Military Mindset

And proud I was when I found myself all attired in His Majesty's royal livery.[1]

First, a retrospect of the 44th (East Essex) Regiment of Foot. When William Roworth enlisted in the regiment in February 1786 the regiment was just 45 years old, having been raised by Colonel James Long in January 1741, so was known by the name of its colonel. Its first test came just four years later at the Battle of Prestonpans in Scotland on 21 September 1745 when, being one of six regiments under the command of Sir John Cope (memorialised by Adam Skirving's words to traditional tune in 'Hey, Johnny Cope') against equal numbers of Highlanders, the royal regiments broke and ran, except for a small number of groups under the command of Lieutenant Colonel Peter Halkett of the 44th Foot. Of a total of 2,300 men only 170 of the foot escaped.[2] The defeat was put down to the inexperience of young soldiers. In 1748 the regiment was given the number 55 briefly which was then changed to the number 44 in 1751.

In 1755 the 44th Foot was involved in the French and American War under the command of Major General Edward Braddock. At a stiff confrontation at the Monongahela River where the two brigades of 'some 1400 regulars and 700 colonials' … were ambushed by 'some 224 French troops accompanied by approximately 600 Indian warriors'.[3]

Braddock and the 44th Regiment's own commanding officer, Colonel Peter Halkett, together with his son, James, were all killed during this battle on 9 July 1755.[4] The regiment itself saw considerable losses, partly by trying to counter the attack from a formal column, as ordered. A total of 976 British and Americans were killed or wounded, left without their commanders and

---

1 Glover, (ed.), *A Short Account*, p.7.
2 'The Battle of Prestonpans', *British Battles*, <https://www.britishbattles.com/jacobite-rebellion/battle-of-prestonpans/>, accessed September 2022.
3 Richard Holmes, *The Oxford Companion to Military History* (Oxford: Oxford University Press, 2001), p.597.
4 'Battle of Monongahela 1755 – Braddock's Defeat', *British Battles*, < https://www.britishbattles.com/french-indian-war/battle-of-monongahela-1755-braddocks-defeat/>, accessed October 2022.

MEN, MISCREANTS AND MARRIAGE: THE MILITARY MINDSET

were soundly beaten into an ignominious retreat. This was one of those instances which persuaded the British army to adapt to 'American warfare by creating [the equivalent of] ranger units and light infantry companies that could confront the threat of Indian [First Nations] and Canadian irregulars in the woods'.[5] Later, these tactics would become the basic modus operandi of the nineteenth century British Army and was employed whenever difficult terrain precluded the use of line formation, the latter being effectively abandoned after the Crimea. The 44th were ordered to Ireland 1763–1775, followed by another eight-year stint in America, during the American War of Independence 1775–1783.

Too late to be present at the Battle of Bunker's Hill, not arriving from Cork until 12 May 1775, the 44th Foot, with others, garrisoned Boston.[6] The following year the regiment fought at the Battles of Brooklyn, 26–29 August 1776; then Brandywine, 11 September 1777, when the 44th were in reserve; Germantown, 4 October 1777 (where the regiment lost its Lieutenant Colonel James Agnew) and Monmouth, 28 June 1778. Brooklyn, Brandywine and Germantown were British victories and Monmouth was deemed inconclusive. In retrospect, despite the American defeat at Germantown, the battle served to encourage and strengthen American determination.

In 1779, the 44th was camped at Staten Island and that autumn eight of the 10 companies moved to Paulus Hook, with a fort seaward of a large salt water marsh on two sides and sea on the other two sides, before all companies left New York for Canada on 15 May 1780.[7] Paulus Hook was where some of those men could be found, who threaded their way through the military life of William Roworth until the end of his service in 1797. Some of the men feature in his letters, like Sergeant Samuel Fetherston, who suffered from rheumatism and his wound from the Battle of Brandywine, but who served for 22 years, until his discharge in 1792.[8] Private James Dougherty (to be Roworth's groomsman at his marriage) was in Captain George Benson's Company 6 July 1780 at Paulus Hook.[9] He died in 1796 in St Lucia. Brown-haired, hazel eyed Serjeant William Duff, above the average height at 5 feet 11 inches, was wounded twice in America, in the right thigh at Princeton, 3 January 1777 and in the right ankle at Brandywine. He was discharged in 1803 aged 52 after 25 years of service.[10] So some survived Roworth, but many did not.

With the death of General James Abercromby, Colonel of the 44th in 1781, the colonelcy of the 44th was given to Major General Charles Rainsford

---

5   David.L. Preston, 'Braddock's Defeat — The Battle of Monongahela and the Road to Revolution', *Military History Now*, <https://militaryhistorynow.com/2018/06/03/braddocks-defeat-the-battle-of-the-monongahela-and-the-road-to-revolution/>, accessed October 2022.
6   Burrows, *Essex Regiment*, p.18
7   Thomas Carter, *Historical Record of the Forty–Fourth, or the East Essex Regiment* (Chatham: Gale & Polden, 1887), p.26.
8   TNA: WO 121/13/305: Fetherston, certificate of service.
9   TNA: WO 12/5637: Muster Roll, Captain George Benson's Company. Paulus Hook, 6 February 1780
10 TNA: WO 121/160/150 & WO 121/29/65: Duff, certificate of service and discharge papers.

(of whom more later). In 1782 King George III ordered the regiments in the British Army to be assigned county names, primarily chosen by their colonels, with the hope that it might aid recruitment from those regions. Rainsford, through his family affiliations, chose East Essex. Rainsford had been born in West Ham, Essex, on 3 February 1728 and maintained links with that county for the rest of his life including, in 1773, being elected as MP for Maldon. By this time the 41year-old regiment was in Quebec and there it remained for a further five years until 1786 and a lifetime away from the 'inexperienced young soldiers' of Prestonpans.

Now is the time to look at the military hierarchy of the 44th Foot when Roworth joined his regiment at Hilsea in September 1786 since, as with any regiment, many comrades remained constant throughout the whole of their service. On any muster roll, the names of all officers and private men were recorded under specific headings. The full muster had lists of the officers in command from the colonel, lieutenant colonels and majors, followed by captains of companies, the captain-lieutenant, lieutenants and ensigns – all commissioned officers.

First published in 1802, Charles James's *Military Dictionary* has been (and still is) the go-to source of contemporary terms and information, concerning the titles and responsibilities of the different ranks in the military hierarchy, in the long eighteenth century.[11] He informs us that:

> A COLONEL of a regiment … is … the head of a given number of men; the clothing, &c, of whom is exclusively entrusted to him, as well as the appointment of an agent, who receives the pay and subsistence of the corps, but for whose solvency and character, the colonel is responsible to the public … He cannot be too careful to maintain union and harmony among his officers … to keep up subordination with unalterable firmness; to do justice to everyone, to employ all his credit to procure favours to the corps in general, and to the officers in particular, without ever losing sight of the health, comfort and contentment of his men.

The title of 'Colonel of the Regiment' carried certain obligations. Although the presence of the colonel was rarely required, as a conscientious man it behoved him to care for the welfare of his men, to engender goodwill and support for his officers, to be ready to advise on all aspects of the recruitment of officers, to visit and review the regiment, to act as a representative for the regiment and to maintain high standards at all times. A regimental colonelcy was an appointment and not a rank, and they did not have to be present with the regiment as it was commanded day-to-day by a lieutenant colonel. James states:

> A Lieutenant-COLONEL is the second person in command of a regiment. Under his direction all the affairs of the regiment roll. His military qualifications should be adequate to the size and importance of the corps he has the honour to serve in.

---

11   C. James, *A New and Enlarged Military Dictionary, or, Alphabetical Explanation of Technical Terms* (London: Egerton, 1810). The following extracts are taken from the relevant entries.

MEN, MISCREANTS AND MARRIAGE: THE MILITARY MINDSET

> The next rank to serve under a lieutenant colonel is a major and is generally promoted from the eldest [most senior] captain: he is to take care that the regiment be well-exercised, to see it march in good order, and to rally it in case of being broken in action: he and the adjutant are the only officers among the infantry that are allowed to be on horseback in the time of action, that they may the more readily execute the colonel's orders.

Below the major were the captains.

> He is both to march and fight at the head of his company … a captain has in most services the power of appointing his own serjeants and corporals, but cannot by his own authority reduce or break them; neither can he punish a soldier with death, unless he revolts against him on duty.

Between the captains and lieutenants came a captain-lieutenant and captain; the commanding officer of the colonel's company, as the colonel was not usually present with the regiment. Below the captains were the lieutenants. They could be involved in recruitment, but their prime function was to be able to, 'take the command upon the death or absence of the superior officer.' In regiments of foot the lowest of the commissioned officers were the ensigns, two of whom bore the Regimental and the King's Colours.

The most senior of the non-commissioned officers was the serjeant-major:

> … of great merit and capacity, subordinate to the adjutant, as the latter is to the major … He is, in fact, an assistant to the adjutant. It is his peculiar duty to be perfect master of anything which relates to drills: and it is always expected, that he should set an example, to the rest of the non-commissioned officers, of manly, soldier-like, and zealous activity.

The duties of a serjeant-major were many and onerous, for example, amongst them was the responsibility of drilling all young officers who entered the regiment, in the manual and platoon exercises, in quick and slow marches and the art of wheeling, for which he was paid by the individual officers. Another aspect was to oversee the training of all the 'awkward' soldiers until their drill was perfect. An important aspect of his duties was in organisation, keeping accurate rosters of the privates, together with details of all corporals and serjeants and dates of their appointments, therefore it was a necessity for him to be literate.

With the serjeant major were his fellow serjeants, of whom there were usually three to a company. James informs us that a serjeant was: 'armed with a pike, and appointed to see discipline observed; to teach the private men their exercise; and to order and straiten, and form ranks, files, &c. He receives the order from the serjeant-major.'

Drummers were essential to the effective workings of the regiment. The over-riding purpose of the drums to the military army was for communication. James cites 10 individual beats to inform the men of what should happen and when, to give an exact routine to their day. That helped to instil a discipline and order to the day and all soldiers would be aware of their message the drumbeat carried at any time of the day or night. The beats the drummers used most frequently are recorded by James as follows:

> *The general*, is to give notice to the troops that they are to march.
> *The assembly*, to order the troops to repair to the place of rendezvous, or to their colours.
> *The march*, to command them to move, always with the left foot first.
> *Tat-too, or tap-too*, to order all to retire to their quarters.
> *The reveillé*, always beats at break of day, and is to warn soldiers to rise, and the centinels to forbear challenging, and to give leave to come out of quarters.
> *To arms*, for soldiers who are dispersed to repair them.
> *The retreat*, a signal to draw off from the enemy. It likewise means a beat in both camp and garrison a little before sunset, at which time the gates are shut, and the soldiers to repair to their barracks.
> *The alarm*, is to give notice of sudden danger, that all may be in readiness for immediate duty.
> *The parley*, is a signal to demand some conference with the enemy.

Serjeants and drummers formed up outside of the ranks and files of the regiment, those ranks and files were made up of corporals and privates. A corporal was, 'a rank and file man with superior pay to that of common soldiers and with nominal rank under a serjeant. He has charge of one of the squads of a company, places and relieves centinels, and keeps good order in the guard.' The privates, or private men, were the ordinary soldiers and made up the bulk of the regiment.

All soldiers, whatever their rank, were recorded on a muster roll, under regular headings with any relevant individual comments, such as 'on command' (meaning on duty either in the barracks or elsewhere) or 'recruiting', 'discharged', 'drafted', 'on furlow' or 'died' beside a soldier's name. As shown above Roworth's name has already appeared twice since enlistment and the muster rolls will continue to follow his passage throughout his time with the army, as they will with each and every man for good or ill.

In times of peace, part of the army's duties was to provide assistance and constabulary service to the civilian authorities. Within a couple of weeks of Roworth's arrival at Hilsea Barracks, that assistance was likely to have been called upon (as for example, the 44th would do in Leeds, Isle of Man, Scotland and Ireland) storms laid waste to parts of the southern half of Britain on 14–15 September 1786.[12] There was immense damage to hundreds of buildings, livestock and people. Many ships were lost at sea with all their crews, as evidenced by the number of bodies lying on beaches. Part of the Battery at Brighthelmstone (today's Brighton) was washed away by the sea. As all available redcoats from Hilsea helped in the gruelling aftermath, many must have been eternally grateful not to be at sea themselves.

---

12   Boult, *Christian's Fleet*, pp.63–76.

MEN, MISCREANTS AND MARRIAGE: THE MILITARY MINDSET

Private Thomas Howarth, however, was not involved in the harrowing clear-up as, with nine others, he took his chance and deserted on 25 September. Unfortunately for him, his freedom was short-lived as he was apprehended in Frome in Somerset for stealing clothing from a shop in Catherine Street on 28 October with two others, William Foster (also a deserter from the 44th) and a woman, Elizabeth Hutchinson. Howarth, who had 'landed from Quebec about a month since, and has been a deserter from the 44th regiment, late at Hilsea barracks', was described as 19 years old from Manchester and a horse-breaker by profession.[13] The three had stolen clothing for men, women and children, probably for themselves and families, but seem to have developed a fetish for waistcoats as they had purloined all of 20! These might have been attractive and therefore saleable. All three were found guilty and 'capitally convicted', but Howarth had made a voluntary confession, which probably helped save his life.[14] He was reprieved, which at the time meant transportation, commencing with some time on a hulk, before embarkation. That could be for months or even years in the most filthy and inhumane conditions. At this time, transportation destinations were in flux. Officially America had closed her doors to British convicts in the spring of 1775 at the beginning of the American War of Independence. Transportation to Australia commenced on 13 May 1787 with the First Fleet leaving Portsmouth for Botany Bay.

John Clarkson, who had enlisted with Roworth in Manchester the previous February, was among 23 of the latest recruits to be discharged, on 13 December 1786. Whatever happened to individuals, new recruits would have spent many hours each day learning the finer points of drill and familiarising themselves with their weapons and how to fire with live ball. Nothing was so instructive as to fire live rounds at a target. Roworth entered his chosen profession just at the right time as 'until 1785, battalions received per annum … roughly 1,200 balls, [that is just] two to four rounds of ball each man could expect to fire in a year'.[15] Fortunately, in 1786, the ball allocation was increased to 9,600 rounds a year for each battalion – the equivalent of 30 balls per man. However, much of the practice would be with blanks, as the mechanics and speed of firing were of greater consideration than complete accuracy at this stage.

Burrows, historian of the regiment, tells us that as soon as Rainsford received his colonelcy in 1781, he wrote to Lieutenant Colonel Henry Hope, the commanding officer, requesting to be informed of 'the state of the Regiment' and 'that of the accoutrements … if you think of anything that may be necessary for me to concur in I shall be happy to show my readiness to comply with it'. He also added details of his agents, father and son, John and George Hesse, so that Hope could keep him informed of any concerns of the 44th at all times, via his agents. In 1782, Rainsford wrote to Hope again concerning his efforts at organising recruitment for the East Essex. Ten years later, in 1792, the 44th Foot were headed for Dublin and while they were there,

---

13   *Salisbury and Winchester Journal*, Monday 6 November 1786.
14   *Northampton Mercury*, Saturday 24 March 1787.
15   Reid, *The British Redcoat*, p.23.

'Colonel Rainsford's attention was drawn to the fact that new equipment and accoutrements were required for the drummers, pioneers, light infantry and grenadiers for "as the corps here vie with each other in appearance and discipline, I am sensible you would not desire the 44th to be eclipsed."'[16]

In 1794, Rainsford was again notified that the '44th, in common with other regiments in Ireland, had been increased to 12 companies, and that recruiting was active in that country'.[17] Holmes pointed out that 'a colonel who took his regiment's welfare seriously ... could spend large sums of his own money on it'.[18] A colonel could lavish money on the regiment's uniforms or fund a band, but likewise they could scrimp and save where possible to minimise their costs. Rainsford may have travelled to Northumberland in August 1795, when the 44th Foot, as part of the army fresh home from the War of the First Coalition, was reviewed by Colonel George Osborn at Blyth – or more likely the review at Southampton in the following September, attended by His Majesty, together with the Duke of York and other dignitaries.

So, was Rainsford an effective colonel of his regiment? He had a large family, was a Fellow of the Royal Society and the Antiquarian Society, was a free-mason with interests in alchemy and magnetism, and supported several benevolent societies. Upon his death on 24 May 1809, he left many volumes of manuscripts about his interests. He had served as MP for Maldon (1772–1774), Bere Alston (1787–1788) and Newport in Cornwall (1790–1796). His military service was long and varied, having risen from a cornet in 1744 to equerry to William, Duke of Gloucester until 1780 and then king's aide-de-camp (1777–1782). Also, that military service extended from Flanders, Fontenoy, the Jacobite Rising, Gibraltar, Germany and Portugal to Governor of Gibraltar (1794–1795), finally coming to rest as Governor of Cliff Fort, Tynemouth – clearly a full and overflowing life. Whether he had the time to perform his rightful duties to his colonelcy of the 44th Foot, it is recorded that they were at least partially fulfilled. He is known to have expressed his concerns on paper about their uniforms and methods of recruitment. He probably left all else to Lieutenant Colonel Henry Hope.[19]

In the circumstances, it was to be hoped that the regiment was left in the capable hands of its lieutenant colonel. Henry Hope had succeeded James Agnew as lieutenant colonel in 1777. However, by 1786, Hope was another absentee officer, who by that time had been sworn in as Acting Lieutenant Governor of Quebec Province on 2 November 1785 and was thought by the Canadians to be 'an efficient administrator', as well as 'hot-tempered' but 'very polite'.[20] Port Hope, the township municipality of Hope, and the municipality of Hope Town, Quebec, were named after him. He finally expired on 13 April 1789, having died from 'his Improper Gallantries ... the most shocking object that can be imagined – his Features & the greatest part of his Face

---

16 Burrows, *Essex Regiment*, pp.24–28.
17 Burrows, *Essex Regiment*, p.27.
18 Holmes, *Redcoat*, p.110.
19 A.J.H. Richardson, *Dictionary of Canadian Biography, 1771–1800* (Canada: University of Toronto Press, 1979) vol.IV, p.367.
20 Richardson, *Canadian Biography*, vol.IV, p.367.

MEN, MISCREANTS AND MARRIAGE: THE MILITARY MINDSET

entirely destroy'd'.[21] This was a somewhat roundabout way of saying that he died of tertiary syphilis. Whatever the cause, there is a monument to him by the sculptor John Bacon to be found in the north transept of Westminster Abbey.[22] He was marked absent in the muster rolls 'by the King's leave' from 1785–1789.

Colonel David Dundas, concerned by the poor discipline in the British Army in general, published the *Principles of Military Movements* in 1788. It was an endeavour to improve army discipline, based on 'many of the principles and reasons on which the Prussian practice is founded'.[23] Dundas had observed the Prussian army in Silesia (as had Sir John Moore as a young boy). Dundas's work was later adopted as the *Rules and Regulations, for the Formations, Field Exercise and Movements of His Majesty's Forces*. So, Roworth and his comrades would have had to learn the new drill, although many commanding officers were slow to adapt to the new regulations.

With Hope absent, the regiment appears to have been left in the hands of Major Bryan Blundell. In 1783, he had been appointed a major in the 44th Foot, aged 33, and was in command when Roworth, Clarkson, Goodbody and Newton arrived at Hilsea. He remained with the 44th for the next 10 years, serving with distinction at the capture of Guadeloupe, 1794, and was then promoted to lieutenant colonel in the 45th Foot.[24] He was married on 28 July 1795 in Shrewsbury to Sarah Mason, and was a brigadier general before he died aged only 46 in 1799.

There were considerable fluctuations in both numbers and reasons for officers taking leave of absence. The Reverend Thomas St Clare Abercromby, chaplain to the 44th Foot (listed as 'Absent Major's leave'), was ordered to return – but he never did and continued to be absent until finally being struck off in 1797, 10 years later.[25] In his defence (if anything), it must be said that the military rarely appeared to chase after their absentee chaplains, of whom there were many. It was all part of the prevailing lax mores of the army in the later years of the eighteenth century. Reverend Abercromby's final dénouement was probably accelerated by the royal warrant of 23 September 1796, which 'abolished regimental chaplains', which until that date had been attached to individual regiments.[26] However a new Army Chaplain's Department was established on the very same day, being one of the many reforms the Duke of York brought to army life in his position as Commander-in-Chief, and the post of regimental chaplain was later reinstated.[27] With the status quo those new recruits of 1786 would have glimpsed neither their chaplain's surplice nor his preaching bands.

21　Richardson, *Canadian Biography*, Vol.IV, p.367.
22　Henry Hope, *Westminster Abbey*, <http://www.westminster-abbey.org/our-history/people/henry-hope>, accessed March 2021.
23　David Dundas, *Principles of Military Movements, chiefly applied to Infantry* (London: T. Cadell and Davies, 1795).
24　Richardson, *Canadian Biography*, p.367.
25　TNA: WO 12/5639: Muster Roll for 25 June to 24 December 1796.
26　Reid, *Redcoat Officer 1740–1815* (Oxford: Osprey, 2002), p.8.
27　Michael Snape, *The Redcoat and Religion: The Forgotten History of the British Soldier from the Age of Marlborough to the Eve of the First World War* (Abingdon: Routledge, 2005), p.89.

Also, on the regimental staff of the 44th Foot at the time was Adjutant David Stark, whose duties included carrying orders from the brigade major, administrative duties, and keeping 'an exact roster and roll of duties and have a perfect knowledge of all manoeuvres', the latter necessary in his training of subalterns.[28] Quartermaster John Tuffie's duties were primarily concerned with the provision of accommodation, food and provisions. His name occurs from time to time in Roworth's letters. Surgeon William Stark and George Graham, his Surgeon's Mate, as expected saw to all things medical, both at home and abroad, where their skills would be required especially in times of conflict or epidemic.

When Roworth enlisted in 1786, the army as a whole was in a similar state of flux as it always had been between its wars, due to the lack of an effective standing army. The American War of Independence had ended three years earlier with defeat for the British. As previously mentioned, consecutive British governments were never prepared for the next war but, in spite of losing the American War of Independence, army tactics were not in quite the same chaotic and incompetent circumstances which have been bandied about in often recurrent reportage of the late 1700s ever since. In fact, there were individual British officers who (as early as the 1750s, for example, Dalrymple) had appreciated the necessity of reading the terrain to configure a looser form of warfare and the freedom to make use of a soldier's initiative. Paul Knight in his book about the 47th Foot, *A Very Fine Regiment*, stresses that the soldiers were not the incompetent automata they were purported to be. Indeed, Knight states, they went to war in America supplied with the 'a new drill manual introduced in 1764, new uniform in 1768 and the new Short Land Pattern Musket in 1769.' As well as innovative instructions for light infantry tactics from Lieutenant General George Townshend and Major General William Howe.[29]

With the winter of 1786–1787 over, preparations were made for the upcoming review by Major General Sir George Osborn (1742–1818). He could be an exacting commander and was an experienced and battle-tried soldier from the recent wars with America. A few days after the Battle of Brandywine, he and another officer discovered two guards grenadiers plundering. Each man received 500 lashes for his misdemeanours.[30] While in America, Osborn served as the inspector to the German auxiliaries. The Americans did not like him for remarks he had made concerning a dead American soldier, which, though witty, were thoughtless and unpleasant.[31] He could be a very tough man; the whole regiment, or what was left of it, together with the newest recruits, would have been worked hard by their non-commissioned officers to prove their abilities. The review was to be held on 16 May 1787.

---

28   James, *Military Dictionary*, p.455.
29   P. Knight, *A Very Fine Regiment* (Warwick: Helion, 2022), p.61.
30   Thomas.J. McGuire, T*he Philadelphia Campaign* (Mechanicsburg: Stackpole Books, 2006), vol.I, p.294.
31   McGuire, *Philadelphia Campaign*, pp.29–31.

MEN, MISCREANTS AND MARRIAGE: THE MILITARY MINDSET

At Hilsea, Osborn's complete report on the 44th Foot was both a revelation and a salutary lesson. The report was damning for the most part and his words are quoted verbatim here:

OFFICERS. A very young Corps, mostly exchanged since the Peace. Dressed uniform. Attentive under arms.

NON-COMMISSIONED OFFICERS. Mostly recruiting, the few with the regiment worn-out.

DRUMMERS AND FIFERS. The Fifers are quite boys, the Band very young MEN. Very indifferent at present, the Recruits obtained for the Regiment before they arrived were many of them discharged from other Corps. The regiment received transfers in Canada which were indifferent, not yet discharged.

RECRUITS SINCE LAST REVIEW. 129. Not at all promising. They have not been successful in Recruiting in E. Essex. They have a Captain's party in London.

NO. OF MEN TO BE DISCHARGED. 21 Approved to be immediately discharged. Worn out or undersized. When the Regiment is relieved from Fort Cumberland, they will require a still greater Discharge.

MARCHING. The Few Men who appear'd under arms, amounting to 132 marched well in slow and quick time.

MANUAL EXERCISE. Performed in Time, accordingly to the Regulations.

FIRINGS. Performed with Exactness and Attention.

ARMS. Received New very lately, but not good, being the arms bought in Holland during the War.

ACCOUTREMENTS. All Good.

CLOTHING. Very good, and well fitted.

REGIMENTAL ACCOUNTS. Regularly kept.

COMPLAINTS. The Duty at Portsmouth prevents their sending out Parties for the Recruiting of the Regiment.

OFFICERS ABSENT. None – The Lieut. Colonel being Lieut Governor of Quebec, without Leave. The Regiment has been for some time commanded by the Major. [Bryan Blundell]

GENERAL OBSERVATIONS. The Regiment having had 134 of their best Men transferr'd to other Corps in Canada, and having hitherto not been successful in their Recruiting, will be sometime before it can be complete in Numbers and Appearance.[32]

Additional comment was given for an 'Exercise according to the Regulation'. Osborn recorded that 'the Regiment Manoeuvred little more than changing their several Fronts, owing to the Smallness of the Battalion', only 132 men which barely constituted two companies. His report was a full and frank statement of facts, as he saw them.

So, it appeared that despite small numbers of personnel, the drills and manoeuvres, manual exercises, firing, marching and accoutrements were all good, but the calibre of the men, non-commissioned officers and methods of recruiting were all sadly lacking.

---

32   TNA: WO 27/60: Inspection 44th Foot, May 1787.

As Osborn indicated above, all responsibilities had fallen upon the shoulders of Major Bryan Blundell, who had joined the service as an ensign in May 1775, gazetted lieutenant in February 1777, captain in January 1778, and who had fought through the American War, so was not inexperienced. But from Osborn's report, it was evident that Blundell was training up a mix of very raw recruits, together with exhausted and worn-out veterans, This was not the last time the redcoats of the 44th Foot would be reviewed by Osborn.

The regiment appeared to be really struggling. Only three commissioned officers were present at this point, Captain Benjamin Fish, who had recovered from the leg wound he received at Brandywine, Lieutenant Rufane Shawe Donkin and Ensign Montague Thorley. Four captains were away recruiting – Colin Campbell, William Rogerson, George Kennedy and James Gage. They were having little success, according to Osborn. Lieutenants Thomas Brown and Henry Holland had been absent since 22 March 1787 by the King's leave, and neither were due to return until the following September. Lieutenant William Bathurst Pye, absent from 15 November 1786, had not joined since appointed in the East Indies. He could take months to arrive. Lieutenant George Kennedy, absent since 21 March, had not yet re-joined and Ensign Richard M. Dickens was recruiting. This was not an unusual state of affairs for any regiment, but the absence of so many officers would not have been helpful to those 'worn and tired-out' or 'raw' rank and file.

A 'General Return of Officers' was also taken, which included nationality, whether English (buttressed by the Welsh, who were thrown in under that soubriquet), Scotch, Irish or Foreigners. Age and length of service were noted, plus dates of commissions.[33] Next, the men were grouped by age, which graduated in steps of five years after the initial 18 to 20, 25, 30 and so on up to 55. On this return, there were eight men over 50 years, 12 over 45, and 49 between 20 and 25. Height and size were recorded, graduated in half inches from five feet six inches to six feet two inches. Only three men were over six feet, while there were 68 under five feet six inches, although that may have been due to the inclusion of 'raw' boy soldiers who had not finished growing. Finally, the return covered also the years of service; a total of four men had completed 30–35 years, those completing 10 and 15 years were 39 and 47 men, respectively, and over 91 had just between one and two years service.[34]

On 1 May 1787, on the muster roll for 25 December 1786 to 24 June 1787, Roworth's name appeared indicating his first step up. On 9 October, he and seven others – William Forester, John Beatty, James Redfern, John Rockcliff, Edward Smith and James Ratchford – were appointed corporals.[35] Roworth had served for one year and 249 days before his first promotion. In contrast, James Redfern – promoted with him and originally a hosier from Mansfield, in Nottinghamshire – who had enlisted in 1774, had been 13 years a private,

---

33 TNA: WO 27/60: Inspection 44th Foot, May 1787.
34 TNA: WO 27/60: Inspection 44th Foot, May 1787.
35 TNA: WO 12/5638: Muster Roll 25 December 1796 to 24 June 1787.

MEN, MISCREANTS AND MARRIAGE: THE MILITARY MINDSET

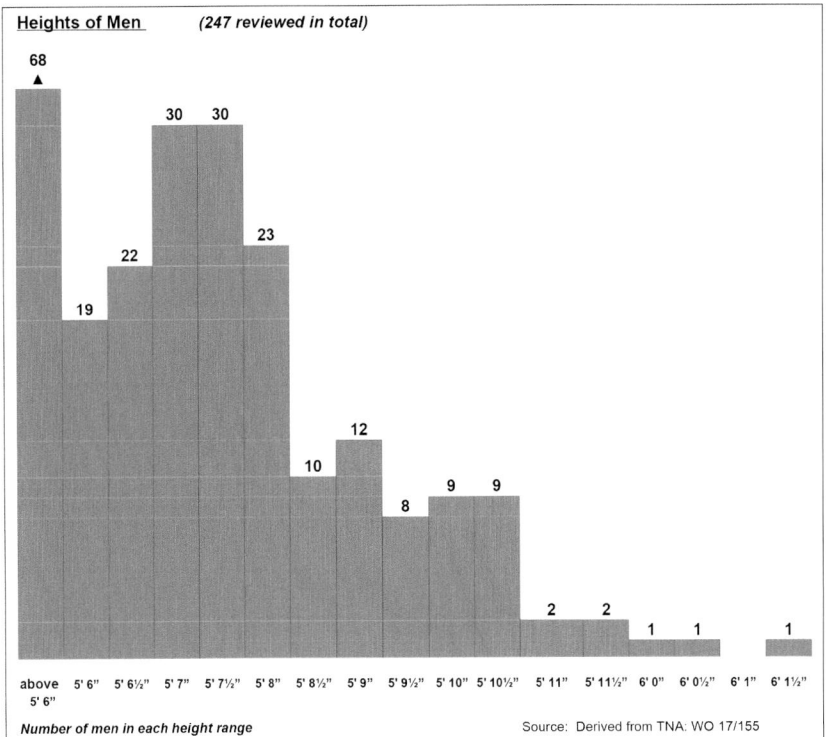

44th Regiment of Foot. Analysis by Height. 16 May 1787

mostly in America.[36] This promotion was Redfern's first, at the top of the middling range in height at five foot nine inches, he eventually totalled (on discharge) 24 years in the service, with eight years as a corporal and three as a serjeant.

Redfern was discharged in Dublin on 16 February 1794 (20 years from enlistment) at the age of 45. He may have completed another five years as a veteran, but there appears to be no record as such.

This first promotion would have been a significant step for Roworth and provided an indication of his personality. Ideally, the rank was given to those perceived to be intelligent and enthusiastic, who took care of their uniform and appearances and who wanted to succeed and climb the ladder. If a corporal was to progress to the rank of serjeant, he had to be able to control a small group of soldiers under his command. Throughout his career, Roworth appears to have made only one major mistake but was never found to be demoted once he had attained that first step up from a private man, apart from the blanket anomaly mentioned below. He would have felt that he was on his way just 21 months after volunteering and been proud of the loop of white cord attached to the right shoulder of his red coat, which denoted the position of corporal for an eighteenth-century soldier.[37] Having said that, it was certainly not unusual for men to be promoted and demoted several times during the course of their service, depending on the measure of their

---

36 TNA: WO 97/595/124: Royal Hospital, Chelsea: Soldiers Service Documents, 1760–1854.
37 Reid, *British Redcoat*, p.13.

NOT SO EASY, LADS

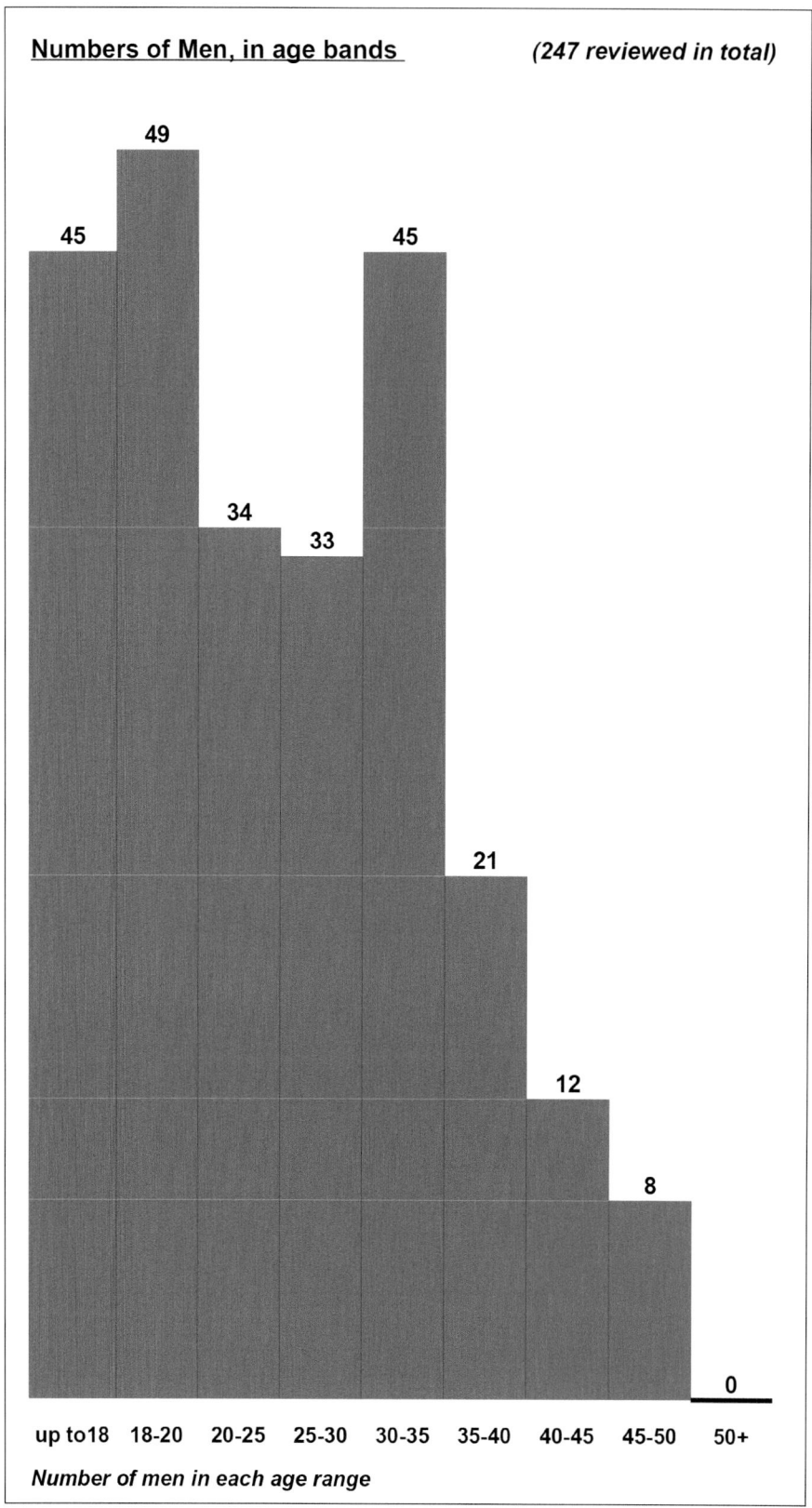

44th Regiment of Foot. Analysis by Age. 16 May 1787.

MEN, MISCREANTS AND MARRIAGE: THE MILITARY MINDSET

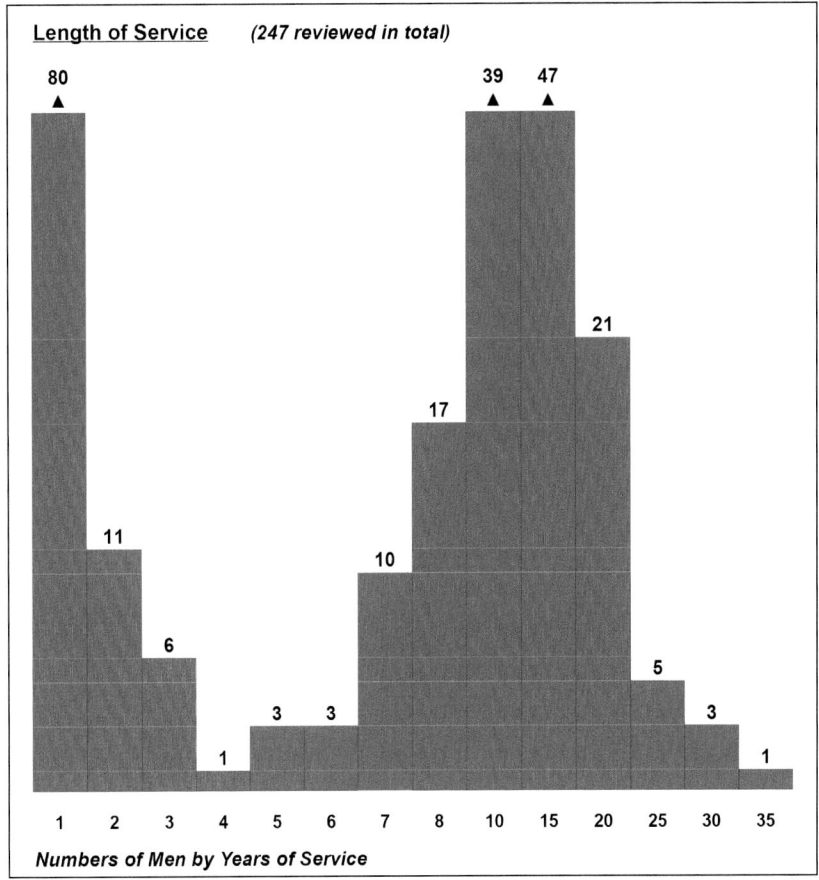

44th Regiment of Foot. Years of Service. Hilsea. 16 May 1787

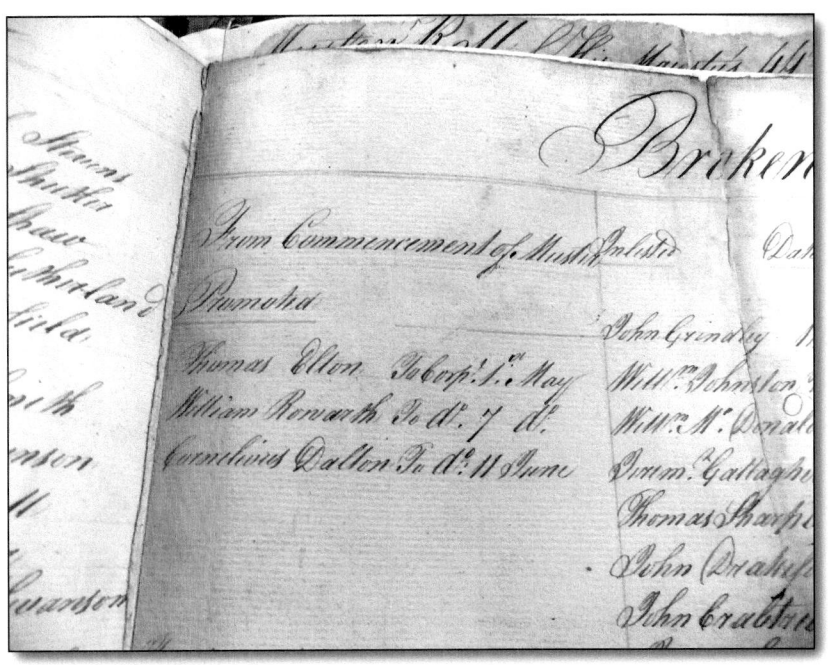

Roworth's promotion to corporal 7 May 1787 on the Muster Roll for 25 June to 24 December 1787. ()TNA: WO 12/5638/1)

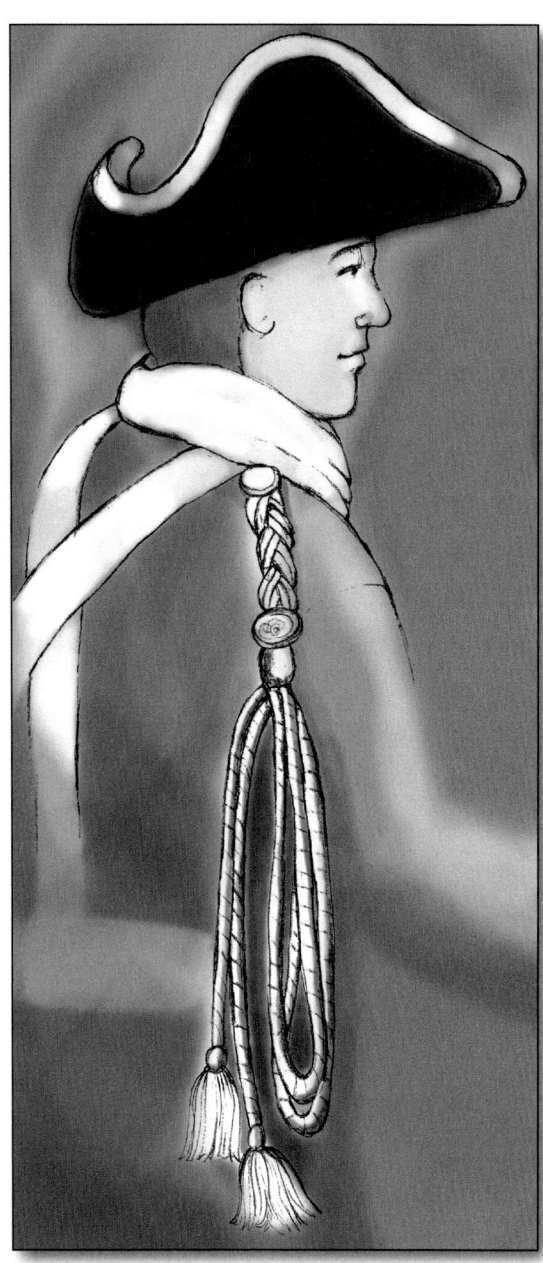

As a newly promoted Corporal Roworth would have worn a white cord on his right shoulder, similar to this one. (Illustrated by Jo Davies)

transgressions, most often drunkenness. The anomaly mentioned above was on the muster for 25 June to 24 December 1787 as all corporals were shown as promoted briefly for about a month and then returned to corporals again. For example, Peter MacNamara, Thomas Elton, John Smith, Thomas Askey, James Mairs, James Cochran and William Griffin were grouped together and marked to be serjeants on 24 September and returned to corporal 10 November. Roworth was marked to be serjeant with two others on 18 October to return to corporal on 10 November 1787. As were all the men, in various groupings, to return to corporals on 10 November, having done one or two months as serjeant, except for eight of them, which included Thomas Legge, who was promoted to serjeant with no return to corporal.

Roworth's company was among eight destined for Guernsey at this time. The 44th Foot with the 55th and 17th Foot embarked at Southampton on the six transports waiting for them 'toward the end of October 1787'.[38] The weather at sea was stormy and the voyage equally so. The inimitable John Shipp, who made the same journey in similar weather a number of years later, described himself on disembarkation as looking like a 'squeezed lemon'.[39]

Their destination was Fort George, Guernsey, in the Channel Islands. The fort was a work in progress which sat on its large promontory at St Peter Port. Begun in 1780, it was not completed until 1812. There was always concern about a possible attack from France, especially as the French had been America's ally in the recent war.

The first monthly return of the 44th Foot at Fort George, dated 1 November 1787, stated that there were 14 serjeants, 10 drummers and fifers; and 135 rank and file fit for duty, 17 were sick in quarters (though there were none in general hospitals), 21 were out in recruiting parties and five were on 'furlow'.[40]

---

38 Carter, *44th Foot*, p.27.
39 Shipp, *Memoirs*, p.29.
40 TNA: WO 17/155: Monthly Return for 1 November 1787.

MEN, MISCREANTS AND MARRIAGE: THE MILITARY MINDSET

State of the 44th Foot, Fort George, Guernsey, 1 November 1787, TNA: WO 17/155.

Present					Rank & File					Number Wanting		
Officers	Staff	QM	Sjt	Drum	Present	Sick	On Com'd	Other	Total	Sjt	Drum	R&F
15	2	1	14	10	135	17	-	26	178	-	8	442

The stalwart and hard-working Major Bryan Blundell was present with the regiment. Six out of eight captains were also present, including Fish, Campbell, Hassard, Gage, Dunne and Wynyard. Lieutenants Brown and Pye were absent, the former by the King's leave, the latter had not joined since appointed and was presumably in transit somewhere on his journey from the East Indies – leaving four lieutenants present. Of the five ensigns, Holme and Beddle were absent; the first was ordered to join, the second marked down as not joined since appointed. The chaplain was absent by an officer's leave – as per usual. Eight corporals were appointed serjeants, two private men were made drummers, one man was claimed by and turned over to the Portsmouth division of the marines, and 58 recruits had not joined. Even though the 44th's numbers were low, 70 rank and file were drafted into the 55th (Westmorland) Regiment of Foot. Why is not clear as they do not seem to have been about to be posted overseas, but this was not the first last time, nor the last, that members of the 44th were to be drafted into the 55th.[41]

The monthly return for 1 December 1787 notes that 37 recruits had joined since the previous return; eight serjeants had been demoted to rank and file, the same demotion applied to seven drummers, 87 recruits had still not returned from England and one drummer had been discharged.[42]

There are no records in journals or diaries of the celebrations of Christmas 1787 in the Guernsey barracks, but there are many memories of other redcoats and other Christmases scattered through memoirs and journals. They were naturally varied according to circumstances, geographical positions and whether at peace or war and are examples of where and how different those seasons might be for any soldier of any rank.

Jonathan Leach described his own experience:

> [A]fter a six weeks' voyage from Portsmouth, we anchored on Christmas day in Carlisle Bay, Barbadoes [sic]. The sky was cloudless, and the heat sufficiently intense to satisfy a salamander. We could scarcely, at first, be reconciled of it being Christmas, with a blazing sun over our heads; every tree and plant seen on the island being as green as we have them in England in Midsummer; and, above all, the total absence of snow, frost, and the dark and lowering clouds emblematic of that season in Europe.[43]

Leach and his comrades must have felt quite alien.

In a forerunner to the informal 1914 Christmas truce that is so often quoted, and despite several days of 'fights or skirmishes with the enemy',

---

41 TNA: WO 17/155: Monthly Return for 1 November 1787.
42 TNA: WO 17/155: Monthly Return for 1 December 1787.
43 Jonathan Leach, *Captain of the 95th Rifles* (Driffield: Leonaur, 2005), p.15.

exactly 100 years earlier, Edward Costello described a similar fraternisation with the enemy:

> We still kept up an excellent private feeling on both sides at the outposts. As an instance, although I must remark a General order had been promulgated prohibiting all intercourse with the enemy on pain of death, our company was on picquet … we clubbed half a dollar each, and sent a man into the French picquet-house to purchase brandy. It was, I recollect Christmas night.[44]

A soldier of the 71st (Highland) Regiment of Foot describes the 'thrill of joy which ran through my whole body' when 'on the 25 December 1807, after an absence of seventeen months from Britain … I landed at the Cove of Cork in Ireland'.[45] Wonderful indeed – but just 12 months later, on Christmas Day 1808, the comparison could not have been more extreme as Todd and the 71st Foot found themselves on the first day of the British retreat to Corunna. Here, a final battle between the French and the British took place and brought the loss of (the revered by many and disliked by some) Lieutenant General Sir John Moore and fame for all those there. What a difference a year could make!

It was likely that the newly promoted Corporal Roworth attended church on Christmas morning 1787 in Guernsey. He was a non-conformist later in life, but, as a lad, he had grown up in Dunham in Cheshire with his parents and seven siblings under the patronage of the Stamford-Grey family at Dunham Massey. They would have attended the parish church on Sundays and holy days, which would have been the norm, while William Roworth Senior – as a manservant to the Greys – was likely to have worshipped up at the chapel in the 'big house'.

Quartermaster John Tuffie's family were staunch Methodists and would have been happy to worship with the newly emerging company of Methodists on the island of Guernsey. There was more than one unexpected link with the British Army when Methodism was introduced to Guernsey, just three years earlier, in 1783. This was brought about by 'a few soldiers' on service, who requested 'a preacher from Mr Wesley's connection, if one could be obtained'. A Lincolnshire man, French-speaking Mr Robert Carr Brackenbury, who was accompanying the preacher, John Wesley, when he received the letter, 'viewed the request of the soldiers as a providential opening for preaching the gospel in the Channel Islands, and instantly offered his services'.[46] Religion is often ignored when considering the British Army, but it was frequently as much part of the fabric of soldiers' lives in the late eighteenth century, as it was in the wider social scene. Revisiting briefly those 47 young soldiers from Chapter 1 who put pen to paper to record their experiences and make reference to their faith to a greater or lesser degree, just under half – 23

---

44 Edward Costello, *Rifleman Costello* (Driffield: Leonaur, 2005), p.196.
45 Anon., *Journal of a Soldier of the 71st, of Glasgow Regiment* (Edinburgh: Tait, 1819), p.46.
46 Jonathan Duncan, *The History of Guernsey with Occasional Notices of Jersey, Alderney, and Sark, and Biographical Sketches* (London: Longman, Brown, Green, and Longman, 1841), pp.357–362.

MEN, MISCREANTS AND MARRIAGE: THE MILITARY MINDSET

– declared themselves, in their personal accounts to be openly Christian, although the vast majority of people in Britain would have called themselves Christian at the time. Brackenbury arrived in Guernsey in December 1783 to be 'welcomed by a number of pious soldiers … to whom he preached in the barracks'.[47]

Nearing the end of the account of his service in the British Army, Quartermaster William Surtees of the 95th Rifles seemed to encapsulate the essence of these Christian soldiers:

> It is true my occupation had not been, strictly speaking, of a Christian character, but I believed I was fulfilling my duty; hence the peace of mind which I enjoyed … I cannot see why a Christian soldier should not be as zealous in the defence of his own king and country, as those who are activated by other motives; and it is certain, I believe, although I once doubted whether there was such a precept, that in whatever calling or occupation a man is in when called to become a Christian, that therein he should abide.[48]

It appears that religion could often make a soldier into a quieter and balanced man, concerning himself with his duties to God and the army – in fact, just the kind of man described above by William Surtees. In 1807, the Dean of Ripon handed out copies of the prayer book to the men of the 68th Foot, one of whom was John Green, he of *Vicissitudes*, who carried his book with him on the Continent. When he left the army in 1814, he remained convinced that his survival and contented life was due in thanks to the God whose hand he felt brought him through all his perils and injuries as a soldier of the king.[49]

With Christmas over, the 44th Foot remained in Guernsey until April 1788. Those last few months were spent, as always, on the service of recruiting; which occupied four lieutenants, four ensigns, four serjeants, four drummers and an indeterminate number of private men. During that time, Surgeon William Stark died on 21 February 1788. He was marked as absent by His Majesty's leave on the previous muster, so he may have already been ill. The surgeon's mate, George Graham, probably hoped for promotion but was overlooked this time and Archibald Douglas, surgeon's mate from the 11th Regiment of Foot, was promoted surgeon in Stark's place.

The 44th Foot returned to Portsmouth on board the *Montague* and *Peacock* transports on 26 April, accompanied by the 17th Foot from Jersey in the *Albion*. The regiment marched for London and there is a graphic account given by the *Leeds Intelligencer* (13 May 1788) of the men taking their leave from the capital on 8 May:

> The 44th regiment, lately arrived from Guernsey, passed over Westminster-bridge on Thursday from Kingston in Surry [sic], on their route to Leeds in Yorkshire; they marched down the bird cage walk in St. James's-Park, and formed the line in the hollow before Lord Milford's House. His Majesty came from the Queen's

---

47 Duncan, *History of Guernsey*, pp.357–362.
48 Surtees, *95th Rifles*, p.255.
49 Green, *Vicissitudes*, p.223.

Palace, attended by their Royal Highnesses the Dukes of York and Gloucester, General Faucitt, Lord Cathcart, and several officers – and road [sic] along the front and rear. The regiment then passed his Majesty in different columns, to slow and quick time, and afterwards proceeded to Barnet, up Grosvenor gate, to which place the King accompanied them. The appearance of the regiment was highly creditable both to the officers and men, particularly the grenadier and light infantry companies. The regiment marched with pioneers in front, and the baggage-waggons were fourteen in number. These veterans had suffered materially during the late war in America.[50]

By the end of the second week in May, the 44th had reached Leeds, in Yorkshire. Corporal Roworth had left them at some point, together with Private James Dougherty, so that Roworth could marry Mary Osborn of Nottingham, which he did on Friday 16 May 1788. The ceremony was held at the Parish Church of St Mary's by special licence, and the marriage was solemnized by the Reverend Nathaniel Haines, while Dougherty was groom's man. Both bride and groom were declared to be of full age – 21 or over (Roworth would have been about 24 or 25). All marriage ceremonies had to be held in the local parish church at that time, whatever the denomination of the consenting persons involved.[51] Corporal William Roworth and Mary were not the only couple in the 44th Foot to be married that spring. The *Caledonian Mercury* for 5 June 1788 announced that Lieutenant Murray Babington married a Miss Gordon just over two weeks later, on Monday 2 June, at Halleaths, near Lockerbie, in Scotland.[52]

Marriage in the military was very controversial. Once a man volunteered in the army, at whatever rank, marriage was not a step to be taken lightly and all men, without exception, had to ask permission of their commander. Marriage was a challenge – not just for the wedded couple – but for the military as a whole. 'Marriage is to be discouraged in the Regiment as much as possible'. So said the Adjutant General, William Fawcett. He continued,

> The Regiment has already more women than could possibly be allowed to embark for foreign service … Officers must explain to the men the many miseries that women are exposed to, even in England, when there are too many of them, and particularly on service; and, by every sort of persuasion, they must prevent their marrying, if possible.[53]

In Roworth's case, he must have received permission well ahead of the actual event, as his marriage was planned with care. The ceremony was booked in for a specific time on a specific day, as there were weddings both before and after his own that day. He would also have had to organise for a licence from the church authorities, though he would not necessarily have had the banns read on the statutory three Sundays preceding the marriage, as the license

---

50 *Leeds Intelligencer*, 13 May 1788.
51 Nottinghamshire Archives: St Mary's Marriage Records 1788, no.679.
52 *Caledonian Mercury*, Thursday, 5 June 1788.
53 William Fawcett, *Rules and Regulations for the Cavalry* (London: J. Walter, 1795), p.74.

would have taken into account that he was a soldier and could not live in the parish at the time. But before all this, he had to request leave to marry from his commanding officer – in this instance, Major Bryan Blundell – and also gain permission for his friend, James Dougherty, to take leave to act as the groom's man. With Roworth, now a corporal and aged 24, it was likely that since his enlistment Blundell had the gauge of his character. However, the groom was not the only one to be scrutinised. The prospective bride had to be as well, and Roworth would have been questioned carefully as to Mary's character. There appear to be no documents extant for the 44th Foot but, for example, in 1813, the 62nd Foot ordered: 'Marriage must be discouraged as much as possible, and before any application is made to the Commanding Officer for his consent, every reference must be made by the Officer commanding the company to which the man belongs, as to the character of the female, with respect to her honesty, good conduct, and ability to support herself.'[54]

That last assumed without hesitation that the 'female' in question would not be travelling 'on the strength'. That would actually be a subject to be discussed between the soldier and his intended, as will be discussed later in this book. Even then, if the wife wished to 'follow the drum', due to the military's method of lottery to limit the numbers – a lottery by its very nature would be too precarious to be a certainty – it was only so much wishful thinking for the majority of the wives.

Because there was no enshrined military law on marriage for commanding officers to follow, it appears that many regiments cobbled together their own versions, all of which endeavoured to establish parameters around the numbers of wives and children that would have to be supported by them. In wartime, service overseas, or on home duties, the Treasury could not afford to support innumerable family members with their accompanying baggage, as well as to transport what could turn out to be an unwieldy horde.

Roworth's marriage plans seem to have gone like clockwork, but if a soldier did not seek (or was refused) permission, his wife (and children if there were any) could be barred from virtually all aspects of barrack life and even refused access to the barracks and its grounds at all. If the soldier brought his wife into the barracks without permission, he could be condemned to the lash. Henderson cites the expansion of these rules by the 29th Foot, that the wife would not be considered 'as a woman of the regiment, or [receive] the smallest indulgence as such.'[55]

The army had to rely on the soldier's personal honesty, of course, which could come in a number of guises, ranging from completely honest to no honesty at all or even roguery. Some soldiers had multiple wives and families, not willing to be outdone by their naval brothers who, by repute, were known to have wives in every port. Marrying (or living with) a soldier could have grave results for a woman and their children if she had no other recourse than to rely on her man's pay. If she was an 'unofficial wife' with no access to the benefits of being a woman 'on the strength', then the outlook was pretty

---

54   Robert Henderson, 'A Soldier's Family in the British Army during the War of 1812', *War of 1812*, <www.warof1812.ca/family.htm>, accessed March 2021.
55   Henderson, 'A Soldier's Family'.

A view of Nottingham as William and Mary Roworth would have known it. 1822. (Author's Collection)

poor and as an 'unofficial wife' she had some other form of income, help from relatives or part-time work, or she might find herself literally out on the street, having to work as a prostitute or, at the very worst, go into the workhouse, where the children would be separated from her and from each other. If, on the other hand, she passed 'muster' and found herself living in the barracks, then her bed was paid for by her work at the laundry, cleaning, mending, cooking and even stints at nursing. She would, along with all the men, have food to eat and a bed to sleep on. The bed, though shared with her husband, might be hidden behind a curtain if she was lucky but well within earshot of between 10 and 20 or so private soldiers. If she was marrying a serjeant, by the end of the century, they were able sometimes to have their own room. Serjeant Thomas Jackson, while in the Stafford Militia stationed at Windsor Barracks, described the 'sleeping rooms' as holding 29 men, the serjeants as having rooms of their own and the 'attics … appropriated to married soldiers'.[56] A rare situation well-ahead of its time.

Whatever the sleeping arrangements at Bearwood Lane, once the few days respite was over for the Nottingham couple, Mary stayed with her parents, and Roworth and Dougherty took to the road again to march the 70-odd miles north-west to Leeds to rejoin the regiment.

---

56   Jackson, *Coldstream Serjeant*, p.28.

3

Smallpox to Smuggling: Leeds to the Isle of Man

'Strongest impressions of their truly meritorious conduct'[1]

For much of the second half-year's muster of 1788, Roworth spent his time on recruiting duties in Leeds. Some two years since volunteering, he and his comrades would have learned this part of their duties from watching and listening to every dramatic move and every impressive shout and patter that the recruiting serjeant employed to attract any impressionable young man who was dissatisfied with his lot. Once they had sufficiently imbibed the theatre, the privates would then have participated. After the day's exertions, the recruiting parties would have returned to their billets. Chapeltown Barracks were still some 32 years from being built, so the regiment was probably encamped on outlying fields or billeted with inn-keepers, or the local populace.

For the 44th Foot, the period spent in Leeds was not without its incidents, nor its public approbation. The regiment had been in the town for only a couple of months when local papers waxed lyrical, particularly so about the events of Tuesday, 3 July 1788.

A large procession was held for the passing of the new Wool Bill. The town's clothiers and the 'worsted and carpet manufacturers' came out in force to celebrate. Around 500 people were in the procession. The town band of music – together with the band belonging to the 44th Foot, fresh from their quarters – assembled early that morning in the White Cloth Hall yard, dressed for the occasion and the regiment suitably blackballed and pipe-clayed. Much hyperbole was flaunted in the *Leeds Intelligencer*, with many vivid descriptions of the local people dressed as well-known figures throughout many eras – from Hercules, with his club, suitably dressed in wool fleece (what else?) attended by Jason in his goatskin to 'King George III' and 'Mr Brumfit's carpet weavers', carrying – you guessed it – a carpet.[2] All were bound together by the theme of the day, that all-important commodity – wool. For once, recruiting may not have entered the soldiers' minds at all,

---

1   *Newcastle Courant*, Saturday 23 May 1789.
2   *Leeds Intelligencer*, Tuesday 8 July 1788.

but some young lad's heart may have beaten faster on seeing the soldiers with their scarlet tunics and yellow facings.

By the time of this spectacle the military band was not restricted to fifes and drums, but had among their instruments clarinets and oboes (known as hautboys) then, with bassoons and horns. They might have included drummers and fifers from the regimental signal players, but not necessarily. They would have entertained the Leeds crowds with their versions of 'Over the Hills and Far Away', a traditional English tune from the late seventeenth century (so familiar to Sharpe fans today) and so many others. What was not in doubt was the good impression the band left on the enthusiastic Yorkshire crowds.

But not everything was music and dancing in Leeds. While the private men were continuing with their drill and recruiting, some of the officers found other things to do away from the parade ground. On the 30 September, the *Leeds Intelligencer* recorded 'An account of the Certificates for Killing Game, granted by the Clerk of the Peace for the said Borough, from the first Day of July, 1788, to the 26 September in the same Year.' The hunting certificates were granted to Major Bryan Blundell and Lieutenant David Kennedy, both of the 44th Foot.[3]

The second item which made the news was partly due to some quick action by the men of the 44th Foot, which may well have included Roworth. Either way, they were on hand to help when at about six o'clock on the evening of 23 August 'a considerable quantity of hemp' caught fire at one of the roperies owned by a Mr Newsom. Although an accident, the conflagration required engines, neighbours, and members of the 44th Foot to bring it under control without incurring too much damage.[4]

Eight days later, the regiment left the town for its next term of duty and arrived in Newcastle on 11 November 1788. The next morning, they marched out of Newcastle, heading for Tynemouth to replace the 55th Foot who were marching for Glasgow. Somewhere between Leeds and Newcastle, Private Thomas Young deserted. Just before Christmas, the papers reported on his whereabouts. He was detained in gaol at Morpeth charged with assault and robbery on the person of a servant, who worked for a 'Mr Armstrong of Glenwhelt'. The latter was a large farm on Colonel Wade's military road at Greenhead.[5]

It was normal for the army to deal with minor crimes within the barracks, but this was usually reserved for ill-discipline. Any crimes outside the barracks or of a more severe nature would be dealt with by the civil authorities. In time of war, Thomas Young would have been taken up by the military, as he would have been subject to the Articles of War. In the event, after nine months in a civilian gaol, Thomas received the worst of punishments. The following August 1789, he was convicted of highway robbery by the Northumberland Assizes and was hanged on the Fair-moor near Morpeth. 'Previous to the execution of this awful sentence he behaved with becoming resignation and fortitude.'[6]

---

3   *Leeds Intelligencer*, Tuesday 30 September 1788.
4   *Leeds Intelligencer*, Tuesday 28 October 1788.
5   *Newcastle Courant*, Saturday 13 December 1788.
6   M.A. Richardson, *The Local Historian's Table Book, of Remarkable Occurrences, Historical Facts, Traditions, Legendary And Descriptive Ballads, Connected With The Counties Of*

SMALLPOX TO SMUGGLING: LEEDS TO THE ISLE OF MAN

Tynemouth Castle where the barracks were built, by H. Gastineau. (Author's Collection)

Tynemouth Barracks – built in 1758 to house 1,000 men – must have been particularly impressive, standing high up on a headland 100 feet above sea level. As with other barracks, they were built not only to defend and to help the locals feel safe but to impress and deter any intended invaders. But the 44th Foot's introduction to their barracks was particularly unpleasant as a frost set in at the end of November and did not break until well into January. The men must have been glad of their drill to work up a sweat.

The year 1789 was to be an epidemic year for many places in Britain, primarily for scarlet fever and typhus. The people of Tynemouth experienced an extremely bad time in the early months of the year, as many died of measles and smallpox, particularly the children, and more than 200 funerals were held during the three winter months. Numbers of ailing rank and file in the regiment rose from 31 to 44 sick in April and May. Two of the soldiers were recorded 'dead' on the return for 1 March 1789 and another on the return for 1 May 1789. Surgeon's Mate Ralph Green was absent with leave at this time.

Newcastle-Upon-Tyne, Northumberland And Durham (Newcastle-upon-Tyne: Richardson, 1841), vol.2, p.325.

State of the 44th Foot, monthly return, Tynemouth, 1 April 1789, TNA: WO 17/155.

Present					Rank & File					Number Wanting		
Officers	Staff	QM	Sjt	Drum	Present	Sick	On Com'd	Other	Total	Sjt	Drum	R&F
13	3	1	13	6	273	31	34	16	354	-	-	46

The 44th Foot was called upon as a constabulary in the middle of March 1789, when an urgent letter was sent to the Tynemouth Barracks from Newcastle. It requested the immediate assistance of the regiment to help with the control of 'an immense multitude of pitmen' who had committed 'divers acts of violence to the machinery' at the mine.[7] In the event, five companies marched into Newcastle from Tynemouth on the same day. Further details were given by the *Saunders's News-Letter* of 27 March, which described 'a number of ships, and some of them large, are getting ready to proceed to the Baltic to load wheat and rye for this place, where we have for some days been in an unpleasant situation from an insurrection of the pitmen.' They reported that the military had 'seized some of the ringleaders last night [and] it is hoped that this matter will soon be got under for the present.'[8] This incident appears to be the only time the 44th was required to help the local population during their stay.

For the final few months in Tynemouth, the regiment concentrated on recruiting. The enlistment numbers varied but slowly improved, with numbers in December reaching 228.[9] In January, two men only enlisted, while February figures were considerably better at 13. March saw nine men enlisted, and April brought a satisfactory leap to 25. However, April's Monthly Return records 275 rank and file with 31 sick in quarters, well over double since Osborn's review in May 1787.

By May, Major Blundell had returned fresh from an eight-week furlough and was again signing the monthly returns. He would have been gratified to find that other than quelling the riots in Newcastle, there was nothing else worthy of report. Captain Benjamin Fish was preparing the regiment for a review by Major General George Scott 'when they [went] through their various manoeuvres in such a manner as to merit the highest praise.'[10]

The 44th Foot left Tynemouth on Tuesday 19 May to be replaced by the 29th (Worcestershire) Regiment of Foot which marched in the next day from Scarborough. The *Newcastle Courant* of 23 May 1789 reported: 'The general behaviour of the 44th regiment during the time of their being quartered at the Barracks, has left the strongest impressions of their truly meritorious conduct upon the inhabitants of that neighbourhood, and evinces the great regularity of the military principle established in that corps.'[11]

So often, reports of soldiers' behaviour towards the latter end of the eighteenth century were quite damning, particularly when soldiers were

---

7   *Derby Mercury*, Thursday 19 March 1789.
8   *Saunders Newsletter*, Friday 27 March 1789.
9   TNA: WO 12/5638: 25 June to 24 December 1789.
10 *Saunders Newsletter*, Friday 27 March 1789.
11 *Newcastle Courant*, Saturday 23 May 1789.

billeted upon an unhappy local populace. Not so on that occasion – a glowing report was good for military morale and the soldiers' good behaviour would have improved their relationships with the local community.

As regiments were on the move on a regular basis during the eighteenth century, those movements were made public in a variety of newspapers and helped the populace of the relevant towns to ready themselves for the next arrivals. Such was recorded in the *Caledonian Mercury* of 25 June 1789, which gave a flavour of the complex manoeuvring required for whole regiments, usually made up of 700–1,000 men, so that they left or arrived at the destinations on the days denoted.

It can be imagined that such occasions were looked forward to with varying expectations by both civilians and the military. Inns and hostelries, in particular, might anticipate an upturn in sales and profits and where there were no barracks, soldiers were likely to be billeted on the locals and at those same hostelries. When the military came to town with its bands playing and flags and ribbons flying, nothing could provide a greater spectacle for a population with little else to entertain them. Even the hearts of young women could be turned by a uniform, and where there were soldiers, there would be food on the table the next day for the local ladies of the night. A newspaper report of the route would therefore give notice to the cities and all small towns and villages in between.

Often when a regiment was sent out on command, their various companies could be split up and sent to wherever help was required, at short notice, as when members of one regiment were drafted into another to help make up numbers in that regiment. The *Newcastle Courant* reported that a battalion of the Royal Artillery was to march through on their way to Perth.[12] This notice gave the locals an opportunity to line the way and cheer the marching gunners. In addition, the music of regimental bands and the colour of the uniforms would add some interest and brightness to what was often a hard life with little distraction. Such processions were not only a thrill for the locals but a pleasure for the men involved, swinging in or out of town to claps and cheers.

One hundred and sixty miles and one month after the 44th had left Northumberland, the *Caledonian Mercury* of 25 June announced the arrival of five companies of the regiment in Glasgow before they marched on to Ayr. It meant an early start for Ayr at four o'clock on the following Monday morning, the 22nd.[13]

It was around this time that a momentous event happened in William Roworth's life, the birth of his son. The baptism occurred on 22 June 1789, and the record is to be found in the Castle Gate Meeting Baptismal Register, entry number 1467, as 'William, son of William and Mary Roworth, of the parish of St Mary, Nottingham, baptised by R Plumbe.'[14]

---

12 *Newcastle Courant*, Saturday 23 May 1789.
13 *Caledonian Mercury*, Thursday 25 June 1789.
14 Nottingham University Library (NUL): Doc. CU R3/1: Castle Gate Meeting Baptismal Register.

The news of the birth probably did not reach Roworth for some weeks. Those weeks might have been shrouded with worry until the news arrived that both child and mother had survived the birth. A third of infants died before their fifth birthday in Britain in 1800.[15] The custom of naming a first boy-child after his father was prevalent in the 1700s, as was the naming of a daughter after her mother. In Roworth's family, the first boy was called William for at least four generations beginning with Roworth's own father. Also, it said a lot for the Osborns and Mary that Little Billy, as he was to be known, survived past his first five years. It probably helped that he was their only child. In the event, Billy turned out to be one of the most long-lived, successful and influential citizens of Nottingham in the nineteenth century, dying at the ripe old age of 96.[16] Roworth would have been so proud had he known.

In the meantime, he and the 44th Foot continued on their way to the sparsely populated town of Ayr, with its population of under 2,000. The rank and file, serjeants and drummers, were probably directed to a large open field on the south side of the harbour to pitch their tents. Barracks would be built on that site in 1795, but not in time for this regiment's term of duty.

By 14 July 1789, the regiment would probably have still been settling into their new surroundings and not have known for some time that world-changing events were happening across the Channel in France on that very day. The fall of the Bastille in Paris was one of the key events of the French Revolution; the reverberations affected millions, including the 44th Foot, in the coming years, and they would see war with the French on the Continent and in the West Indies as a result. Many would not survive their experiences.

No records appear to have survived of the regiment's time in Ayr. For information, only newspaper reports are revealing. The *Caledonian Mercury* reported that Lieutenant David Stark received orders on 19 December to march from Ayr to Stranraer and Girvan on anti-smuggling duties.[17] Despite the mildness of the winter that year, the 44th struggled against gale-force winds as the men fought their way along the coast roads. It seems the storms did their job for them and a real disaster had occurred by the time the redcoats arrived at the beaches. At least 10 vessels and fishing boats had been driven ashore, with considerable loss of life. The soldiers, together with local people, may have endeavoured to save any lives they could and to help with the dead where they could not. Once the gales died down and their usefulness ended, the 44th would have been ordered back to policing the coastline and searching for smugglers and their booty.

On 3 April 1790, Ensign William Tuffie married Grizell Campbell (later called Grace) in the town of Ayr.[18] The marriage was officiated by Mr Carter. If widely known within the companies, the time would have been one of joy

---

15 'Child mortality rate (under five years old) in the United Kingdom from 1800 to 2020', *Statista*, <https://www.statista.com/statistics/1041714/united-kingdom-all-time-child-mortality-rate/>, accessed July 2023.
16 *Nottingham Evening Post*, Friday 16 April 1886.
17 *Caledonian Mercury*, Thursday 24 December 1789.
18 Extract from a Register of Proclamation of Banns and Marriages dated 3 April 1790, <https://scotlandspeople.gov.uk/>, accessed July 2023.

Whitehaven Harbour showing detail of jetties and ships, from the south, by W.H. Bartlett. (Author's Collection)

and congratulation and probably some leg-pulling for Tuffie. The rest of his family, his father, Quartermaster John Tuffie, his mother, Mary, who was on the strength and his older brother, Ensign Samuel Tuffie, were present with the regiment, a real army family, so it may have been quite a party with the redcoats doubtless happily joining in the toasts.

Later in the month, there were three desertions from the camp at Ayr. The men who ran were William Nailor, John Caurd and Christopher Thompson. Two of them were over six feet tall. Nailor – a stonemason from Redman in Yorkshire, (possibly Redcar or Redmire) – was purportedly 17 years old, with dark hair, two front teeth missing, a large scar on his top lip and a mole on his right eye-lid, while Caurd – a shoemaker from Ireland – was 23 years and altogether less piratical with light brown hair and a fair complexion. The third, Christopher Thompson – a husband-man from Brompton, near Northallerton in Yorkshire – was about five feet six, dark-haired and with a scar on his right cheek.[19] The advertisement seeking their capture went on to ask anyone to secure them, put them in gaol, and inform the commanding officer at Ayr.[20] There is a Christopher Thompson on the full Muster Roll for June to December 1791 (so he seems to have returned, one way or another), but no sign of Nailor or Caurd, so they must have succeeded in their bid for freedom and made new lives elsewhere.

---

19 *Newcastle Courant*, Saturday 17 April 1790.
20 *Newcastle Courant*, Saturday 17 April 1790.

State of the 44th Foot, monthly return, Whitehaven, 1 July 1790, TNA: WO 17/155.

Present					Rank & File					Number Wanting		
Officers	Staff	QM	Sjt	Drum	Present	Sick	On Com'd	Other	Total	Sjt	Drum	R&F
6	-	-	7	9	84	2	9	5	100	-	1	136

Four companies of the 44th were 'detached from Scotland to the Isle of Man' via Whitehaven, where the monthly return for July 1790 was taken. The soldiers left the mainland on the *John and Esther* on 23 July 1790 and landed in Douglas later in the day. Yet again, the detachment of the 44th Foot, commanded by Brevet Major Benjamin Fish, received an excellent reference from the people of Whitehaven in the local *Cumberland Pacquet* newspaper for Wednesday 28 July: 'From the good order and discipline, so observable in the 44th during their residence in this town, it is presumed, the inhabitants of the Island will find them very agreeable successors to the corps they have lost.'[21]

They would have marched the nine or 10 miles from Douglas to Castletown, which was the capital of the island at the time. Despite the well-documented history of the Manx Militia (understandably), details of the British regiments on the island are much more sketchy. For example, although the Duke of Atholl was fairly derogatory as to the condition of the castle garrison barracks, announcing the castle itself as being a 'pile of ruins' and that there were 'some very indifferent barracks built where no man in his senses would ever have placed them in the Ditch of the Castle'.[22] It was likely he was wielding his own verbal weapon, as contemporary prints reveal a neat castle of which the people were rightly proud. Soldiers and officers would have been barracked both in the castle and in the town where there is still a barrack building contemporary with the time, now the Barracks Tapas Bar, a clue to its origin. Douglas retains its Barrack Street, but not the buildings. According to Charles Guard, Chairman of Manx Culture and Heritage, the picture was fluid, with regards to the barracking of the British regiments.[23] As with all visiting British military, the 44th was employed in its usual duties of recruiting and policing for the next 20 months, with regular recruiting parties in Castletown and Ramsey.

All monthly returns were recorded in Castletown and the early returns were countersigned by Colonel Richard Dawson, Lieutenant Governor, until Colonel Alexander Shaw succeeded him on 26 November 1790.

A year earlier, Richard Townley – a visitor to the Isle of Man – gave a neat description of the town and the current regiment's duties:

> The Castle stands in the centre of the place, close to … the harbour. It is a very irregular building, though tolerably large, visibly constructed at many different times, and for different uses … There is a handsome opening behind it, terminated by a neat, small church, or chapel, which forms one side of a small

---

21 *Cumberland Pacquet and Ware's Whitehaven Advertiser*, Wednesday 28 July 1790.
22 B. O'Neil, 'Castle Rushen, Isle of Man', *Archaeologia*, vol.94, 1951, pp.1–26.
23 Charles Guard, email to the author, 2022.

SMALLPOX TO SMUGGLING: LEEDS TO THE ISLE OF MAN

View of Douglas, Isle of Man, as the 44th would have seen it on their approach in the *John and Esther*, by W.H. Watts, 1841. (Author's Collection)

Castle Rushen, Isle of Man, February 6 1775. The Duke of Atholl referred to the castle as '… a pile of ruins', by Godfrey (Author's Collection)

Castle Rushin [sic] on the Isle of Man, May 20 1775. The Duke of Atholl referred to 'indifferent barracks built … in the Ditch of the Castle'. By S. Cooper. (Author's Collection)

quadrangle; and that serves, both for a market-place, and a parade, for the troops in the Castle-barracks; now consisting of two companies of soldiers. The other companies cantoned within the different towns in the island, to assist the customhouse officers against the smugglers, that are still hovering about the island, though the illicit trade carried on by those daring people, is very trifling to what it was before government became possessed of the port duties.[24]

The four companies were commanded by Brevet Major Fish, Captains George Kennedy and Charles Semple, with Captain Edward Dunne on his way to join (Dunne finally arrived in August). Of those, Kennedy and Semple were recruiting with Lieutenants Rufane Shaw Donkin and James Cordner, and Ensign Edward Wilson. There were seven serjeants in total, two were on command and five were recruiting, plus five drummers. The companies totalled just 98 with 138 rank and file wanting to complete. The August return taken in Castletown corroborated these numbers. One man was discharged and was claimed by, and turned over to, the Durham Militia. Five men were recorded as having deserted, two from Dunne's company, two from Kennedy's, and one from Semples'.[25]

24　Richard Townley, *A Journal kept in the Isle of Man* (Whitehaven: J.Ware and Son, 1791), vol.1, pp.32–33.
25　TNA: WO 17/155: 1st August 1790, Monthly Return of 4 Companies 44th Regiment, Castle Town.

State of the 44th Foot detachment, Castle Town, Isle of Man 1 August 1790, TNA: WO/17/155.

Present					Rank & File					Number Wanting		
Officers	Staff	QM	Sjt	Drum	Present	Sick	On Com'd	Other	Total	Sjt	Drum	R&F
3	-	-	5	1	95	2	7	13	117	-	-	43

Recruiting was to prove somewhat difficult. British soldiers had been arriving on the island only since 1765 after the island's Act of Revestment. This afforded the British Crown freedom to place military regiments on the island to (try to) put an end to the lucrative practice of smuggling, which had such a negative and disastrous effect on the privy purse. It was also the practice of the British Army to recruit wherever duty took them.

The Manx were a very self-contained nation. An idea of this may be gleaned from a memorial that was presented to Lieutenant Governor Dawson, a little over 10 years prior to the arrival of the 44th Foot, elucidating on the mindset of the Manx inhabitants towards a regimental existence:

> Your Honour, from your long residence and experience, needs not to be informed that the Genius of this people in military matters differs much from that of the neighbouring kingdom [Britain], that they have in general so great an aversion to the Land Service that His Majesty's Troops in this Isle from the Vesting Act till their departure could not procure even five recruits.[26]

Of course, the British were trying to recruit soldiers from a much tinier island nation than their own, where the sea, for many of the Manx, was both their place of work and the view every day of their lives. The 44th remained on the island for 18 months while the army recruited in Castletown, Douglas and Ramsey, as well as at 45 annual fairs throughout the island. For the first five months, the parties comprised five officers, four or five serjeants and four drummers, during which time they recruited 37 men, the best month being December 1790, with 23 recruits and only five deserters.[27]

Recruiting came to a halt briefly for the Ramsey party when, as the *Cumberland Pacquet* reported on Saturday 3 November:

> ... on Sunday the 17th ult. in the evening, a large lugger, mounting 18 guns, six and nine pounders, (and said to have 70 men) came to an anchor in the bay. The next morning, Mr. Gammell, the collector, assisted by a party of the 44th regiment seized 14 kegs of brandy and gin, which had been landed, and hid near the town.[28]

The luggers and their crews were not to be taken lightly. They were ferocious men who used their weapons without compunction and like so many of their smuggling brothers from the coastal towns around the Irish sea, would not hesitate to kill if things were not going their way. A ship of 18 guns with

---

26 B.E. Sargeaunt, *The Royal Manx Fencibles* (Aldershot: Gale and Polden, 1947), p.10.
27 TNA: WO 17/155: Return, Castle Town, 1 December 1790.
28 *Cumberland Pacquet*, Saturday 3rd November 1790.

70 crew might easily beat a customs cutter. Smuggling was so lucrative that smugglers would not hesitate to defy and assault any authority, including the military, attempting to prevent them from landing their goods. With an armed crew of maybe 50 coming ashore with barrels of rum and brandy at Ramsey, the 15 or so redcoats would be hard put to overcome the smugglers and help save the goods for the customs officers.

In the following year, 1791, the companies recruited 35 men, 32 of those in June. The annual total of deserters was 13. The number of officers, serjeants and drummers recruiting slowly lessened over the period, as numbers were sent back to headquarters in Ayr. The first six weeks of 1792 produced eight recruits and three deserters before the 44th left for Ireland. However, in total, the regiment successfully enlisted 81 recruits and lost 20 to desertion – quite a remarkable number considering the Manx love of the sea.[29]

For a soldier to desert was a personal and momentous decision. Considerable thought and planning may have gone into that decision, or it may have been purely opportune. Either way, there would have to be specific reasons, especially when the soldier himself would be aware of the consequences. The Articles of War were read out to the regiments on a regular basis so that a deserter could not claim he had never heard them. James tells us that 'It is ordained, that the Articles of War shall be read [at the minimum] in the circle of each regiment belonging to the army every month'.[30] If caught, the miscreant would be punished severely and often irreparably by court-martial, which might result in death by hanging or shooting. Other sentences included flogging, imprisonment, transportation and branding, the latter of which had been devised by the army in the Civil War of the seventeenth century. Branding was carried out with heated irons, but this practice came to an end in 1829, being replaced by tattooing, which was itself mercifully rejected 50 years later.

As late as 1847, an order had been issued by Horse Guards directing that deserters should be branded with the letter D – as opposed to the hand brand pictured on the next page, presumably. Some might rather have been shot since this draconian measure was taken so that the deserter in question could never rejoin the British Army. Joseph Hume, MP, commented that he 'was aware that it was very important to discountenance desertion in the regular Army, at the same time he 'thought it very discreditable to mark men as beasts were marked'.[31]

The reasons cited by soldiers were many and varied. Often desertion was the final option for a soldier (however long his army career) if he perceived himself to have been unjustly dealt with by a superior. Whatever the reason, it was likely to have been thoroughly considered before going on the run. Drunkenness was often to blame and a soldier might not even remember where he had been, or for how long, once he finally found his way muzzily back to barracks or camp – more as a matter of absence without leave than intended desertion. Then much depended on his commander as to the

---

29   TNA: WO 17/155: Monthly Return, 1 February 1792.
30   James, *Military Dictionary*.
31   Joseph Hume, MP, 1775–1855, *Hansard*, House of Commons Debate 20 July 1847, vol.94 cc 607–608.

punishment. Occasions were known when alcohol did the job for them and the soldier was so addicted that he died without any further assistance. Donaldson of the 94th wrote, 'the besetting sin of the British soldier is drunkenness (the parent of many others), produced in a great measure, by the leisure time he has in general hanging on his hands.'[32] While Harris, when in the 95th, 'danced, drank, shouted and piped thirteen Irish miles from Cashel to Clonmel.'[33]

Others less drunk and more cunning were multiple deserters who made it their occupation, keeping one step ahead of the military by moving from regiment to regiment in order to collect the bounty offered. One such was described by Private Benjamin Harris just three months into his military service. He referred to the event as 'my first lesson in the stern duties of a soldier's life'. The deserter in question was a 'private in the 70th Regiment [who] had deserted from that corps, and had afterwards enlisted into several other regiments'. In fact, he accomplished that ignominious achievement 16 times. Finally caught, he was brought to Portsmouth for a general court-martial and sentenced to be shot. Four young soldiers from each of four regiments, including Harris's 66th, were to make up the firing party, as a cautionary lesson. Harris, then aged 22, was one chosen from the 66th, and all 16 attended the place of execution at Portsdown Hill, overlooking Hilsea Barracks. Several thousand soldiers were sent to witness the execution as a stiff lesson:

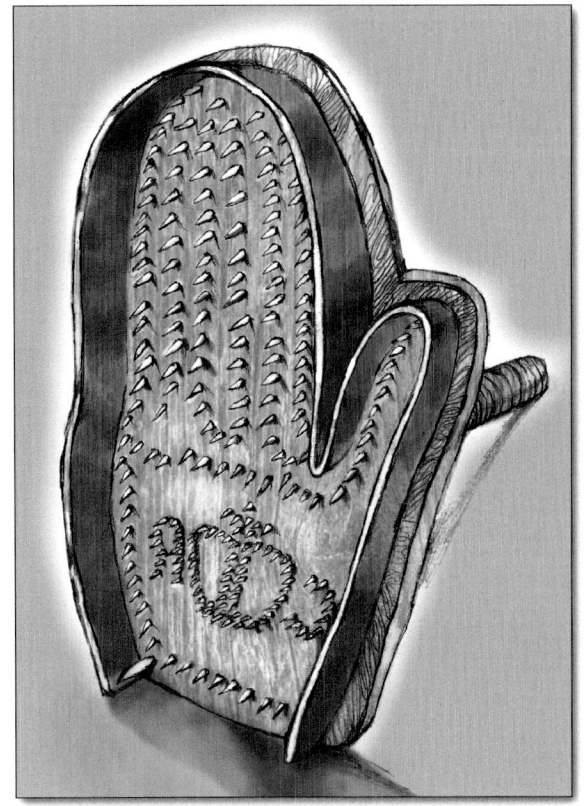

Depiction of a hand brand used on deserters, similar to those used by royalists during the Civil War in Britain. (Illustrated by Jo Davies)

> The culprit was brought out. He made a short speech to the parade, blaming 'drink and evil company' for his downfall [and] behaved firmly and well, and did not seem to flinch. After being blindfolded, he was desired to kneel down behind a coffin, which had been placed on the ground. The drum-major … gave us an expressive glance, and we immediately commenced loading. This was done in the deepest silence … There was a dreadful pause for a few moments, then the drum-major, again looking towards us, gave the signal before agreed upon – a flourish of his cane – and we levelled and fired. We had been strictly enjoined to be steady and take good aim, and the poor fellow, pierced by several balls, fell heavily upon his back … his hands wavered for a few moments, like the fins of a fish when in the agonies of death. The drum-major also observed the movement.

---

32 Joseph Donaldson, *Recollections of the Eventful Life of a Soldier: Including The War In The Peninsula and Scenes And Sketches In Ireland* (Staplehurst: Spellmount Library, 2000), p.341.
33 Hathaway (ed.), *A Dorset Rifleman*, p.19.

> Making another signal, four of our party immediately stepped up to the prostrate body. Placing the muzzles of their pieces to the head, they fired, and put him out of his misery. The different regiments then fell back by companies, and the word was given to march past in slow time. As each company came in line with the body, they were ordered to first 'mark time', and then 'eyes left' in order we might observe the terrible example.[34]

This happened so early in his career that – as far as Harris was concerned – it was a lesson well learnt.

Homesickness or the love of a sweetheart, loss of family, or illness were among the reasons cited for desertion during the eighteenth century. It might be that the expectations promised on volunteering had not come up to snuff. Those dreams of high adventure had imploded, and the reality of constant drill and discipline had replaced them. For some soldiers, boredom became the norm. The beautiful red jacket was not enough after all.

But why desert on the Isle of Man? It is hard to say, for records are scanty. Were the deserters men who joined for the bounty on the island, only to run? There were plenty of places to hide and not be found, especially if your mates looked after you. Were the deserters from the men who had joined in previous months and years? What was the draw? Perhaps the beauty and peace of the place. Perhaps the pull of love, for a pull of love there definitely was.

During their tour of duty, there were three marriages of private men of the 44th stationed on the island to local girls. On 1 March 1791, Vicar John Moore married John Brown to Elenor Johnston at Braddan, the Manx Parish Church for Douglas, flanked by three Manx witnesses, John Buskirk, Nicolas Quirk and Thomas Curphey.[35] Both John and Elenor signed the register. George Gibb was married to Elinr [sic] Quirk on 13 July 1791 at Malew, the Manx Parish Church of Castle Town, by Vicar David Harrison.[36] Malew was the Garrison Church for the military. George and Elinor made their marks. Their witnesses were again Manxmen – Arthur Bridson and John Clague. Lastly, on 22 October 1791, the Reverend Moore married Thomas Thorne to Isabella Cretney at Braddan, before witnesses William Esmond and Thomas Curphey, the couple each signed their names.[37] A daughter, Selah, was born to Thomas and Isabella in 1796, and her baptism is to be found in the parish records for 3 February that year.

Just five days after the Brown-Johnston marriage tragedy struck another company of the 44th, which was on duty in Scotland. The *Caledonian Mercury* of Saturday 19 March 1791 described how a corporal and seven privates were ordered to Stirling from Fort Augustus on 6 March. They were overtaken by heavy snow while crossing the hills and took refuge in a hut, when they discovered that the wife and baby of one of the men were missing. They were finally found by a search party. The mother had died,

---

34 Hathaway, (ed.), *A Dorset Rifleman*, pp.17–18.
35 Manx National Heritage (MNH): MS 09073/3/2: Marriage record.
36 MNH: MS 09769/4/3: Marriage record.
37 MNH: MS 09769/4/3: Marriage record.

but the nine-month-old was lying well wrapped in its mother's clothes, which she had taken off to keep the child warm – a redcoat's wife with her own brand of courage.[38]

The summer of 1791 returned to normal for the 44th Foot, with nothing out of the ordinary happening on the island other than the usual rounds of duty, drill, recruiting and policing. Whatever the current state of the regiment and its need to recruit, it did not prevent the young officers from pursuing their personal interests. When back in Ayr, it may be remembered, Major Bryan Blundell was able to find time for grouse-shooting. While on the Isle of Man, however, the 17-year-old Lieutenant Rufane Shaw Donkin was able to pursue his passion for Greek. Donkin would not have had far to go for his Greek lessons. Cambridge MA Thomas Castley, grammar school master and academic master for tertiary education, probably taught just across the road from Rushen Castle in Bishop Wilson's Library, built specifically for the use of academic students. Teaching in Castletown from 1757 until 1817 Castley was known for his fine mind and rigorous teaching.[39] But while Donkin was learning his Greek other soldiers may have felt uneasy and edgy as news arrived regularly from home, with the newspapers bringing vivid and confusing accounts of unrest and violence among the population of Britain, rather more accentuated by the relative peace of the Isle of Man punctuated only by smugglers' exploits.

The nearest unrest to the island appeared to be in Whitehaven and was settled by the 4th (Queen's Own) Dragoons and the civilian authorities. On the Isle of Man, it would seem that no such disorders required the 44th's involvement. Being the centre of the smuggling trade in the Irish Sea, it was these concerns that occupied the 44th from one end of the island to the other. In 1791, one particular lugger built for purpose, the *Morgan Rattler*, with 10 guns mounted and a 50-man crew, terrorised the revenue cutters from the island. In one run-in with the cutter *Badger*, the *Morgan Rattler* captured the captain and crew and shot the cook so badly that both his legs were later amputated. The smugglers plundered the *Badger*, cut down her mainmast and left the crew to float back to Douglas without oars, while the *Morgan Rattler* delivered its cargo unhindered.[40]

The *Newcastle Courant* for 19 November 1791 described a landing of smuggled goods on the Isle of Man on 29 September, naming the lugger, *Morgan Rattler*:

> … landed 100 ankers of spirits and a quantity of tea, at Port Eynon [Port Erin] and Le Murray [Port St Mary], in the Isle of Mann. Of these, 71 ankers and 3 boxes were then seized (on shore) by the crews of the Pigmy, Pilote, and Prince Edward cutters, together with some horses and carts, employed in conveying the articles into the interior parts of the island.[41]

---

38 *Caledonian Mercury*, Saturday 19 March 1791.
39 Airey Robert (ed.), *Feltham, A Tour through the Island of Man, in 1797 and 1798* (Bath: 1798, reprinted in *Manx Society*, vol.VI, 1861, p.93.
40 *Cumberland Pacquet, and Ware's Whitehaven Advertiser*, Tuesday 15 November 1791.
41 *Newcastle Couran*, 19 November 1791.

The Smugglers, by J. Steyn. (Author's Collection)

No doubt they were using the well-trodden route across the moors, still known today as the Whisky Run. It is almost certain that some of the 44th helped with the recovery of these goods by supplementing the number of customs officers.

The *Morgan Rattler* finally got her come-uppance as a smuggling lugger on 1 August 1801 when she was brought captive into Falmouth, together with her illicit cargo of 644 casks of spirits (smuggled from Guernsey), by Captain Robert Jope Kinsman in the revenue cutter *Active* – and active she must have been finally to foil the able crew of the infamous *Morgan Rattler*.[42]

Orders arrived for the 44th early in 1792 to sail for Ireland on 17 February. No doubt a few recruits would have left wives behind and for the Browns, the Gibbs and the Thornes, the farewells would have been harder than most. The transport sailed for Dublin, where the 44th's numbers were swelled by their other companies joining them from Portpatrick in the south-west of Scotland. On 21 February 1792, the full muster for the whole 44th Regiment recorded 199 rank and file, about a quarter of a completed regiment, so a lot of successful recruiting would have to be achieved in Ireland – which country had its own problems.

---

42 *London Courier and Evening Gazette*, Monday 3 August 1801.

4

The Land of the Irish: Home of Hostilities

'Remember soldiers, that first and foremost you are citizens.
Let us not become a greater scourge to our country than the enemy themselves.'[1]

Since the fall of the Bastille in 1789, the hunger of the French to replace their monarchy with a republic was being played out on the world stage, and the unrest in France touched many countries and many peoples. By the time the 44th Foot arrived at their Dublin barracks in February 1792, Ireland was quietly seething with unrest of its own, some clearly affected by the French Revolution, others through sectarian discord between Catholic and Protestant. The latter was nothing new, but the general unease in the country presented opportunities for various factions to (at the very least) contemplate rebellion and conflict.

There was considerable disquiet as the British Government found itself potentially besieged from many directions and the British army was stretched to breaking point in its efforts to police its empire in far-flung corners of the globe. The former realised that threats to society at home were multiplying both from within and without. There was still some way to go before Britain embraced democracy and there was no intention of allowing rebellion of any sort to take hold of the British people, but the signs were there. In fact, the Government had developed a 'spy complex' and responded to its own anxieties with an iron glove, though not quite a fist as yet. That is not to say that spies and plots were an entire figment of the Government's tribal response, but it was a fact, as historian Kenneth Johnstone asserts, that 'there were more trials for sedition and treason in the 1790s in Great Britain than ever before or after in its history'.[2] Over 100!

The concerns of the Government, touching that which they considered to be the unstable heart of the Irish people, were inspired primarily by the knowledge received (from its own spies, no less) of the real possibility of an

---

1 Kevin Kiley, 'Thumbing through the Napoleonic Wars: The words of Napoleon and Others Who May Have Influenced His Methods', *The Napoleon Series*, <https://napoleon-series.org/researchnapoleon/c/quotes>, accessed January 2023.
2 Johnston, *Unusual Suspects*, p.12.

uprising, on the lines of the social and political upheaval currently in France. An example of such unrest in Ireland – and which served to make the British Government twitchy – was a poster given space on the front page of *Finns Leinster Journal* for Wednesday, 7 November 1792:

> Union to Irishmen
> The Divorce of Church and State
> Rights of Man
> May Tyranny be banished the World
> Irishmen! – Look at France
> Perfect Freedom, and Equal Liberty
> The Triumph of Reason over Despotism
> Vive la Republique
> The Right of Man Established
> Despotism Prostrate
> L'Esprit de Jour
> Liberty and Equality
> Despotism is fled – let the people rejoice
> France is free – so may we – Let us Will it
> Fourteenth of July 1789 – Sacred to Liberty
> Tenth of August 1792 – The People Triumphant
> Twenty-second of October, 1792 – The Exit of Tyranny
> Eight of September 1793 – The armed citizens of Ireland spoke[3]

Ten days after this advertisement appeared, the same newspaper reported an incident concerning a colony of French Jacobins who, living in Clontarf, Dublin, were inciting the townspeople to rise up against the constitution and the laws of the country. The accusation was that a Frenchman, Francis Potain – who, together with other foreigners – had raised a mob and rescued a man taken for debt by a bailiff, carrying him off in triumph and shouting 'Vive La Republique Francaise' – an invasive public act requiring swift and corrective punishment.[4] This kind of action further stimulated an already agitated people that, together with the rejection of the application of the Catholic Emancipation Bill, served to give the members of the British Parliament a collective political migraine.

Catholic Emancipation apart, the Government was very aware that war with France was inevitable and a matter of 'when' not 'if'. The need to police at home in Britain and Ireland – to stave off incipient insurrection – was almost as urgent as the need for a fully trained army to throw at the French when the time came, preferably on French soil rather than British. More troops were needed on the Irish mainland to combat unrest and what was perceived as sedition – such was the mutability of Ireland in 1792 when the 44th took up their duties in February and March of that year.

The 44th left Douglas, Isle of Man, on 17 February and by 29 February had landed in Dublin and already marched the 75 miles south-west to Kilkenny,

---

3   *Finns Leinster Journal*, Wednesday 7 November 1792.
4   *Finns Leinster Journal*, Saturday 12 November 1792.

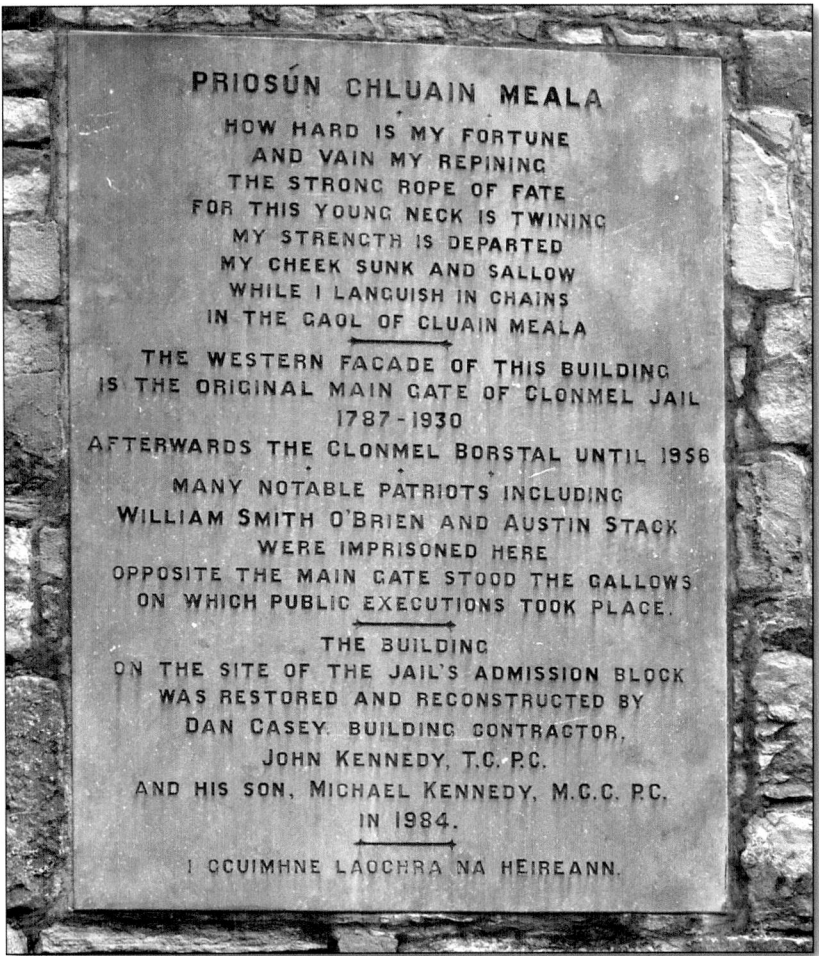

Plaque recording original site of Clonmel Barracks. (Donald Roworth)

leaving a detachment of two companies behind in Dublin. Kilkenny appeared to be a regular hub for regiments marching through to their next place of duty. This was most fortunate for *Finns Leinster Journal*, published in Kilkenny, the manoeuvres of all regiments being recorded meticulously twice weekly, on Wednesdays and Saturdays, together with their destinations.

The 44th passed through Kilkenny a number of times before they left the shores of Ireland again. On this first occasion, they marched straight through, two companies splitting off to the south-west towards Clonmel and two more were left behind at the barracks on the north side of Barracks Road in Kilkenny itself. The remaining four continued on beside the River Suir, south through Waterford, to the barracks at New Geneva, whose name provoked some comment from interested parties.

This area of land, 'some 11,000 acres around Passage East', had been put aside for a grand project which would – had it ever come about – have changed the face of Southern Ireland forever.[5] At the time, much of continental Europe

---

5   Julian Walton, *Geneva in Waterford* (Unpublished Work, 2008), via email, January 2017.

was in flux, not least because of religious and autocratic oppression. One such group was the Genevans, who decided that leaving home was their only option. Britain was among many countries to offer them an alternative home, an area large enough to build a city, which commenced in 1782. The project would have been a huge undertaking if it had ever happened. In the event, second thoughts were had on all sides and it never took shape. But what to do with a spare 11,000 acres? In the end, the New Geneva Barracks were built on the site and the name continues to this day, though without the barracks, and perplexing many a visitor to County Waterford. Today, all that can be seen are the large perimeter walls and a plaque to explain the derivation. The area is so peaceful, but with a little imagination, one can almost hear the boots of those thousands of soldiers who marched the road from Waterford.

The only description of the New Geneva Barracks the author has discovered to date is that written by Irishman Andrew Bryson, a tanner and farmer's son born in 1779. He was an explosive mix of devout Presbyterianism and United Irish rebel, rising to colonel. By 1796, he had attracted the attention of the British Government as a colonel of the military wing of the United Irishmen. Bryson was arrested after the rebellion of 1798 and tried by a military court. He was found guilty and sentenced to service in the army overseas for life. Some years after the event, he wrote a letter dated 28 May 1801 to his sister, which included his impressions of the New Geneva Barracks:

> The Gates were Opened with as much precaution as if there had been an Enemy blockading the Fortress … The Ground, Enclosed by an 18 feet wall, was about Twelve Acres directly Square & at each corner now converted into coal yards. In the Centre of the Square, fronting the Sea, was a Large Gate, on the outside of which, at the distance of 10 yards, was Che Va De Frize [Chevaux de Frise] erected, between which and the Gate the Guard was placed. At the distance of 12 yards from the wall Stood the Barracks, the 4 Sides of which were divided in the middle to allow the men to pass to the Pumps etc which were in the rear. 1 of the Sides the Officers occupied, 1 we occupied, 1½ the Soldiers & the other half was made into 2 hospitals, one for the Soldiers & One for the Cropeys [Croppies]. In the open opposite the Gate was the market, the back Ground from which to the Extremity of the Culprit's Square was closed in with railing 6 feet high, Spiked on the top, and into this Yard we were put into at 8 o'clock in the morning. At 11 we came in to breakfast. As Soon as we had finished which, we were turned out again till Dark, Leaving in each room 1 Man to buy provisions & another to Cook it. The rooms were allowed to contain 18 men.[6]

These were the barracks where the 44th arrived in 1792, as events both at home and abroad were stirring the political and sectarian pots. The soldiers serving in Ireland became familiar with such terms as 'Defenders', 'Whiteboys' and 'Break-o-Day' or 'Peep-o' Day Boys' (the latter to morph eventually into the more familiar Orange Order).

---

6   Michael Durey (ed.), *Andrew Bryson's Ordeal* (Cork: Cork University Press, 1998), pp.59–60.

THE LAND OF THE IRISH: HOME OF HOSTILITIES

Remains of New Geneva Barracks with its 18 foot high walls. (Donald Roworth)

'Defenders' were essentially agrarian groups of Roman Catholic workers who gathered to defend themselves (hence the name) against the predations of a Protestant group, the 'Peep 'o Day Boys'. The latter were formed (in the 1780s) initially to raid the homes of Roman Catholics to remove any arms found which were prohibited by law. Peep o' Day Boys were so named for the timing of their raids in the early hours. But, as with many such groups, the original principles evolved to become lost, diffused or modified. The British Army's involvement was to put down disturbances and uprisings within the community, from whichever quarter, in effect, policing.

This involvement of the military as a police force often left them in a 'damned if they did, or damned if they didn't' situation. During the years 1792–1794, when the 44th were doing their duty in Ireland, there were numerous occasions when the British Army was looked on as the enemy, and sometimes with good reason. The regiment was rarely mentioned in the Irish newspapers (except when on the march), and only three muster rolls for the period appear to have survived, although there are some monthly returns. Unfortunately, it appears that all other military records for Ireland were lost in a hugely catastrophic fire in 1922 during the Irish Civil War. The late Gregory O'Connor, archivist at the Irish National Archives, said that documents 'included in that collection [were] Muster Rolls described as "quarterly lists of commissioned and non-commissioned officers and men of each regiment in Ireland covering the years 1741 to 1795"'.[7] A disastrous loss for the Irish nation and for all historians in the future but, particularly, for those researching both Irish and British military history.

There were to be times when British soldiers in Ireland were involved in incidents that brought disgrace upon themselves and the army in general. The *Finns Leinster Journal* described one occurrence in Dublin, which involved

---

7   Gregory O'Connor, Archivist, Irish National Archives, email to author, 2015.

The Peep O'Day Boy's Cabin, by Sir David Wilkie. (Author's Collection)

a number of soldiers from one of the regiments in garrison, who attacked (unprovoked it was claimed) and injured a number of citizens. When they experienced resistance, the soldiers returned to the barracks, only to appear again – fully armed and headed by some officers – to renew the attacks, firing into houses and injuring a number with their swords, some mortally. This aggression was finally subdued but understandably left an outraged and frightened populace and appeared totally uncalled for.[8]

The report of the shameful occurrence placed the blame squarely upon those 'heroes of the scarlet'. It appeared that the military had run amok among the local population. No reason was forthcoming. If there were any more measured reports of this incident, then the author has found none. It was suggested that all soldiers might be better split up and billeted on the people to prevent such collective aggression or otherwise barracked away from centres of civilisation entirely. An interesting and opposing point of view was that of His Majesty's Government in other parts of Britain, which, in the late 1700s, was in the process of building barracks throughout Britain. Although primarily to house the military for defence from France, the barracks were to prevent just such scenes of confrontation which, by all accounts, were often fuelled by alcohol. The Irishman Charles O'Neil in his *Military Adventures*

---

8   *Finns Leinster Journal*, Saturday 21 April 1792.

THE LAND OF THE IRISH: HOME OF HOSTILITIES

Part of the parade ground of Dublin Barracks (now Collins Barracks), familiar to so many British regiments during the eighteenth and nineteenth centuries. (Donald Roworth)

provided a reasoned and balanced comment when he observed: 'It is my humble opinion that much of the disobedience and disrespectful language from the men might be avoided, and consequently many of the punishments dispensed with, if this custom [of serving a daily ration of grog] were wholly discontinued.'[9]

Drunkenness and billeted soldiers were the subject of an article by G.O. Rickword in 1956, quoting from the *Gentlemen's Magazine* of 1743. Rickword was discussing the trials and tribulations of imposed-upon innkeepers who, in the eighteenth century, regularly complained and with good cause if their 'caustic comments' were to be anywhere near the truth: 'The Landlord looks upon the Soldier as an Intruder forced into his House, and rioting in Sloth at his Expense; and the Farmer and Manufacturer, have learned to call the Army the Vermine of the Land, the Caterpillars of the Nation, and the Devourers of other Men's Industry, the Enemies of Liberty, and the Slaves of the Court.'[10]

Strong words indeed and what an awful indictment on the men who (in other circumstances) used their bodies and weapons to keep their country, their king and his subjects safe. But the debacle which happened in Dublin

---

9   O'Neil, *Military Adventures*, pp.40–41.
10 G.O. Rickword, 'Billeting in Inns in the Eighteenth Century', *Journal of the Society for Army Historical Research*, vol.34, no.138, June 1956, p.86.

(above) involved not only the privates but disturbingly their officers also. Officers were well aware of how their regiment should behave towards civilians and although some of them might not have been of the best calibre, it must surely have been alcohol that took them onto the streets to attack and cause unrest. Local yeomanry and militia regiments were often less disciplined than the regular regiments.

Early in May 1792, five regiments of infantry and the regiment of cavalry then quartered in Dublin Barracks were reviewed by the Commander-in-Chief and the Lord Lieutenant in Phoenix Park, after which the whole body of soldiers was moved 'to country quarters', much to the rejoicing of the general public, no doubt.

There must have been occasions when the more thoughtful and observant soldier carried out those policing duties with some heartache, having sworn allegiance to king and country, but (at the time) not necessarily understanding fully what that might involve. So many different calamities assailed Ireland at this period, some of the people's own making, but some not. Many redcoats would become inured to their duty and maybe even enjoy it.

At the end of May 1792, there was a general reshuffle of regiments and companies. Specifically, five companies of the 8th (King's) Regiment of Foot marched through Kilkenny on 29 May, on their way from Cork to Dublin. Similarly, five companies of the 33rd (1st Yorkshire West Riding) Regiment of Foot marched through Kilkenny, also on their way from Cork to Dublin. By the end of the first week of June, the other companies of the 44th were on their way to join their comrades at New Geneva – five companies under Captain William Hamilton, Lord Belhaven, three under Captain John Ormsby, and three under Brevet Major Colin Campbell.

The 44th companies waited for their first call for policing duties and it was not long in coming. On the last day of June, a party was ordered to Waterford to apprehend a person named Callaghan, who had forcibly entered his uncle's home 'with intent, it is supposed, to commit some depredations'. But the uncle, being forewarned, hit him over the head with a slean when he arrived. This instrument – a sharp, two-sided turf-cutter – 'so completely disabled [Callaghan] that he was incapable of the least resistance till taken into custody'. The soldiers were called to do their duty and took him to the local gaol to await his trial at the assizes, followed by a nine-mile march back to barracks.[11]

At the beginning of August, mutiny broke out amongst the 64th (2nd Staffordshire) Regiment of Foot, stationed at Limerick. From time to time, instances occurred when redcoats felt aggrieved or imposed upon and it took very little to set a wave of discontent throughout a regiment. The mutiny of the 64th resulted from a very 'trifling cause'. The men, accustomed to drawing water for their own use, had been ordered to draw water for the whole barracks. They refused the order, the consequence of which was a court-martial for disobedience of an officer's order. A general court-martial was held in the council chamber at Limerick. After evidence was heard, all

---

11   *Finns Leinster Journal*, Saturday 7 July 1792.

18 soldiers 'threw themselves on the mercy of the court' while their officers spoke up for them.[12] They were found guilty of mutiny and a severe sentence was expected – the death sentence for mutiny remaining until 1998 – but these young men may not have equated what they did with mutiny. They were simply seeking justice.

Two weeks later, the 18 redcoats were drawn up in the square at New Geneva to hear their fates. After a long introductory speech by the commanding officer, the judgement of the court-martial was given: one soldier was to be shot, another to receive 1,000 lashes and a third 500 lashes. The remainder were acquitted. One can imagine the horror with which they heard these sentences.

With typical military theatricality, the officer paused 'for about a minute and a most awful solemnity pervaded the whole corps'. He finally broke his silence to the 'repenting prisoners' and with appropriate phrases which gave emphasis to the gravitas of the situation including 'sincere contrition', 'culprits manifested for the error', 'foolishly plunged themselves', twinned with 'youth and inexperience', and more in the same vein, the commanding officer solemnly announced that which he had intended before he commenced, namely that 'his Excellency the Lord Lieutenant had humanely granted them a free pardon'.[13] The joy was complete. A very hard lesson had been taught, but the army would think it a necessary lesson well-learned. Such examples were always *pour encourager les autres.*

In the somewhat wider world of London and its environs, changes were afoot as fearful migrants fleeing from the terrors of Paris arrived from the Continent. This huge influx appeared overwhelming. The English aristocracy were providing for the French equivalent, but what to do with approximately 40,000 lesser mortals already in the country? The government had to 'do something' came the cry of the masses, who were disturbed and confused by the sheer numbers. It was said that the government would intervene by fitting up temporary residences like the old Palace of Winchester, in Southwark, originally the London home of the bishops of Winchester. It had already been used as a prison and by 1792 as tenements and warehouses for over 100 years – so, if its function was to be changed again, the current tenants would have felt a real grievance.[14]

During the winter months of 1792–1793, the redcoats themselves, whether in Britain or Ireland, were at least secure in the knowledge that in times of peace, their needs would be met by their quartermasters. The soldiers' daily bread and meat, though somewhat monotonous and arriving with equally monotonous regularity, was at least plentiful and nourishing. Whatever the rights and wrongs of military life, the men were grateful that they themselves were taken care of by the huge machine that was and still is, the British Army. They would have been aware that many of the population outside of the barrack walls were starving. At 42 shillings

---

12　*Finns Leinster Journal*, Wednesday 16 August 1792.
13　*Finns Leinster Journal*, Saturday 1 September 1792
14　History of Winchester Palace, *English Heritage*, < https://www.english-heritage.org.uk/visit/places/winchester-palace/history/>, accessed October 2022.

a quarter,[15] the grain to be had (much of which was exported) was very sparing, and for many citizens throughout Ireland, times were incredibly hard, as their empty bellies and shivering bodies constantly reminded them. It had started after the poor grain crop of 1789, with another the following year. Poor harvests were to continue through much of the final decade of the eighteenth century. In 1791, a new corn law was passed, which increased the price of grain imports. The advent of war made things worse, and 'as a result, the clause which enabled the act of 1791 to be modified in case of need was employed every year from 1793 to 1801.'[16] Those at the bottom of the human heap were starving, and as desperation made men bolder, the military often found itself either saint or bogey-man.

Neither civilian nor military authorities could be blind to the efforts to draw the Irish into the vortex of the French Revolution. Hunger would always provide fodder for insurrection. The military was called upon to help put down uprisings of hungry people who attacked mills and corn stores to take away corn and flour. The Waterford poor were reduced to stealing to feed themselves, as were so many communities. The mills in Waterford were reported to have been attacked by 2,000 men. The army was called in to put a stop to it and they did. The mayor and councillors gave their thanks and indebtedness to the military for their 'great promptness and steady good conduct', their 'zeal and alacrity', and attributed to them the 'suppression, or rather suspension' of the event.[17] Yet, how many redcoat consciences blenched on those occasions?

But the morning after the insurrection, enterprising and (probably scared) inhabitants set up a subscription 'to buy provisions, and sell them to the poor at a reduced price during the winter.' The response to the subscription by 26 worthies of Waterford 'exceeds eleven hundred pounds' – a considerable amount of money, worth around £145,500 today. The wealthier inhabitants of Cork set up a similar scheme.[18] The winter wore on and neither Britain nor Ireland boiled over into that expected insurrection so feared by Pitt's government. Yet the astounding news received in Britain from France of the execution of Louis XVI by guillotine on 21 January 1793 served as a warning of what might happen on British soil if the government should lose their hold on their home-grown and visiting anarchists.

The British Government's response was swift. Within three days of the execution, the French Ambassador to Britain in London, M. Francois-Bernard de Chauvelin, was expelled from the French Embassy in Portman Square.

On 1 February 1793, France declared war on Britain. As usual, Britain was unprepared and only able to make a military gesture of sorts. At the time, nearly half the British Army was outside of the British Isles, and those regiments at home could not all be extracted from their normal policing

---

15   George Crosby, *Crosby's Parliamentary Record of Elections in Great Britain and Ireland* (Leeds: Crosby, 1847), p.480.

16   W.E. Minchinton, *Agricultural Returns and the Government during the Napoleonic Wars* (Newton Abbot: David and Charles, 1968), p.29.

17   *Finns Leinster Journal*, Saturday 1 December 1792.

18   *Finns Leinster Journal*, Saturday 24 November 1792.

THE LAND OF THE IRISH: HOME OF HOSTILITIES

duties. The somewhat rushed honour of confronting the French army was given to those who were available at the time – the Foot Guards – 'consisting of the 1st Battalion of each Regiment, together with a fourth or Flank Battalion formed from the grenadier and light companies'.[19] After a brief ceremony at which the brigade paraded in St James's Park and was reviewed by His Majesty George III, they marched to Greenwich, where they embarked at the hospital stairs for the Continent. Amongst their numbers were Captain Roger Morris and Corporal Robert Brown, both of whom would (helpfully) keep personal journals of their experiences.

News of the French King's violent death at the hands of his people would have quickly spread amongst the redcoats in Britain. Oaths they had taken at attestation would not preclude shock, sympathy, anger, or any other response, including *volte-face*. But probably an unease would set in, an expectation, maybe an excitement.

The Guards left for France in February under the command of Major General Gerard Lake, Colonel of the First Guards. Historian Julian Paget described their condition as 'extremely ill-equipped with no transport, no reserve ammunition and few stores.'[20] How much more unprepared could they be? Added to which, orders were to 'remain within immediate reach of their transports in case their services should be required elsewhere'.[21]

Britain would be at war with France for some 20 years, excluding a short and fragile time of peace from 25 March 1802 to 18 May 1803, the Peace of Amiens. To supply the army with the men it needed, as usual, the British Government was involved in an imperative and inexorable quest for available men for its regiments. Recruiting continued with renewed vigour in all parts of the country. Despite the efforts of the recruiting parties in Ireland, relatively few were successful.

Concerns grew.

One quite extraordinary report from Cork brought news that, on 14 February, the French had invaded the River Lee, where it flows from Cork into the Celtic Sea, and succeeded in cutting out 'five vessels laden with provisions'.[22] This brazen act served to rattle the nerves of the establishment and bring smiles to the faces of the pro-French, the numbers of whom were growing.[23]

Despite the large barracks already at Clonmel, news broke on 6 April that a further encampment was to be formed nearby, within a month, for 'twenty regiments of horse and foot, with a train of the Royal Artillery'.[24] They were to be commanded by a lieutenant general and two major generals.

The authorities in Ireland were aware of the strong possibilities of insurrection and were on the constant lookout for transgressors. Every effort was made to prevent the proliferation of illegal arms, in one case digging up a beach when information was received of Defenders hiding cannon under

---

19   Julian Paget (ed.), *Coldstream Guards 1650–2000* (Barnsley: Leo Cooper, 2000), p.15.
20   Paget, *Coldstream*, p.15.
21   J.W. Fortescue, *A History of the Army* (London: Macmillan,1899), vol.IV, Part 1, pp.80–81.
22   *Finns Leinster Journal*, Wednesday 20 February 1793.
23   *Caledonian Mercury*, Saturday 6 April 1793.
24   *Caledonian Mercury*, Saturday 6 April 1793.

the sand.²⁵ In another, a sheriff's bailiff had a stash of 15 stands of arms in his 'lock-up house'.²⁶ Pikes were removed from the home of a gun-maker and with their owners' consent, cannon were removed from a number of the landed gentry's houses to Dublin's arsenal. The military was always involved in the removal of weapons of any shape or size. 'Sixteen pieces of heavy cannon and several waggons loaded with ammunition' were sent under guard to the south of the country – possibly Cork, for use should there be a rebellion, an invasion or even as a shipment to the Continent.²⁷

By the middle of the year, the time had come for extreme action to swell military numbers. Between 1 April and 30 September 1793, all regiments sent out their recruiting parties across the British Isles. The 44th in Ireland was no exception, but to recruit in such disordered and anarchic times could not have been easy. There were many occurrences reported in the newspapers of the citizenry stoning soldiers and pelting them with clods of earth.

Simultaneously, there were rumblings further afield, in the West Indies, of the possibility of French attacks and the need for four regiments to be sent out to Jamaica, ready to counteract any unrest.

The government seized on the obvious answer – the raising of militia by ballot in the Irish establishment to free up the necessary regiments. Militia troops were raised on a part-time basis to police the population on home soil. They would never be required to go abroad. This was an important measure when balloting the Irish, who believed to the contrary. Meanwhile in England, many rushed to join the English militia regiments to defend the country from invasion – one of those being Henry Austen, brother of Jane – who 'took a commission as a Lieutenant in the Oxfordshire Militia in the spring of 1793 and joined the regiment at Southampton in readiness to guard the coast'.²⁸ Once the Royal Assent was granted for the [Irish] Militia Act 1793, on 9 April, it enabled 38 militia regiments to be raised.

There appeared to be multiple reasons why the raising of militia in Ireland was, to say the least, unpopular but mostly feared and hated to the extreme. Specifically, the likelihood of being sent overseas, the destitution of families if their breadwinners were taken from them (this was an only too real threat if correct), opposition to the ballot system employed, the compulsion in the raising of the militia, and the obvious economic factors.²⁹ Enlistment into the militia meant none of these things, in fact the opposite. It seems that there was a general lack of understanding which had not been dealt with by the authorities. It was possible that once all questions had been addressed, then the raising of militia would be understood for what it was. So a real effort was then made by the authorities through the medium of the newspapers to lay out clearly the reasons for raising militia and the steps that would be taken.

---

25   *Finns Leinster Journal*, Saturday 2 March 1793.
26   *Finns Leinster Journal*, Wednesday 6 March 1793.
27   *Finns Leinster Journal*, Saturday 20 April 1793.
28   Irene Collins, *Jane Austen, The Parson's Daughter* (London: Hambledon Press, 1998), p.129.
29   Charles H.E. Philpin, *Nationalism and Popular Protest in Ireland* (Cambridge: Cambridge University Press, 2002), p.213.

THE LAND OF THE IRISH: HOME OF HOSTILITIES

Drawing for the Militia was resolved in Ireland after considerable misunderstanding. Engraving after by J.Phillip. (Author's Collection)

This stratagem worked. The *Saunders News-Letter* of Friday, 14 June 1793 enthusiastically trumpeted its delight, 'all misapprehensions of its intentions being removed, the people see its salutary tendency, and offer with joy to become the legal and constitutional defenders of themselves, their families, and their property'.[30]

Well, maybe not quite 'joy' – but though there remained some dissension, the greater populace responded well to the clarity of the explanations. The results of this could be seen all over the country with organised non-violent gatherings and deep curiosity of the people as to the results. With the assurance that the new militia raised would not serve overseas, that families would be recompensed, and that service would be for a maximum of four years, the anxieties felt were mainly dispelled.

In years to come, when given the opportunity, many Irish militiamen chose to volunteer for the regular British Army, continuing with the voluntary code. They proved themselves to be a nation of fighters – and were it not for the Irish spirit and dogged aggression, the army would have found many bad situations untenably worse.

As the raising of the militia in Ireland continued, the city of Valenciennes in France was laid siege to from 13 June–28 July 1793 by the allied troops of the First Coalition. The Duke of York made his positive mark by both commanding the siege and taking its surrender.

---

30   *Saunders News-Letter*, 14 June 1793.

The Bombardment of Valenciennes, which surrendered to His Royal Highness the Duke of York. Drawn by Godefroy. Engraved by J. Pass. (Author's Collection)

As the raising of the 38 militia regiments swung into action, the evacuation of the island by regular British regiments required elsewhere was at last enabled. In November 1793, the flank companies of light infantry and grenadiers of all regiments currently on the Irish Establishment were split off and sent to support other commands, in particular, in the West Indies. This included the flank companies of the 8th, 33rd and 44th. The flank companies of the 44th were commanded by Brevet Lieutenant Colonel Bryan Blundell. They included Captain Rufane Shaw Donkin's company and that of Captain John Lees. The return for 1 May 1794 taken at Liverpool shows the detachment of those companies mentioned above together with four lieutenants, Henry Holland, Montague Thorley, John Charles Phipps and Charles Phillips.[31] In that single move, the first battalion of the 44th was deprived of the cream of its regiment and two of the better officers, Blundell, an experienced officer aged 45 and Donkin who, although just 21 years old, was to become an able soldier and eventually Governor of Port Elizabeth in South Africa. The remaining companies of the 44th Regiment of Foot in Ireland were still nonetheless constantly involved in recruiting. The flank companies were missed for their specific skills by all their respective regiments.

---

31 TNA: WO 17/155: Return 1 May 1794, Liverpool.

The flank companies joined the expedition of Lieutenant General Sir Charles Grey, who was sailing in HMS *Boyne*, captained by his own son, George Grey, heading for Martinique. Leaving Portsmouth on Sunday 24 November, the *Boyne* arrived in Martinique on 6 January 1794 to find that some ships were already there, and by 10 January, all transports had reached their destination, except the one containing the 44th and 55th flank companies, which had returned to Ireland having lost its masts in a storm. The transport repaired, the *Peggy* arrived carrying the flank companies of the two missing regiments, in good order and without any sick. At that time the flank companies contained the tallest and most steady men in the grenadier company, and those adept at skirmishing in the light company.

The eight companies of the 44th left behind for service on the Continent now totalled 766 effective men, so the recruitment efforts in Ireland must have eventually borne fruit. The preparations regarding the regiments left in Ireland had taken some 10 months to finalise the withdrawal and the 44th was one of the very last to leave. Many of the regiments, having embarked on transports at Cork, would have passed the *Sarah* anchored in the Cove of Cork. A contagion running through the 40th (2nd Somersetshire) Regiment of Foot was so severe that the sick soldiers were removed from the military hospital in Cork and put into quarantine on board the *Sarah*, which had been converted into a hospital ship for the duration. Seventy of the 40th were suffering from dysentery and a putrid fever.[32]

Sir Jeremiah (sometimes known as Jerome) Fitzpatrick, who as well as being 'the Inspector of Jails and Madhouses In Ireland', had offered his services to accompany the 40th as surgeon on their passage from Ireland – as had Dr Richard Harris of Clonmel – to assist in the immediate emergency. The *Sarah* made it across the Irish Sea to Portsmouth. A reference in a Home Office memorandum dated 1 March 1794, mentions transports which were 'lately employed in bringing over the 40th regiment – have been cleaned & fumigated and are now supposed to be fit for the reception of Troops'.[33] Sir Jeremiah hoped to fit up all carrying either troops or horses and (as late as mid-July) 'requested permission to replace the bad water on the troop and war ships'.[34] For the sake of speed it was not unknown for unused casks of water to set out on another sailing!

Once the regiment reached Plymouth, the commander, Lieutenant General Lord George Lennox, equated the mortality rate to 'a regiment attacked by yellow fever in the West Indies'.[35] As yellow fever in the West Indies claimed some half to three-quarters of private men, the mortality rate of the fever among the 40th would have laid waste to those sick, so this was more likely to have been typhus. Nevertheless, this illustration of how a contagion could so devastate a regiment and virtually obliterate its fighting capacity gives a sad portent of what was to come.

---

32 *Finns Leinster Journal*, Saturday 4 January 1794.
33 TNA: HO 42/29: Fitzpatrick to Nepean, 1 March 1794, p.3.
34 TNA: PRO 30/8/135: Fitzpatrick to Brooke Watson, 16 July 1794.
35 Catherine Kelly, *War and the Militarization of British Army Medicine, 1793–1830* (London: Pickering & Chatto, 2011), p.23.

Major William Harness of the 80th (Staffordshire Volunteers) Regiment of Foot had a similar problem at Deal, onboard the *Mary and Elizabeth* transport the following September, when he wrote to his beloved wife, Bessy,

> This dreadful delay is the ruin of our Regiment, confined as they are in close Transports. [This] is a shocking Ship; she has been in service all the War, is but lately returned from the West Indies. Our poor Fellows have a nasty Fever broken out amongst them and I have prevailed upon Lord P[aget] to take all the men in health out of her. In consequence I have removed to the *John*. I hope by this timely arrangement the health of our Men will be preserved and that of the Sick restored. Forty were taken ill in two days. The Surgeon is removed to her and tells me this morning that most of the Sick are better.[36]

As Sir Jeremiah fought the fever in Cork Harbour in January 1794, news arrived with the 44th that they had a new lieutenant colonel, Robert Riddell. He, who was to be an important player in Roworth's life, came from an old Scottish family, and was related to the Riddells of Ardnamurchan. He appears to have languished as a captain in the 32nd Foot from 17 November 1780 to his exchange into the 12th Light Dragoons as captain, on 31 October 1792, when he paid the difference. Just five months later on 31 March 1793 he became a major in the 18th Light Dragoons, followed by lieutenant colonel in the 44th, 26 November 1793.[37] He may well have languished as a captain during peacetime, but must have had an infusion of money to rise so swiftly from a captain to a lieutenant colonel just 12 months.

While Lieutenant Colonel Riddell was finding his feet in the new job, the community of Kilkenny made a collection of 'warm clothing for the army serving abroad, or under orders for embarkation, and to sending to their respective homes, the wives and children of such soldiers as have embarked'.[38]

As well as the sum of £20.9s.6d, there were 554 flannel waistcoats, 349 pairs of drawers, 121 caps, 60 yards of flannel and 26 blankets. This generosity of spirit was recognised a couple of months later when the good people of Kilkenny were thanked by Lieutenant Colonel Hon. Arthur Wesley, who received a letter from Captain Stewart of the 33rd Foot's light company then arrived in Barbados. Stewart attributed the 'most perfect health of the soldiers on arrival, (with infinite gratitude to their benefactors) the flannel waistcoats delivered to Cork for their use on voyage'.[39]

The regiments slowly withdrew their troops via Ireland's various ports. The 8th Light Dragoons embarked at George's Quay for Chester early in March 1794. The 12th Light Dragoons left from Drogheda on transports taking them to England on their way to the Continent. The militia

---

36 Duncan-Jones, *Trusty*, p.53
37 TNA: WO 65: Army Lists.
38 *Finns Leinster Journal*, Wednesday 4 December 1793.
39 *Finns Leinster Journal*, Saturday 8 March 1794.

THE LAND OF THE IRISH: HOME OF HOSTILITIES

regiments were also on the move to position themselves as the regulars moved out. The inimitable Mrs Catherine Finn (widow of Edmund) of *Finns Leinster Journal* carefully noted all those who passed its portals in Kilkenny and gave the usual succinct overview on Saturday 29 March 1794: 'The Royal Irish Invalids into Kinsale; Meath Royal Regiment into Cork; the County of Louth Regiment into Cork; the Derry Militia to Drogheda; Tyrone militia to New Geneva; the Queen's county Militia to Derry; Wicklow Militia to Strabane; Wexford Militia to Enniskillen; the Clare Militia to Ballyshannon.'[40] The constant moving, marching and embarking continued.

The newly raised militia regiments were already fulfilling their duty. Just one example was the members of the Carlow Militia who, near Kinsale, were ordered to fire on insurgents. They obeyed, killing and wounding a number of them.[41] By the time the regular regiments had nearly all left the island of Ireland, the militia was getting in plenty of practice.

At last, the 44th was also ready to leave Ireland. In mid-April, the soldiers were on duty in Dublin Barracks 'holding in instant readiness for foreign service'.[42] By 1 May, they were in Liverpool recording their monthly return, including 26 serjeants, 17 drummers and fifers, and 537 men fit for duty, 139 on command, 50 recruiting, two on furlough, with a total of 767; sick in quarters were 22 and 18 sick in hospital.[43]

Spike Island in the Cobh of Cork as it is today. (Donald Roworth)

---

40   *Finns Leinster Journal*, Saturday 29 March 1794.
41   *Finns Leinster Journal*, Saturday 22 March 1794.
42   *Finns Leinster Journal*, Saturday 19 April 1794.
43   TNA: WO 17/155: Monthly Return 1 May 1794, Liverpool.

State of the 44th Foot, monthly return, Liverpool, 1 May 1794, TNA: WO 17/155

Present					Rank & File					Number Wanting		
Officers	Staff	QM	Sjt	Drum	Present	Sick	On Com'd	Other	Total	Sjt	Drum	R&F
12	2	1	26	17	537	40	139	51	767	3	1	433

State of the 44th Foot, monthly return, Dartford, 1 June 1794, TNA: WO 17/155

Present					Rank & File					Number Wanting		
Officers	Staff	QM	Sjt	Drum	Present	Sick	On Com'd	Other	Total	Sjt	Drum	R&F
17	3		33	18	544	50	142	24	766	3	2	434

By the first week in June, the regiment was in Dartford, Kent. This was the final opportunity for Roworth to meet up with his wife, Mary, before leaving her at Gravesend, where the regiment waited to embark for the Continent.

There was no sign of Lieutenant Samuel Tuffie, who was still marked as 'sick in Dublin'. Yet it seems that Samuel, eldest son of Quartermaster John Tuffie, did eventually arrive in Dartford some time after the regiment had left but he did not recover from his illness. There is a record of his burial at Holy Trinity Church in Dartford on 4 November 1794. He is recorded there as a lieutenant in the 44th Regiment. It may be that he was that Samuel Tuffie who was born in Canada, as his family was there in 1764. If so, he would have been just 29 or 30 at death. Soon tragedy would strike the Tuffie family again.

At that time, the 44th contained few effective soldiers experienced in war. The previous war was the American War of Independence, which had ended in 1783. Many men, who had spent 10 years of their lives in North America and Canada, were discharged and retired soon after, worn out. Some, like Serjeant Alexander Andrew – the servant to James Agnew – had been discharged at the end of his service in Ireland. As referred to above, with other regiments, the 44th's grenadier and light companies had been diverted to fight the French in the West Indies. That meant that many experienced officers were gone, too. Of those 766 men remaining, few of the non-commissioned officers were veterans of the American War. Only five serjeants had been in the 44th since 1780 or before, though only one as a serjeant at that time. The remainder, including Roworth, were recruited after 1783 and had no war experience at all. The nearest they had got to shots in anger was their experience with rioting civilians in Ireland or determined smugglers on the Isle of Man and Ayr.

While the 44th had been preparing to leave Ireland, British troops had been fighting in the Low Countries and the 44th were now ordered to join them. In his history of the Flanders campaign, Captain Lewis Tobias Jones of the 14th (Bedfordshire) Regiment of Foot voiced his reservations concerning the attitude of the Allies, who considered quitting the Netherlands even before the reinforcements had left British shores. The reason he gave was the opposing numbers of troops. The 'whole [Allied] force, which, in the beginning of the campaign, amounted to one hundred and ninety thousand men, was now only eighty thousand, while that of the enemy had encreased

THE LAND OF THE IRISH: HOME OF HOSTILITIES

[*sic*] to above three hundred thousand fighting men'.[44] The 14th, under its commanding officer, Lieutenant Colonel Welbore Ellis Doyle, was the first regiment of the line to arrive at the scene of war at Helvoetsluys, on the Island of Voorn, on 19 March 1793. They had continued fighting on the Continent for 16 months before the reinforcements arrived in June 1794.

All transports at Cowes and Southampton were fitted up for the imminent reception of troops, most of whom were gathering at Scholing Down, east of Southampton. The 8th, the 33rd, and the 44th were to join separately – as part of the reserve of Major General Lord Moira's army of reinforcement for the Duke of York on the Continent. Embarking from Cork, it took nearly three weeks for the 33rd Foot and the 14th Light Dragoons to arrive at the Nore.

The 2nd Brigade consisted of those same three regiments from Ireland. They arrived in Flanders at a considerable disadvantage. Some of the 8th and 44th Foot, as well as the raw recruits from Gravesend, were sent without some of their equipment and with inadequate clothing:

> These unfortunate men, on being drafted into the depots in England, received what was called slop-clothing … a linen jacket and trousers … it is an actual fact that many of them were sent on active service in this dress, without waistcoat, drawers or stockings. The result was that the Duke of York's corps was in a worse state in respect of clothing than had hitherto been recorded of any British army.[45]

Many of those recruits had barely seen a parade ground, let alone felt the pride that the precious red uniform would have given them – a step up in the community, identity and respect. As in any uniformed organisation, it was the uniform itself that started to instil that initial training and distinction. The famous red coat marked them out. Somehow a linen jacket and trousers failed to come up to expectations. It was fortunate for those so clad that it was still high summer.

The regiments despatched to Flanders so ill-prepared contained relatively few experienced veterans mixed with a large number of recruits who were without adequate training and discipline. 'Many of them do not know one end of a fire-lock from the other,' wrote Colonel Sir James Craig, York's adjutant general, 'and will never know it … Six of the battalions had been deprived of their best men in the flank companies and no sooner did the new levies find themselves released from the crimping-house … and the gaol for active service, than they fell to plundering in all directions.'[46]

That was Fortescue's opinion, too, but was he right? As mentioned earlier, the British Army, at this time, did not conscript men – it only recruited. A judge may have offered a convicted man the option of transportation or the

---

44   L.T. Jones, *An Historical Journal of the British Campaign on the continent, in the year 1794: with the Retreat through Holland, in the year 1795* (Birmingham: Swinney & Hawkins, 1797) p.77.
45   J.W. Fortescue, *History of the Army*, vol.IV, Part 1, p.299.
46   Fortescue, *History of the Army*, vol.IV, Part 1, p.295.

army, but both the offender and the commander always had the choice (See Chapter 1).

In July 1794, the Duke of York found himself at the head of about 26,000 men, in seven brigades, with only four generals – David Dundas, Alexander Stewart, Ralph Abercromby and Henry Edward Fox.[47] The elite flank companies had been sent to the West Indies leaving, perhaps, less experienced men for duty in Flanders. Fortescue described the commanders of the new battalions as 'boys of twenty-one who knew nothing of their simplest duties. Though they went cheerfully into action, they looked upon the whole campaign as an elaborate picnic.'[48]

Indeed, these young men made sure that they were not without their 'picnic' as they travelled forth with all their home comforts on what they perceived as grand adventures. The hard-pushed quartermasters had to find room for huge quantities of baggage, full of clothes, food and cases of wine and brandy. However, these adventures were not necessarily of their own choosing but wished upon them by the parental mores of the time, according to Fortescue: 'Thrust into the army to satisfy the claims of dependents, constituents, importunate creditors, and discarded concubines, many of these young men were at once a disgrace and an encumbrance to the force.'[49]

This sounded somewhat harsh, but it might have been termed second-son syndrome, where the first son inherited, the second joined the army or navy, and the third entered the church, irrespective of the young men's own wishes. Nor was it always a failure, if not the career the young man might have wished for, indeed some flourished and became effective officers but for many it was not the ideal, nor, more importantly, for the calibre of the army.

An example of the problems this caused was highlighted by Captain John Gaspard Le Marchant early in the war in May 1793 when commenting on a detachment of Light Dragoons, who 'met a detachment of Dutch troops on their march from Furnes to Ypres, took them for French, and were so dreadfully frightened that they galloped away like madmen. They rode their horses so hard, that several died the same evening, and others were seriously wounded'.[50]

A competent dragoon commander would have known better and acted differently, instead incurring a humiliating debacle by failing to recognise an allied uniform. Leadbetter's own comments on the above were telling: 'Such was the army with which the Duke of York, a youthful and inexperienced commander, took the field to oppose an enemy whose numerical superiority was directed by a succession of veteran leaders of established military reputation and skill.'[51] In later years, Lieutenant Colonel John Gaspard Le Marchant became Lieutenant Governor of the Royal Military College at High Wycombe in Buckinghamshire for the training of officers. The college

---

47 Fortescue, *History of the Army*, vol.IV, Part 1, p.296.
48 Fortescue, *History of the Army*, vol.IV, Part 1, pp.296–297.
49 Fortescue, *History of the Army*, vol.IV, Part 1, p.297.
50 Denis Le Marchant, *Memoirs of the late Major-General Le Marchant. 1766–1812* (Staplehurst: Spellmount, 1997), p.14.
51 Le Marchant, *Memoirs*, pp.14–15, n.29.

was his own brainchild, of which the Duke of York thoroughly approved and set into motion.

It was not that Britain was without success since that March day when the Foot Guards had landed in France. In 1793, there had been seven early successes for Britain against the French, as a member of the First Coalition – Raismes, Famars, Valenciennes, the Battle of Caesar's Camp, Lincelles, the Siege of Toulon, and Courtrai. In 1794, there were Allied successes at Villers-en-Cauchies on 24 April, Beaumont on 26 April and at Tournay on 22 May. But it seemed there were to be no more. Time for reinforcements.

The *Chester Chronicle* reported that, 'Troops embarked under the command of Lord Moira are the 19th, 27th, 28th, 40th, 42nd, 54th, 57th, 59th, 87th, and 89th regiments, forming a body of 8000 effective men'.[52] They had arrived off Portsmouth on the evening of the 21st of June. The fleet was convoyed by large ships of war, gunboats and two floating batteries. The artillery 'portion of the force comprised a field officer in command – the 5th Company of the 4th Battalion – with 110 of all ranks, and also 114 sergeant-conductors and gunner-drivers'.[53] Two of the artillery officers who would leave their names for posterity were already fighting on the Continent, Major William Congreve was one. He would go on to invent the Congreve rocket in 1805. One of the inspirations for Francis Scott Key's 'Star-Spangled Banner' in 1814 was the red glare of Congreve's rockets, now sung as part of the American National Anthem. The other officer was Lieutenant Henry Shrapnel, who had already invented the spherical case round in 1787 that would later be known by his name. The fleet was joined by the 8th, 33rd, and 44th Regiments at the Nore. On 28 June, they sailed for Ostend, passing through Lord Howe's Fleet, who had returned from his victory over the French – known as the Glorious First of June. The army and navy cheered as the ships passed each other.

That was to be the last 'huzzah' for some time.

---

52 *Chester Chronicle*, Friday, 27 June 1794.
53 Francis Duncan, *History of the Royal Regiment of Artillery: Compiled from Original Records* (London: Naval and Military Press Ltd, 2004), vol.II, p.58.

5

Laxity, Lawlessness and Loathing: Allies or Enemies?

'Compared with which number all our army is but a small piquet.'[1]

Little had changed in the 44th between the May and June monthly returns, although Rufane Shaw Donkin had returned from St Lucia and Bryan Blundell had not, the latter had been promoted a lieutenant colonel in the 45th Foot. Brevet Lieutenant Colonel Colin Campbell (still a regimental captain) and Captain Edward Wilson were still on the road to join the regiment. There were to be six captains with the 44th when all had arrived, Colin Campbell, David Ogilvie, George Johnston, William Blaquiere, Edward Wilson, William Tomkinson, and a seventh unnamed officer for '12th' company. Ensign Francis Morris was ignominiously 'Detained by an Arrest of the Civil Powers', with three men in the same position. Adjutant David Stark was on leave. Both the surgeon and his mate were marked present though not recorded. Further details include 33 serjeants, 18 drummers, 544 rank and file present and fit for duty, 31 sick in quarters, 25 in hospitals, with 142 On Command making 766 in total. Needing to complete there were three serjeants, two drummers with 434 rank and file. The alterations show 39 joined, three dead, three discharged but not recommended, and 13 deserted.[2]

A few months later from France, Roworth was to remind his wife of the morning they lay in bed in Dartford. The letter, written in October, says that he had not slept in a bed since.[3] In an earlier letter we learn that the regiment 'did not sail [until] the Tuesday after you Left me and then we sailed [probably from Blackwall] to the Nore and joined the rest of the fleet', prior to meeting up with the Earl of Moira and his army sailing for Flanders.[4] The Nore sandbank was in the Thames Estuary, used as a rendezvous for shipping.

The flank companies, both light infantry and grenadier, would have been a huge advantage to the 44th. The campaigns of eighteenth century, particularly the two wars the British Army had fought in America, emphasised the need

---

1   Brown, *Impartial Journal*, p.170.
2   TNA: WO 17/155: Monthly Return 1 June 1794.
3   NA: DDWR 3/25: Roworth to Mary, Tiell, 10 October 1794
4   NA: DDWR 1/25. Roworth to Mary, Camp near Rosendale [sic], 27 July 1794

LAXITY, LAWLESSNESS AND LOATHING: ALLIES OR ENEMIES?

for light infantry to British commanders. The men of the light companies needed to be light on their feet, with an ability to think for themselves as well as to be part of the line when needed. They had to assess a situation and their response to it, to be able to skirmish, to annoy the enemy, to be aware of the use the enemy could make of cover, to use cover themselves and, importantly, not to waste their fire by using it to no effect. Some would come from rural backgrounds and be naturally familiar with functioning in the ways of countryside, whether their own or in adapting to foreign climes. For these types of troops, in America 'British Generals selected the most enterprising officers … [who] engaged the enemy in his own way, opposed Light Troops to Light Troops, repulsed him with advantage, and secured and facilitated the operations of the army'.[5] This type of fighting skill was also to be so important in a number of the campaigns to come, including those between the French and English in the Caribbean in the 1790s.

In spite of early successes in 1793 and early 1794, for Britain and the allies, the War of the First Coalition on the Continent had begun to descend into a shambles. The British commissariat, which supplied food and equipment, was totally inadequate to keep up with the movements of an army of approximately 40,000 men, whether advancing or retreating, plus horses and camp followers. The hospitals were in a parlous state and the men who staffed them were often barely adequate or downright rogues. Historian John Fortescue's seemingly constant state of apoplexy knew no bounds in his demonisation of Dundas, at whose feet he squarely placed the disastrous state of medical affairs in the army on the Continent at this time: 'Dundas's idea of putting an army in the field was to land raw men on a foreign shore, and to expect discipline, arms, ammunition, clothing, victuals, medical stores and medical treatment to descend on them from Heaven.'[6] In July 1794 Henry Calvert (aide de camp to the Duke of York) in a letter to his friend Sir Hew Dalrymple had asked rhetorically, 'Explain to me the reason of the recruits joining the army [in Flanders] without arms or any appointments necessary for soldiers. I am often asked the question and can't resolve it.'[7]

Whether Fortescue was biased in his opinions or not, he and others highlighted the supreme difficulties into which the Duke of York was thrust. It would have taken a man of the stature of Wellington (who was currently cutting his military teeth and fast learning 'what not to do') to have handled the intricacies and multiple personalities of the members of the First Coalition. Indeed, it is possible that even Wellington might have come to grief as the various leaders seemed unable to grasp the meaning of 'coalition'. There were other factors working against York, not least of which was his own inexperience. That, together with the sheer weight of conscripted manpower

---

5   Thomas Cooper, *A Practical Guide for the Light Infantry Officer: Comprising Valuable Extracts From All the Most Popular Works on the Subject with Further Original Information* (London: Robert Wilks, 1806). pp.xiii–xiv.
6   Fortescue, *History of the Army*, vol.IV, part 1, p.300.
7   H. Verney (ed.), *The Journals and Correspondence of General Sir Harry Calvert* (London: Hurst & Blackett, 1853), p.277.

Général de division Jean-Charles Pichegru, 1835, by Lacouchie & Couché. (Author's Collection)

on the French side would prove too much for the rather rocky coalition in the long run.

Britain was but one member in an allied European army which resembled a many-headed hydra, with Spain, the Dutch Republic, Austria, Prussia and Sardinia being the other heads. These were led by multiple commanders fighting for their own countries' best interests, while Britain was not only bankrolling its own forces but subsidizing its allies. Those facts came to prominence when Britain drew on a treaty made with the Prussians that would provide the former with 60,000 troops to recover the lost ground of West Flanders. Prussia could only provide 40,000, which were not only short of stores, supplies and transports but of which the Austrian Emperor claimed back 30,000 to shore up the borders of his own empire. This all brought Britain to the brink of bankruptcy and (by September) York was left facing *Général de division* Jean-Charles Pichegru and his Army of the North. As the year went on York was to find himself virtually denuded of allies.

In the meantime, York – although Commander-in-Chief of the British and Hanoverian forces – was in effect also fighting a war with his own country, in the shape of Henry Dundas, Secretary of State for War and his own father, King George III, as well as many other civilian and military administrators. It seems outrageous today – but not beyond the realms of fantasy – that even the Duke of York's request for maps of the area around Bois-le-Duc, together with 'military surveys', to be sent from England, resulted in a single copy of a map of Hanover found in his father's library.[8]

By the end of June 1794, the infantry had been organised into seven brigades. Things were tricky for Moira. He was at Ostend with 10 regiments; the 3rd, 19th, 27th, 28th, 40th, 42nd, 54th, 59th, 63rd, 87th and 89th – numbering 7,000 men in total – waiting in the Sand Hills, unpleasantly placed with Bruges and Ypres on either side, both held by the enemy. He made the unilateral decision to relieve the Duke of York and the allies, so he marched 'through the town and crossed the river at the ferry, and halted until daybreak [still] within two miles of Ostend'.[9] On 28 June, information received the previous day persuaded him to join the Duke as soon as possible. On 29 June, the 42nd Foot, marching with Moira in the direction of Bruges,

---

8   Richard Glover, *Peninsular Preparation: The Reform of the British Army 1795–1809* (Cambridge: Cambridge University Press, 1963), p.19.
9   Jones, *An Historical Journal*, p.81.

LAXITY, LAWLESSNESS AND LOATHING: ALLIES OR ENEMIES?

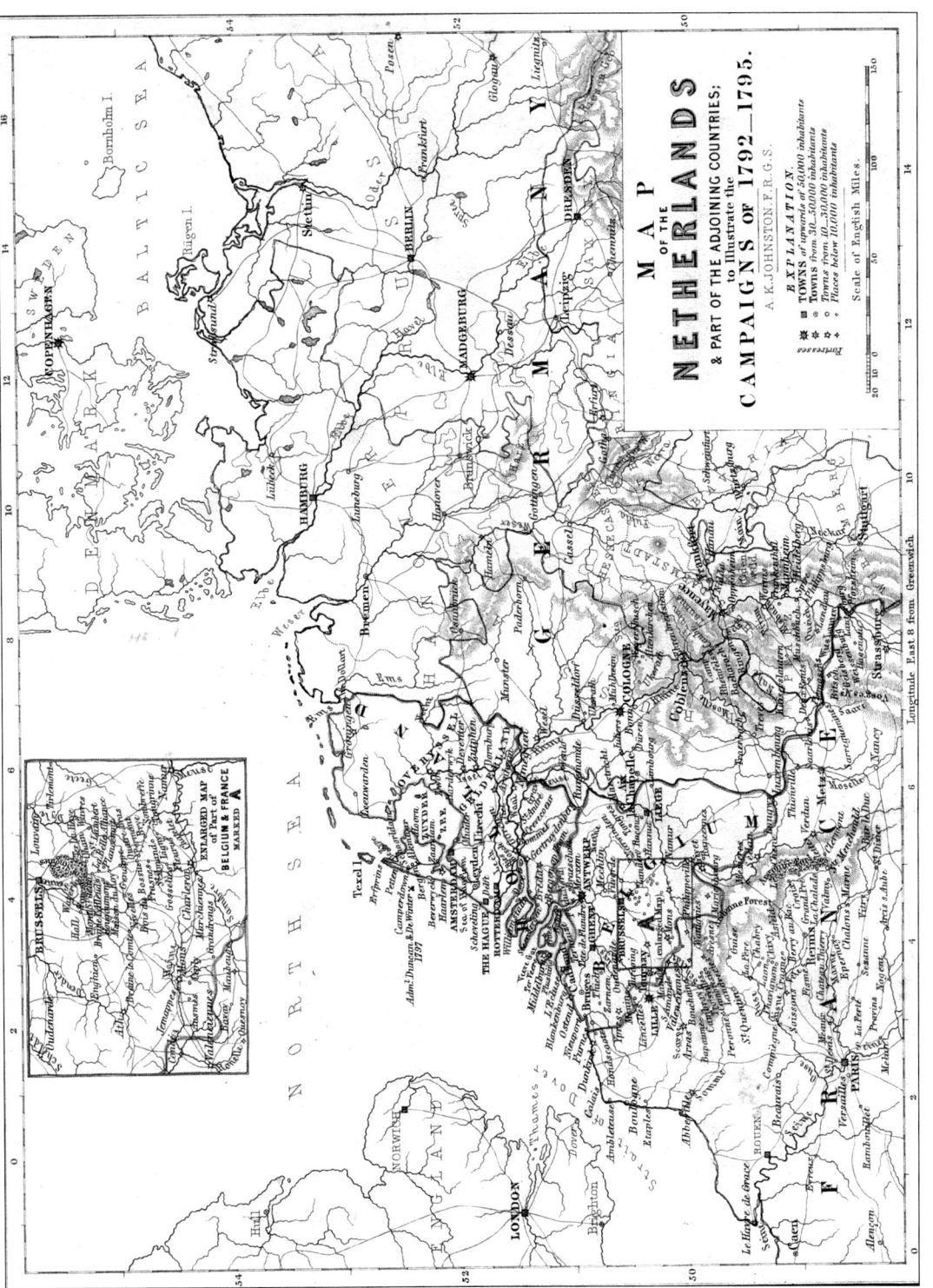

The Campaigns of 1792–1795. Flanders. (Author's Collection)

were inadvertently entertaining the inhabitants who thought the kilts of the men were skirts and they acquired the nickname of 'English Frows' (women). Moira and the Duke finally met up at Alost on 5 July.

Meanwhile, the 8th, 33rd and 44th, including raw recruits, had arrived at Ostend on 22 June 1794. In his first known letter to Mary, dated 27 July 1794 and written from Roosendaal, near Bergen op Zoom, Roworth added some small minutiae for her, which also provided corroboration of dates and whereabouts of his own march:

> My Dear we did not sail while the Tuesday after you Left me [at Gravesend] and then we sailed [22 miles] to the Nore and joined the Rest of the fleet; at which place [we] Anchored there two days, and then proceeded on our Voyage to Ostend and arrived on the 22nd of June. And we Disembarked on the 23rd, at which place we only stayed eight days. Ostend is a Very pleasant place, but Very ill-destroyed on account of the War.[10]

It was at Ostend on 27 June 1794 that Lord Moira had given the following order to, 'Colonel Vyse, Commandant of the Town, will please for the present to take the command of the Brigade consisting of the 8th, 33rd [and] 44th Regiments. Captain Earl of the 24th Foot having been appointed by his Majesty a Major of Brigade to those Corps, will assume the Functions of that station under the order of Col: Vyse.'[11] Vyse gave instructions to the Guard of the Gate to refuse entry into the town from the camp to any soldier who did not have a pass. His intention was to avoid trouble with the local people.

At this time any private letters from abroad that were considered to be of public interest were often published (by the recipients) in the newspapers, to provide a bona fide source of news. The *Caledonian Mercury* printed a letter from Colonel Vyse, from Ostend dated 29 June 1794, to say that 'he was embarking the 8th, 33d, and 44th regiments, and the rest of the troops, artillery, and stores, intending to evacuate that place'.[12] It has been suggested that this brigade was given to Lieutenant Colonel Arthur Wesley (the future Duke of Wellington) as a rearguard by Moira in order 'to settle matters at Ostend … then come away as quick as I could'. So, according to this version of events, the evacuation, though supervised by Vyse, gave Wesley the opportunity to 're-embark his men, put them ashore at Antwerp and [they in fact] reached the Duke of York [at Alost] before the leading files of Moira's force'.[13] However, in Rory Muir's recent biography of Wellington he states that on 29 June Moira with the bulk of his troops left Ostend to march overland to join the Duke of York. He also states that the 33rd remained behind as part of the rearguard, commanded by Vyse (not Wesley), which would protect the reloading of stores, heavy equipment and the sick, and

---

10 NA: DDRW1/25: Roworth to Mary, Camp near Rosendale [*sic*], 27 July 1794.
11 National Army Museum (NAM): 1985-12-9: Orderly book Earl of Moira's Army.
12 *Caledonian Mercury*, Saturday, 5 July 1794.
13 J.M. Brereton & A.C.S. Savory, *The History of The Duke of Wellington's Regiment (West Riding) 1702–1992* (Halifax: Duke of Wellington's Regiment, 1993), p.93.

join the main army by ship'.[14] The rearguard re-embarked on 30 June and arrived by 11 July.[15]

Roworth mentioned an exchange of fire with the French and the renowned difficulties of getting into the tidal Scheldt:

> ... we went on board of the transports again on the 31st ... We had not got on board from Ostend half an hour but the French Army came on the opposite Side of the River, where there is a ferry that parts the town. Our Shipping that Lay before the town kept a constant fire on them [the French] and did some little Execution. Night Coming on our Shipping got aground and there Lay for the Next tide, when we got off without any damage. But the Roberts struck, I Suppose, twenty times, against the Bottom, and when we [finally] got off, our Fleet Set Sail ... And proceeded up the Scheldt to Antwerp ... at which place we all arrived Safe and went to Camp.[16]

By 3 July, Moira had requested that the commanding officers instruct their men to refrain from throwing broken bottles around the camp avenues as injuries were inflicted on the hooves of Dragoon horses. Orders were given to bury the bottles or at least throw them in the ditches. Only two days later, the first complaints came in about plundering by British troops. Again, he called on the officers 'by every sense they have of Military discipline & national credit to exert themselves in suppressing a Conduct so disgraceful to the Army'.[17]

The 8th, 33rd and 44th arrived at the port of Antwerp on 5 July, and Roworth was much impressed and thought it a beautiful place – the people and the houses were very clean and the people were Roman Catholic with rich churches, but he found the fashions very curious.[18]

He was probably among those who arrived in the afternoon when, according to Van der Straalen, who was an eyewitness, 'great transport of English luggage passed through the St Joris gate and was stationed at Casteelplein [Castle Square]. Many of the soldiers stationed outside the village marched to the square'.[19] This continued throughout 6–8 July. As the 44th was part of the 6th Brigade, now commanded by Major General Nisbet Balfour, they, and 8th and 33rd, were likely to have camped together in the area of the Castle Square. The chapel of St Jacob in the Keyserstraat (among others) was used as a hospital for the English troops.

Moira, at Malines, was having difficulty with his troops. On 7 July, his comments were at the least robust, ordering the provost martial 'to patrol in the vicinity of the Camp [and] to punish on the spot every man who shall be found committing the smallest outrage'.[20] He also gave orders that

---

14 Rory Muir, *Wellington: The Path to Victory 1769–1814* (New Haven: Yale, 2015), p.31.
15 NA: DDWR1/25: Roworth to Mary, Camp at Rosendale, 27 July 1794.
16 NA: DDRW1/25: Roworth to Mary, Camp at Rosendale, 27 July 1794.
17 NAM: 1985-12-9: Orderly book for Earl of Moira's Army.
18 NA: DDRW1/25: Roworth to Mary, 27 July 1794.
19 Jan Baptist van der Straalen and Jan Fran van der Straalen, *Der Kronijk van Antwerpen, Deel 4 1791 tot en met 1794* (Antwerp: Maatschappij, 1932), p.210.
20 Van der Straalen, *Der Kronijk*, p.212.

An example of the Dutch clothing Roworth found 'very curious', by Lacauchie & Couché. (Author's Collection)

no soldier would be allowed to leave camp unless accompanied by a non-commissioned officer because of the marauding in the neighbourhood of Alost. The indications were not good. Moira's army had been on foreign soil for less than a month and was already pillaging from their allies. Their officers seemed incapable of maintaining discipline.

Back in Antwerp, the British troops and the inhabitants were soon to develop a love/hate relationship. If the British Army had any reputation for decency, it was lost as soon as it disembarked. Van Der Straalen kept a daily account of the reprehensible outrages and atrocities committed by numbers of the British and Hanoverian soldiers over the days and weeks which followed. On 10 July, he wrote, 'Our city is full of soldiers, particularly English ones. Every one fears the English as there are so many wanton people among them.'[21] Accusations included robbery, indiscriminate damage such as breaking into nunneries and churches and laying waste to the contents,

---

21 Van der Straalen, *Der Kronijk*, pp.212–214.

LAXITY, LAWLESSNESS AND LOATHING: ALLIES OR ENEMIES?

desecrating churches by using them as stables for horses, setting fires for cooking in the aisles and naves, and the ripping out of ancient and valuable woodwork to stoke those fires.

Van Der Straalen described the masts of the English ships as looking like a forest on the Scheldt. These had sailed from Nieuport and were filled with men and horses. On 14 July, soldiers, wagons and baggage continued to pour through the city. The French were rumoured to have reached Mechelen and by noon on the 16th, cannon fire could be heard. In Antwerp the soldiers emptied those chapels and cloisters and the Church of St Carolus, which were being used as hospitals, and sent the sick back on the empty transports. The sick were the lucky ones.

British soldiers began to move out of the city, leaving sufficient to garrison the place and keep a constant lookout to the west. The sheer number of soldiers amazed the inhabitants to the extent that they felt like strangers in their own town. There were those who were grateful for the defence, and when the cannon roared and rumours swirled of the arrival of the French, the citizens either upped and fled or stayed to defend where they could. But the fear of the French was as all-encompassing as the fear of the British. They knew that the atrocities and cruelties of the French would not only be to the infrastructure but to the citizens themselves.

Captain Roger Morris, who had ridden from his camp at Kontich where his company of the Coldstreams was based, rode into Antwerp by the side of the Scheldt and close to the Citadel. He noticed 'a great quantity of Forage in large ricks, looking like a Street with houses'.[22] This was probably the forage the British set on fire before they vacated the city, anxious to remove anything which might help the French continue their pursuit of the allies. It burned all day.

The next day, 15 July, Morris left via the Gate of Antwerp, worked his way south-east to Boechout, then Hove and onto the main Antwerp road opposite the British Park of Artillery. He took advantage of his wanderings to describe in his journal the positions of picquets, manoeuvres of regiments, skirmishes, incidents by either of the protagonists, and positions of camps. The Coldstreams had passed through Malines on the 9th and so on to Duffel, but three days later the French were virtually on their heels and by the 16th had 'possessed themselves of Malines'.

It is at this point that the full content of Morris's entry dated Wednesday the 16th requires careful scrutiny for the corroboration or otherwise of Roworth's account. Morris states:

> I am on the Picq't advanced about a 200 yards, in front of the Qr: G'd: of the 1st Reg't.–At 11 a heavy Cannonade commenced in front which continued till 6 in the evening: the Hessians, who burned the [Walheim] bridge over the river Niethe on the Chausee to Malines, left the village standing on the other side, & the French being in possession of it, their sharp shooters kept up a destructive fire

---

22 Roger Morris, *With the Guards in Flanders: The Diary of Captain Roger Morris 1793–1795* (Warwick: Helion, 2018), p.88.

on our men on the windows of the house – All night I heard continued reports of rifles but no cannon shot.

Thursday 17 [July]
I was relieved at 9 – 11 we were joined by 4 Comp's of Lt Inf'y from England I rode down the Chausee tow'ds the Neithe there was nothing going on but some sharp shooting. The 12, 38 & 55 Regt's are hutted near the river.[23]

This statement holds importance for the 44th Foot as Jones claims that they were involved in this incident, together with the 12th and the 38th Foot.[24] It seems unlikely as they left Antwerp on the 23 July then marched for two days arriving at camp in Roosendaal on the 25th from where Roworth wrote his first letter to Mary on the 27th. If such an encounter had happened to the 44th, gauging by the contents of his letters to her, Roworth would be sure to have mentioned it, but even more likely is that Jones made a simple error. Immediately after Morris's journal entry, he recorded details of the brigades, which regiments were in which brigades and their brigade commanders.[25] The second brigade, that of Brigadier General Stuart was made up from the 12th and the 38th, being two of those fighting at the Bridge at Walheim, the third regiment being the 55th Foot, therefore much more likely to be fighting in its own brigade. So, what of the 44th? The list of brigades accounts for them as being in Antwerp, with the 8th and 33rd regiments – which is exactly where they were on 16 July 1794, officially under the command of Balfour.

Morris had ridden to Duffel on 21 July (noting that some of the meadows were inundated with water). Lord Moira had returned to Britain, due to a 'misunderstanding', so that his army (now under the command of Lieutenant General Ralph Abercromby) was hutted at Duffel and was due to march at 3:00 a.m. on the 22nd. They arrived at their destination within nine hours and encamped close to Wijnegen, thereby missing an unpleasant incident at Antwerp.

In Antwerp on that day, there had been a huge explosion caused by some small gunpowder magazines within the castle, which started a fire and killed and injured about 20 people – with body parts scattered in all directions. Roworth's report of this incident in his letter home seemed to indicate that the three regiments from Ireland were indeed camped together in the Castle Square, '… one of the 33rd being Sentinel, was unfortunately blown to pieces and a number [of] More Lives besides. I was in My tent when the Explosion went off and … I went to see it and to see the poor Souls … It was a Shocking Sight.'[26] So, Roworth was an eyewitness to the aftermath.

The incident was reported widely in the British newspapers. The next day, the 44th, 33rd and 8th left Antwerp to march the 50 miles to Roosendaal, south-west of Breda, which was to be the new headquarters. The army

---

23   Morris, *With the Guards*, p.89.
24   Jones, *An Historical Journal*, p.93.
25   Morris, *With the Guards*, p.89.
26   NA: DDRW1/25: Roworth to Mary, Camp at Rosendale, 27 July 1794.

crossed a 'Large Barren heath' with small copses of trees. It took them two days, arriving on the 25th.²⁷ For Roworth, it was the first time he had seen such a large army all camped in one place and he was staggered by the size of it. 'You would not [believe] what ground we cover – all the English Horse and Foot – and all the other Powers. We are all encamped together and in good Health and Spirits, willing to bring those French to action, but they take care never to come to an Engagement in the open field.'²⁸

Fortescue gives an estimate of all officers and men at 40,000.²⁹ Morris reported on that part of the ground covered by the guards alone: 'The Right flank of the Brigade of G'ds is in line with the Church of Nispen at the distance of about a League & the left flank is in line with the Church of Sprindel [Sprundel] at about 2 leagues distance.'³⁰

On Sunday 26 July, Morris was the orderly officer for the day. Even so, he still found time to indulge in his passion – that of looking at churches and church organs. Roosendaal was 'a neat town', but the local church organ was 'indifferent'. Meanwhile, Roworth continued with a running letter to Mary whenever time allowed. He mentioned the rumoured possibility of troops being sent to the West Indies. That was not the first nor the last time during these months on the Continent that this particular subject was aired between them on paper. The West Indies was writ large on the minds of all redcoats as it was looked upon as certain death from the tropical diseases, which would always kill far more of them than war.

In July, the Duke of York also had to deal with the ongoing question of what to do about Nieuport. The garrison there comprised about 2,000 Hanoverians and some 500 émigrés. As the line of the Scheldt was abandoned, the troops were drawn back from Belgium into Holland, and Nieuport was left unsupported. York wrote to Dundas urging the evacuation of Nieuport, in particular, that the émigrés 'should not for pity's sake be exposed to the risk of capture'.³¹ He knew full well what their fate would be. In response, Dundas promised boats to evacuate the émigrés, but too late. The garrison surrendered to the French. The captain of a cutter which arrived in Deal from Nieuport brought the news of the catastrophe, which the *Hampshire Chronicle* duly reported:

> The garrison capitulated on the 18th, after a two-week siege, at six o'clock on Saturday morning; and at noon, the Hanoverians and two English officers, of whom Captain Wilson of the artillery was one, were marched out as prisoners of war to Lille. Lieutenant Reedy, of the *Redoubt* floating battery, who was said to have been guillotined, was alive in the town. One hundred and thirty emigrants are said to have been put instantly to death, 24 of whom were tied to the mouth of a 24-pounder, and blown off.³²

---

27 NA: DDRW1/25: Roworth to Mary, Camp at Rosendale, 27 July 1794.
28 NA: DDRW1/25: Roworth to Mary, Camp at Rosendale, 27 July 1794.
29 Fortescue, *A History of the Army*, vol.IV, Part 1, p.296.
30 Morris, *With the Guards*, p.91. An English league is three miles.
31 Fortescue, *A History of the Army*, vol.IV, Part 1, pp.285–286.
32 *Hampshire Chronicle*, Monday 28 July 1794.

Estimates of the number of émigrés executed in this incident vary from the figure quoted above up to 500. York was much blamed for this, and he also had the problem of the ongoing plundering to stretch his mind. However, a clue as to the obvious cause is to be found to the excessive and continual theft from vegetable plots, recorded in the Grenadiers' General Orders, – but no recourse to alleviate the problem was made, only the punishment given:

> As the situation of that Corps under the Command of Earl Moira with respect to provisions ha[d] obliged the Men frequently to subsist on the Country by Picking such Roots and Vegetables as could be found in the Fields it [wa]s necessary that they should now be warned that [it be] understood as plundering to all intents and purposes and the Provost had orders to punish on the spot any man he … detect[ed] in injuring any garden or field.[33]

The problem of plundering was never resolved, however. No matter what size the army – 20,000 or 200,000 – all its constituent parts needed to be fed. An army on the march could not starve indefinitely. There were further orders from the Duke of York on 29 July and 5 August repeating that 'no Regt or Corps is ever to Forage in the Country without particular directions from the QMG.'[34]

Food was on Roworth's mind even in his first letter home, though he saw it differently: 'Provisions here are pretty Reasonable Considering the Number of troops which are in the Country.'[35] Bear in mind, however, that he was not part of Moira's army. Those men had not the privilege of sailing from Ostend to Antwerp – nor had he experienced the fast and hard 100-mile march from Ostend to Malines over poor terrain. Soldiers so often had to march on empty stomachs.

State of the 44th Foot, 1 August 1794.[36]

Present					Rank & File					Number Wanting		
Officers	Staff	QM	Sjt	Drum	Present	Sick	On Com'd	Other	Total	Sjt	Drum	R&F
14	3		34	18	540	33	54	83	710	1	1	140

State of the British Troops under the Command of His Royal Highness the Duke of York. Camp at Oosterhoute, 5 August 1794.[37]

Present					Rank & File					Number Wanting		
Officers	Staff	QM	Sjt	Drum	Present	Sick	On Com'd	Other	Total	Sjt	Drum	R&F
43	-	-	100	49	2,290	235	-	-	-	-	-	-

---

33 NAM: 2016-10-23-4-11: Grenadiers' General Orders, 24 July 1794.
34 NAM: 2016-10-23-4-11: Grenadiers' General Orders, 5 August 1794. Eight o'clock.
35 NA: DDWR1/25: Roworth to Mary, 27 July 1794.
36 R.N.W. Thomas, *No Want of Courage: The British Army in Flanders, 1793–1795* (Warwick: Helion & Company, 2022), p.276.
37 Thomas, *Courage*, p.277.

Roworth's next letter was written from the 'Grand Army Camp near Oosterhout'. Both he, Brown, and Morris, mentioned the digging of wells to provide the army's needs 'above six feet deep'. These excavations uncovered much older wells, while the plain itself bore witness to previous confrontations with 'many raised platforms, batteries, redoubts, etc., still retained nearly in their original form'. Morris believed them to be part of an encampment left by the Dutch army in 1747. James Russell, 1st (King's) Dragoon Guards, thought they were likely to have been left over from the days of Marlborough.[38] The latter was correct.

All four men wrote of seeing the remains of five individuals left hanging on various gibbets on the plain, near the outskirts of Breda. They affected Corporal Brown greatly, who described them graphically and added that the men had orders to take them down and bury them and to burn the gibbets.[39]

Roworth alluded briefly to the attendance of the whole army, on 18 August, at the execution of 'John Gorman, a private in the 8th Light Dragoons, who was shot' for mutiny, following a court-martial.[40] Russell, 1st Dragoon Guards, recorded in his journal:

> At 8 a.m. in the morning the whole of the British army assembled in front of the encampment to see a soldier ... shot for mutiny, the army was drawn up in two lines–the prisoner after being conducted along the first line under a strong escort (of Horse and Foot) was taken to a small eminence (where grave was already made) when after a few minutes in prayer, he gave the signal and met his fate with a calm resignation.[41]

Gorman's brother, a private soldier in the same regiment, was present to see his brother's execution – this unfortunate youth was no more than 16 years of age.[42] Captain John Atherley of the Coldstream Guards added that 'Piquets of a Capt, 2 Sub & 50 Men from each Regt were present at the execution.'[43] Typically that scene would be replayed whenever and wherever there was such a sentence, at home or abroad.

Execution was used as the ultimate deterrent, with reference to the Articles of War. Many of the regiments, including the 8th (King's Royal Irish) Light Dragoons (of which Gorman was a member), had been in Flanders from April 1793, just weeks from the beginning of the war. The army had been on the move almost non-stop. Gorman was shot, not only as a mutinous soldier, but as an example to discourage others. Various papers in England picked up on this event, the *Cumberland Pacquet* on Tuesday 9 September, adding that

---

38 NAM: 1987–07–31: Typescript taken from a diary reputed to be that of Lt Col James Russell 1st Dragoon Guards Flanders Campaign, 1793–1796. However, there is no officer named Russell in the 1st Dragoon Guards in the army lists of the 1790s.
39 Robert Brown, *An Impartial Journal of a Detachment from the Brigade of Foot Guards, Commencing 25th February, 1793, and ending 9th May 1795* (Huntingdon: Ken Trotman Books, 2006), p.188.
40 NA: DDWR 2/25: Roworth to Mary, Grand Army Camp near Oosterhoot, 24 August 1794.
41 NAM: 1987-07-31: Russell, Diary, p.11
42 NAM: 1987-07-31: Russell, Diary, p.22.
43 NAM: 1997-10-131: John Atherley, Manuscript Journal.

the soldier 'was shot ... for firing at his commanding officer. After he was shot the whole army marched past the body, which was afterwards burnt'.⁴⁴

The following day, at about 3:00 p.m., there was a flash flood. Brown described the rapidity with which it came on: 'a most terrible storm of hail and rain, accompanied with one continued roar of thunder and flashes of lightning; it lasted about thirty-five minutes, and set the country all afloat'.⁴⁵ Roworth reported that the tents were all torn up from the strength of the water.

The Duke of York must have felt flooded himself with the continuing discipline problems of his troops. Only days later, he offered 100 guineas to anyone who could deliver the perpetrator of the murder of a local man, killed by sword wounds, the body being found between Oosterhout and the camp. It was rumoured to be one of the British light dragoons who was the killer. It was just after both incidents of mutiny and murder and the continuing struggle against looting and drunkenness that Roworth wrote his second letter to Mary, dated 24 August, from the Grand Army near Oosterhout. He was obviously so disturbed by the crimes that – without reference to specifics – he appealed to Mary to 'take care of My Son and keep him from all Military People for it Is but a Troublesome Life here at present'.⁴⁶

This was something of an understatement and obviously not the kind of life he wanted for Billy. It was also on that day that Private Robert Wood of the 44th was prosecuted for robbery at a court-martial, at which Major General Hulse was the President, together with a panel of officers. At the same court-martial session, Private Edward Glover of the 56th was charged with mutiny. Both men were found guilty, and each sentenced to 1,000 lashes. Such large numbers of lashes were not unknown, but nor was it frequent, and not all lashes in a sentence were always inflicted. It often depended on the ire or relish of the officer whose order it was. Flogging was used as a deterrent. The man to be flogged was stripped to the waist then, if an infantryman, tied to a triangle made from serjeants' spontoons and if a cavalryman, to a ladder. There was a bucket of water and a chair, and the regimental surgeon stood close by to monitor the prisoner's condition. When arrangements were complete, the adjutant reported to the commanding officer, who gave the order to proceed. The first cat o' nine tails was removed from its bag, and a farrier (for cavalry) or drummer (for infantry) struck the prisoner with it, the serjeant major calling out each stroke.

Historian Harry Hopkins, using examples from Sergeant John Teesdale's *Military Torture – A Letter Addressed to the People of England*, published in 1835, reports that:

> Teesdale spares his readers nothing ... the gallant Sir Thomas Picton had three men flogged on the field of Waterloo, forming the usual hollow square for the gory ritual although the enemy were then advancing. Two of the miscreants had

---

44 *Cumberland Pacquet*, 9 September 1794.
45 Brown, *Impartial Journal*, p.189.
46 NA: DDRW 2/25: Roworth to Mary, Grand Army Camp near Oosterhoot, 24 August 1794.

LAXITY, LAWLESSNESS AND LOATHING: ALLIES OR ENEMIES?

been guilty of falling out to get a drink of water, the third of firing a comrade's musket to free a charge damaged by heavy rain.

All three, says Teesdale, were 'remarked for general good conduct'.[47] One of the men was shot and killed at Waterloo – as was Picton.

Once Roworth became a serjeant major, in August 1795, he would presumably have performed this duty, though his private thoughts on such punishment are not known. The punishment continued – the cats being exchanged until the man with the bloodied back was no longer conscious, or the surgeon stopped the flogging, as could the commanding officer. With far fewer than a thousand lashes, a man would be taken down and his back treated (for a number of weeks if necessary) until the wounds were scabbed over. Then his punishment would resume where it had left off. It was not unknown for men to die from flogging and it was also not unknown for soldiers to take their own lives rather than submit to a flogging.

The day following the court-martial, 29 August, the brigades were re-ordered once again. The 44th, together with the 12th, 33rd and 42nd, were in the 3rd Brigade, commanded by Balfour. Captain Morris helpfully recorded both infantry and cavalry numbers in the British and German contingent at that time. The infantry, including British, Hanoverians, Hesse Cassell and Hesse Darmstadt, totalled 34,153 men, while officers totalled 1,238 men, serjeants 1,693 men, and drummers and trumpeters 884 – in all, a total of 34,153.[48]

On 22 August 1794, a gentleman by the name of Charles Pitt was made an ensign (vice Hamerton who was promoted), in the 44th without purchase.[49] Nothing unusual there until, less than 24 hours later, he was appointed Assistant Barrack Master General which sounds remarkably fast and lofty until you know that there were four other junior staff assistants in that department. Ensign Charles Pitt surfaced again in the pages of the *London Gazette*, less than a year later when he was promoted to lieutenant, vice William Tuffie, still in the 44th. Both he and Ensign McNamara were promoted lieutenants on 1 September 1796 while Tuffie was promoted captain, vice Donkin, who became major.[50] The following month Pitt left the regiment when the 44th were getting ready to sail for the West Indies and, ironically, became a captain in one of the West India Regiments that were being formed but he seems to have dropped off the *Army List* soon afterwards.[51]

---

47 Harry Hopkins, *The Strange Death of Private White: A Victorian Scandal that made History* (London: Weidenfeld and Nicolson, 1977), p.17.
48 Morris, *With the Guards*, p.103.
49 *London Gazette*, 27 December 1794.
50 *London Gazette*, 8 September 1795.
51 *London Gazette*, 6 October 1795.

Infantry Brigades, November 1794.[52]

HQ Arnhem 15th November 1794		
The Infantry of the Line to be in the following Order		
1st Brigade.	3rd, 40th, 55th, 59th, 79th.	Major General Stewart
2nd Brigade.	8th, 37th, 44th, 57th, 88th.	Major General Deburgh [sic]
3rd Brigade.	12th, 33rd, 42nd, 78th.	Fox's
4th Brigade.	14th, 38th, 63rd, 80th.	
5th Brigade.	19th, 54th, 84th, 89th.	
6th Brigade.	27th, 28th, 53rd, 85th.	

Source: NAM: 2016-10-23-4-11. Book no. G152.

Roworth and the 44th had not yet had any real contact with the enemy in the shape of a battle or even a skirmish or two. Admittedly they had only been on the continent for two months, but during that time the mood had become unsettling for the British Army. On 30 June Robert Brown had reported that 'the enemy has above three hundred thousand effective men on this frontier, compared with which number all our army is but a small piquet so that we have begun to retreat: it is probable that we may continue to do so, till we find a proper place to make a stand against such unequal numbers.'[53]

He was right and an opportunity to face the enemy proper would arise just two weeks later. It would be the first time for the 44th Foot.

---

52 Thomas, *Courage*, p.279.
53 Brown, *Impartial Journal*, p.170.

6

The Battle of Boxtel: 14–15 September 1794

'Defeat is one thing; disgrace is another'.[1]

The long-awaited action for the redcoats of the 44th finally arrived on 15 September. The flashpoint was the movement on Sunday the 14th by *Général de division* Jean-Charles Pichegru, when he attacked the Duke of York's advanced posts at Boxtel. Pichegru was commander of the Army of the North and his orders were to take the offensive where an opportunity to strike at the allies presented itself.

The village of Boxtel was defended by allied troops commanded by *Generalmajor* Georg von Düring and numbering fewer than 2,000 – mostly from Hesse-Darmstadt. The defenders held the post for four hours, before being overwhelmed, with many taken prisoner. The Duke of York reported to Dundas that a '… sudden Attack, in which it appeared that the Enemy were in great Force, was made upon all my Posts of the Right; and that of Boxtel, which was the most advanced, was forced, with considerable Loss to the Hesse Darmstadt Troops, who occupied it'.[2]

The Duke decided to try and retake Boxtel the following day. He determined to send out the reserve corps and ordered Lieutenant General Abercromby to march at night, reconnoitre at dawn and after assessing the situation and the number of the enemy force, make his decision. It should be noted here that Abercromby was known to be extremely short-sighted, a fact which was mentioned by a number of officers in other war arenas and therefore a matter about which they were concerned since it might have given him different perspectives on what was happening at greater distances.

Abercromby's infantry consisted of the Brigade of Guards and the 3rd Brigade (12th, 33rd, 42nd and 44th Foot), with supporting artillery. The infantry were accompanied by a cavalry brigade consisting of the 1st Dragoon

---

1   Winston Churchill, *The Second World War, Vol.IV: The Hinge of Fate* (Boston: Houghton Mifflin, 1950), p.344.
2   John Grehan and Martin Mace, *British Battles of the Napoleonic Wars, 1793–1806* (Barnsley: Pen & Sword, 2013), p.72.

Sir Ralph Abercromby 1734–1801. Mezzotint by S.W. Reynolds after Hoppner. (Anne S.K. Brown Military Collection)

THE BATTLE OF BOXTEL: 14–15 SEPTEMBER 1794

Guards, 8th, 14th and 16th Light Dragoons, under the immediate command of Colonel Richard Vyse.

Captain Roger Morris, the Coldstream, on his way back from Cleves via Grave on the evening of the 14th was surprised to see the heavy baggage of the army on the move, 'which had left the Camp in consequence of an attack made upon Our Posts at Boxtel'. He retired to bed, only to be woken half an hour later '…ordered under arms immediately, & to march with the rest of the reserve (except the Coldstream, which was at the picquet at Erp) to Boxtel where the French had surprised the Hessian Troops & taken possession of the Post'.[3] Morris added that Abercromby had orders to retake the village of Boxtel 'without any other instructions'. He was apparently unaware of the proviso added by the Duke of York.

This would be the first time that Roworth had ever been in action, other than in general fracas and affrays on the streets of Ireland. Roworth even referred to himself as an eyewitness in his letter home.

Russell's account of Boxtel started late in the evening of 14 September:

> Our Brigade, with some regiments of Infantry, marched from the camp at 11pm in the evening, and proceeded to the village of Boxtel, where we arrived in the morning of the 15th at daybreak, when we began an attack upon the advanced post of the enemy but were repulsed, they having taken up an advantageous position in the woods, likewise having a great superiority both in men and cannon which rendered it impossible for our small force to dislodge them – and not being able to bring them to a fair combat (which was much wished by our men who were in high spirits) we were at length obliged to retreat which we did in good order without any material loss – of the King's Dragoon Guards. We had one horse killed and one man and horse wounded. Of the 8th Light Dragoons they had two horses killed and one wounded by one shot from the enemy. On our return to camp (about 1pm in the afternoon) we found the whole army under arms, expecting to have brought the enemy to a general engagement but not being able to accomplish our design we proceeded on our march at 3pm in the afternoon and in the evening halted near Grave where we remained the whole night without tents.[4]

Serjeant William Roworth's personal experience of the battle was included in a letter to Mary:

> My Dear Wife here Follows [his own] Exact account of the Engagement. On the 15th September, as I can possibly form an idea of, for I was an Eye Witness of it from the Beginning to the Ending of it, and Some of my Brother soldiers fell that Day, which fought Like British Soldiers. My dear Mary, it was on the 14th of September on Sunday Night at 8 o'clock, an Aid de Camp from the Duke of York came to our camp with orders for our Brigade to March at Nine that Night, under the Command of that Bold Commanding officer General Abercrombie, to Dislodge the French from the Village Boxtel, which only Consisted of the

---

3 Morris, *With the Guards*, p.110.
4 NAM: 1987-07-31: Russell Diary, 26 April.

following Regiments, the 1st and 3rd Regiments of Guards: the 12th, 33rd, 42nd, 44th Regiments of Foot, which was only A handful to the French, for their Cavalry Consisted of as Many Men as our foot and horse was, and for all that they Could not Stand our Charge. Their foot was placed in a Very thick wood to our right and Left, and our 2 British 24 pounders with their grape Cut them down Like grass, both their horse and foot. Their loss was considerable and ours not so Much as we Expecked [it] would be, as our Brave General Abercrombie Conducted it So well, otherwise we Should have been all killed or took prisoners, as their Reinforcements Came Down So Strong, we was obliged to retreat to our former Ground. We expect some Bomb shells in here to Night. We found our tents struck and the Baggage Marched through a town called Graves, which is fortified a Long the River Muse.[5]

When Roworth commented on the fact that the French cavalry numbers appeared to be more than the whole of Abercromby's army put together at the time, there were some 6,000 French cavalry in and around Boxtel, whereas outside Schyndel (see historian Garry Wills's analysis below) they only encountered one regiment of Hussars – about 400 men. 'For all that they could not stand charge' could only refer to the initial withdrawal of the French Hussars, who were at a considerable disadvantage to the British cavalry because of their smaller horses and lack of carbines. The 24-pounders that Roworth refers to were the pieces of artillery attached to each infantry battalion. These, according to Wills, would be 5.5-inch howitzers which were also known as 24-pounders and not long guns or cannon.[6] It is no exaggeration for Roworth to say that but for Abercromby's withdrawal, they would 'all have been killed or taken prisoners' and that as the reinforcements 'Came Down So Strong' it was likely to be the six battalions of Daendal's Brigade. Abercromby's forces would have been surrounded. Wills says that in retrospect, Abercromby was given a 'mission impossible' by the Duke of York.[7]

Carter, historian of the 44th, described it thus:

> ...the enemy advanced in great force, and attacked the British posts on the right. The outpost at Boxtel, the advanced post of the allies, was forced, and the troops of Hesse D'Armstadt, which occupied it, sustained a severe loss [around 1,500] … the 44th, with the other regiments of their brigade, proceeded under Lieutenant Colonel the Honourable Arthur Wellesley [sic]… who then commanded the 33rd, to recover possession of Boxtel. The 44th had thus the honour of serving under England's greatest chief in his first brigade command, and in his first experience of active warfare.[8]

---

5   NA: DDRW 3/25: Roworth to Mary, Tiel, 10 October 1794.
6   Garry David Wills, *Wellington's First Battle: Combat for Boxtel, 15th September 1794. A Guide for Military Historians & Wargamers* (Grantham: Caseshot Publishing, 2011). Email to author, 17 December 2016.
7   Wills, email to author, 17 December 2016.
8   Carter, *44th Regiment*, p.29.

THE BATTLE OF BOXTEL: 14–15 SEPTEMBER 1794

Wesley's role in the battle is uncertain, as some sources, like Carter, place him in command of the brigade, which he would have been as the senior lieutenant colonel if Balfour were absent. The following account was dictated by Lieutenant Colonel John Coape Sherbrooke, the 33rd's other lieutenant colonel at the time, to his daughter-in-law in 1830, the year of Sherbrooke's death:

> When he (Sherbrooke) had obtained the rank of Lt-Col., he served under the Duke of York in Flanders, and during this unfortunate and memorable retreat, the 33rd was appointed to cover it. Two regiments of French Cavalry were seen coming down with the intention of charging the 33rd ... Col. Sherbrooke faced his Regt to the rear and gave the word 33rd 'Steady'. In this awful crisis not a man moved, but with determined fortitude they awaited the attack. When the first French Regt. was within 50 yards the command was given to Fire!'– the steady coolness of the men gave it full effect... men and horses were precipitated to the ground – those who were neither unhorsed nor wounded, halted and attempted to retreat, but before they had gained a very short distance a second volley completed the work of destruction and the whole Regt. lay stretched on the ground. The second Regt witnessing the dreadful over-throw faced about and were seen no more. This brilliant action Sir John (Sherbrooke) always declared was more satisfactory to him, and he took more pride in it, than any affair in which he was ever engaged.[9]

Wills, who also includes the above account in his section of personal accounts, believes that Wesley probably did command the brigade at Boxtel. Sherbrooke's account supports this because if Wesley was commanding the brigade he could not also be commanding the 33rd. Wills believes also that the battle took place, not at Boxtel itself, but at Schyndel 'some 5 miles north-east of Boxtel'.[10] As to the place where the battle was actually fought Schyndel seems to be a persuasive likelihood, much as Waterloo was not the actual scene of battle for the battle of the century. Interestingly, Philip Ball, in his book *Neither Up Nor Down*, covering the Flanders Campaign, states that 'Some sources give Wesley as commander of this brigade but this is unlikely given his junior rank and lack of experience'.[11] The speculation continues.

The army had marched at about 11:00 p.m., reaching Moddeven at around 2:00 a.m. Abercromby received news of *Generalmajor* Hammerstein's evacuation of Oedenrode. At this point Abercromby sent to headquarters for advice. That which returned ordered him to take counsel from *Generalmajor* Rudolf Von Hammerstein, 'and act according to his directions'.[12]

At around 5:00 a.m. the march continued and Abercromby and his troops – having just passed through the village of Schyndel at daybreak at around 6:15 a.m. '& having advanced from thence about 3 miles we formed our line in

---

9   Brereton & Savory, *Wellington's Regiment*, p.93.
10 Wills, *Wellington's First Battle*, p.20.
11 Philip Ball, *Neither Up Nor Down: The British Army and the Flanders Campaign 1793–1795* (Warwick: Helion & Company, 2020), p.418.
12 Brown, *Impartial Journal*, p.219.

a Lane leading out to the Heath' where could be seen the French picquet line on the plain.[13] It was also clear that Abercromby was made aware of numbers of the enemy moving in the trees. As mentioned earlier, Abercromby had very poor eye-sight so that it is not really known what he thought he saw and what he actually saw, but based on an approximation of enemy strength, he was concerned enough to send back to the Duke of York for further orders. The Duke had ordered him to attack, but 'with prudence'. A mixed message, some might say. Obedient to orders, Abercromby did both!

So commenced a number of skirmishes described by Morris of the Coldstreams as they led their way out of the lane onto the heath where they found:

> Wood & Enclosures in our Front, & at no great distance on our Right Flank – we advanced our 2 Batt'n guns & a 12 P'r (of which 2 accompanied us, & 2 howitzers, but the latter were left in Moddeven) & fired some shot into the wood in front, in which we saw the French Riflemen, who fire many ineffective shots at us – they were soon driven off, as was a French howitzer placed at the Corner of the Wood. A large body of French Cavalry, were soon on the Plain who attracted several Shot from us, which I believe did them little mischief. While we were occupied with them, the Enemy brought a Gun to their Right, which (from a Masqued situation) they made to bear on Our Battalion. Having received some well directed shot from this Gun, and a report being made that the 12th Regiment were all surrounded at Gestel, & had been taken, Gen'l A.– ordered a retreat which was conducted … thro' Schindel & Moddeven, having had a narrow escape from being cut off by the Enemy …[14]

It is at this point that a company of the 1st Foot Guards supported by the 33rd and the 44th were sent forward to skirmish. The Guards were too far forward to avoid being taken prisoner when Abercromby ordered a retreat.

Morris blames a specific gun, hidden by foliage, which made the circumstances too warm for 'Our Battalion', together with a report that the 12th Foot had been 'surrounded at Gestel'. Carter claimed that the 12th and the 42nd had been kept in reserve while the 33rd and the 44th had supported the Dragoons.[15] Abercromby put on his prudence hat and commenced an orderly retreat. 'On the plain, the British cavalry [kept] the French Hussars back with their light infantry in the surrounding woods for perhaps 30–60 minutes' to facilitate this retreat.[16] Unfortunately, there was a bottleneck of both dragoons and infantry as they proceeded into a narrow lane.

The 33rd stopped the pursuit of the French 8th Hussars by standing calmly, muskets at the ready, to wait until the hussars were within 50 yards before delivering their withering fire. This was what Sherbrooke talked in his description of the two volleys that caused the 'whole regiment [to] lay

---

13   Morris, *With the Guards*, p.110.
14   Morris, *With the Guards*, pp.110–111.
15   Carter, *History of the Forty-Fourth*, p.30.
16   Wills, *Wellington's First Battle*, p.22.

stretched on the ground'.[17] Roworth witnessed this stand of the 33rd and says, 'our 2 British 24 pounders cut them down like grass'.[18]

Historian Steve Brown writes that the 'British retired to Schijndel ... the French did not pursue past that point', but he does mention that a company of the 12th Foot were taken 'wholesale at Voet, just north of Schijndel', with 49 of them taken as prisoners of war.[19] There certainly appears to have been some confusion concerning the whereabouts of the 12th Foot during the combat at Boxtel but there seems little doubt that they marched with the rest of the brigade from the camp towards Boxtel. Brown corroborates that by saying 'The flanks of the column were protected by the Coldstream Guards on the south side and the 12th Foot with a detachment ... on the north side'.[20] Both Morris and Roworth agree that the 3rd Brigade was ordered to retake Boxtel and that it comprised the 12th, 33rd, 42nd & 44th Regiments. There also seems some uncertainty as to whether Balfour had yet arrived to join his brigade, which would add weight to Wesley commanding it at Boxtel.[21] The whereabouts of the 12th on the battlefield seems somewhat muddled probably due to what happened to them later.

After the event Roworth was able to add some small detail relevant to the men of the 44th when recalling to Mary that 'Mrs. Whittle [who] was Quartered with us ... Her husband was Either Killed or taken Prisoner [and has] not been heard of since'. He must have been one of the four rank and file missing from the 44th, and then he continued, 'My Dear, you know that Serjt [in] The 33rd Regt which [had] Such a bold walk ... He was the Drill Sergt and he was killed.'[22]

Wills says that on the relevant six-month muster roll for 25 June to 24 December 1795 there were no deaths of serjeants during that period, except one, George Kay, who died on 27 November 1794.[23] Obviously, a mistaken assumption on Roworth's part, the much more likely scenario being that the man was missing, presumed dead and actually made it back to his regiment, in due course. Morris described the retreat ordered by Abercromby as 'without the loss of a gun, or any confusion'.[24] They retreated through Schyndel and Moddeven and met up with the 12th Foot at the latter, when Morris states categorically that 'The loss of the 12th Regiment was false report & we were happy to see that Corps at Moddeven, as we returned home'.

Divall opines that Pichegru was marching east and might have overwhelmed (indeed thrashed) both the main British army and Abercromby's detachment, but due to the latter's realisation of the position his men were in, he withdrew them 'in good order'. Even so, the loss was not trifling. Ninety men were lost, one third killed, the others taken prisoner.[25]

---

17 Brereton & Savory, *Wellington's Regiment*, p.93.
18 NA: DDWR 3/25: Roworth to Mary, Tiel, 10 October 1794.
19 Steve Brown, *The Duke of York's Flanders Campaign: Fighting the French Revolution 1793–1795* (Barnsley: Frontline Books, 2018), p.220.
20 Brown, *Flanders Campaign*, p.219.
21 See, Brown, *Flanders Campaign*, p.224; Thomas, *No Want of Courage*, p.204.
22 NA: DDRW 3/25: William Roworth to Mary, Tiel, 10 October 1794.
23 Wills, emails to author 27 May and 7 December 2016.
24 Morris, *With the Guards*, p.111.
25 Divall, *Abercromby*, p.55.

Few battles are without casualties. In total, Jones records: six rank and file killed; two serjeants, 14 rank and file wounded; two officers, four serjeants, two drummers and 64 rank and file missing.[26] One officer had been taken prisoner, namely, Captain George Bristow of the 1st Foot Guards. The 44th had just four rank and file missing.

After the excitement of the withdrawal and the return to the camp at about 1:30 p.m. the troops found that the tents were being struck and the army on the move yet again. Morris, a captain in the Coldstream Guards, was forewarned, having seen all the heavy baggage at Grave the evening before. 'The Reserve [including Roworth] and the Light Cavalry were left to Cover the retreat.'[27] Then men marched on through the night, through Grave, to their next encampment, Morris and the Coldstream Guards a mile further on near a windmill, which they finally reached about 6:00 p.m. the following evening, the 16th. The 44th were stationed near the Waal, aspects of which they were to become very familiar over the next two months – so some very welcome respite in the meantime.

After Boxtel, the sense of uncertainty and movement may have persuaded the more criminally minded to take advantage of the ever-shifting scenario, for their ulterior purposes. This was born out by the continual plunder and 'outrage' which was still evident, indeed so extensive that after only eight days, on 23 September the Duke of York was moved to pronounce a very long speech and order some retribution concerning the 'scandalous scenes' which 'disgrace the army under his command'. He listed a number of specific men caught in the act and who were condemned to death, but which order had been reduced to 'severe Corporal punishment.' The Provost and his assistants were immediately given extra powers 'to execute on the spot the First and Every Man whom they may catch … in any act of plundering or outrage'.[28] The behaviour of the soldiery did not improve.

It was not just the rank and file who plundered the land and the people of Flanders. On the 26th a general court-martial was held against two soldiers of the 53rd, one a private and the other a serjeant, Edward Milner. Both were charged with robbery and rape against the same woman. The soldier was acquitted on both counts, but Serjeant Edward Milner, though found not guilty of robbery, was found guilty of rape. The serjeant's punishment was reduction to private and 700 lashes. The Duke of York confirmed the demotion but let him off the corporal punishment.[29] Another opportunity to exert discipline and make an example, appears missed.

The next move for the 44th was as part of the 2nd Brigade to relieve the Commissary General's detachment at Nijmegen on 19 November. The 44th was now brigaded with the 8th (King's); 37th (North Hampshire); 57th (West Middlesex) and 88th (Connaught Rangers) Regiments of Foot, under the command of Major General John Thomas de Burgh.[30]

---

26 Jones, *An Historical Journal*, p.125.
27 Morris, *With the Guards*, p.111.
28 NAM: 2016-10-23-4-9: Grenadiers' General Orders, HQ Groesneck, 23 September 1794.
29 NAM: 2016-10-23-4-9: Grenadiers' General Orders, 26 September 1794.
30 Burrows, *Essex Regiment*, p.30.

7

Indeed a Hostile Shore: Sint Andries and Nijmegen

> '… the Dutch are as great enemies to us as the French are …'[1]

In October 1794, Brevet Lieutenant Colonel Colin Campbell of the 44th, who had been on furlough, made his way back to his regiment. He started by arranging transport with William Huskisson, clerk to Secretary of State for War, Henry Dundas. Huskisson, in turn, asked his friend, Captain Hugh Christian, then of the Transport Board, to arrange transport for a number of persons, including Campbell, together with his servant, luggage and two horses.[2]

So much depended on wind and tide that it took 27 days from Campbell's arrival in London on 11 October, until his arrival at Arnhem on 6 November. By 27 October he disembarked at Helvoetsluys from the *Bellona* transport and spoke with a serjeant of the 44th who informed him that the regiment was in reserve at Tiel.[3] During his journey along the canals he had intimations that all was not well between the British and the Dutch, when 'they pretend never to understand those who speak their language, & they exercise the most barefaced impositions in every transaction one may have with them'. The Dutch skipper took them to the correct address, but refused to let them disembark without considerable extra pay, 'we were therefore obliged to debark, & send waggons for our baggage, [which] was somewhat less than his demand.'[4] After disembarkation, like Morris, Campbell took every opportunity to visit great buildings and was much taken with the organ in Sint Eusebius, the Grote Kerk at Arnhem, both the sound and the price, £12,000!

The low and foggy country, near to the Waal, was taking such a toll on the soldiers' health that numbers were falling sick daily. Both Roworth and Campbell wrote to their wives about the natural death of 'old Mr Tuffie, the

---

1   NA: DDWR 4/25: Roworth to Mary, Country Quarters on the Banks of the River Waal, 5 December 1794
2   TNA: WO 6/156: Huskisson to Christian, Commissioners of Transport, 16 October 1794.
3   NAM: 2002-08-144-55: Campbell to Polly, 25 October 1794.
4   NAM: 2002-08-144-59: Campbell to Polly, 5 November 1794.

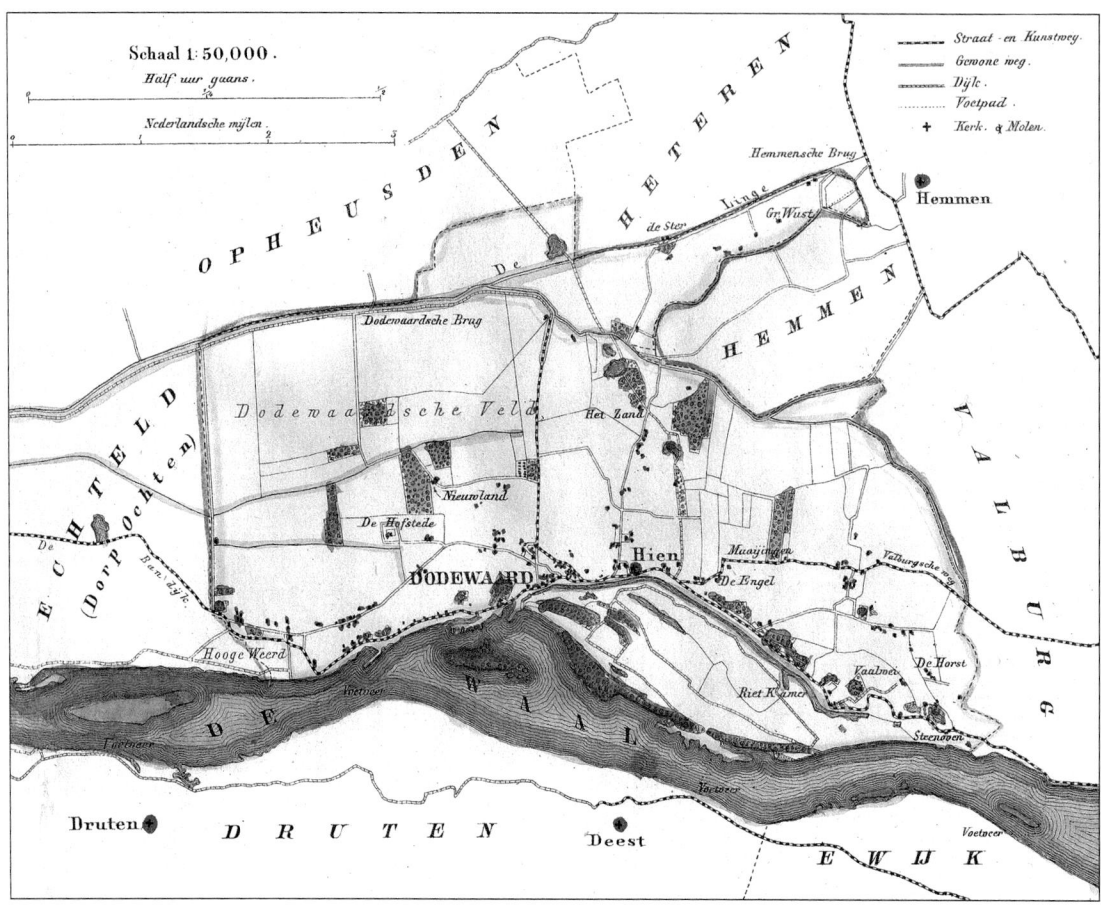

Dodewaard on the Waal, burial place of Quartermaster John Tuffie, 44th Regiment, edition Hugo Suringat. (Author's Collection)

quartermaster … The very day old Mrs Tuffie heard of the old man's death she died immediately'.[5] Campbell reported to Polly that Tuffie had succumbed to a cold which brought on a fever and consequently his death.[6] Campbell added that this had been John Tuffie's 'third war'. He was buried at Dodewaard on the banks of the Waal and the whole regiment attended his interment. It was in his letter dated 5 December that Roworth corroborated the death of Samuel Tuffie in Dartford some weeks earlier. Eighteen years previously, on Friday 4 October 1776, Lieutenant Colin Campbell, then of the 55th Foot, had been made captain-lieutenant and captain in the 44th, without purchase on the very same day that Serjeant John Tuffie was promoted to quartermaster. Campbell, who finally caught up with his regiment at Dodewaard on 29 October, was therefore too late to see his old comrade laid to rest. Tuffie had been in the 44th since its raising in 1741, a total of 53 years, making him likely to be in his seventies. Strange that both the Tuffie parents and their oldest son, Samuel should die in the same month in 1794. That must have been hard on William Tuffie.

---

5   NA: DDRW 4/25: Roworth to Mary, 5 December 1794.
6   NAM: 2002-08-144-60: Campbell to Polly, 9 December 1794.

INDEED A HOSTILE SHORE: SINT ANDRIES AND NIJMEGEN

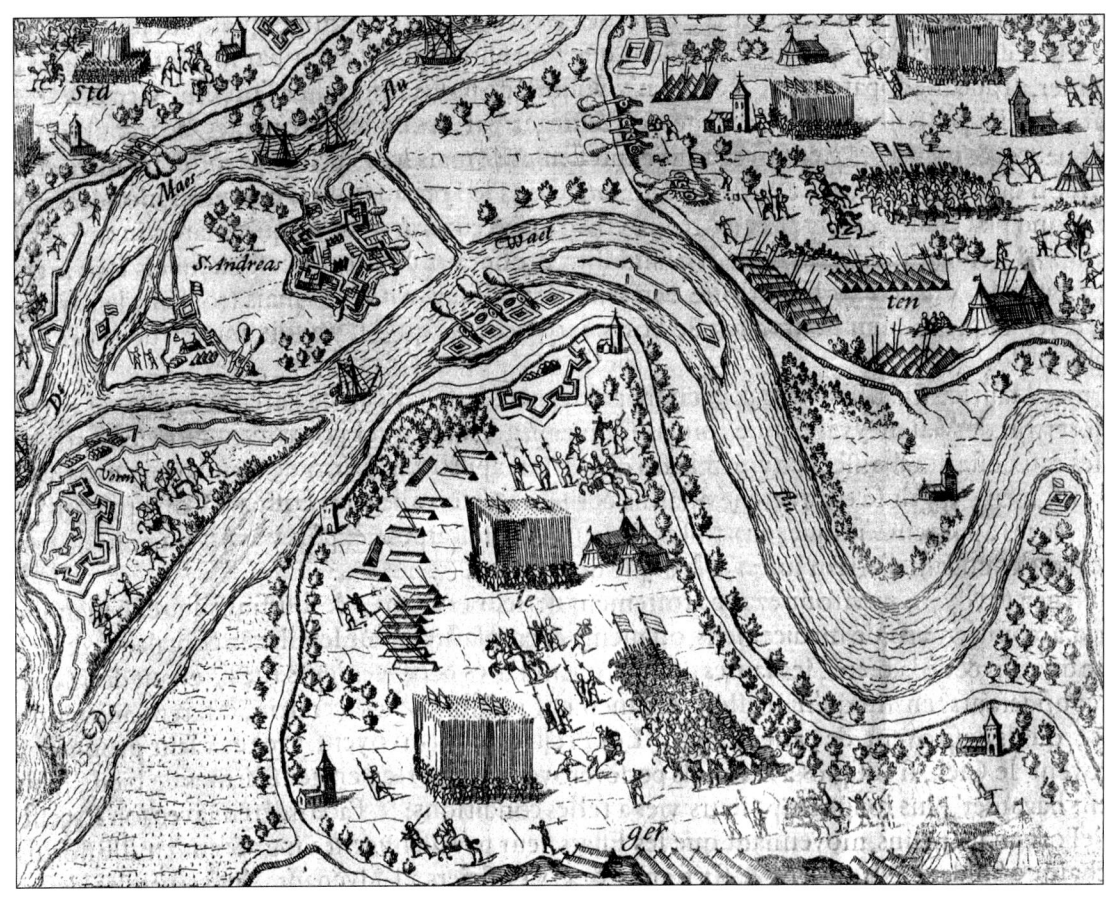

Original seventeenth century map showing the River Waal & Sint Andries. (Author's Collection)

Lieutenant General Ralph Abercromby and *General der Cavallerie* Count Walmoden were ordered by the Duke of York to take Fort Sint Andries, the five-sided star-shaped fort with bastions, situated on the Bommeler Waert.

On 9 October, Morris was one of a number of officers to attend the funeral of Serjeant Malpas of the Grenadiers. Morris was disgusted that no other serjeant attended the occasion. He then rode from Bommel to the village of Rossum, where he had a good view of Fort Sint Andries across the water and watched British engineers 'erecting Batteries & [digging] trenches' in preparation to take the fort.[7] They were working under the French guns, whose gunners appeared to be ignoring the British. The plan was to take the fort on the night of 10 October. Roworth was among the 20 soldiers of the 44th who were told off to take the fort, along with others from various regiments:

> I have Been on Command a While at a place called Fort St. Andrew, which you might See In the London Papers … In the Night we landed two pieces of cannon on a Small Island opposite to the fort and made a Battrie and planted the

---

7   Morris, *With the Guards*, p.117.

cannon by daylight in the morning, where we gave them both shot and shell as warm as possible [which] they abandoned in about four hours ... likewise all the inhabitants leaving Most of Their Effects Behind them.[8]

The inhabitants had sensibly taken all their livestock with them, except for a cow and two pigs which soon fell prey to the soldiers. Roworth and his comrades also found a little boy 'like My Billey which we turned into the French lines to follow his friends'.[9]

On the morning of the 11th Morris described the 'heavy Cross Cannonade [which] was brought on Fort St André, which the French ... were obliged to evacuate, & our people took possession of it with'[ou]t the loss of a man'.[10]

The Coldstreams received orders to make ready to embark for Fort Sint Andries at 10:00 a.m. on the morning of the 13th, furnishing a subaltern, two serjeants, two corporals and 34 privates. The grenadiers and the light infantry were to meet up at Rossicum, opposite the fort where boats would be waiting to ferry them across. The 44th were to assemble at Tiel under the command of Captain Borthwick. This could possibly have been Captain William Borthwick of the Royal Artillery. The 33rd and 44th were also to furnish 20 men from each company and these men would relieve each other for garrison duty. Later that day Morris rode to Fort Sint Andries and noted the few small, deserted houses within its walls. He was still there when the sound of the 44th Foot's long drum roll, requesting their relief in the fort, resulted in shots fired from both sides, but again without any loss of life.[11] Roworth's moment of glory over, he returned to Tiel where the majority of the 44th was based.

The picquet, some 400 strong together with artillery, retained the fort (being relieved every 48 hours) for some weeks, although efforts were made almost daily by the enemy to regain the fort. Lieutenant General Abercromby also set up his quarters at Bommel. From then on, the sound of cannon fire between the men holding Fort Sint Andries and the French became a daily constant in the area. Major Harness of the 65th was also at Bommel, in his 'excellent quarters'. He looked forward to the army moving into winter quarters because 'I shall, I hope, be at liberty to pass a month with you and our sweet children ... We live well and the Officers have but little to do.'[12]

In previous years it had often been the custom of opposing armies to go into winter quarters, sit out the winter weather conditions and then resume hostilities when those conditions improved. Many officers took the opportunity to leave the army temporarily in the winter and go home. Harness was indeed a product of his time, 'A [campaign] in this delightful Country for an Officer of my Rank furnishes much instruction, much to amuse the mind in its progress, with almost every comfort, at a risk which when compared to

---

8   NA: DDRW 4/25: Roworth to Mary, 5 December 1794.
9   NA: DDRW 4/25: Roworth to Mary, 5 December 1794.
10 Morris, *With the Guards*, p.117.
11 Morris, *With the Guards*, pp.115–116.
12 Caroline Duncan-Jones, *Trusty and Well-Beloved, The Letters Home of W. Harness, an Officer of George III* (London: SPCK, 1957), p.56.

that of the subaltern Ranks becomes contemptible.'[13] It was not that he was necessarily flagrantly lazy or uncaring (though some were), it was that he and many of the young officers appeared to believe that their army life was there for enjoyment and personal progression. Neither were they disabused, by their own commanders, from this apparently enshrined belief. The system was such that many of these young officers left the rank and file well alone and enjoyed themselves, while any active indiscipline of an army of 40,000 men appeared to have no bearing on, or reaction from, them at all.

Major Harness unwittingly highlighted yet another practice of which officers took advantage. He, like many of his young compatriots, did not appear to see any reason to alter his behaviour. He comprehended the social difference between himself and the non-commissioned officers and the rank and file, but not the injustice. So many letters written home were concerned with promotion. He broke the news to his wife that his lieutenant-colonelcy was imminent, closely followed by the observation that 'We continue dreadfully sickly, having four hundred unfit for Duty, including two hundred left in the General Hospital at Dort. Those Dye daily. It is a melancholy thing.'[14] Again, two distinct sides of the military coin. Roworth corroborates the mention of illness amongst the men: 'These are trying times here in the army in Regard of Sickness, as Numbers go off Daily, as the Country is Very Low and Very Foggy. We have Some Frosty weather lately, which I hope will Continue For a while, which it is better for us when we take our Out posts at Night.'[15]

The guards and artillery took over the daily grind of holding the fort and shelling the enemy on the other side of the river. Brown and the Coldstreams marched some 20 miles down-river through Tiel to be cantoned on the riverside. Roworth wrote of the Duke of York still holding the lines of the Waal and the Meuse with batteries and sentries.[16] The sentries were stationed at posts of regular intervals to the east and west of Tiel.

The Grenadier Guards were opposite Bommel, with the light infantry and the other guards stretching away to the east. The whole line of British and Hessians reached as far as Emmerich, where the Austrian troops were encamped. Stretching westwards from Bommel were the Dutch troops and those British troops who were occupying the area around Bommel, about 60 miles in total.[17] This may have proved an unfortunate juxtaposition for the British and the Dutch as Roworth mentioned to Mary that 'the Dutch are as great enemies to us as the French are and would rather receive them than the English. They have Murdered several English soldiers lately'.[18] Two Britons had been killed the previous night on the road to the British headquarters

---

13 Duncan-Jones, *Trusty*, p.54.
14 Duncan-Jones, *Trusty*, p.56.
15 NA: DDRW 4/25: Roworth to Mary, Country Quarters on the Banks of the River Waal, 5 December 1794.
16 NA: DDRW 4/25: Roworth to Mary, Country Quarters on the Banks of the River Waal, 5 December 1794.
17 Brown, *An Impartial Journal*, p.201.
18 NA: DDRW 4/25: Roworth to Mary, Country Quarters on the Banks of the River Waal, 5 December 1794.

NOT SO EASY, LADS

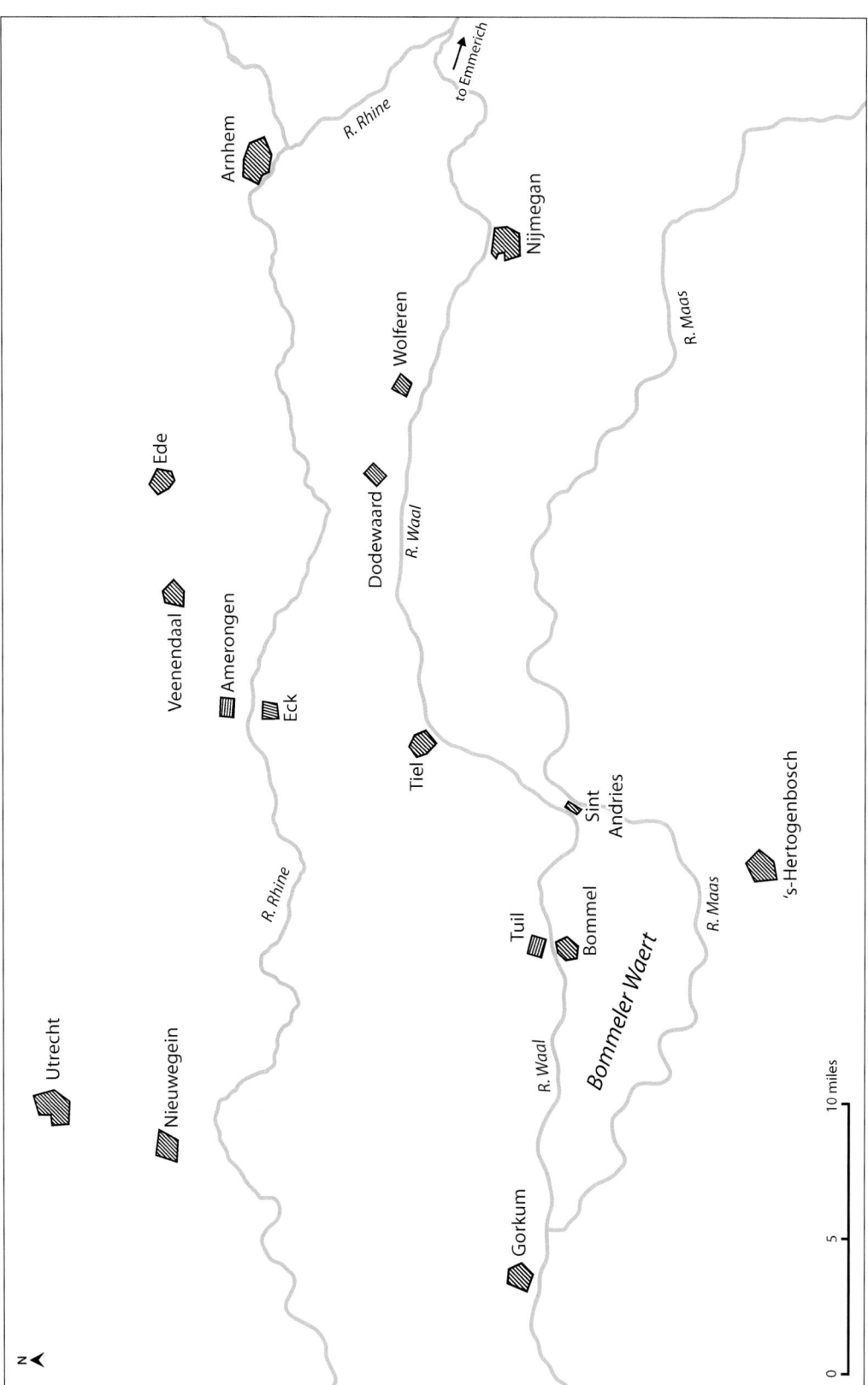

The rivers Waal, Meuse/Maas and Rhine. The Meuse and the Waal rivers show the extent that the Duke of York's batteries and sentries were posted along their length from Gorkum (today's Gorinchem) in the west to Emmerich in the east. The Grenadier Guards were opposite Bommel, with the light infantry and battalions of the other guards stretched away to the east. The whole line of British and Hessians reached as far as Emmerich, where the Austrian troops were encamped. Stretching westwards were the Dutch and those British troops who were occupying the area around Bommel, about 60 miles in total.

at Arnhem. The continuing enmity between the Dutch and British was to outlive the transient British occupation. The official enemy, the French, was still very numerous, making multiple attempts to retake Fort Sint Andries as well as shelling Tiel. Roworth was in Tiel when 'they Begun to Bombard The place. The first Shell which fell in the Town was the Very Next house where I was In, which Disturbed Me and My Comrades of our Supper … The Bombardment did not Last Long but They Destroyed two Houses joining to where I was, and never Hurt ours the least'.[19]

A very strong observation came from that anonymous officer of the guards around the same time:

> … much has been said, and with truth, of the want of discipline that existed among the British troops; but a detail of the shameful treatment they experienced through their different marches through Holland, which was to them, 'indeed a hostile shore!' would in some measure account for their taking by force those necessaries, which our good and faithful ALLIES refused to supply them with for money. The implacable hatred evinced by the Dutch towards the English, can scarcely be conceived; extending even beyond the grave. They have been known to dig up the dead bodies of British soldiers in the night, to mutilate and deface them with the long assassin's knives, which all of them conceal about their persons, and to leave them in that state for their former comrades to feast their eyes upon the next mornin'.[20]

There was no doubt that the British Army had a difficult time through lack of food supplies and not only of food. Morris had an encounter with the 89th and their officer on Tuesday 4 November when he was relieving their picquet at 3:00 p.m. He seemed quite startled at the sight - 'A Ragamuffin crew, whose appearance beggared all description'. It may well have done, but he leaves a description nevertheless. 'The Centries [sic] at the guardroom had neither shoes, or stockings, & the whole picquet, from their rags and filth, had more of the appearance of a jail delivery, that anything else'.[21] This in early November when heading towards one of the worst winters in living memory.

It can be said that those British excesses in the city of Antwerp in July most definitely had not been an aid to camaraderie. The regular plundering, the depredation of the countryside caused by thousands of men trampling over the corn fields, the rape of local women, all engendered a poisonous hatred between the two allies, which became legendary. Dutch tales of British depredations were myriad; British tales of Dutch hatred and animosity were equally as numerous. In fact, it would not be too long until the Dutch capitulated to the French, whom the British and Hanoverians were fighting on their behalf. But with the British in retreat the Dutch were well aware of whom their future rulers would be (however, temporary) and

---
19 NA: DDRW 4/25: Roworth to Mary, Country Quarters on the Banks of the River Waal, 5 December 1794.
20 Anon., *Officer of the Guards* (London: Cadell and Davies, 1796), p.102.
21 Morris, *With the Guards*, p.123.

many appeared to be as malleable as possible towards the French. To be caught between the marauding British and the revolutionary French must have been a heavy trial. But Pichegru and his Army of the North who, having been given orders not to go into winter quarters and to continue on the offensive, answered the call.

By 20 October, the British headquarters had moved to Arnhem and the enemy prepared to lay siege to Nijmegen. On that day the French attacked the 'whole of the advanced posts of the Duke's army, particularly that at Drutin, which was defended by the thirty-seventh regiment, and at Appelthern, where the light battalion of Rhoan [sic] was posted'.[22] The story varied somewhat according to whichever account was heard, but in essence, the French turned their attention to the outposts at Nijmegen and endeavoured to deceive the 37th Foot by dressing in the uniform of the Rohan hussars, who were British allies. The ruse worked (if ruse it was) and the French hussars were able to cause considerable death and injury to the unsuspecting British regiment, leaving just 50 men and their commander, Major Charles Hope, to survive the ordeal. Writer Edward Cust gave a slightly different slant, by describing the regiment as under orders to retire along the bank of the Waal, and 'having mistaken the French Hussars for Rohans, had no room to form [square]' and added that there were about 80 men slaughtered together with another officer 'and one colour and some field artillery [which] fell into the enemy's hand'.[23] Perhaps an amalgamation of both was near the mark. One Serjeant and seven privates were killed on 20 October from the 37th regiment. Three officers and 11 rank and file were wounded, while 10 officers and 402 rank and file were reported missing.

An incredible waste of manpower for a silly, but crucial mistake. It appeared that this was probably a ruse on the part of the enemy (as mentioned above), but there were certainly a number of regiments whose uniforms bore a sufficient resemblance to an enemy regiment, on either side, which could be mistaken for their own. Ruse or mistaken identity, it appeared to boil down to the same cause – a lack of serious officer instruction and of not using their innate intelligence.

It was time to change tactics, with Nijmegen the goal for both allies and enemy. On 24 October there seemed to be distinct movements by the enemy to indicate an all-out push against Nijmegen, the result of which the various British regiments were to be moved into different positions on the nights of the 30th and 31st. Still the British persisted in their marauding of the populace: 'The excesses committed by the Garrison on the Morning of the 25th before they were relieved – disgraces the Troops and shews how little attention is paid to Order and Discipline'.[24]

They did not have to wait long for retribution. Brown recorded that 'The enemy are very numerous opposite us, and make some attempts to retake the Fort St André almost every day.'[25] On the morning of the 27th Morris

---

22 Jones, *An Historical Journal*, pp.131–132.
23 Edward Cust, *Annals of the Wars of the Eighteenth Century* (London: Murray, 1862), p.252.
24 NAM: 2016-10-23-4-11: Grenadiers' General Orders, 26 October 1794.
25 Brown, *An Impartial Journal*, p.202.

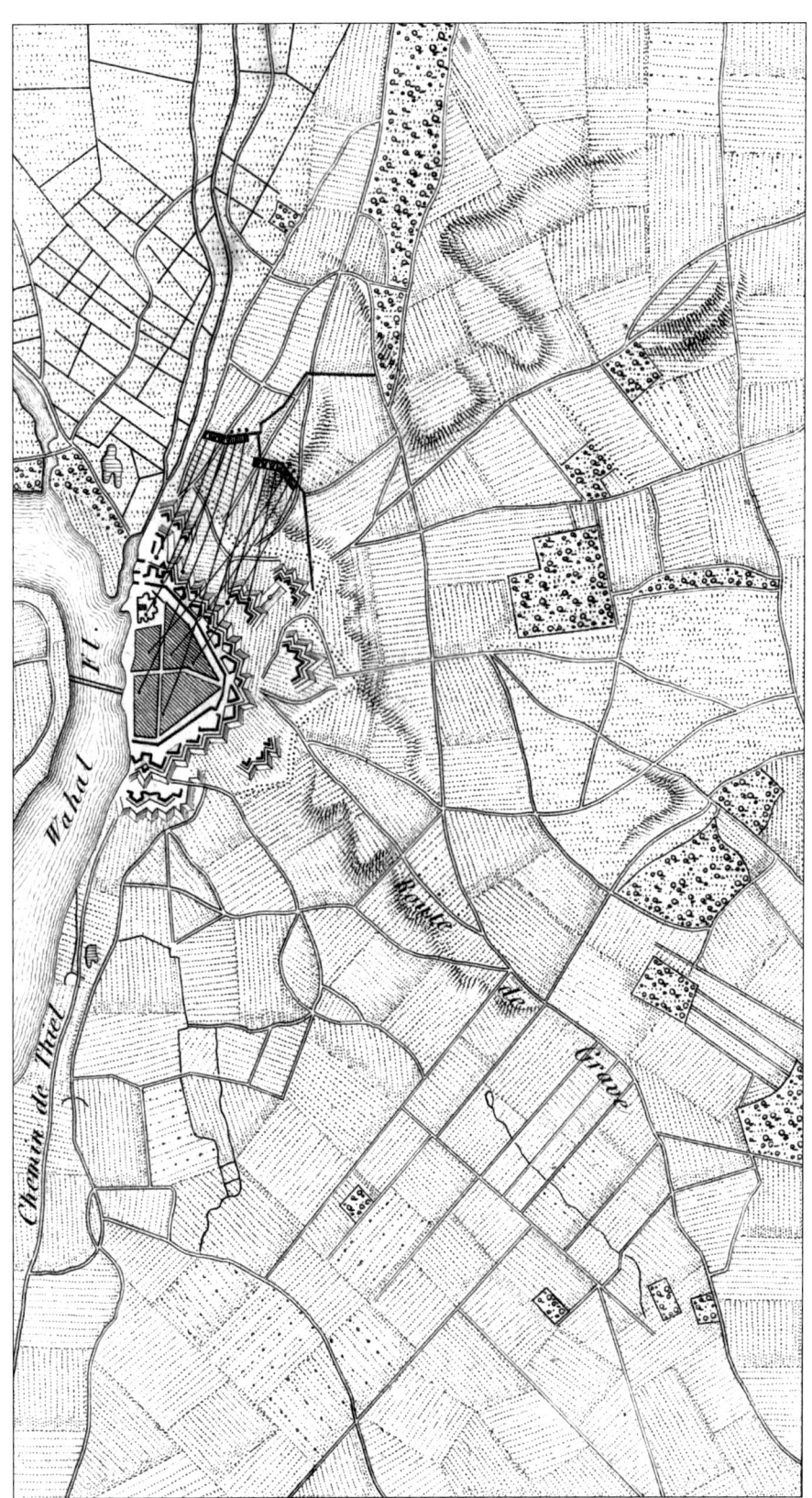

Siege of Nijmegen on the River Waal, Guelderland, 1794. (Author's Collection)

reported an attack upon the village of Herewaarden, with French infantry and hussars, which drove in the Guards picquet close to Fort Sint Andries and 'ab't 30 men of the 44th Reg't wounded, or taken, & 7 or 8 of the Guards'.[26] The campaign bulletin concurs with Morris that these same outposts fell back upon the fort, the French guns keeping up a constant barrage, adding that Lieutenant General Abercromby and Lieutenant Colonel Sir William Clarke were 'slightly wounded in the Skirmish'.[27] Abercromby was wounded in the arm.[28]

Surgeon James McGrigor of the 88th was by this time caring for both the wounded of his own regiment and that of the 78th Foot, as their own surgeon was so ill. McGrigor was manning a hospital within a church. He recorded 'many poor fellows' of the 88th, some mortally wounded. Captain Monro of the 78th was badly injured, blinded by a shot to the head. McGrigor worked on while the church hospital took direct hits from the French cannonade despite a hospital flag flying from the steeple.

The regiments involved had held on to their position for two weeks until the 29th when the Dutch undertook to defend the island of Bommel and the fort. Bommel remained with the Dutch just five days until 3 November when the French took possession of it. Major Harness wrote, 'The Bommelwaard has been ceded by the perfidious Dutch … the want of confidence in Allyed armies is always mischievous, but the present hatred of the Dutch is ruinous and would destroy better hopes than we can form.'[29]

By 31 October the sick-wagons had come under French fire as they were being moved along the dyke to the hospitals, but neither men nor wagons received any damage. For the next four days the sound of the French shells intermittently bombarding Tiel and Fort Sint Andries continued, as described by Roworth above, but the French troops besieging the town of Nijmegen were quietly preparing their considerable earthworks and trenches.

The Dutch citizens continued their complaints against the British when soldiers used empty houses as billets and destroyed the contents, even that of the church. One inhabitant recorded on 1 November: 'everything that is flammable is destroyed even in the houses, and burned, doors, windows – yesterday the beautiful organ in the church was found to be damaged.'[30] A week later, on the 8th, the church itself was burned during the evacuation. The same diary continues: 'November 2nd, at eleven o'clock in the evening, the alarm was sounded. The garrison came [under] arms between half past eleven and twelve o'clock, a Corps of foot soldiers of 3 to 400 men [marched] out of the Crane gate. At night the shooting … with howitzers is much more violent than during the day.'[31]

Jan van Hulst, the diarist, recorded about 3,000 soldiers crossing the river from the town, on Monday, 3 November 'with the intention of clearing the

---

26 Morris, *With the Guards*, p.122.
27 *London Gazette*, 8 November 1794.
28 Carole Divall, *Inside the Regiment* (Barnsley: Pen & Sword, 2011), p.56.
29 Duncan-Jones, *Trusty*, p.64.
30 Jan van Hulst, *'Dagboek van Nijmegen 1794-1795'*, blz.72, <https://www.noviomagus.nl/Gastredactie/Kam/Hulst/Hulst.htm>, accessed June 2022.
31 Van Hulst, *'Dagboek'*, blz.76–77.

INDEED A HOSTILE SHORE: SINT ANDRIES AND NIJMEGEN

Capture of Bommel by Pichegru on 23 December 1794. Winter had not interfered with French operations. (Author's Collection)

city, almost all of them were also driven through, each time [with] army wagons and packs'.[32] He also stated that the rest of the garrison made a sortie and penetrated the French trenches and that the Hanoverians reported 40 of their own men dead and 60 injured.

Van Hulst made reference to the amount of heavy artillery that the garrison threw into the harbour, plus tons of flour and provisions, indicating their intentions to retreat. Many of the citizens later retrieved what provisions they could. After a visit by the Prince of Orange and *Generalmajor* Hammerstein there was a late change of plan and many of the weapons, including cannon, had to be recovered. This was a clear indication of the difficulties experienced by an allied army and the farcical chaos which ensued.

On 4 November Wallmoden made a sortie against the French. The troops involved were the 8th, 27th, 28th, 55th, 63rd and 78th Foot, together with the 15th Light Dragoons. Under heavy fire the British 'swept the enemy out of their trenches without drawing a trigger'.[33] The cavalry inflicted a heavy loss on the enemy but the Allied casualties were over 300 killed and wounded. Van Hulst claimed that the French fire was so fierce that the English fled back into the city, bringing with them wounded, a number of prisoners and 12 Rohan Hussars, who died from their wounds. He further claimed that even

---

32 Van Hulst, '*Dagboek*', blz.77.
33 Fortescue, *History of the Army*, vol.IV, Part 1, p.312.

during the fighting, English thieves plundered in the city, mistook some of their own for citizens, shot them and buried them near the shore.[34] A diarist's hyperbole? Perhaps, but hard to verify in the circumstances.

Brown concurs with Fortescue that on the afternoon of 5 November, those British still in Nijmegen made a sortie from the town and 'without firing a shot, entered the enemy's entrenchments, and put all … to the bayonet'.[35] The following day, the 6th, the French began in earnest to batter the city and the bridge of boats which was thrown across the river as part of any necessary retreat. It was at this time that McGrigor's hospital came so heavily under fire. He and his assistants were warned to be ready to leave via the pontoon bridge over the Waal and to wait for orders. This was finally achieved about two or three in the morning. In his autobiography McGrigor wrote:

> All had been hitherto darkness; but as we were crossing the bridge, the moon began to rise. By the time the animals and batt-horses and baggage which followed us had passed, the moon shone bright, the noise of their passing was considerable, and a very heavy fire opened on the bridge by the enemy. On the other side of the bridge, we were anxious lookers on; at length, one of the centre boats which formed the bridge was detached and swung round. Measures were taken by the engineers to repair this … but the enemy's fire redoubled. By the time daylight broke in upon us, the centre of the bridge was demolished.[36]

Until this point at Nijmegen, the River Waal was a large naturally meandering river being part of the Rhine and 350–400 metres wide and in winter up to two kilometres (1.2 miles) wide, but it narrowed somewhat at the city. The first bridge to be built over the Waal was not until 1936, its total length was 604 metres (1,982 feet). This gives an indication of the difficulties overcome in building a bridge of boats in the winter of 1794, before the ice and snow set in.

Captain Morris was ordered, early on the 7th, to march with his battalion to Drumpt, near Tiel, as a precursor to evacuation. Tiel was also under heavy fire by the enemy.[37] The 44th were still in Tiel at this time, being held in reserve. The Allied and British troops began their evacuation of Nijmegen, in total about 2,500 men, which was completed by 9 November. This involved a retreat across the Waal using the pontoon bridge with a flying bridge reserved for the rear guard. On 5 October, Morris had ridden into Nijmegen where he saw a bridge of boats. The sight must have made Morris a little anxious as 'Several of the boats are very leakey, & in so bad condition that will require attention to baling, etc., to enable the Heavy part of the army to pass over it.'[38] He need not have worried.

---

34 Van Hulst, '*Dagboek*', blz.77.
35 Brown, *Impartial Journal*, p.205.
36 J. McGrigor, *The Autobiography and Services of Sir James McGrigor, Bart: Late Director-General of the Army Medical Department; With an Appendix of Notes and Original Correspondence* (London: Longman, Green, Longman, and Roberts, 1861), p.31.
37 NA: DDWR 4/25: Roworth to Mary, Country Quarters on the Banks of the River Waal, 5 December 1794.
38 Morris, *With the Guards*, p.115.

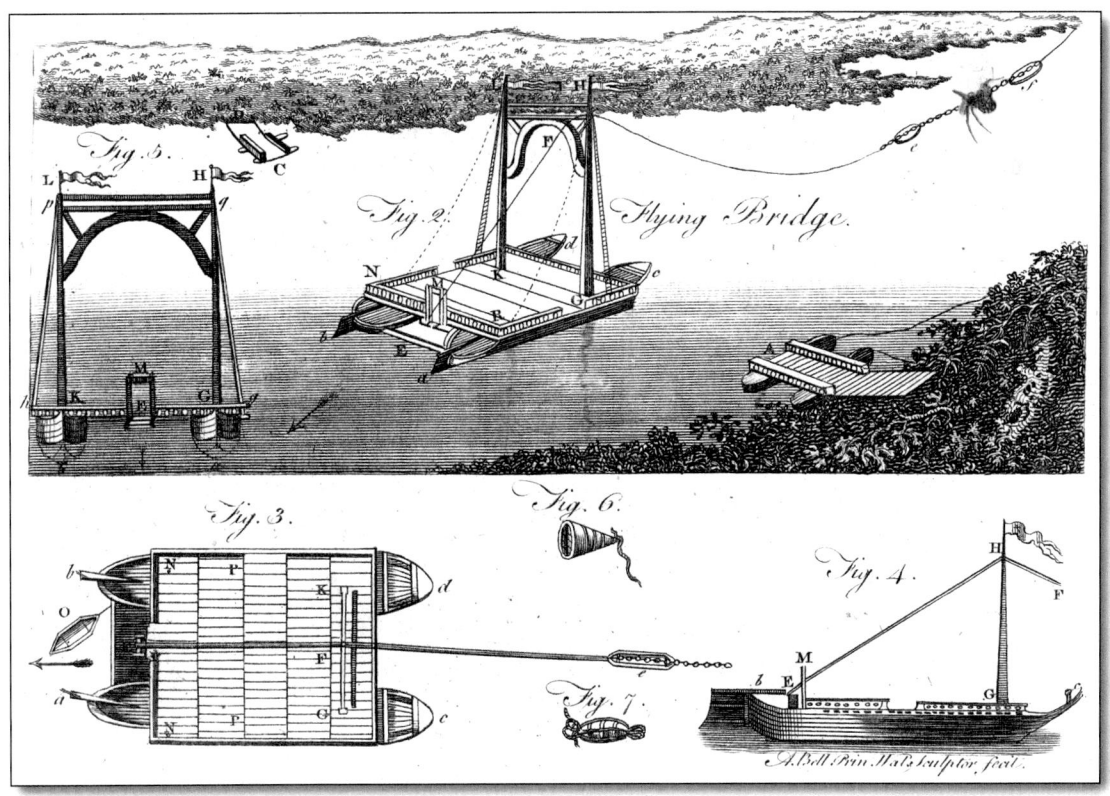

An Eighteenth-Century Flying Bridge, probably similar to the one on which the allies relied at Nijmegen. By A. Bell. (Author's Collection)

Jones believed that if it had not been for the energies of the Royal Navy's Lieutenant Home Riggs Popham, currently serving with the army as Superintendent of Inland Navigation and soon to be promoted to Master and Commander, who had been repeatedly mending the pontoon bridge despite constant shelling, the British and Allies may never have got over.[39] Van Hulst, too, described the efforts of Popham when, 'at 9 o'clock a ship shot under the bridge, where carpenters were immediately appointed to make the bridge useable again by means of beams, which also happened in the middle of the shooting'.[40]

Van Hulst wrote some 30 pages of a blow-by-blow account of the evacuation in his diary, covering 8 November alone. As soon as the troops were across the pontoon bridge, it was destroyed. Roworth, although not an eyewitness, stated baldly that the whole of the army got across except for 'some Dutch Troops that [were] left in the town … [then] we set fire to the bridge and Burnt It Down'.[41] According to Fortescue, the British offered to bring the Dutch troops across on the flying bridge, but the offer was refused. He blamed their capture by the French on their officer, whose histrionics resulted in 'eleven hundred' men who apparently preferred capture by the

---

39   Jones, *An Historical Journal*, p.141.
40   Van Hulst, '*Dagboek*', blz.77
41   NA: DDRW 3/25: Roworth to Mary, 5 December 1794.

French, than rescue by the British.[42] Brown's estimate was 800 and Atherley's 600, possibly more accurate. However, an account was given by the anonymous 'officer of the guards' who, as an eyewitness, painted a somewhat different and more balanced a picture:

> About 600 Dutch were left to pass over on a temporary flying bridge. They had nearly effected a safe landing, when a chance shot from a French battery on the opposite side of the river, carried away the mast to which the hawzer (or chain) was attached, on which the flying-bridge depended; and it consequently swung round, and was hurried by the mercy of the current towards the town. The troops upon it, ere they could by any means obtain a parley, suffered severely from the incessant fire brought to bear upon them.[43]

Campbell's view made reference to his own regiment: 'Troops got all safe out by a well-constructed bridge of [large river] Boats on the Waal wch was immediately distroyed. The 44th had no share in that duty tho it was intended that they should go in had the place been kept longer'.[44] They were, in fact, some eight miles from Arnhem on the 5th, cantoned in houses, then removed to Dodewaard on the 9th.

Major General de Burgh, who had commanded the sortie from Nijmegen on the 5th, was now in charge of the 2nd Brigade (from the 13th November), which comprised the 8th, 37th, 44th, 57th and his own 88th, the Connaught Rangers. The 33rd and 42nd were still part of the 3rd Brigade commanded by Major General Balfour. Unbeknownst to any of them at this stage, five of the regiments in the Low Countries, the 27th (in the 6th Brigade), 33rd, 42nd, 44th and 88th, were all ear-marked for service in the West Indies.

The 88th also made for Arnhem. Their surgeon, Dr McGrigor was struck by the young age of many of the troops in that regiment, using the word 'raw' and described them as exhausted by forced marches and bad quarters, yet they were able to commit 'excesses and outrage' on the local people. He remarked on the ongoing enmity between the British and the Dutch, the latter of whom would make efforts to aid the French. The British were also attacked by that other old enemy, typhus. McGrigor and Captain Maconnochie of the 88th both succumbed and were rushed forward to Emden in a sprung wagon. McGrigor was extremely ill, as were two of his friends. They were carried by others – in the former's case, lying across his horse with a soldier at his head and feet to prevent him falling. He became unconscious for several days and was fortunate to survive. His two friends did not.[45]

Now, however, they and the rest of the army were all to suffer the ignominy of a five-month retreat, in a winter so severe, that it has since been compared to Moore's retreat to Corunna in 1809 and to that of the French army from Moscow in 1812. Throughout those harsh months, rumours swirled about the likelihood of the removal of some regiments for service in the West Indies.

---

42 NAM: 1997-10-131: Atherley, MS Journal, 3 November 1794
43 Anon., *Officer of the Guards*, p.99.
44 NAM: 2002-08-144-60: Campbell to Polly, 12 November 1794.
45 McGrigor, *Autobiography*, p.37.

There were also rumours concerning the fate of the Duke of York. In fact, York had known for some time that there were queries about his suitability as commander-in-chief. As far back as 4 September he had accepted 'the proposal to appoint Lord Cornwallis as supreme commander, Allied Forces', but in the event of this happening he asked leave to return home as he would not want to serve under a junior officer.[46] Cornwallis refused the position. York was still in post a month later, when the King insisted that if both Brunswick and Prince of Orange declined the offer, that he would insist that York continued 'with assistance of General Walmoden; Sir William Erskine; Sir Ralph Abercromby; [and] William Windham'.[47] Another seven weeks elapsed before the King received a letter from the Prime Minister, William Pitt, about the perceived shortcomings of the Duke and advised his 'removal from supreme command'. King George was 'deeply hurt' by Pitt's words and blamed the allies – the Dutch, the Prussians and the Austrians – for York's failures.[48] So York's fate was sealed; it was just a matter of when. The post had been a minefield. Historian R.N.W. Thomas says that: 'Apart from expressing his views, there was little else the Duke could do … he had no real power base at home. This may indeed explain why his reputation could be impugned so readily following the campaign's failures'. Thomas's general consensus was that York had done the best he could under the circumstances.[49]

Back at the beginning of October Henry Dundas, Secretary of State of War, had decided to pull the monetary plug. As early as the 4th he advised 'the Duke of York that the Government … was growing weary of paying subsidies to Austria and Prussia for service which they never rendered … and had resolved to give them no more money'.[50] The Duke must have felt assailed at every turn, poor man – a steep learning curve indeed and not finished yet. For bank-rolling the First Coalition was not the only thing with which the Government was becoming tired. In a letter to banker Brook Watson on 30 September, just before heading out for the Continent, William Windham (then Secretary at War, a different post to Dundas) answered Watson's previous communication. He was concerned about the objections raised by Lord Cornwallis to the suggestion that he (Cornwallis) should take over the position. He suggested an alternative possibility:

> … if it is presented, the removal of the Duke of York, even if he were to continue with the Army, would not seem to be attended with all the Difficulty, than Ld C stated. The question would not so much be of destroying his character (and establishment) as a Commander, as of removing it to another part of the Combined Army.[51]

---

46 TNA: PRO 30/8/106: 4 September 1794. Letters of Frederick, Duke of York.
47 TNA: PRO 30/8/103/3: 12 October 1794, Viscount Palmerston Letters.
48 TNA: PRO 30/8/103/3: 24–27 November 1794, The King.
49 Thomas, *No Want of Courage*, p.269.
50 Fortescue, *History of the Army*, vol.IV, Part 1, p.309.
51 TNA: PRO 30/8/190: Windham to Brooke Watson, 30 September 1794.

The Duke still hoped to put the army into cantonments for the winter and following the burning of the pontoon bridge, William Harness writing from Elst 10 November, claimed that 'the Army now occupy Villages on the left bank of the Waal and are busy in erecting works to prevent the Enemy crossing that River'.[52] Little did they know that within a month all their work would come to nothing. Not only was it determined that Pichegru and his Army of the North should continue the campaign throughout the winter, but the very weather which was to kill so many British soldiers and their camp followers, was the same weather which so conveniently froze the rivers to allow for ease of passage of the enemy army. Captain John Carter Atherley, Coldstream Guards, listed the movements of the officers in his own abbreviated form of record, which lends detail:

> Sunday 30th. Sir W. Erskine set out for England. MGenl Coates, Gordon & Ld Cathcart arrived a few days ago. The Duke set off for England – Wednsy [sic]. The Aide de Camps set off for England. Thursday 12th. A Small Party of French crossed the River & surprised a Hanoverian Regiment. Genl Bush was killed by a Cannon shot. Sunday 14th. Genl Bush buried in the Cathedral. 22[n]d Monday. The Bridge over the Rhine has been removed on account of the great ice that comes down the River. Genl Crosbie is not to return. Genl Hulse has set off for England. 27th – Several people walked over the Rhine. 28th. The Acct came that the Dutch had evacuated and that the French had crossed the Waal at Tuil.[53]

Tuil was a small village on the Waal opposite Zaltbommel and the fort. Captain Atherley himself had less than a month to live. He would die in Flanders on 22 January 1795.

With the apparent desertion of York and a number of the commissioned officers, historian Carole Divall indicates that:

> Not until 1795, after his failed adventure in Flanders, did the Duke of York become Commander-in-Chief of the army and begin the prodigious task of cleaning the Augean stables ... Even the Duke of York, though, could not completely amend the damage of a decade or more when self-interest had been rampant ... Nor could he sweep his new broom through the antiquated system of military administration.[54]

In fact, his removal from command allowed the Duke of York the space and time to step back and take stock, to see the army as an insightful minority already saw it and to take rigorous action when and where he could. In reality, it would be nearly another 80 years until that invidious and wrecking ball of interest and preferment 'promotion by purchase' was completely abolished in the British Army, through the Cardwell Reforms of 1868–1874. Yet York was the man with enough clout to pick up the ideas and ideals of others and to run with them, or at least to shake this amorphous animal that was the

---

52   Duncan-Jones, *Trusty*, p.61.
53   NAM: 1997-10-131: Atherley, MS Journal, 30 November 1794.
54   Divall, *Inside the Regiment*, p.15.

INDEED A HOSTILE SHORE: SINT ANDRIES AND NIJMEGEN

British Army, until its outlines began to take on the shape of the excellent creature that it was to become.

However, in the Low Countries winter was beginning to make itself felt and to worsen. When there were no fires then the men had to rely solely on their blankets or greatcoats, if they had them. It was often a different story for the officers. While the redcoats lay shivering in their cold barns and sodden tents near the riverbank, Major Harness, quartered in Nijmegen, wrote home to Bessy:

> … it has rained almost incessantly for the last four days … I am very comfortably lodged. We have an excellent Coffee House where everybody meets. Nothing can be more sociable. But for the Guns from our Batteries, I should scarce know I am in a Garrison Town, but it is dreadfully hard upon the poor fellows, as very strong Picquets are obliged to be kept day and night unprotected from the weather and not permitted to light fires lest they should attract the fire of the Enemy … I have all sorts of things to keep out the rain [and] I have four horses, two of them carry my Trunks, one with hampers of wine and porter and cold meat, and soup which I make into a jelly, and by cutting a piece out can immediately warm a bason [*sic*].[55]

Some of Harness's views were reiterated by the young Henry, Lord Paget:

> The fact is that barring excessive fatigue & constant night marches we have lived like Princes. In all the Villages & farm houses where we cantooned [*sic*], Officers and men alike had always excellent dinners provided for them by the owners gratis. Their civility to the body has been unboundless, but *en revanche*, they have murdered most of our Stragglers.[56]

However, Roworth refers to the same barns as 'Very Cold, and no fire in them'.[57] In those few words of Paget's, the two extremes of army life were there – clear for all to see. The revenge taken by the Dutch was hardly surprising. If one's country was depredated by its allies, then revenge is better served on a cold plate. On the other hand, if the Dutch allies had been more welcoming, the soldiers would not have had to burn any wood they could find to keep warm. Harness, despite his early tendency to ignore his men's conditions on the continent, went on to become Wellesley's right-hand man in India, being a tough fighter and leader of his men. He died of fever on 2 January 1804, a successful and brave commander.

In the meantime, Lieutenant General William Harcourt replaced the Duke of York as Commander-in-Chief and then had to oversee the British retreat throughout the spring of 1795 – something of a thankless, though necessary, task. Cust commented upon the Duke of York and his relationship with the British Army:

---

55 Duncan-Jones, *Trusty*, p.59.
56 Marquess of Anglesey, *One Leg: The Life and Letters of Henry William Paget First Marquess of Anglesey. K.G., 1768–1854* (Barnsley: Leo Cooper, 1996), p.51.
57 NA: DDWR 4/25: 5 December 1794.

> Frederick, Duke of York had not, it must be confessed, the qualities requisite for a General commanding an army in the field, but his Royal Highness has scarcely had the full credit given him for the services he rendered to the allied arms in the campaigns from which he now retired. He evinced thus early, and through life, the qualities of an excellent military administrator, and was never deficient either in boldness or activity, but he was too easy of temper for the command of an army.[58]

Meanwhile the remnants of the British army slowly worked their way towards Bremen and Cuxhaven, with a French army (bolstered by idealistic fervour) snapping at their heels. Before they reached their goal, the winter of 1794–1795 set in with a vengeance.

---

58 Cust, *Annals*, p.256.

An earlier uniform of the 44th Foot: *Grenadier, 44th Foot 1755 (Braddock's Campaign)* by Don Troiani. (Bridgeman Images)

Serjeant Major William Roworth, 44th Foot, ca 1795, by Alix Baker. (Author's Collection)

The Duke of York, reviewing troops during the Flanders Campaign ca. 1794 by William Anderson. (Image Courtesy of the National Army Museum, London)

His Royal Highness the Duke of York, colour mezzotint by Hodges after Hoppner, published 1791. (Anne S.K. Brown Military Collection)

The West Prospect of His Majesty's Dockyard at Chatham, 1738, by S. & N. Buck. (Author's Collection)

Entrance to Portsmouth Harbour, 1846 by J. Lynn. (Author's Collection)

View of the Harbour of the Carenage, St Lucia, by Lieutenant Charles Forrest, 1781. (Author's Collection)

View from Morne Fortuné, St Lucia, showing the tombs of four governors who died on the island. (*Scenery Of The Windward And Leeward Islands*, London: Ackermann & Co., 1837)

Castries before the disastrous fire of 1796, by Lieutenant Caddy, Royal Artillery. (David Druett, Pennymead)

Pigeon Island, St Lucia. A causeway was built in 1972. (Donald Roworth)

The military cemetery on Pigeon Island. (Donald Roworth)

The Pitons, volcanic mountains south of Soufriere. (Donald Roworth)

Old military buildings carpeted in lush vegetation. (Donald Roworth)

8

Winter Retreat: 1794–1795

'We Serve No Redcoats Here'[1]

After the raising of the Siege of Nijmegen and the collapse of the First Coalition the British troops began to make their way home – the long way round. Like Major Harness of the 65th, Brevet Lieutenant Colonel Colin Campbell of the 44th had prophesied an early return to Britain before winter set in but this was prevented by this grimmest of all winters for some years. Over the months the men and their camp followers suffered untold miseries, following those routes of march set by the quartermaster general's department, which was part of the Duke of York's staff, and who were in no way to blame for the weather. The troops were spread across many miles of desolate and unrecognisable ice-encased landscapes.

Corporal Robert Brown, of the Coldstream Guards, poured his anxieties into his journal, as many of the troops were suffering from illness and the lack of basic requirements:

> Nov 13th 1794. The sick have been frequently sent to the general hospitals, totally destitute of necessaries, the fatal consequence of which is evident in this severe season. His Royal Highness, always attentive to the good of the soldiers, issued an order, directing the commanding officers to pay very particular attention to this object; and likewise ordering the surgeons, purveyors, &c., at the hospitals, to provide them with what is necessary.[2]

In spite of the Duke's goodwill and effort, in the months that followed much was lacking in the care of the sick and injured men. By the end of November army provisions had been stopped by the Dutch, as well as a refusal to allow the sick-wagons to travel through Delft, the 30 miles on their way to hospital at Helvoetsluys on the southern Dutch coast, making the journey longer. 'Upwards of 8000 sick and wounded British soldiers are now waiting at Helvoetsluys for an opportunity of being conveyed to England,' recorded the *Hampshire Chronicle* as late as January.[3]

---

1   Rudyard Kipling, *Ballads and Barrack Room Ballads* (New York: Macmillan, 1892), p.136.
2   Brown, *Impartial Journal*, p.207.
3   *Hampshire Chronicle*, 5 January 1795.

Morning State of the British Infantry, 24 December 1794.[4]

Infantry Brigades	Present				Sick			Artillery				
	Officers	Serjeants	Drummers	Rank & File	Officers	Serjeants	Rank & File	Cannon	Officers	NCOs	Gunners	Infantry Attached
Brigade of Guards	70	127	50	2,081	4	20	1,161	10	5	10	60	93
1st Brigade	79	138	82	1,712	10	36	988	8	4	8	32	132
2nd Brigade	89	113	63	1,838	5	48	948	8	4	8	53	127
3rd Brigade	70	100	57	1,837	5	35	1,033	6	4	19	60	82
4th Brigade	67	90	52	1,299	6	33	1,318	8	3	8	40	145
5th Brigade	65	72	54	1,097	12	57	892	6	3	6	40	84
6th Brigade	73	102	58	1,634	4	24	1,020	4	2	4	26	41
Totals	530	753	428	11,704	46	254	7,418	79	25	63	311	900

The 42nd Foot, the Black Watch, understandably changed their kilts for trousers. 'The frost had set in so severe that it was found the Troops could not exist in their double Tents during the severe Cold and orders were given to build huts of Sods and thatch them.'[5] On 6 December 1794 the Duke of York received his orders to leave for England immediately and Hanoverian *General der Cavallerie* Wallmoden took overall command with Lieutenant General William Harcourt just commanding the British troops.[6] After his promotion to the rank of field marshal in February 1795, the following April the Duke of York was appointed Commander-in-Chief of the British Army, replacing the 80-year-old Lord Amherst, although this appointment was not confirmed for another three years.[7] The Duke was to do more for the British soldier in the army during his tenure than, arguably, any other commander-in-chief before or since.

The French army displayed no indication that it was going into winter quarters that December – in fact Pichegru had received orders to keep fighting – and so the long and appalling retreat of the British army began. The written record of this retreat was left to the voices and memories of those who experienced it and those to whom they told it. The actual experience that winter would have been much the same for all the redcoats, of whatever rank, who survived it – and for the women and children, many of whom did not.

Lieutenant Colonel Robert Riddell had been promoted into the 44th from the 18th Light Dragoons the previous January, before embarking for the Continent. Unfortunately, to date no written record by Riddell of his experiences (if he put pen to paper), has seen the light of day. Colin Campbell, on the other hand, usefully for the researcher, penned a constant stream of letters home to his wife, Polly, at every opportunity. Although he gave her few graphic pen pictures of the extremes of weather experienced by the army that winter (probably not to worry her), he helpfully dated most of his letters and noted his whereabouts. He also left a notebook in which

---

4 Thomas, *Courage*, p.281. Attached Artillery is Infantry serving with the Royal Artillery.
5 NAM: 1968-07-158: Digest of Services, Royal Highland Regiment the Black Watch, 23 November 1794.
6 TNA: WO 16/53/7: GO, Arnhem, 2 December 1794.
7 *London Gazette*, 3 April 1798.

he kept a very brief record of the route taken by the regiment and their movements. These two documents appear to be the only records extant for the 44th Regiment during the six months after his arrival in early November. The other possibility was that the single letter written by Roworth to Mary as he passed through Deventer never reached her, so therefore there is no record of Roworth's retreat.

As the 44th was not required at the Siege of Nijmegen, they were on duty further upriver from Arnhem, where Campbell arrived at the headquarters on the evening of 4 November and then at Dodewaard where he met up with them again, on the 8th. He mentioned to Polly that he had shared his sleeping quarters, on his arrival there, with Lieutenant Colonel Riddell, but was moving to new quarters a mile away from him.[8] As well as route information the Campbell letters and notebook reveal the only character picture extant concerning Riddell and the perceptions of him held by the regiment.

Before winter set in in earnest, Campbell's letters were full of his ambitions both for himself and his son, Guy, born in 1786, so eight years old in November 1794. Writing from Dodewaard on 12 November, he told Polly that he intended to request an ensign's position for Guy and added that 'he [Riddell] seems desirous to keep on good terms with me having frequently had differences with all the other Officers he may probably not wish to offend me by a refusal'.[9]

Riddell seems to have been a difficult and probably lonely man. Four days later, Campbell wrote again and commented on Riddell's personality, which gave some indication of the latter's way of thinking. Although Riddell had agreed to recommend Guy for the post of ensign, he was 'not the sort of man to be turned from the way he wd [sic] walk and as it is doing me a favour to Recom[mend] Him in any shape I must submit to his own mode'.[10] His precise words to Polly were thus: 'The Death of an Ens[ign] who was left ill in England a son of the late Mr M gives me an opening and Col[onel] Riddell agrees to recommend him to the Com[mander] in Chief'.[11] This is interesting as it was usually the Colonel of the regiment, in this case Lieutenant General Rainsford, who would have the commission in his gift, which was then confirmed by Horse Guards. Nowhere in the letters is Rainsford's name mentioned and it appears that Riddell goes straight to the York.

The mode in question was that before Riddell put forward the request, he (Campbell), must promise that Guy would immediately be put on half-pay and that the Duke must be informed of Guy's true age. In other words – the facts. Nothing wrong with that although it might make Campbell's proposal more difficult and he may not have foreseen that degree of Riddell's conscientiousness. Further down, in the same letter to Polly of 16 November, Campbell writes: 'Riddell went to Head Qu[arters] yesterday on this & other Recommend[atio]ns and not yet returned'.[12] Whatever, the truth was accepted so Guy was successfully appointed to a vacant ensigncy in the 44th

---

8   NAM: 2002-08-144-60: Campbell to Polly, 12 November 1794.
9   NAM: 2002-08-144-60: Campbell to Polly, 12 November 1794.
10   NAM: 2002-08-144-62: Campbell to Polly, 16 November 1794.
11   NAM: 2002-08-144-62: Campbell to Polly, 16 November 1794.
12   NAM: 2002-08-144-62: Campbell to Polly, 16 November 1794.

by the Adjutant General, without purchase. The date given in the Army List is 9 December 1794. Campbell exchanged Guy on half-pay with an ensign from an Independent Company as soon as he could, so that the 44th would not be without an officer and that Guy would not yet be called upon to serve.[13] Campbell later wrote, 'Guy's Recomn is gone from here to the Duke of York in England & I dare say will take place'.[14]

This arrangement demonstrated clearly (with hindsight) how ludicrous the circumstances were which would allow an eight-year-old child to be nominally on the muster as a commissioned officer and be paid £30 annually, for no service whatsoever. Campbell added jokingly, 'I must follow your father's account of someone who had his daughter appointed [Quartermaster] and get my Dear Pam & all the others Commissions each'.[15] Rufane Shaw Donkin, currently fighting under Grey, with the flank companies, in the West Indies, was another such son (of Colonel Robert Donkin) who had been appointed ensign in the 44th Regiment in New York 21 March 1778, when he was just five years old and advanced to lieutenant on 9 September 1779 at the age of seven purely on paper.[16] There was an even more extreme example of purchase and interest from Henry Nevin, a quartermaster in the 85th (Bucks Volunteers) Regiment of Foot, in July 1799. He wrote to his colonel, George Nugent, requesting a commission for his six-month-old son as a quartermaster and an ensigncy for himself, by purchase. He suggested he would fulfil the duties of his son's commission as a quartermaster himself.[17] This ploy demonstrates the lengths to which officers went for ambition and money, and maybe the best they could do for their sons, according to the mores of the army at the time.

Campbell also told Polly that the regiment had moved further upriver to Wolferen and that he had acquired 'quite a good chateau'. This must have been the one described as '… not exactly at Dodewaard but at the Chateau of Osen, two miles further down the River Waal where Half the Regiment is with me – in a large house & lodges most of the Officers of the Detachment in the Summer residence of a Dutch family'.[18]

Campbell did indeed have only half of the regiment with him, 'He [Riddell] told me on my arrival that he wd share the Comd of the Regt with me and I have had one half under my own directions Since', so that when Campbell referred to half the regiment, that is what he meant. He commented again concerning Riddell who had 'been very polite and from getting on bad terms [with] the Officers, wished my coming out much before my arrival … they had sent him to Coventry [which] brought him to his bearings'.[19]

Things must have been at a pretty pass for fellow officers to refuse to speak to their commanding officer, although those circumstances must have been only in the mess or socially, otherwise the junior officers would have been

---

13   TNA: WO 65/44: Army List 1794.
14   NAM: 2002-08-144-66: Campbell to Polly, undated.
15   NAM: 2002-08-144-6: Campbell to Polly, Undated.
16   TNA: WO 65/29: Army List 1779.
17   NAM: 1968- 07-174: Nugent Letters, Isle of Wight, 29 July 1799, p.46.
18   NAM: 2002-08-144-62: Campbell to Polly, 12 November 1794.
19   NAM: 2002-08-144-66: Campbell to Polly, undated.

court martialled. If such behaviour between the commissioned officers and their superior were common knowledge, its fall-out could be detrimental to the redcoats as a whole. It was around this time that the officers of the 44th were able to hunt for hares and partridges with hounds and pointers. So wine and fine food were not the only luxuries they took to war with them.

Campbell's wing of the 44th was still at the chateau and its environs in Wolferen where the whole regiment had been able to get together for Christmas Day. There had been one or two skirmishes for other regiments. The 27th Foot was involved at Bueren between the Waal and the Rhine, for which 'the Whole Army was put in motion' but, after some cursory exchange of fire, the French retired, as did the British. Campbell was awaiting orders to move. 'All the Spare Horses and Baggage [took precedence and] are gone on their way to Germany where we follow and will embark for England whenever transports can be procured.'[20]

This corroborates Walmoden's words which he had written to the Duke of York in England: 'To their immortal shame, the officers of the British Army lost most of their enlisted men while they saved their personal baggage.'[21]

The table below, based on Colin Campbell's papers, shows the progress of the 44th across Germany.

The 44th's line of retreat from 4 January – 29 April 1795, approximately 80 days march.

WAYPOINTS	Miles	Days march for stage when known	COMMENTS
Wolferen	16	5	Left on 4th January
Eck en Wiel	3		
Amerongen	12		
Lunteren	22		
Appeldoorn	11		Ice crossing of frozen R. Issel
Deventer	13	Halted 8 days	
Holten	17	Halted 6 days	
Delden	11	1	
Oldenzaal	15		Leaving Netherlands for Saxony
Schüttorp [Schüttorf]	20		Across moorland
Lingen	26	7	Returning southwards[22]
Bad Bentheim	45	9	
Osnabrück	81	20[23]	Leaving Saxony for Bremen[24]
Bremen	37		
Bremerhaven	24		
Cuxhaven			At mouth of R. Elbe[25]
Total Distance	350[26]		

---

20 NAM: 2002-08-144-76: Campbell to Polly, 8 January 1795.
21 Glover, *Peninsular Preparation*, p.3.
22 From Schüttorp, it was a long march northwards to Lingen. The next move was a reversal of direction, southwards to Bad Bentheim (only six kilometres from Schüttorp). It seems likely that the original intention had been to board ship at Eemshafen, north of Lingen and at the mouth of the river Ems, but the place of embarkation was then changed to Bremerhafen, north of Bremen.
23 There were several overnight bivouacs on this long stage.
24 The main body of men embarked at Bremen.
25 The officers sailed from Cuxhafen on 19 April, and landed at Yarmouth on 22 April.
26 Approximately 80 days were taken, from leaving Wolferen to arrival in Bremen.

Campbell and the 44th left Wolferen on 4 January 1795. Wolferen was on the north bank of the Waal about four miles northwest of Nijmegen. The grenadiers and the light infantry of regiments which still had them (many were in the West Indies) were already on the move and had marched for Dodewaard and Ochten on New Year's Day. The winter weather had closed in, and the rivers had frozen solid making them passable by both the allies and the enemy. As the 44th left Wolferen making for Eck en Wiel to cross the river Rhine, known in that district as the Leck, destruction began of the artillery's guns, limbers and carriages, as the weather made it impossible for the removal of larger pieces of ordnance and they could not be left for future use by the enemy. On 2 January Morris's diary recorded, 'Our defence seems to consist in Batteries without Guns, & Guns without Artillerymen'.[27] Brown, at Rhenen on the 7th, described the hospital arrangements at that place, which included the church, a monastery and temporary hospitals on adjoining fields, all of which were filled with soldiers, and 'upwards of four thousand men [have] been buried here within the last three months'.[28] The Guards ringed the hospital area with posts, utilising tobacco sheds for shelter. The dead, placed in coffins 'are piled regularly one above the other … to within a foot or two of the surface' to fill a space 'twelve to twenty feet square … and twelve to fourteen feet deep. They are not many days in filling a hole'.[29] Once filled over with earth, another was dug.

Brown talked of a 'speedy movement' including the sick from Rhenen's general hospital, but was at a loss to hazard where the army might 'make a stand' against the enemy. He recorded that the army crossed the river at several places on the ice, but that the Coldstream and the 3rd Foot were retained to skirmish with the ever-present French.[30] There were numerous small clashes during the retreat, resulting in a constant trickle of dead and dying soldiers. The beginning of the retreat for the 44th appears somewhat confusing from the first descriptive notes made by Campbell. It is worth reading parts in full.

> 1795 The 7th Jany to Eck, Arrived yesterday 13th Jany. [This last crossed out.] Marched to Linden with an expectation of attacking the Enemy the 10th, after some fire from the Sharp Shooters in front retired across the Rhine at Rhenen Halted at Abt …March next … the 11th. To Eck took up our former position – Retired again across the Rhine on the 13th Janry Halted at – Amerongen – The whole army moved 15th inst. At 3 morning. Our Boys halted at Leinteren – 16th marched for Leoneri at 6 in the morning and Under arms at 5 O'Clock'.[31]

The 44th had crossed the Leck at Eck on the ice which in normal circumstances was served by a ferry, then they made their way to Amerongen (having retired twice back across the Rhine), where they halted for a couple of days

---

27   Morris, *Diary*, p.139.
28   Brown, *Impartial Journal*, pp.214–215.
29   Brown, *Impartial Journal*, p.217.
30   Brown, *Impartial Journal*, p.214.
31   NAM: 2002-08-144: Campbell, notebook. Undated entry, probably 17 January 1795.

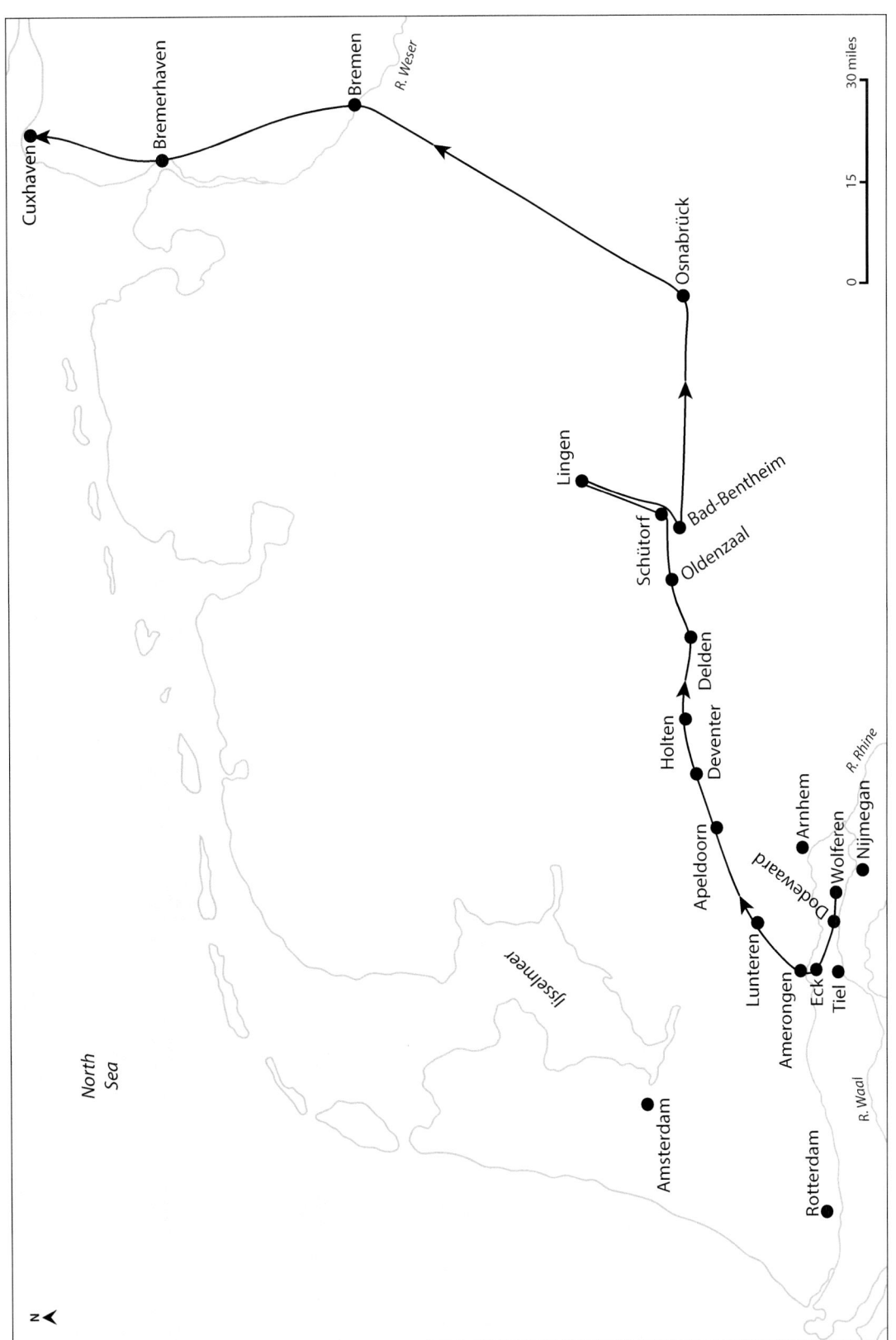

The line of retreat of the 44th Foot, from 4 January – 29 April 1795. Approximately 80 days march.

and were then moved out at 3:00 a.m. on the morning of the 15th, to trudge the nine miles to Lunteren.[32]

In his letter to Polly dated from Eck, 12 January, Campbell writes: 'there has been a pretty smart skirmish near a place called Bueren between the Waal and the Rhine in wch the 27th Regiment has chiefly suffered. The 44th was not concerned. We expect every moment orders to move… all the Spare Horses and Baggage are gone on their way to Germany where we follow and will embark for England whenever transports can be procured'.[33]

In the meantime, the Coldstreams had, after arriving at Rhenen, been ordered to retrace their steps, recross the Leck and to return to Tiel to attack the enemy there. But the enemy knew better and were already attacking Major General Dundas's outposts. Apart from one of the émigré hussars being shot by an allied Coldstream sentry, by mistake due to confusion over uniform (again), the troops were all back at Rhenen by the 10th, another example of Morris's understandable gripes with the collective commanders' inability to get a grip on the overall picture.

While Campbell noted his passages across the Rhine, Captain Morris recounted so many manoeuvres in a handful of days, which were either aborted or involved a change of mind or order:

> The Indecision of Head Quarters of the last two days, in ordering us backwards & forwards across the Rhine appears Most extraordinary, & is not to be accounted for by ordinary Capacities.
>
> Everything is in Such Confusion & our whole System is so extraordinary that it is morally impossible to form any conjectures on our present Situation or future Operations – Our Artillery on the Waal having all been Spiked & the banks rendered defenceless, it is difficult to account for our last movement across the Rhine as this position is undoubtedly more insecure than the one we left, & possesses no visible advantages to account for the preference given to it'.[34]

The retreat continued in weather reminiscent of polar exploration, when the frost and snow whipped up by vicious winds, hung in icicles from eyelashes, noses and clothing. Not one of those who survived the night of 16 January, would have forgotten the experience. Many, if not all the regiments, struggled through an area called the Veluwe, which Brown referred to as 'an immense desert.'[35] Despite wrapping their heads in coats and blankets, every breath was hung with ice. Campbell recorded in his notebook, although not to his wife:

> 6 in the morning, and Under arms at 5 o'Clock, a High Wind & intense Frost. The Guides mistook the Road wch brought it to 12 at night before we reached Leonen [probably Lunteren] – we had 34 men freezing, 20 of whom joined 4 more froze to death … for many froze of the Army … from the length of the March, Severity of

---

32 NAM: 2002-08-144: Campbell, notebook. Undated entry, probably 17 January 1795.
33 NAM: 2002-08-144-75: Campbell to Polly, Eck, 12 January 1795.
34 Morris, *With the Guards*, pp.142–143.
35 Brown, *Impartial Journal*, p.220.

the weather. Many women and children [were] left dead. We [marched] without any Halt for 18 hours so that the ground we went over must have been nearly 40 miles.[36]

All this with women and children travelling as part of the Regiment!

On the morning of the 16th, Morris reported that 'Whole Regiments were missing & scarce a Brigade compleat', such was the chaos and confusion – and search parties had to be sent back to find the stragglers.[37] He wrote:

> The March of Yesterday was the most scandalous business that ever was planned – After the Troops had been twelve hours under arms & marched about 14 miles they had a trackless waste to pass about four leagues [twelve miles] & not a house to be found the whole way – Many regiments had their routes marked for 40 miles ... Accounts are coming in every instant of the loss of men frozen to death, who are laying on the Waste we crossed – Women & Children, Soldiers & Servants, are all included in this dreadful account; their numbers cannot be at present ascertained.[38]

Morris's distress and anger were as evident here as was Brown's, in his own account:

> Waggons were sent out and A great number were found dead near the route of the column, but a greater number who had straggled farther off ... In one place seven men, one woman, and a child were found dead; in another a man, a woman and two children; in another a man, a woman and one child; and an unhappy woman being taken in labour, she, with her husband and infant were all found lifeless. One or two men were found alive, but their hands and feet were frozen to such a degree as to be dropping off by the wrists and ancles [sic].[39]

It was in the weeks following this event that Morris referred to those suffering from bullet fever to be found amongst hospital patients.[40] This was the term for self-inflicted wounds. He found the numbers were considerable and shameful to the British Army, though hardly surprising considering the conditions experienced. For some the continual hardship and strain was obviously too great. Bullet fever took another sort of courage.

The advanced posts of the Guards were set up there and at Loo and Appeldoorn. Brown's distress is palpable:

> Never did a British army experience such distress as our does at this time ... some dead and others dying, or unable to walk ... the country here is a desart [sic] without roads ... every tract [sic] filled up with the drifting and falling snow. Add to all this, the inhabitants are our most inveterate enemies, and where opportunity

---

36 NAM: 2002-08-144: Campbell, notebook, undated entry, probably 17 January 1795.
37 Morris, *With the Guards*, p.147.
38 Morris, *With the Guards*, p.147.
39 Brown, *Impartial Journal*, p.223.
40 Morris, *With the Guards*, p.154.

offers, would rather murder a poor, lost, distressed Englishman, than direct him the right way.[41]

There was a short respite in the weather around 9 February when a sudden thaw set in briefly 'which lays this country all afloat'.[42] Thus the Earl of Cavan, on 9 February 1795, had ordered spirits to the value of £15.4s.4d. to be issued to the Grenadier Battalion of Foot Guards 'after crossing the Waters at Scoutthorp [sic] and on the march to Rene'.[43] This action was taken by the Earl after the following incident described by an officer of the Guards:

> The Flank Battalion and first Regiment of Guards passed through the water almost up to their knapsacks, and several of the men were nearly drowned, owing to the great difficulty they found of bearing up against the current. It became absolutely necessary to break the enormous masses of ice, and clear a passage for the waters through the bridge, to render the march of the main body with artillery and batt horses practicable, in which service the troops in Scuttorp [sic] were busily employed for two days.[44]

On 29 January, Campbell referred to the further 'fatiguing March' to come on their way to Osnabruch, when he thought every mile 10 and although 'moving in the most frozen Location our Army has suffered tho' not so much as might be expected'.[45] Perhaps Campbell was just reassuring his wife

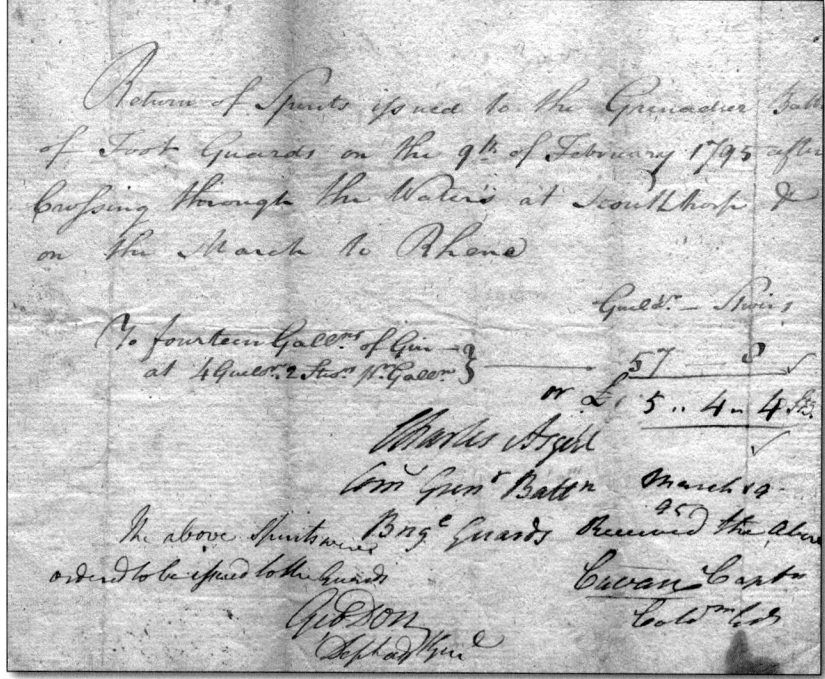

Seventh Earl of Cavan issued spirits to all his men to combat cold and damp. Signed by Sir Charles Asgill, commander Grenadier Battalion and Lieutenant Colonel George Don. (Author's Collection)

41 Brown, *Impartial Journal*, p.224.
42 Brown, *Impartial Journal*, p.231.
43 Richard Ford William Lambart, 7th Earl of Cavan, 9 February 1795. Original document, in author's collection.
44 Anon., *Officer of the Guards*, p.126.
45 NAM: 2202-08-144-75: Campbell to Polly, Oldensael, 29 January 1795.

WINTER RETREAT: 1794–1795

Crossing the Ijssel river at Deventer in the snow, 1794. Possibly camp followers. (Mary Evans Pictures)

whose only news for the last three weeks came from the horrors described graphically in the Edinburgh newspapers.[46]

The 44th then continued on again to reach Deventer on 21 January, where they stayed for six days and would have crossed the River Ijssel there to reach their next destination of Holtern on 27 January. On the 28th they marched to Delden, the 29th to Oldenzaal, and on the 30th to Scuttorf, where they halted until 2 February. They then marched to Nierberken, where, according to Campbell, they halted for 11 days. On the morning of 13 February they marched on to Bentheim, 'where 250 men were quartered in the Castle [and] the rest in [the] Town.'[47] It is possible that the 44th Regiment remained at Bentheim for some weeks as, at some stage, they would have marched a further 87 miles to reach Bremen, while Campbell's notebook ignores the next couple of months, when it leaps neatly from Bentheim to the coast, arriving sometime in April. Interestingly Campbell's letters to Polly deviate somewhat from his record of the regiment's march in his notebook. He, like Morris and other officers, was mounted. So next, he was in Munster, Nienkerken (probably Neuenkirchen) on 11 February, followed by Bentheim,

---

46 NAM: 2202-08-144-75: Campbell to Polly, Oldensael, 29 January 1795.
47 NAM: 2002-08-144: Campbell, notebook, undated entry, likely to be mid-March 1795.

Hanover, on 20 February, Osnabruck seven days later, where he 'went to … make particular enquiry into the reports of the 44th being destined for the West Indies'.⁴⁸ In this letter he reports that the 44th 'move to a Village near to Lingan on the Ems this day' and mentions that because of the continuing severe weather no ships have been able to sail on either the Elbe or the Ems. He reiterates his promise to Polly, 'I can only now repeat what I before wrote you that I will on no account whatever go to the West Indies [should] the 44th be ordered for that service.'⁴⁹

From then there is a gap of a month when he writes from Bremen on 28 March. His last four letters from the Continent, all to Polly, came from 'Geistendorff on the Weser', three written on 3 April 1795 and the fourth on 7 April. Geistendorff being right next to Bremerhaven, at the very mouth of the Weser, Campbell was well placed to jump onto some form of water transport. He had asked Harcourt if he could leave on the mail packet boat, but Harcourt had already refused Riddell, so the answer was in the negative. However, the last letter reports 'I have the greatest satisfaction in telling you that the 44th with other Regts … embark this day at ½ past 2 o'Clock [this] afternoon.'⁵⁰

In all, the retreat for the 44th was some 350 miles in about 80 days, not counting the many deviations and rescinded orders. From there the men were left to wait for transport to England until the march to Bremen Lehe to meet their transports. The officers, including Campbell, found their way to Cuxhaven (another 25 miles) from where they sailed on 19 April 1795. He made a note that there was a shortage of transports and that in all 'men Women & Children will count to about 19,000'.⁵¹ When Campbell arrived in London he wrote 'I am just returned My Love, from Kissing the King's Hand on my coming from foreign Service.⁵² That was written on a Friday. The next was the following Monday when he was able to tell Polly that 'You will see me in the last Gazette Lt Col to the 81st. I from that moved to the 6th Infantry'. Thus he kept his promise to Polly to avoid the West Indies.

The French had continued to harry the British to the borders of the German states. Throughout the four-month retreat there were constant alarms and many skirmishes caused by the large numbers of French in proximity to British picquets. Campbell does not refer to any of the latter involving the 44th. It is much to be regretted that the one letter which Roworth wrote home to Mary from Deventer did not arrive as it would have shone more light on this and the regiment's experiences during that awful winter march.

Captain Lewis Tobias Jones believed the War of the First Coalition was lost through the disparity of numbers: the enemy were formidable only in their numbers, and to those numbers alone were they indebted for their

---

48   NAM: 2002-08-144-82: Campbell to Polly, Osnabruck 27 February 1795.
49   NAM: 2002-08-144-82: Campbell to Polly, Osnabruck 27 February 1795.
50   NAM: 2002-08-144-87: Campbell to Polly, Geistendoff on the Weser, 7 April 1795.
51   NAM: 2002-08-144: Campbell, Notebook, undated, probably mid-April 1795.
52   NAM: 2002-08-144-90: Campbell to Polly, London, undated, probably early May.

conquests.[53] That the 1793–1795 war on the Continent was a catastrophe for the British is not to be argued with. With the benefit of hindsight, there are multiple reasons for that catastrophe. The British seem fond of finding blame in others for their own failings and there were many who would lay the blame at the feet of the Duke of York. For others it lay solely at the feet of Government, in the guise of Henry Dundas, as Fortescue so angrily implied. Without doubt, the army as an institution or a machine was probably near to its lowest ebb – certainly since the successes of Marlborough at Blenheim. Looking at the wider picture, in this particular war, the failure of the Allied armies as a whole must be attributed to just that – their failure to be loyal to their alliance. As to the British army and its German auxiliaries, the officers at all levels certainly required a thorough shake-up, while the Government had still to learn the lesson of keeping a larger, disciplined standing army, ready to move at a moment's notice. This never happened, as can be seen by the paring down of the British Army numbers in the third decade of the twenty-first century. As of 1 April 2023, the British Army (the largest of all the British armed services), stood at only 77,540 men and women.[54] As opposed to some 900,000 active personnel in the Russian army, which also supports 2,000,000 reserves, although the war in Ukraine has cast doubt on the quality of the Russian forces. There are similar comparisons with the standing armies of other countries. One thing is certain, in all the wars since Waterloo, when Britain has been called to fight, men have had to be recruited on every occasion to fill up those necessary holes, the two exceptions being in the World Wars when recruiting was not enough and the government had to conscript to make up the numbers.

---

53 Jones, *An Historical Journal*, p.183.
54 Quarterly Service Personnel Statistics, 2023, *Gov.uk*, < https://www.gov.uk/government/statistics/quarterly-service-personnel-statistics-2023/quarterly-service-personnel-statistics-1-april-2023#uk-regular-personnel>, accessed July 2023.

9

From Bremen to Nursling

*I was overjoyed To See your Dear Handwriting, for you and
My Billy are always in my thoughts.*[1]

Major John Patterson, of the 50th Foot, writing long after the wars, stated cogently that:

> In time of war matrimony is a serious drawback to a soldier. Constant uneasiness about the family he has left at home, when he himself is called abroad, and their anxiety for him are painful to think of; his happiness and peace of mind are marred, and all his best exertions paralyzed, by reflecting on his situation; and he hinders his advancement in the service.[2]

This reasoned comment will be corroborated clearly (as will be seen), by the series of letters which passed between William Roworth and his wife, Mary, over the period of 30 months, when Roworth was away from England, on service on the Continent and in the West Indies – especially in the West Indies. It also echoed true in Campbell's letters to Polly on the Continent and his journey home. Naturally both men tailored their words to be character-specific to their very different wives to take account of sensibilities. Not only are Campbell's words formed with care but also his actions are altered to take into account Polly's wishes. If Campbell had been single whether he would have acted differently is difficult to discern, but it is entirely possible that, without a wife and family, as a serving officer he may have simply followed orders and headed for the West Indies under Abercromby.

Campbell wrote to Polly in April:

> I have the greatest satisfaction in telling you that the 44th wth other Regts [are] making the first Embarkation [at Bremen] … this day at ½ past 2 o'Clock after noon. [W]e hear no orders to sail so that I fear we will wait the embarkation of the whole Army tho' its expected, that may take place in the course of a week.[3]

---

1 NA: DDRW 4/25: Roworth to Mary, Country Quarters on the Banks of the River Waal, 5th December 1794.
2 John Patterson, *Camp and Quarters, Scenes and Impressions of Military Life* (London: Sanders and Otley, 1840), vol.1, pp.113–114.
3 NAM: 2002-08-144-87: Campbell to Polly, 7 April 1795.

The transports took their time to move away from Bremen Lehe. Although Robert Brown embarked (seven days after Campbell) at 5:00 a.m. on 14 April, his transport did not actually make sail until the 20th when it weighed anchor and attempted 'to drop down the river, but the wind failing cast anchor again'.[4]

The following entry from the Grenadiers' General Orders made on 9 April at Bremen after the General Orders for the day were given, are of interest. It concerned stragglers. 'Such soldiers as have been straggled in the course of the different Marches and are still attached to and are doing duty with other regiments are to join their respective Corps'.[5]

After waiting two weeks for the wind to take them down and out of the River Weser, the fleet of some 200 ships, finally sailed for home on 24 April 1795. Within two days they were lashed by storms which blew them 300 miles north of the Thames Estuary and their first sight of Britain was the Cheviot Hills, the border between Scotland and Northumberland.[6] The storm was severe enough for the transport, *Three Brothers*, 'to lose her bowsprit and part of her head'.[7] Finally they turned south to sail past Bamburgh Castle for South Shields. By Friday 1 May the fleet could be seen lying off Tynemouth, with 10 naval escorts, including the *Prince of Wales* of 98 guns and the *Scipio* of 64. Twelve transports arrived in Sunderland Harbour and the 8th, 37th, 44th, 55th, 84th and 89th Foot were disembarked and marched to their barracks, while the rest of the fleet sailed south for Harwich and Portsmouth, including the Coldstream Guards as they sailed on for Greenwich, to meet His Majesty on 8 May, and march on to St James's Park. Even at a distance home soil must have never looked so beautiful, especially for those who had the added misery of sea-sickness.

In spite of the initial euphoria of reaching England, many of the 44th were in poor health. On disembarkation, Carter says that '… the strength of the battalion companies was then eighteen officers, twenty-eight sergeants, twenty drummers, and four hundred and eighteen rank and file'.[8]

This was just over half of the 1,000-odd men who left Britain the previous June. However there is the monthly return taken at Sunderland 1 June 1795, which should be an accurate state of the regiment for that day. Those fit for duty number 352, with 51 sick in quarters and 206 sick in hospital – a total of 609. So, a loss of about a third.

An immediate letter was scribbled on the 1 May, followed on the 9th by a certain serjeant writing from his current quarters: 'These are the Happiest Moments that Ever I experienced, to think I am once more In My Native Country.'[9]

Roworth's relief to be back on home soil was palpable and probably represented the majority of the redcoats who had survived that appalling

---

4   Brown, *Impartial Journal*, p.253.
5   NAM: 2016-10-23-4-12: Grenadiers' General Orders, Bremen, 9 April 1795.
6   Brown, *An Impartial Journal*, p.255.
7   Brown, *An Impartial Journal*, p.254.
8   Carter, *44th Foot*, p.31.
9   NA: DDRW 6/25: Roworth to Mary, Sunderland, 9 May 1795.

North Shields, Northumberland, with ships off-shore, by William Daniell, 1822. (Author's Collection)

winter and the miserable storm at sea: 'I take this opportunity of Letting [you] Know of My safe Arrival at this place, and with the Blessing of God, I hope These few Lines will find you and My Son In Good Health … for My part, My Dear Mary, I never thought I Should Make the shore alive.'[10] Many of the 44th would have agreed.

One could imagine the relief and elation of the men as they finally reached their nearest home ports in England. Even the English weather would not have dampened their spirits and when the troops disembarked at Shields it was to a genuine welcome. The previous winter had been hard in Britain as well, when people had suffered badly. Those who had read their news sheets had a fair idea of what the conditions had been for the troops. The stalwart *Newcastle Courant* on Saturday 9 May, just nine days after the disembarkation, proclaimed that the men 'were received with loud acclamations, and treated by the inhabitants with all that respect their fatiguing situation in the service of their country merits.'[11] It must be said that this was not the situation country-wide.

Their welcome was in sharp contrast to that of the 88th and Dr McGrigor. That sense of revolution which was in the air in Ireland before the regiments were bound for the continent was, if anything, even more pronounced in the south of England. When the redcoats first arrived in Norwich they were

---

10   NA: DDRW 5/25: Roworth to Mary, South Shields, 1 May 1795.
11   *Newcastle Courant*, Saturday 2 May 1795.

constantly insulted by the populace, who aimed their venom at the officers in particular, even to knocking them down after dark, '… attempts were even made to sow disaffection among the troops.' Desertion appeared to become the watchword and it was not unusual for 20–30 to desert in a night. To add insult, typhus broke out yet again in all the regiments in the garrison. A large building was hired as a hospital and James McGrigor was ordered to assume 'the superintendance of the whole'.[12] He had an assistant surgeon and two mates. Within months the 88th was sufficiently fit to be on the road to Chelmsford and then on to Southampton to join that camp where thousands would gather for their next tour of service.

Back in Northumberland, as early as 4 April, temporary barracks had been in preparation in Sunderland for 4,000 returning troops. Roworth had been one of the sick 'with a gripeing of the bowels' for two weeks, on board the same transport which had one and a half companies of the 37th Foot, all suffering with black fever, which had caused a number of deaths. 'Some of ours have died since landing,' he wrote.[13] The *Newcastle Courant* reported the return of 250 sick and wounded men who had been left behind on the Continent. They arrived at Newcastle via Harwich, and Ferrybridge on the River Aire. A number of serjeants, who had been left in the hospitals in the Low Countries, were never heard of again, so presumably did not survive, or may have taken the opportunity to end their time in the army. Not all those still alive returned and the monthly return of 1 August 1795 noted that 85 men who were 'left Sick in Hospitals & of whom no Intelligence can be gained have been struck off since the last return [9 July] in Consequence of an order of the War Office'.[14]

Before they moved out of their barracks in Sunderland, the troops made ready for a review by Lieutenant General George Osborn less than three weeks after their disembarkation, on Tuesday 23 May. This was to be the very same George Osborn who reviewed the 44th eight years earlier, on its return from North America in 1786. They must have been issued with new clothing for this occasion as the general 'expressed great satisfaction at their appearance and discipline', pronounced the *Newcastle Courant* on the very same day.[15] For the 44th Foot that would have been due to Rainsford's organisation of new uniforms for each man. The troops were intended to be issued with new uniforms at the end of each year (though for some items every two years), so it seems likely that they had not had the last issue and it had since caught up with them.

12   McGrigor, *Autobiography*, p.41.
13   NA: DDWR 7/25: Roworth to Mary, Sunderland 20 May 1795.
14   TNA: WO 17/155: Blyth Bay, 1 August 1795.
15   *Newcastle Courant*, Saturday 23 May 1795.

State of the 44th Foot, Sunderland, 1 June 1795. (TNA: WO 17/155)

Present					Rank & File					Number Wanting		
Officers	Staff	QM	Sjt	Drum	Present	Sick	On Com'd	Other	Total	Sjt	Drum	R&F
14	5	1	29	17	352	257	19	1	629	-	1	221

Leaving Sunderland, the regiments marched out of town and north, up the coast 24 miles or so, to Blyth Bay, where they would prepare for their next big military event some three months away and in the meantime, there was family business to catch up with.

Two men in Riddell's company were marked down as sick in quarters and 30 sick in the hospital on the monthly return for 1 June 1795. It was likely to have been from that severe diarrhoea on board the transports crossing from Bremen to the English ports, mentioned by Roworth to Mary, which he himself had for a couple of weeks.

The State of the 44th Foot. Blyth Bay, 1 September 1795. (TNA: WO 17/155)

Present					Rank & File					Number Wanting		
Officers	Staff	QM	Sjt	Drum	Present	Sick	On Com'd	Other	Total	Sjt	Drum	R&F
19	3	1	37	21	547	29	-	4	500	19	4	540

During the time the 44th was encamped at Blyth they, together with the West York Militia and the short-lived 115th (Duke of Gloucester's) Regiment of Foot, lay between Gloucester Road and Lysdon. In front of Gloucester Lodge the 21st Light Dragoons were encamped while the 55th and 84th Foot, the 7th and 16th Light Dragoons, the Leicestershire Militia and part of the Royal Artillery were at Cowpen Camp.[16]

Roworth's wish to see his family would have been mirrored by the majority of redcoats in the camp. He went to some length to persuade Mary to visit him at Blyth. He sent her a money order for three guineas to draw from the post master in Nottingham to cover the cost of her travel, but to come alone, as 'I Could Wish to See My Dear Boy, but It will only Learn him Bad ways to be Here.'[17] It appears that he did not want Billy to be swayed by either the attraction of the red jacket or the behaviour of its wearers, particularly scenes of drunkenness. Like Campbell, Roworth talks instead of his friends in the regiment:

> My Dear … Serjeant Grigson and his Wife was took Prisoners by the French when we Left Holland, and [so were a] great many Privates. Mrs Gardiner has got a fine Boy born in Holland Last Winter. Sergt Page is Left Behind … Ja[mes] Woods and [his] Wife, [sends] Love to His Mother and he recd Her Letter … He wants her to send Some Stockings By You if Convenient … My Dear Mary, I could wish you to bring me a good Stout purse of Some kind if Possible.[18]

---

16 John Wallace, *The History of Blyth* (Blyth: John Robinson, 1869), p.49.
17 NA: DDRW 7/25: Roworth to Mary, Sunderland, 20 July 1795.
18 NA: DDRW 7/25: Roworth to Mary, Sunderland, 20 July 1795.

Whether Mary's visit was all that they wished, or if she carried James Wood's stockings with her, or even if the long-awaited visit ever happened at all, we are not privy to, as Roworth's next letter was dated 31 August, by which time he had travelled to see his family in Nottingham and he was, by then, Lieutenant Colonel Riddell's company pay serjeant, 'which is a 'Benefit to me'.[19] This meant a personal pay rise of two shillings a day but also involved a lot more work. Company pay serjeants were likely to have assisted their company commanders with the company's pay and reported to the battalion pay serjeant. Not a job for the dishonest nor the faint-hearted and it would have required an appropriate level of literacy and a fairly sound knowledge of accounting and arithmetic.

Yet another review was looming, which would have involved hours spent by the men, with the routine pipeclay, blackball for their boots, and the spit and polish of their short land pattern muskets. One week later, at 7:00 a.m. promptly on 28 August, Frederick, Duke of York, together with his brother, William Frederick, Duke of Gloucester and Edinburgh and General Sir William Howe, Commander of the Northern District, reviewed the troops on the sands at Blyth Bay. The line of cavalry and infantry stretched along the sands and the two royals inspected and reviewed the men. The whole army on this occasion 'consisted of thirteen regiments of horse and foot, comprising seven thousand men, took ground on Blyth sands, extending, when in line, about three miles'.[20] As York rode along the line with Howe, reviewing the men he had commanded throughout the early part of the allied war, although it had ended in defeat, he must at least have felt proud – if not stirred – by the sight of them performing their discipline, those familiar movements and evolutions.

There would have been weapon firings and maybe a *feu de joie* in salute of His Royal Highness, a familiar figure to all the men. Other notable figures present included other generals, aristocrats and politicians, together with their ladies. Even so, the last time the men had seen so many people gathered together, would have been on the Continent, a far cry from these excited and enthusiastic spectators, assembled to cheer them on. John Wallace, a Blyth inhabitant, reported that 'This grand military spectacle, being so novel in this part of the country, attracted an immense number of spectators, calculated to amount to thirty thousand.'[21]

However, unknown to the regiments present, the Duke of York was not as happy as he seemed. Winterbottom tells us that only three months earlier, in May 1795, Frederick had ordered that those *Rules and Regulations for the Formations, Field-Exercise and Movements of His Majesty's Forces* which had been assembled by General Sir David Dundas and 'issued by direct command of the king in 1792', be followed by the military – to the letter.[22] It appeared that on this occasion his command bore virtually no fruit

---

19 NA: DDRW 7/25: Roworth to Mary, Sunderland, 20 July 1795.
20 Wallace, *Blyth*, p.49.
21 Wallace, *Blyth*, p.50.
22 Derek Winterbottom. *The Grand Old Duke of York* (Barnsley: Pen & Sword Military, 2016), p.78.

whatsoever. It was this review on the beaches at Blyth, in which the 44th took part, that demonstrated an almost total disregard for his order. The Duke wrote to his father 'that all but one of the regiments he had inspected were drawn up two-deep' as opposed to the three men deep as required in the instruction manual.[23] It is not known which regiment stood out for its order. Was it the 44th? From Campbell's reportage of Riddell's pedantry and a follower of rules it may well have been – but that is purely speculative. What can be said with fair accuracy, is that ironically, the three deep line was abandoned in almost all the subsequent campaigns, even though it remained in the manual.

Although the grand review itself was complete by mid-morning the celebrations continued and fulfilled the spectacle of the greatest pageant that many would ever see gathered in their home-town, or elsewhere in the region. John Wallace commented later on the difference so large a number of soldiers made to the life and prosperity of the town. 'The old tradesmen used to refer to the time of the Camps as the golden age of business in Blyth. Such a number of people being brought to the neighbourhood turned the little out-of-the-way town upside down, and made money plentiful to a degree as had not been previously known.'[24]

There must have been many tradespeople who benefited from the extra income, not just the inns and taverns. The soldiers' money may even have stretched to a trinket or two for those at home.

Three days later Roworth was able to write to Mary with even more exciting news than the review:

> My Dear Mary You will Excuse My Short Letter But … I have to Inform You That on Saturday Morning last Lieut. Col. Riddill [sic] Sent for Me and has Been So Good as to Make [me] Serjt Major in the 44th Regt In Room of Sergt Major Legge Promoted to Quarter Master and Promised Me the adjutantcy if any thing Should Happen, as he Says it Shall always fall to the Serjt Major.[25]

The rank of serjeant major was introduced in the British Army early in the eighteenth century. Roworth would have been rightly feeling pleasure at his appointment and anxious for Mary to know of it. Although Mary's letters to Roworth have not survived, from the phrasing in his letters to her it can be seen that she would regularly ask him about his possible promotions or 'steps up'. As a serjeant major his duties were precise, onerous and busy. James in his *Military Dictionary* states them thus:

> The serjeant-major is the first non-commissioned officer in the regiment after the quartermaster. He is, in fact, an assistant to the adjutant. It is his peculiar duty to be perfect master of everything that relates to drills; and it is always expected, that he should set an example, to the rest of the non-commissioned officers, of manly, soldier-like and zealous activity. He must be thoroughly acquainted with all the

---

23 Winterbottom, *Grand Old Duke*, p.78.
24 Wallace, *Blyth*, p.50.
25 NA: DDRW 8/25: Roworth to Mary, 29 September 1795.

details which regard the interior management and the discipline of a regiment. For this purpose he must be a good penman, and must keep regular lists of the serjeants and corporals.[26]

On 25 August 1794 Serjeant Major Peter MacNamara had been promoted without purchase to adjutant, vice Starke, and he appears on the *Army List* as adjutant from 8 October that year.[27] He was then gazetted ensign in the 44th on 7 July 1795, and then appointed a lieutenant in the 39th Foot on 5 September 1795. He died in 1796.[28] The day after the review Roworth was appointed serjeant major. MacNamara left the 44th on 12 September as Roworth verified in his letter dated the following day. After which MacNamara's name disappeared from the muster rolls of the 44th Foot. It had first appeared during the period 30 September–11 October 1786. He was promoted to corporal on 10 October 1787 and to serjeant on 24 August 1788. Between that date and his promotion to adjutant he was made serjeant major. Although Peter MacNamara was not mentioned in Roworth's earlier letters, his rise through the ranks was swift – less than two years from private to serjeant and nine years in total from enlistment to adjutant. Not only a driven man, but presumably meritorious.

Roworth's friend, Thomas Legge, was also an ambitious man, although records show him in the 44th as far back as 19 May 1781, still in America, being reduced from serjeant to private, but not for too long. On 9 September the same year he was promoted to corporal again. He stayed in that position for seven years, rising to serjeant in the first half of 1788. Legge became serjeant major between that date and his promotion to quartermaster on 25 September 1795.[29] However, he resigned as quartermaster in November and instead was commissioned as an ensign, rising to lieutenant in May 1796.[30]

Ambition shines through Roworth's letters to his wife. From enlistment on 2 February 1786, he rose to corporal on 19 October 1787 (one year and seven months), to serjeant on 9 May 1790, another two years and seven months, then gained his title of serjeant major in just under five and a half years on 29 September 1795, nine and a half years in total. Not as fast as he would have liked, no doubt.

Although volunteering in 1786, MacNamara had overtaken both Roworth and Legge in the promotion stakes. He must have been an indispensable soldier and a high-flyer, who made no mistakes. Unfortunately, MacNamara left no written accounts so there is no record of the man himself or his career other than army records. That together with the lack of reference in Roworth's letters leaves no clue to his personality. Riddell's promise of the adjutancy to Roworth would have depended on the current adjutant's promotion or move into another regiment, death, discharge or retirement.

---

26   James, *Military Dictionary*.
27   NAM: 20-16-10-23-4-9: Grenadiers' General Orders, HQ Groesbeck, 25 September 1794; TNA: WO 65/45: Army List 1795.
28   *London Gazette*, 7 July 1795; TNA: WO 65/46: Army List 1796.
29   TNA: WO 12: Muster Books, 44th Foot 1781–1795.
30   *London Gazette*, 7 November 1795; TNA: WO 65/46: Army List 1796.

Within a fortnight of his new appointment it appeared that Roworth had apparently scuppered his own chances of the adjutancy, when he admitted (despite his serjeant major appointment) that he had been:

> … very Impertinent to Col Riddle [sic], Which I believe the B[e]rth will Not Be a Gift any More Though Some of the Regimt Is of an Oppinion It will fall as it formerly Did – If I keep this Station for a few years I Shall Be Content But as we are going on foreign Service Something Else will fall out to me If I have But my health and I hope to do Something for the Benefit of you and My Son if It pleases God to Grant it.[31]

With reference to what was known about Riddell's interaction with his officers, from Colin Campbell's comments while on the continent, Roworth's 'impertinence' may have been saying just the wrong thing at the wrong time. Elsewhere he mentions that Riddell often asked for his (Roworth's) advice, so perhaps he gave too much! Whatever the 'impertinence' it appears to have set back Roworth's chance of a further promotion for the foreseeable future. The other reference to promotion came in the words 'Something Else will fall out to me If I have But my health' – a very clear indication of understanding that there were likely to be many deaths through battle or disease.

On the 44th's muster roll for the 25 June–24 December 1795 there were several other promotions recorded. The same physical roll was also used to record the deaths of the men in the West Indies over the course of the next 18 or so months; when the redcoats returned in July 1797, it was later marked 'Stains 24th March 1798' and signed by David Ogilvy, the commanding officer, Richard Chaloner, paymaster, and John Donaldson, adjutant. In the meantime, 'Serjeant Donaldson joined from the Flank Comps & put on the Strength as a Supernumerary Serjt till 25th Aug' on the monthly return for the 1st September 1795. Richard Chaloner (not William Roworth) was appointed adjutant in McNamara's stead on the 19th and resigned on 6 September 1797 and Thomas Mackrell was marked as the new adjutant the following day. When Legge resigned as quartermaster to take up his commission as ensign, Sergeant Thomas Gardner took on the roll on 4 November.[32]

To return to May 1795, promotion was the same for all the serjeants, drummers, and rank-and-file, in that it was awarded on merit alone, unlike, as previously mentioned, purchase and interest in the commissioned officer ranks. It is not known what kind of a serjeant major Roworth became – other than busy, which was his constant excuse for the paucity of letters he wrote, but that rang true for serjeants and serjeant majors alike.

Thomas Jackson of the King's Own Staffordshire Militia drew a pen picture of his own serjeant major, at 'about six foot two … and with his stentorian voice used to make us young chaps tremble … [was] a fine noble fellow; and so he was, and an excellent disciplinarian … I then called him

---

31 NA: DDRW 8/25: Roworth to Mary, Camp at Blyth Bay, 13 September 1795.
32 TNA: WO 65/46: Army List 1796.

surly, I afterwards found him no tyrant, but a very good man'.[33] Apart from the matter of height it is to be hoped that Serjeant Major Roworth was of similar steadiness.

The next letter that Mary received, informed her that her husband and the regiment were definitely 'going on foreign service' although there was no specific destination given at that stage. But the officers of the 44th were in preparation, promoting a number of men to serjeants and corporals in order to maintain five serjeants and five corporals per company. The numbers of men were to be augmented by drafts from the 14th (Bedfordshire) Regiment of Foot, the 19th (1st Yorkshire North Riding) Regiment of Foot, and the Royal Glasgow and Loyal Sheffield Volunteers to bring the total number of men to 1,000. After the large loss of men in the Low Countries through fighting the enemy, then the hundreds dying from disease and hunger during the retreat in particularly evil weather, many of the regiments to go for foreign service would have been augmented as the 44th was.

Roworth constantly requested Mary to stay with him while he was in England, citing every positive aspect of army life he could think of, even if she chose not go abroad with him: 'We Could have been Very Comfortable here ... as I have got a Tent to my Selfe & Everything almost is as agreeable as I could wish for, only for want of you, My Dear Mary, to tell My mind to ...'.[34]

That was a real cry from the heart. She had some unexplained illness during the six months the regiment was in Britain, but nothing specific could be inferred from Roworth's letters. Her letters to him did not survive. He dangled tempting carrots under her nose – to let Mrs Woods (she of the stockings gift) know that her son, James, and his wife were well and gave 'their duty to her'; the wife of Serjeant Foxcroft was thinking of going with her husband abroad and desired to be remembered to Mary; Captain William Tuffie's wife, Grace, was also going with her husband, as well as Captain Allen's wife, inferring she would not be without suitable female companions. This in itself might have concerned her as, unlike Roworth, who was obviously certain of his own capabilities and used to associating (at least to some extent) with commissioned officers and their wives, she may have felt not confident to espouse her husband's rigorous army life.

Once their son, William, was an adult and part of the wider political life of Nottingham, himself used to public speaking, fraternising and taking a leading role in the council chambers and in public life, with Mary living at home with him and his family, she may well have coped with integration to a much greater degree. But this is only surmise. No doubt there were many redcoats whose wives preferred to stay on solid ground, but with none of the letters Mary wrote having survived there are no clues other than reading between the lines of those Roworth wrote home.

In the meantime, the 115th had already embarked at Shields early in September, so Roworth expected that the 44th's turn would come sooner rather than later. From the wording in the remaining letters it seems clear

---

33 T. Jackson, *Thomas Jackson, Militiaman and Coldstream Sergeant, 1803–1815* (Solihull: Helion, 2018), p.24.
34 NA: DDRW 9/25: Roworth to Mary, Camp at Blyth Bay, 13 September 1795.

that Roworth and Mary did not meet again, regardless of his efforts. There is no record of the number of times they saw each other, with or without Little Billy. Billy was six years old at that time and it was never clear if he visited his father during William's seven months back in England, although they must have met on that solitary visit of Roworth to Nottingham in the summer. He was certainly not alone. So many soldiers must have had complex lives and relationships with some, perhaps, only too pleased not to receive visitors.

On Tuesday 22 September, Roworth put pen to paper again when he wrote to tell Mary he was embarked on board the *Isis* transport since 19 September.[35] He was expecting to sail the next day for Southampton – barring any storms – and a relatively short time onboard. Sometimes soldiers were embarked for several days or weeks, those days were usually spent waiting to catch the offshore wind to sail. Other causes might be waiting for missing officers or even to discourage desertion, as often men were unable to swim, but most likely was to wait for that favourable wind. In this case the wait was not long, as the *Isis* sailed on 26 September, when the whole fleet of 37 sailed for Portsmouth, having on board three regiments of infantry, the 44th, the 55th, and the 115th, together with the 21st Light Dragoons.

The actual voyage took just two days, the troops landed on the 28th and marched to their campground 'after a Very Pleasant passage from North Shields'.[36] The camp was at Nursling Common, about three miles to the north-west of Southampton town centre. It was an area of over 700 acres, ideal for a large army camp, within a short distance of the embarkation point.[37]

By the time of the 44th's arrival, the camp had already grown to 17 regiments; about 10,000 rank and file and 600 officers. Disease was an ever-recurring problem and was rife yet again among the soldiers. Local historian John Oldfield wrote that 'between August and October 1795, no less than eight men from the camp were buried at St Boniface's Church, Nursling, together with 15 children'.[38] One regiment arrived at Nursling from Jersey of whom Lord John Manners noted that they had left behind them 250 lost to fever.[39]

Safely ensconced in pleasant surroundings, Roworth wrote from Nursling, returning to the theme of their personal difficulties, which continued to be the reluctance on Mary's part to spend time with him in camp, or even to put her name forward in the lottery for joining her husband on his journey abroad. The cause of her reluctance did not appear to be money as William could provide for her, without too much of a problem. The constant refusal (for whatever reason) served to highlight, not just their difficulties, but the extra pressures on Roworth's military life. The Roworth letters corroborate throughout the effect that an army marriage had on the sheer functioning of either party.

---

35 NA: DDRW 10/25: Roworth to Mary, on board the *Isis* transport, 22 September 1795.
36 NA: DDRW 11/25: Roworth to Mary, Camp at Nursling Common, 29 September 1795.
37 John Oldfield, 'From Spa to Garrison Town', in Miles Taylor (ed.), *Southampton, Gateway to the British Empire* (London: I.B. Tauris, Bloomsbury, 2007), p.5.
38 Oldfield, 'From Spa to Garrison Town', p.5.
39 Oldfield, 'From Spa to Garrison Town', p.7.

Officially the commanders were supposed to know only where their destination was after they had left shore and opened the envelope containing orders. But the rumour mill ground round the regiments (and thoroughly), so there was not much of a surprise left to be had. All redcoats were very much aware of the fact that the West Indies was renowned as much for death by disease, as death through battle, so perhaps it was this knowledge which inhibited Mary Roworth, like Polly Campbell, from joining those hundreds of women frantic to join their husbands; perhaps her parents, with whom she and Little Billy lived, persuaded her of the dangers of ships and foreign climates. Roworth was quite desperate in his efforts to persuade her to see him just one more time, as some of the regiments were already embarked and onboard their transports.

Contrary to his expectations, he was still at Nursling Common on 9 October and wrote that day, much more positively and business-like as he planned for the future and reported on happenings concerning them both. Family matters of a different kind took his attention. Serjeant Gardiner had brought him a letter (a few days previously) from one of Roworth's brothers, John, who wrote from London to tell him to expect a visit in the not-too-distant future. John enclosed a letter of '… recommendation to [a] Mr Sears, Deputy Purveyor of the West India Staff, from one, Mr Beedin … Desiring Him to assist Me In Case of Sickness or any other way that Lay in His power, and I hope I Shall have the pleasure To See him in Some part of our Travels'.[40]

Another reason for John's letter (he worked in textiles in Manchester and London) was to enquire (apparently with an eye to the main chance) as to Roworth's needs in the West Indies as he could get the items at 'first rate in Town' and send them down to Southampton. Roworth sent off for 'Dimetys & Calico, Nankeen and All Such as will Be Necessary for a Hot Climate … And Serjt Gardiner has [also] wrote for a large quantity to him'.[41]

As a serjeant major, Roworth was also the owner of a 'Very Handsome Coat and Epaulette',[42] which was not unlike a soldier's coat in weight and cut, but of slightly better quality and fit. It was also the very first change in uniform specifically for duty overseas, taking into some consideration the conditions of heat and humidity under which the men would have to live and fight. But, true to form, flannel still took pride of place in the matter of 'small clothes'. The weather in the West Indies could range from comfortably warm to uncomfortably hot and was often very humid.

The medical men were aware that the usual uniform dress sapped energy, enthusiasm and the ability to fight, so, in the spring of 1795, uniforms for the military were changed to take some account of the climate. Soldiers in the West Indies were to have the following kit:

> …a round hat as is furnished to recruits on foreign service, a plain red jacket so made to button close to the body and to have a stand up collar, under flannel waistcoat and drawers of the same, a pair of woollen trousers to button over the

---

40 NA: DDRW 12/25: Roworth to Mary, Camp at Nursling Common, 9 October 1795.
41 NA: DDRW 12/25: Roworth to Mary, Camp at Nursling Common, 9 October 1795.
42 NA: DDRW 12/25: Roworth to Mary, Camp at Nursling Common, 9 October 1795.

NOT SO EASY, LADS

Uniform adapted for all infantry troops for the coming expedition to the warmer temperatures of the West Indies. (Illustrated by Jo Davies)

shoes like a gaiter, 2 shirts, 2 pairs of flannel socks, 1 black leather stock, 1 knapsack or pack.[43]

In the autumn of 1795, a medical board further recommended '... regimental coats with the tails shortened and Russian duck gaiter-trousers'.[44] Another seven years and the infantry would have the further comfort and advantage of white linen trousers.

In his continued effort to see Mary once more, Roworth drew her attention to the precarious position of the redcoats' wives who were hoping to 'follow the drum':

My Dear, there is sad work among the women which [are] to go, as it is not Settled on Yet, for there is Only four per Company to Embarke, the Rest is to [be] Left In England and to have 2 guineas to Carry them Home [and] if any Children, halfe a Guinea Each, with a Passage free to Either Ireland or Scotland.[45]

The rule of four women per company applied only to the other ranks because the wives of officers were allowed to go by choice. Some of the officers' wives became famous in their own right because of their own exploits in the field. Lady Magdalene De Lancey, accompanied her husband, Colonel William Howe De Lancey, just two months after their marriage, to the Continent where he was mortally wounded in the Battle of Waterloo on 18th June 1815. Still alive, he was found on the battlefield the morning after, by a staff officer and was removed to a cottage nearby. Lady De Lancey, waiting in Brussels, received a message to tell her of her husband's situation on the 20th. From the time she arrived at his bedside that evening until the 26th when William finally passed away, she and her maid were in constant attendance. At one stage, Magdalene tore up her flannel petticoat to use to apply a poultice to her husband's chest. Later she left her own account of that week spent at Waterloo beside her dying husband.[46]

The records of soldiers' wives were much less frequently recorded, not least because so many were illiterate. But one such who went down in army lore was the much-admired Irishwoman Biddy Skiddy, whom Ensign George Bell of the 34th Foot referred to as 'Mrs Commissary-General Skiddy'. She

---

43 René Chartrand, *British Forces in the West Indies 1793–1815* (Oxford: Osprey Publishing, 1996), pp.8–9.
44 Chartrand, *British Forces*, pp.8–9.
45 NA: DDRW 12/25: Roworth to Mary, Camp at Nursling Common, 9 October 1795.
46 David Miller (ed.), *Lady De Lancey at Waterloo* (Staplehurst: Spellmount, 2008), pp.105–130.

related the story to him which has been repeated many times over the intervening years, as it was here, in Bell's own memoirs.

> Yer honour minds how we were all kilt and destroyed on the long march last winter, and the French at our heels, an' all our men droppin' and dyin' on the roadside, waitin' to be killed over agin by them vagabones comin' after us. Well, I don't know if you seed him, sir, but down drops poor Dan, to be murdered like all the rest. Says he, 'Biddy dear, I can't go on furder one yard to save me life.' 'O, Dan jewel,' sis I, 'I'll help you on a bit; tak' a hould av me, an' throw away your knapsack.' 'I'll niver part wid my knapsack,' says he, 'nor my firelock, while I'm a soger.' 'Dogs, then,' sis I, 'you 'ont live long, for the French are comin' up quick upon us.' Thinkin', ye see, sir, to give him sperret to move on, but the poor crather hadn't power to stir a lim.
>
> Now I heerd the firin' behind, and saw them killin' Dan, as if it was! So I draws him up on the bank and coaxed him to get on me back, for, sis I, 'the French will have yea in half an hour, an' me too, the pagans.' In truth I was just thinkin' they had hould av us both, when I draws him up on me back, knapsack and' all. 'Throw away your gun,' sis I. 'I won't,' says he. 'Biddy, I'll shoot the first vagabone lays hould av your tail,' says he. He was always a conthrary crather when any one invaded his firelock.
>
> Well, Sir, I went away wid him on me back, knapsack, firelock, and all, as strong as Sampson, for the fear I was in. An' fegs, I carried him half a league after the regiment into the Bivwack. Me back was bruck entirely from that time to this, an' it'll never get strait till I go to the Holy Well in Ireland, and have Father McShane's blessin', an' his hand laid over me! An' that's all the thruth, yer honour, I've told ye.[47]

Bell was an Irishman himself and had an obvious gift for reproducing accents in the written word! Biddy Skiddy can be heard both loud and clear.

There were many army wives who held genuine lifelong affection for the army, as did their husbands. They enjoyed the camaraderie and developed a pride in their husband's regiment, that which we now think of 'a band of brothers'. They held this affection and loyalty both inside and outside of the confines of the barrack walls and the battlefield. One such was 'Mary Major, a "widow" of the 44th Regiment of Foot [who] took on the care of another soldier's daughter – despite her own large brood – when his wife died. The girl's father was serving in North America and Major's benevolence only came to light after she found herself unable to support the girl any longer and petitioned for a place in the Royal Military asylum'.[48]

Historian Stuart Reid supplies a good evaluation of the circumstances around the numbers of wives and children accompanying their husbands and fathers:

---

47 George Bell, *Ensign George Bell in the Peninsular War: The Experiences of a Young British Soldier of the 34th Regiment 'The Cumberland Gentlemen' in the Napoleonic Wars* (Driffield: Leonaur, 2006), pp.224–225.

48 Jennine Hurl-Eamon, *Marriage & the British Army in the Long Eighteenth Century: The Girl I Left Behind Me* (Oxford: Oxford University Press, 2014), p.147.

> The only real check upon the number of women attached to an infantry battalion was the allocation of space and rations on the transports taking it to or from a foreign station. Then, and only then, could the 'six wives to a company' rule be effectively enforced. When 1/Royals sailed for Jamaica in January 1790, for example, they embarked 349 effectives in ten companies, plus 62 women and 70 children.[49]

Preparations for the embarkation of the 44th were well advanced, which brought extra duties for Serjeant Major Roworth but also some perks: 'Our Regt is almost 1000 Strong with Drafts from New Regiments … I am Kept Very Busy at present, with the Drill and other matters, But I have a good Clark to help Me [and] I have got a Man to Clean My things and to boil the Tea Kettle as well.'[50]

One can almost hear the kick it gave him to report that to his wife. Still at Nursling Camp on 13 October, the brothers, William and John, had spent two pleasurable days together and William Roworth had entrusted to his brother £1.11.6d which Mary would draw from Mr Bates once she received the letter of proof. Herein lay the foundations of a family feud! Mary did not receive the money or any further monies sent to her via John Roworth and despite multiple letters to his brother on the subject, William eventually washed his hands of his brother and cut off all further communication with him. But that is in the future, back in October 1795 he wrote:

> My Dear, what money I can save I shall give into the hands of the Pay Master of our Regiment, and my brother is to draw it from the agent in London, for which I have given John an order with my [signature] to it and he will remit money at different times to you, in my absence … I have Settled everything that Lays in my Power with John. You Must Give My Son learning … and John will take him to London. … write to John as soon as possible, and don't forget me by return of post.[51]

Roworth was most anxious that his wife and son should not be left impoverished if he should die, neither should Billy be unlettered. Roworth also continued in his personal avid thirst for advancement. He and Captain Lane, who had command of him at Chatham, back in 1786 and whose son was now a lieutenant in the 44th, spent an evening together in Southampton and 'this Day Spoke to me in the Most friendly manner Informing me, upon word and Honour, I was Not to be in the Station long, for which I have Reason to Believe there is Something going forward in My favour'.[52] How promotion called.

He and Mary exchanged locks of hair (as would have many redcoats and their loved ones) and seemingly he had come to terms with not seeing her

---

49   Stuart Reid, *British Redcoat*, p.14.
50   NA: DDRW 12/25: Roworth to Mary, Camp at Nursling Common, 9 October 1795.
51   NA: DDRW 13/25: Roworth to Mary, Nursling Camp, 13 October 1795.
52   NA: DDRW 13/25: Roworth to Mary, Nursling Camp, 13 October 1795.

again before leaving for the tropics.[53] He promised her that 'I shall always take Greatest of care of My Self In Keeping My Selfe in a Sober Steady way and to pay the Greatest Attention to my Duty as I always have Done So far.'[54]

There was one last duty before the camp broke up for embarkation – that of taking part in one of the many grand reviews of which royalty, in this case, the Prince of Wales and the Duke of York, were so particularly fond. Oldfield says that it was 'held on Nursling Common and lasted for eight hours'![55]

On 21 September the 8th, 19th, 31st, 33rd and the 42nd Foot embarked. The 29th Foot was given special treatment. They 'struck their tents and marched of[f] immediately' and onto their transports, *Sally*, *St Sebastian* and *Somerset* on 18 October, 'on account of their desertion in that regiment'.[56] All men destined for the West Indies were aware of what their fate might be – death by disease rather than action – and many took the opportunity to desert.

Many in the officer ranks, once they knew their destination was to be the tropics, in particular the West Indies, looked on such a step with horror and promptly deserted – after their fashion. They searched for ways to evade the posting – exchanging, taking a step up or sideways into another regiment if they could, or in some cases, even retiring, witness Captain Colin Campbell's wife, whose fear persuaded him to move regiments not once, but twice to avoid such a posting.

Because of the purchase system many of the officers of the time were in a position to do this. But for the private men, once they were on the transport there was nothing they could do (apart from jumping overboard) but pray for preservation on their destined island. Reid gives the example of the 130th Foot, who were '… literally wiped out by Yellow Fever on San Domingo: on 1 November 1795 [the regiment] had mustered 166 rank and file fit for duty; exactly a month later it had just seven, with a further 11 in hospital'.[57] The others had died.

Back at camp, while waiting its turn to embark, the 44th Foot received the new issue of round hats and short jackets – the serjeants with loops and a girdle round the crown 'which looks very well'.[58] Knowing it would not be long before they embarked Roworth wrote what he assumed would be his final letter before leaving Britain, sending his love to his parents and extended family and a kiss to his son. Many redcoats would do the same thing or ask a friend to do it for them if they were not able to write.

The 44th marched down the road from Nursling Common Camp for embarkation at Southampton. Then came that part of the embarkation which was always fraught with emotion and sadness for the majority of redcoats, their wives and their children, waiting to find out which of the women were to go with them. They gathered on the quayside that, for many, would be the last time they ever saw and touched each other again. For those left behind

---

53 It is thought that the lock of light brown hair held in the Roworth archive in Nottingham is probably that of Serjeant Major William Roworth.
54 NA: DDRW 13/25: Roworth to Mary, Nursling Camp, 13 October 1795.
55 Oldfield, 'From Spa to Garrison Town', pp.4–5.
56 NA: DDRW 14/25: Roworth to Mary, Nursling Camp, 22 October 1795.
57 Reid, *British Redcoat*, p.5.
58 NA: DDRW 14/25: Roworth to Mary, Nursling, 22 October 1795.

most would have no source of monetary security; in short, the families were often destitute without the army, and their futures bleak. That future was put to the ballot. Small pieces of paper were placed into a hat or ballot box with 'to go' or 'not to go' written on them. When a woman's name was called, she then took a piece of paper from the box and read the fate of herself and her children. The result for the majority on the quayside was stark – 'Not to go'.[59] The consequences could be probable starvation; maybe even prostitution to keep the children fed; or the stark realities of the workhouse.

It was a great pity that Mary Roworth's letters did not survive, to explain the reasoning and circumstances that precluded her and Little Billy from being among the numbers bidding farewell – even if the decision not to ballot for a place was already agreed between them. Busy though he was, Roworth must have felt devastated by it. Mary loved him enough to keep his letters. She met him in Dartford when he joined the transports for the Continent in 1794. But not this time. Whatever the cause, Mary and Billy were not there.

Once the human lottery was over, overwhelmed by the screams and tears of so many women and children, the redcoats waited out the days before their ships sailed.

Even allowing for a generous length of time on furlough, it seems unlikely that in Roworth's eight and a half years, or so, of marriage, he would have been with his family for not much more than six months. Throughout his letters he displays that uneasiness, anxiety, unhappiness, concern and effort as the various aspects of his life – family and duty in particular – pull at him. Duties weigh heavily and are his repeated excuses for not writing more often. The anxieties pointed out by Patterson are only too apparent in those 25 letters Roworth wrote home over the course of two years, although this is purely speculative, of course, and strictly subjective. The Roworth letters require reading in toto to become aware of all the nuances within.

So, when compared with Patterson's cold light of day summation of married soldiers, it would appear that Serjeant Major Roworth was a fair example of how Patterson perceived the constraints of marriage within the day-to-day functioning of the army. However, though his writings represent him as a troubled man, Roworth must have been able to compartmentalise his dealings with the 44th Foot, if he was to be an effective leader. Indeed the serjeants of the 44th appear to have done a fairly good job of it, particularly in the light of those complimentary observations made by the people of Whitehaven who praised the regiment for its good order and discipline;[60] the people of Leeds for the 'attentions of the men belonging to the 44th Regiment of Foot' who helped save life and belongings at a fire at a ropery;[61] the people of Tynemouth for their 'truly meritorious conduct upon the inhabitants' and 'the great regulation of the military discipline established in that corps'.[62] Maybe not such 'bad boys' after all.

---

59   Annabel Venning, *Following the Drum: The Lives of Army Wives and Daughters Past and Present* (London: Headline, 2005), p.28.
60   *The Cumberland Pacquet and Ware's Whitehaven Advertiser*, Wednesday 28 July 1790.
61   *Leeds Intelligencer*, Tuesday 28 October 1788.
62   *Newcastle Courant*, Saturday 23 May 1789.

10

Tragedy in the Channel: Like Nothing in the World

'Twer the great sea itself rose up level like - and come on right over the ridge and all, like nothing in the world'[1]

Britain in the eighteenth century saw many storms, some of huge proportions. The greatest of them was the storm of the night of 26–27 November 1703. It is still the greatest storm in recorded history ever to have hit southern Britain. There was huge loss of property, with many churches and public buildings damaged or destroyed and many ships sunk; vast areas of flooding on land caused the death of thousands of animals. Herbert Lamb and Knud Frydendahl wrote, 'It is estimated that one-third of all seamen in the navy, some ten thousand men were lost on the night of the storm.'[2]

Ninety-two years later in 1795, a stormy October and November presaged a nasty winter. Another hurricane that wreaked havoc, especially in the Channel, became infamous as 'Admiral Christian's Gales'. A British fleet, commanded by Rear Admiral Hugh Cloberry Christian, was gathering together off the Mother Bank outside St Helen's on the Isle of Wight, in the Solent and at Spithead, ready for their voyage to the West Indies.[3]

Christian, whose ancestors came from the Isle of Man, had already had a taste of the West Indies, serving there from 1779 to 1782. In this latest fleet to be despatched, Christian had overall command, with Rear Admiral Charles Pole as his deputy. Christian was working at the newly-formed Transport Board, when his next appointment was ordered. So, he was intimately involved with the fleet for this command, and he raised his flag on board the *Prince George* on 15 September 1795.[4] The troops to be carried in the transports were

---

1   Dorset eyewitness to the 1824 storm surge over the Chesil Beach at Fleet, <https://wessexcoastgeology.soton.ac.uk/chestorm.htm>, accessed July 2023.

2   Herbert Lamb and Knud Frydendahl, *Historic Storms of the North Sea, British Isles and Northwest Europe* (Cambridge: Cambridge University Press, 1991), p.59.

3   TNA: CO 318/18: Christian to Huskisson, Prince George at sea, Recapitulation of Tonnage and Troops embarked, 15 November 1795. p.171. For further reading and history of HMS Glory see William Dillon, *A Narrative of my Professional Adventures, 1790–1839* (Abingdon: Navy Records Society, 1953), p.208.

4   TNA: CO 318/18; Boult, *Christian's Fleet*, p.53.

under the command Major General Ralph Abercromby, an elderly but well respected general.⁵ He was a man of integrity, who had refused to be part of the war with America from 1775 to 1783, but when France declared war on Britain 10 years later, he felt that he could play a positive role. Nearing his 60th birthday, he had left retirement to support the Duke of York and the Allies on the Continent – though with mixed results. Many of the troops in this expedition would have remembered him from Flanders. But now he had been asked to command the army in the West Indies. He and Christian got on well together and appreciated each other's personal skills and abilities.

It was the work of various boards, the Navy, Transport, Victualling, Ordnance and Army Medical Boards to co-ordinate and co-operate in all the necessary logistics for the fleet. At board level all was achieved by writing letters! Not only written but copied multiple times – for administration purposes and therefore for posterity. While ships of the line, frigates, cutters, brigs, store-ships and gunboats were in preparation, letters were flying backwards and forwards between Christian and the secretaries at the War Office, between Christian and the Admiralty, Christian and the Port Admiral, Christian and Dundas, Christian and myriad suppliers. Letters of command came from His Majesty, requiring action at 'His Majesty's pleasure', some concerning great affairs of state down to the health of those troops gathering from all corners of Britain, readying themselves for their next service in the West Indies.

From the outset Christian was plagued by the usual difficulties presented by fitting out, in this case, the largest fleet ever to be sailed from Britain – in essence two fleets, one assembling at Portsmouth, the other at Cork. The logistics must have been a nightmare. The infrastructure was available, but the difficulties of gathering together the number of ships were vast, including hiring the transports from private owners and then equipping and victualling them. Added to which the matériel to supply, equip and support an army performing its service several thousand miles distant would prove another formidable task. That army of thousands of men, once on land, would continue to need the flow of uninterrupted supplies to continue for – maybe – years. The project was to take many months of the most meticulous planning that the various boards involved could provide. A fleet of the size necessary for the expedition proposed, took many months to get ready to sail.

Take a single naval ship like HMS *Colossus*, Captain Henry Jenkins, 74 guns, which had a large crew of about 640. The officers and petty officers she required included a captain, seven lieutenants, a master and second master, one each of a surgeon, carpenter, boatswain, gunner and purser, an assistant surgeon, with three master's mates, and 16 midshipmen. Some 30-odd men with skilled occupations would also be required, ranging from clerks to caulkers, cooks to chaplain, sailmakers to schoolmaster, steward to gunner's mate. Added to that was the complement of marines including its captain, two subalterns, two sergeants, three corporals, one drummer and 98 privates.⁶

---

5   Abercromby held the local rank of lieutenant general on the continent but would have reverted to major general on his return to Britain.
6   Bryan Lavery, *Nelson's Navy. The Ships, Men and Organisation, 1793–1815* (London: Conway Maritime Press, 2013), pp.328–330.

Provisioning just this one ship was a momentous task, comparable to supplying a small twenty-first-century cruise ship with sufficient food, drink, bedding, and so on, for up to, say, three months, but without the constant fresh daily supply and with none of today's modern conveniences. The fare for sailors and troops was somewhat different, too; casks of water, bread (actually a very hard biscuit, renowned for its weevils), rum, small beer, casks of salted beef and pork (often many years old and rotten and passed from ship to ship), vegetables, livestock (pigs, sheep, chickens, ducks) for fresh meat en route, a cow for fresh milk. A veritable floating city inside wooden walls. This was to be the largest convoyed British fleet ever organised on that scale up to that time. Multiply this particular 74-gun vessel three times over, the *Colossus* plus *Irresistible* and *Alfred*; add one vessel – the *Commerce de Marseilles*, formerly of 128 guns but now only carrying 50, intended to carry 900 of the 57th Foot, over and above the crew; two vessels of 98 guns, *Prince George* and *Impregnable*; three of 64 guns – *Polyphemus*, *Lion* and *Trident*; one of 38, *Undaunted*; one of 36, *Leda*; one of 32, *Alcemene*; one of 28, *La Prompte*; one of 22, *Babet*; one of 16, *Albacore*; one armed brig, *Requin*, and four gunboats of eight guns – *L'Eclair*, *Crachefeu*, *Terror* and *Vesuve*.[7]

Multiply all the logistics above, but in differing proportions to the 21 ships of war, with 133 transports, some of which would carry troops, others the baggage, clothing, horses, victuals, water, rum, forage, cannons, ammunition and gunpowder, and even horseshoes.

Many ships would arrive in Britain from the West Indies needing to be fumigated, before they could be turned around, re-fitted, stocked up and sent on their way again. All took time, as a report from the Transport Office demonstrated, concerning extra hazards:

> Twenty five Sail of Transports have arrived from the West Indies … but the precaution was taken, that Those Transports should be placed as they arrived in the River Thames, distinct from all others; a Process of Fumigation, under the particular direction of Sir Jerome Fitzpatrick, M.D was directed; and the time allowed for their cleansing exceeded four Weeks. These Transports were then refitted and supplied with new Beds, Provisions, and every other Article; and not till then considered as fit for Service.[8]

With reference to all things medical Rear Admiral Christian received a report dated 25 September 1795, from the Medical Officers, J. Johnston and T. Trotter at the Royal Hospital at Haslar in Gosport, concerning a physician and hospital ship to accompany the fleet because of the concerns of illness and death in such a climate. Among the suggestions of the 'sub-joined heads' of the doctors were the breakfast and dinner diet, antiscorbutics, additional medicines which the doctors could not provide themselves, transports for convalescents, and appropriate liquids for convalescing patients.[9]

---

7   Boult, *Christian's Fleet*, Appendix 6, p.130.
8   TNA: WO 1/798: Transport Office, War Department In-Letters, 2 February 1795, p.291.
9   Julian S. Corbett, (ed.), *Private Papers of George, second Earl Spencer First Lord of the Admiralty* (London: Elibron Classics Replica Edition, 2005), vol.1, pp.151–152.

The antiscorbutics were prescribed for scurvy – a constant anxiety on board a ship (whether soldier or sailor) when fresh fruit and vegetables had a limited life. The longer the journey the more likelihood of scurvy unless the right antiscorbutics were on hand. Scurvy was nasty and caused by a lack of vitamin C. Sufferers had purple bleeding gums and teeth which were loose. Their eyes bulged and their hair became dry and easily damaged, while dry scaly skin turned brown and bruised easily. The first sign was often exhaustion. The symptoms were so severe that the above letter was a result of a board of military and medical officers which was set up at the suggestion of the War Office, to discuss methods of preserving the health of the troops at sea. Consequently, large amounts of port wine, portable soup, sugar rice and pearl barley and 'sour crout' were included in the inventory.[10]

Another antiscorbutic was loaded on board, essence of spruce which could be made into beer. James Hume at Falmouth Customs House was given prior warning of the delivery by wagon of 'fifty-two cases of the essence, each Case containing thirty Pound of Essence in 6 Jars, intended for the use of H.M's Forces'. Eight cases were to go to St Domingo and Martinico, while Jamaica, Antigua, St Kitts, St Lucia, Barbados, Grenada, Tobago and St Vincent were limited to four cases each.[11] It was an acquired taste but was quite acceptable to many on both sides of the Atlantic.

Christian had raised his flag on the *Prince George*, on 15 September, at Spithead. At the end of the month, Captain John Schank, one of the Transport Commissioners, was concerned by the complaints of Dr Hayes to Abercromby, specifically about the filthy conditions of some of the transports. Together with Colonel Gilman, Sir Jerome Fitzpatrick and the agents, Schank inspected those boats complained of by the doctor. His considered opinion was that some of the officers' berths had not been white-washed and some of the bedding on the *Marquis of Carmarthen* had not been changed. So, he replaced the *Marquis* with the *Rambler* (to be used by the Inniskillings) and ordered the former to be cleaned by the crew to be ready for 10 o'clock the next morning.[12]

Everything had to be accomplished with 'expediency', a frequently used word in both naval and military circles. By 29 October Dr Pinckard was reporting 'It has been stormy and tempestuous beyond all that is usual, even, at the roughest season of the year. On the 29th instant, it blew a perfect hurricane … unlike all that we are accustomed in England'.[13]

Around this time, Admiral Laforey, in the Caribbean, gave warning of 'a most malignant fever'. His flagship, *Majestic,* had lost 110 men to it and he was doing all he could to improve conditions on the ship by 'fumigating, washing with hot vinegar and whitewashing with lime' throughout.[14] This emphasis

---

10   TNA: WO 6/147: Letters to Public Departments, Admiralty, pp.61–62, 12 Nov 1794.
11   TNA: WO 4/338: War Office, Secretary of War, Out-letters, p.447.
12   TNA: WO 1/798: Letter from John Schank, Transport Office, 29 September 1795, p.481.
13   George Pinckard, *Notes on the West Indies: Written during the Expedition, Under the Command of the Late General Sir Ralph Abercromby* (London: Longman, Hurst, Rees, and Orme, 1806), pp.64–65.
14   TNA: ADM 1/317: Laforey to Nepean, on board *Majestic,* 1 October 1795, quoted in Boult, *Christian's Fleet,* p.59.

TRAGEDY IN THE CHANNEL: LIKE NOTHING IN THE WORLD

on cleaning and fumigating was believed to counteract those various diseases common to large communities of people, be they on land or sea. The War Office took it so seriously that, on 10 October 1795, they issued a series of regulations 'to be observed by troops embarked in transports for service abroad, particularly by those designed for the West Indies' – given out by His Majesty's Command and signed by Secretary at War, William Windham.[15] The first part was aimed at preventing fire on board ship. The second part covered fumigation, cleanliness and the sick and covered those three points in much greater detail, but clearly and with obvious good intention.

Transports were coming in on a regular basis, which not only needed to refit, but which had fever on board and so first required the statutory quarantine of 40 days, not far off six weeks. The Transport Office had a list of transports which had come in from the West Indies and were currently in quarantine, having recently arrived at Plymouth. The *Atlantic* 'has a party of the 25th on board', while *Hope*, *Monmouth* and *Planter* carried 'Invalids and French prisoners'. *Thetis* arrived in Portsmouth carrying 54 invalids.[16] The Transport Office requested the release of these ships for refit. There were two ships called *Hope*, in this group, which were refitted – one embarked the 55th on 26 October, the other the 88th on 3 November, while *Planter* was fitted out as a hospital ship.[17]

The beady eyes and pricked ears of the local newspaper reporters garnished information from wherever they could. The *Hampshire Chronicle*, being at the centre of all things naval could, with a degree of certainty, trumpet the regiments at Southampton which were believed to be destined for the West Indies. On 10 October 1795 they included the 2nd, 3rd, 8th, 19th, 25th, 29th, 31st, 33rd, 37th, 38th, 42rd, 44th, 48th, 53rd, 55th, 63nd and 92nd Foot.[18]

It had taken months of frenetic preparation to fit out the fleet, its accompanying convoy and its loudly trumpeted 200 plus ships and transports, but this number was always an approximation. Boult tells us that there never was a categorical list of ships. Christian himself claimed 133 to Huskisson, as mentioned above. Nevertheless, the War Office was awash with papers listing various ships, destined for Christian's fleet, on a multitude of different dates and for a variety of purposes and offices.

One such document (with specific reference to the 44th Regiment) headed 'West India Troop Ships on Freight' provided a sample of tonnage, numbers of men, unfinished tasks and timings of readiness for just six transports:

> *Trelawney Planter*, 300 tons burthen, [already] carrying 150 44th Regt on board – when removed will be ready to receive the Foreign Corps; *Amelia*, 270 tons burthen, 150 of the 55th Regt, wants 25 tons [of] water; *Prince of Wales*, 245 tons, 123 [troops], In Harbour – will be ready tomorrow; *Guernsey Lilley*, 218 tons, 110 [troops], will be ready in about ten days; *Eastridge*, 300 tons, 150 [of the] 44th Regt

---

15 War Office, *Regulations to be observed by troops for service abroad, particularly for those designed for the West Indies* (London: War Office 1795).
16 TNA: WO 1/799: War Department In-Letters, 22 September 1796, Transport Office, p.371.
17 Boult, *Christian's Fleet*, pp.131–132.
18 *Hampshire Chronicle*, Saturday 10 October 1795.

on board – when removed will be ready to receive Foreign Corps [Lowenstein's]; *Generous Planter*, 280 tons, 140 [troops on board] wants to compleat water and will be ready on Wednesday.[19]

From this document there is early warning that 300 redcoats of the 44th currently split between two transports, 150 on board of the *Estridge*, another 150 on board the *Trelawney Planter*, were to be removed onto other transports and replaced with Löwenstein's Chasseurs, one of the foreign regiments in British pay. It was not immediately obvious which transports were then allocated for those 300 troops of the 44th turned out at short notice and also begs the question as to where 300 surplus redcoats were to go while other transports were found for them. Back under canvas at Nursling, perhaps?

The same document listed 12 'Coppered Transports' with numbers of troops fitted for, and ready to receive them; yet a further list of 15 'Common Transports at Spithead & Cowes' included, for example: the *Derwent* – fitted for 123 troops – had been 'separated from the Cork Fleet – 56th Regt on board – several sick, may be ready in 7 days'; the *Mary* – fitted out for 124 troops – 'may be ready in ten days and wants a new main mast & other repairs'; the *Rambler* – 're-caulking, may be ready in 14 days; the *St Mary's Planter* 'wants to be laid on the ways – time uncertain,' in other words she needed attention in the ship yard. She would eventually take part of the 27th Foot, with the *Rambler*.[20]

Of five 'Common Transports at Cowes', the first four 'are under the Shipwright's hands – time uncertain'; *Success*, a hospital ship, 'will be ready in seven days, except what alterations may be made ... by the Inspector'. The results of the inspection might put the ship's readiness back days or even weeks. Of the 10 transports at Southampton – four were ready to receive troops, three were being fitted for cavalry, three others would be ready in seven days and the *Thetis* would be ready in '3 days except for taking on her Hospital Stores'.[21] And so it went on. So many 'maybes,' 'times uncertain' and 'will be,' 'would be,' 'are ready', or 'except'. A clear demonstration of the monumental difficulties involved. Regular mention of 'contrary winds' added to the uncertain mix.

Another constant was the concern of a major sickness in the troops breaking out on board the transports. Sir Jerome Fitzpatrick was one of a number of medical men who advocated a variety of schemes to prevent 'the spread of sickness among troops while on board transports'. His approach 'was to separate the sick from healthy men as much as possible. Upon the first appearance of any acute infection the diseased men were removed into the hospital ship accompanying the fleet'.[22] The same paper stated that the use of a monthly application of whitewash between decks reduced the spread of disease. Probably the only thing to have stopped a sickness from spreading

---

19 TNA: CO 318/18: Secretary of State, Naval Despatches, p.309.
20 TNA: CO 318/18: Secretary of State, Naval Despatches, p.309.
21 TNA: CO 318/18: Secretary of State, Naval Despatches, p.309
22 Mary Ellen Condon, *The Administration of the Transport Service During the War against Revolutionary France, 1793–1802* (University of London, PhD Thesis, 1968), p.107.

TRAGEDY IN THE CHANNEL: LIKE NOTHING IN THE WORLD

would be total isolation of each individual – sick or otherwise. This was an impossibility in a confined space such as a ship, where the men would be sleeping in berths and hammocks, the latter just 18 inches apart. Little chance of that socially-distancing of two metres (so familiar to the world during the pandemic of the early 2020s), so disease would spread like wildfire.

While the troops were on board the transports they were subject to military, not to naval discipline. Specifically, an order made by the Duke of York became public. This was to the effect that 'regular troops serving on board men-of-war shall not be subject to naval discipline; but, in case of any misbehaviour, "they are to be put on board on some other ship or vessel, if any should be in company, and tried upon their arrival in port". This order is taken up in a serious point of view by all the navy; and it is thought it will meet with a unanimous opposition.'[23] The navy bristled at the instruction, presumably it was felt (by the navy) that any misdemeanour on board a ship of war – whoever committed it – should be dealt with by the navy. The Duke of York was adamant. It was fortunate for both soldiers and sailors heading for the West Indies that their two commanders, Abercromby and Christian had developed such a good personal relationship. It appeared that common sense prevailed and when the time came for the expedition to take its leave of Britain. 'It was decided to ignore the regulations and trust to the temper and right headedness of the army and navy commanders.'[24] That good relationship bore positive fruit throughout the whole of the expedition to the West Indies of 1795–1796.

The first of the troops were embarked as early as the third week in October. Often troops were on board their transports for three or four weeks or longer before any possible sailing. This brought difficulties of its own. What did hundreds of men do, bobbing up and down for weeks on end in sight of land, while they waited for their transports to set sail? The only positive might be that some of them got their sea-legs. With the possibility of sea-sickness even at anchor, the first responsibility of any army officer would be to keep his company busy and active where possible, much of which would be exactly what the soldiers did in barracks; cleaning themselves, their uniforms, equipment and their sleeping environment – and exercise. Historian Mary Ellen Condon tells us that the troops were divided into three watches, with one watch upon deck at all times. This helped the troops themselves as both sickness through disease was less likely and the crowding below decks was eased. The army officers, non-commissioned officers and the soldiers took their 'watch', or shift, as they did on shore, but the timings would echo those of the navy. Any soldier on deck, of whatever rank, would be ready for any duty required of them by the naval officers, should the need arise.

After breakfast the troops were kept on deck between 8:00 a.m. and 10:00 a.m. for cleaning purposes, both of their persons and of their quarters, including attention to shoes and clothes. This was followed by a daily inspection by their own officers and the ship's commanding officer. They were paraded at 10:00 a.m. and were then allowed to go below deck.

---

23 *Hampshire Chronicle*, Saturday 7 November 1795.
24 Condon, *Transport Service*, pp.156–157.

Clothes washing took up one day per week. Wet washing was hung in the shrouds to dry. On wash day, the troops assembled at the head of the ship, each company by squads. The ships must have resembled laundries. The oiling and cleaning of accoutrements took place twice weekly, followed by company inspection. These activities came under the aegis of the non-commissioned officers, so serjeants and corporals would be kept busy.

On 23 October, Christian let rip to William Huskisson at the War Office, concerning one of the most important parts of the convoy and that was the non-appearance of all the ordnance transports, carrying the artillery and ammunition amongst other stores. 'D..n the ordnance' – the words nearly bounced off the paper 'I cannot help making this exclamation altho' it is not Xtian like'.[25]

A different tone was used on 26 October as he imparted some good news to Huskisson: 'I have the pleasure to tell you that the two Bat: of Grenadiers the 42nd, the third and the 19th have embarked this Day … the 33rd will embark early in the morning.'[26] On 28 October more frustration was apparent: 'This uncommon weather has checked our instructions of the Day, & it has been impracticable to Embark [the] Men.'[27]

Historian Edwina Boult gives the final embarkation day for the 33rd, onto the *Sullivan* and *Sir Edward Hughes*, both East Indiamen, as 2 November, at Gosport. Both these vessels sailed on 16 November and were caught in the hurricane, both lost their mizen masts and limped back to Portland to wait the storm out. On the second attempt of sailing on 9 December the 33rd Foot was not with the convoy. The regiment had been removed from the fleet and sent to Lymington where it remained until February 1796. On the 30 March following, the men marched from Poole to Portsmouth, under the command of Lieutenant Colonel the Hon. Arthur Wesley, where he left them and from where they sailed, stopping over in Cape Town, before sailing onward to India. Wesley rejoined them in South Africa for the final leg.[28] The removal of the 33rd from the West India fleet must surely be another of those 'what if?' moments. What if the 33rd had been successful in reaching the West Indies at the first attempt? What if Wesley had died of yellow fever? Would Waterloo (or its equivalent) have been a failure for the British? Would it have even happened? It was Wellington who chose the battlefield after all.

It needed a strong admiral to cope with the vagaries of politicians, the Admiralty itself, the army, the shipyards, the butchers, the bakers, the candlestick makers and the ordnance office, to say the least. Add wind, tides and weather into the mix and that could make the situation positively explosive. There were several stormy weeks while the fleet was preparing. Christian, writing to Huskisson on 6 November, spoke of: 'The violent gale of last Night has increased our difficulty, one Transport (the *Elizabeth*) has been sunk … others driven on Shore, some damage of inferior Moment sustained

---

25   TNA: CO 318/18: Secretary of State, Naval Despatches, 23 October 1795, p.91.
26   TNA: CO 318/18: Secretary of State, Naval Despatches, 26 October 1795, p.99.
27   TNA: CO 318/18: Secretary of State, Naval Despatches, 28 October 1795, p.107.
28   Brereton & Savory, *Wellington's Regiment*, p.96.

TRAGEDY IN THE CHANNEL: LIKE NOTHING IN THE WORLD

by others'.[29] This while they were still at anchor! There appear to have been four transports named *Elizabeth* sailing with the fleet during the multiple attempts to reach the West Indies: firstly, the above-mentioned which sank on 6 November; secondly, the vessel carrying the 27th; thirdly, that carrying the 28th; fourthly, the *Elizabeth* carrying the 37th.[30]

On that Friday morning, 6 November 1795, a most tremendous gale of wind arose at about 2:00 a.m. The *Hampshire Chronicle* described the storm as 'more dreadful and terrifying than any thing of the kind that has happened for many years'.[31] Worse was to come.

On Wednesday 11 November there was another attempt to get out into the Channel. The weather was fine with a fair wind but HMS *Impregnable*, 98 guns, damaged her rudder on a sand bank and the fleet was ordered to return again. It was on this occasion that the transport *Stanley*, carrying part of the 48th Foot was 'unaware of the signal' to return and sailed on to be the first to reach Barbados – on Christmas Day, a voyage of 44 days. Lucky them, as it transpired.

What of Roworth and the 44th during those days and weeks of flux and uncertainty? In the 18 days since his last letter to Mary, he embarked, first on the *Boddington* at Southampton and then changed to the *Julius* – 'I have been tossed from ship to ship. My time has been employed so much on the Regiments Business.' The up-to-strength 44th was divided between *Julius*, *Boddington*, *Marion (Mary Ann)*, *Trelawney* and *Estridge*. Three hundred men who had embarked already, split equally between the last two transports, had been removed, as we have already seen. Roworth's 15th letter, dated 9 November, placed the *Julius* at the Mother Bank, a shallow sandbank some three miles from Portsmouth and a mile from the Isle of Wight. It was deep enough for vessels to moor there without going aground and was near to the town of Ryde. 'There is one Captain Baily Commands … this ship and His Lady Came on Board this Day. The Reason I am on board Here [is that] he applied to the Colonel for Me …'[32] That would have been Captain George Bayley, of the 44th, new to the regiment, having been promoted to captain lieutenant in the 78th in May 1795, and then promoted to captain in the 44th in September. The state of the 44th is recorded on the Monthly Return for 1 November 1795, taken at Southampton and on different transports on the South River.

State of the 44th Foot, monthly return, Southampton, 1 November 1795.[33]

Present					Rank & File					Number Wanting		
Officers	Staff	QM	Sjt	Drum	Present	Sick	On Com'd	Other	Total	Sjt	Drum	R&F
23	5	1	51	14	635	34	80	8	757	-	-	433

---

29 TNA: CO 318/18: Secretary of State, Naval Despatches, 6 November 1795, p.139.
30 Boult, *Christian's Fleet*, Appendix 6, pp.131–132.
31 *Hampshire Chronicle*, Saturday 7 November 1795.
32 NA: DDRW 15/25: Roworth to Mary Roworth, 9 November 1795.
33 TNA: WO 17/155: Return, 1 November 1795.

Interestingly, other than the precipitate exodus of Lieutenant Colonel Colin Campbell on his return from Flanders and Peter MacNamara who moved to the 39th, there appear to have been no other flights from the 44th. Most movements were inside the regiment in the forms of promotion. It appears that William Iremonger was made captain from outside of the regiment. Lieutenant Kersopp retired, but then, according to the army list, changed his mind, only to retire again in 1797. Three lieutenants, George Robert Stoney, Ramsey Ogilvie and John Wright, had died and their places were filled within the regiment, by Ensigns Thomas Legge, Adam Ogilvie and John Fernandez. Serjeant McCabe was made quartermaster, succeeding the dead Thomas Gardner.[34]

A trying time for all the regiments, noisy, smelly, chaotic, and colourful in the extreme. Living conditions on board *Julius* were very different to barracks and required both physical and mental adjustment, particularly with the damp and often heaving decks. Settling into any kind of routine was difficult for every redcoat and his regiment.

The letter Roworth wrote on 9 November was the usual mix of news but this one demonstrated a real fear of not returning, as all the troops departing must have felt. Rumour, stories and more personal tales about those who had not returned, were common knowledge. Many of the fevers found in the West Indies were known to the soldiers by other names, for example, the most commonly feared was yellow fever which was also called 'yellow jack, black vomit (for obvious reasons) and bulam fever'.[35] At that time malaria was referred to as intermittent fever and the cause of the disease was not discovered for another hundred years by a young medical officer, Ronald Ross in 1897. Others mortal diseases were dysentery and typhus but the endemic trio were malaria, dysentery and yellow fever, the latter killing the largest numbers. Those who died from wounds in the West Indies were only a fraction of those who died of endemic diseases.

On Sunday 15 November, Rear Admiral Christian wrote Huskisson at the War Office, reporting the actual numbers of vessels and tonnage of the fleet ready to sail with the words 'You have not been correctly informed respecting the Transport or the Tonnage. I therefore transmit you an accurate return'. He gave the number of ships to sail as 133. The tonnage as 35,151 tons. The number of men was 18,740.[36] The decision was taken by Christian, to make weigh and sail on that day, 15 November 1795, although the awaited ordnance had still not made an appearance, but 'conditions were right, with a north north-easterly wind, backing to north'.[37] Slowly the whole fleet got underway and as 'darkness fell they passed the Needles … and *Alcemene* was signalled to keep ahead during the night and look out'.[38]

---

34 TNA: WO 65/46: Army List 1796
35 Tom Scotland, *Sir James McGrigor: The Adventurous Life of Wellington's Chief Medical Officer* (Warwick: Helion & Company Ltd, 2021), p.39.
36 TNA: CO 318/18: Christian to Huskisson, *Prince George* at St Helens under sail 15 November 1795, from Boult, *Christian's Fleet*, p.134.
37 Boult, *Christian's Fleet*, p.59.
38 TNA: ADM 1/317: Ship's log, Monday 16 November, from Boult, *Christian's Fleet*, p.62.

Dawn on Monday 16 November saw the fleet heading west in 'a light north-westerly breeze' although Christian noted an uncertain sky. By 2:00 a.m. on the 17th, the weather had turned decidedly squally and HMS *Babet* (22) 'was signalled to keep ahead during the night and carry a light'.[39] When daylight dawned the wind shifted to the south-south-west, which prevented most of the ships from sailing the last crucial 10 miles into the safety of Torquay's sheltered harbour, so they were forced to put about for Portsmouth and shelter. Only 10 made it into Torbay.

As the squalls increased Christian made the decision to seek shelter in Torbay, but the storm strengthened during the next 24 hours. Only two miles from Torbay the hurricane winds drove him to return to St Helens. Christian was forced to admit that the force of the storms were the worst he had ever experienced. Captain Thomas Drury of HMS *Alfred* knew on the 17th that he could not make Torbay in the storm force winds and had headed for Portland, taking with him 'the infantry transports Hope [55th or 88th], Sally [29th Foot], Lady Jane [28th], victuallers Marquis of Worcester, Fanny, Enterprise, ordnance transports Firm and Harmony, cavalry transport Patty, hospital ship Juba and the West Indiaman General Cuyler'.[40] A good decision, as it transpired.

Meanwhile, incredibly, convoys bringing transports were still arriving from the Continent, with foreign troops and cavalry on board. Urgent letters were flying to and fro concerning the condition of those transports, which required fitting out for their journey to the West Indies. The horses needed to be landed in order to do this and the commissioners for transports needed reassurance of the legality of landing Foreign troops on shore. The King took matters into his own hands and the following orders came before the House of Commons and was reported upon on 12 December 1795:

> His Majesty thinks proper to acquaint the House of Commons that a considerable division of ships, having on-board foreign troops in the service of Great Britain, having been dispersed and damaged, while on their passage from the rivers Elbe and Weser to Spithead, the place of rendezvous appointed for the convoy under which it was intended they should be sent on distant foreign service, His Majesty has found it necessary to order the said troops to be disembarked, and to be stationed in barracks near Southampton, and in the Isle of Wight; and at the same time has given directions that they shall be reimbarked, and sent to the place of their destination, as soon as the transports necessary for their accommodation and conveyance shall be in readiness to receive them, the necessary orders for that purpose having by His Majesty's command already been given.[41]

Dundas acquired permission for them to be 'put on Shore either at Gravesend or at Southampton or at any other place in the River, where they can be disembarked with safety and Expedition, instead of waiting till the tide will

---

39 TNA: ADM 1/317: Ship's log, 17 November, from Boult, *Christian's Fleet*, p.63
40 Boult, *Christian's Fleet*, p.65.
41 *Hampshire Chronicle*, Saturday 12 December 1795.

admit of their being landed at Blackwall'.[42] In the meantime the gales had caused difficulties for HMS *Arethusa* and HMS *Concorde* which had arrived in Plymouth as convoy to a number of transports from Quiberon Bay, which contained troops from various émigré units.[43]

Some men had the good luck to miss the storm. Surgeon James McGrigor had been embarked with the 88th on the *Jamaica* transport, waiting for the fleet to sail in Portsmouth. His services were required on another ship to examine a number of men in levies drafted into the embarking corps. Having completed this service to the new levy which he found to be of 'very indifferent materials' he was too late to get back to the *Jamaica*. The signal to sail was made by the great guns and despite hiring a sloop to find his transport, McGrigor finally sailed on the *Betsey*, officially carrying the 37th (though McGrigor says 48th) and that he was 'most hospitably treated' by them. He saw 'very few ships in sight' and 'they were much ahead of us' and they never caught up with them. He claimed that the journey was quite short and the wind was favourable and that the *Betsey* made it to Carlisle Bay in about six weeks, expecting to see 'the whole of the fleet there before us'. He continued: 'The truth was, the *Betsey* was the only transport of the West India expedition that had arrived … It was later realised that the signal had been for those of the Mediterranean vessels only.' The frigates were sent after the West India fleet 'and brought back every one of them, but the *Betsey*.'[44] There is an anomaly in this claim as both the *Betsey* and the *Stanley* claimed to have been the first into Carlisle Bay. Interestingly, Dr George Pinckard, claimed in his 3 February letter from Barbados, that 'the *Stanley*, [carrying the 48th Regiment] which has sailed with the first fleet in November, and was supposed to have been lost, during the disastrous storm which arose in the channel, had arrived safe in Carlisle Bay, on Christmas Day, being the only ship of the November convoy that made good her passage'.[45] He added that 'nine or ten of the December convoy had [also] reached Barbados in safety, with upwards of two thousand troops on board'.

Over the succeeding weeks and months, the rest of the fleet dribbled in, but the *Jamaica* (with McGrigor's brother on board) had been captured by the French. James himself was believed to have already died as no-one had seen him since early on the morning of that misunderstood signal, together with the fact that an officer had been seen that morning crushed between two ships and it was generally thought to have been McGrigor. As the ships arrived McGrigor was able to serve under the Inspector General of Hospitals and was of obvious use to him, although he commented that 'Mr [Thomas] Young … was a rigid officer and a strict disciplinarian'.[46]

There were many other complicated journeys undertaken, by officers in particular, to reach their appointed positions; in some cases aided by the fleet's delay. One of these was another doctor, George Pinckard who, on

---

42 TNA: WO 6/156: Commissioners of Transport, 17–18 November 1795, p.134.
43 *Hampshire Chronicle*, Saturday 28 November 1795.
44 McGrigor, *Autobiography*, p.51.
45 Pinckard, *Notes on the West Indies*, vol.1, p.225.
46 McGrigor, *Autobiography*, p.53.

TRAGEDY IN THE CHANNEL: LIKE NOTHING IN THE WORLD

5 October was in Southampton, where he joined the army having been appointed a physician to the forces, then obtained 'leave of absence to go to London'. In London, by 9 October:

> [We] found our names upon the list of the St Domingo staff … [and] are now directed to proceed in the *Ulysses*, armed transport, to Cork, to join the expedition under major-general Whyte. But as this ship is now in the Thames, and is to touch at Spithead on her way, it will give us a few days to prepare our baggage, and instead of going round with her by sea, we can put our things on board and meet the vessel in Portsmouth.[47]

Ten days later, Pinckard was in Southampton again where, 'we have now the singular comfort of being told that the destination of this ship is changed … to proceed, forthwith, to the West Indies'.[48] Another four days and in Portsmouth, there was neither sight nor sound of the *Ulysses* or Pinckard's luggage. On 28 October, Pinckard was still in Portsmouth, still awaiting the *Ulysses*, but the orders changed for him 'to repair, immediately, on board the *Bridgewater* transport, and proceed to Cork'.[49] He remained in Portsmouth, however, having missed the boat so to speak, as the *Bridgewater* had already sailed for Cork before the orders ever reached him! 'Greetings from the *Ulysses*!' wrote a very relieved Pinckard, on 12 November. He proceeded to pen a vivid picture of his first introduction to his hammock, which must have been familiar to many a supernumerary:

> Our first night has been restless and disturbed – the unpleasant heaving of the ship – the creaking of bulkheads, and other noises – the uneasy motion of the cot … prevented me from sleeping. At each movement of the ship, or the cot, my feet were struck against the bulkhead at the bottom of the wardroom; or I was bumped upon the huge cannon standing under me; or had Cleghorn's feet roughly presented to my head …[50]

All this while still tied up in port! In the event Pinckard's discomforts were to be alleviated by the gales when the *Ulysses*, amongst others, was appropriated to receive troops from the wallowing *Commerce de Marseilles* and the doctor was transferred to the *Lord Sheffield*, a much superior ship altogether, at least with regards to her suitability for passengers.

By the morning of Wednesday 18 November, 'The ships tossed violently in mountainous seas. A thick fog of driving rain and spindrift enveloped them, and their crews could see nothing. Nor could they hear anything but a howling, shrieking wind from the south-west and so strong, it was beating the ships backwards.'[51]

---

47 Pinckard, *Notes on the West Indies*, vol.1, pp.26–27.
48 Pinckard, *Notes on the West Indies*, vol.1, p.28.
49 Pinckard, *Notes on the West Indies*, vol.1, p.52.
50 Pinckard, *Notes on the West Indies*, vol.1, p.101.
51 Boult, *Christian's Fleet*, p.65.

HMS *Alfred*, despite her badly damaged mainsail and topsails, made it to the Portland Roads and shelter, together with her nursery of transports, most of which bore some damage. Drury's decision turned out to be an excellent move as, to the northwest of Portland along the 18-mile length of the pebble beach that is the Chesil, the winds were now at hurricane force. They drove the convulsing waves to attack the coast in a huge line of lashing surf, with an unforgiving undertow and no shelter from the unstoppable strength of the vast amounts of angry water. 'In such conditions, the … transports were doomed … the Aeolus, borne on the crest of waves the height of a house, was rushed towards the Chesil … her crew … could do nothing but cling, terrified, to any support on deck as Aeolus was sucked back and thrown repeatedly onto the beach.'[52]

Again, and again, the *Aeolus* struck, splintering and breaking with each blow. Eventually, she 'was lifted up by a gigantic wave and thrown onto the beach with a final, great crash, where she lay on her side … the exhausted crew struggled down onto the beach, while locals swarmed round to scavenge what they could'.[53] She was carrying gunboats, masts, and other stores, much of which would be useful to the locals. Records show that Lieutenant Mason and eight other men on board had drowned, while the master (probably Isaac Duck) and eight other seamen survived.[54]

Ultimately, with differences only in the numbers of lives lost and saved, the same fate was to fall on five other ships. Like the *Aeolus*, the 284-ton *Golden Grove* was thrown onto the beach and then broken up by the waves. Lieutenant Colonel Ross jumped to safety as did 17 of the crew, and the captain, W. Hodgzard. The lost included the master, Robert Bagg, Dr Stevens, Mr Burrows and two boys. Her cargo was 'bale goods'. Forty drowned from the 253-ton *Catherine* cavalry transport, including the master, 22 soldiers of the 26th Light Dragoons, Cornet Stukeley Burns, Lieutenants Jenner and Stains, Mr Dodd of the hospital staff, two women and 11 seamen; only Mrs Burns, wife of Cornet Burns, and a cabin boy, were saved.

From the 230-ton *Piedmont,* the captain, 11 seamen, 139 soldiers and officers of the 63rd Foot (including Captain Barcroft, Lieutenant Ashe and Surgeon Kelly) all died. Captain Ambrose William Barcroft, of the 63rd Foot, was a charismatic officer who lived in Colne, Lancashire. Barcroft had fought in the American War of Independence and the local young men of Colne answered his call for volunteers and 'joined almost en masse'.[55] Wearing rosettes in their caps, they had marched from Colne, cheered on by friends and relatives and wept over by wives and girlfriends. None returned. All 126 were later identified from the Muster Rolls and recorded for posterity. 'When the sad news reached Colne … hardly a home in Waterside but mourned the loss of some dead one'.[56]

---

52 Boult, *Christian's Fleet*, p.65.
53 Boult, *Christian's Fleet*, pp.66–67.
54 Boult, *Christian's Fleet*, p.108
55 James Carr, *Annals and stories of Colne and neighbourhood* (Manchester: John Heywood, 1878), p.87
56 Carr, *Annals*, p.89

From the 181-ton *Venus* transport, which was carrying amongst others, invalid soldiers and officers, hospital corps and three officers of the West India regiments, 91 were drowned. A merchantman, the *Thomas*, bound for Oporto in Portugal, lost 13 of the 19 persons carried, including the master and his son. The total drowned on the Chesil that day was 296, only 71 were saved.[57]

Most of the bodies from these six ships, thrown onto the 18-mile-long Chesil Beach, were buried on the lee side of the Chesil beside the Fleet Lagoon. The hazardous Chesil Beach has always been renowned for shipwrecks. The responsibility of the burying of the bodies was, to a large extent, taken on by William Shrapnel, lieutenant and surgeon of the South Gloucester Militia; John Darley, who survived the *Venus*, and Mr Bryer, a surgeon from Weymouth. Major Austin of the 61st (South Gloucestershire) Regiment of Foot, then camping on Weymouth's South Down, who acquired 'the authority from a magistrate to bury the dead … organised a work party of forty men', under the command of Lieutenant Shrapnel. Some of those who were identified were removed for burial in the churchyard at Wyke Regis, but the majority still lie beside the Fleet, within sound of the sea that took them. For six days the South Gloucesters continued their gruesome and laborious task on the beach. Each day they struggled on six miles of shifting pebbles to reach the bodies, then carry them up and over the summit and along to the Fleet, where they buried them by the waterside, raising a pile of stones over each grave to mark where they lay. Two-hundred-and-eight soldiers and seamen were buried in this way – and must still be there to this day.[58]

The men who died from the wreck of the *Piedmont* were among those 208 drowned and whose bodies were found. Others were never recovered. Boult records those whose names were amongst the officers found and buried in the churchyard at Wyke Regis. Captain Ambrose William Barcroft from Colne has been mentioned already. Surgeon John Charles Ker was appointed Military Commandant of Hospitals in the Leeward Islands. His 14-year-old son, James, was travelling with his father in his rank of ensign. Only James's body was found, never his father's.

---

57 Boult, *Christian's Fleet*, pp.108–120.
58 Boult, *Christian's Fleet*, pp.77–83.

11

Attacking the Atlantic: It Makes My Blood Run Cold

Winds ... rend the world, resistless where they pass, and mighty marks of mischief leave behind.[1]

My Dear Loving Wife,
This is the Happiest Opertunity I ever Embraced. I am now in Sight of the Isle of Wight and I mean to Send These few lines on Shore [at] the first opertunity, which I hope to Embrace on Coming to Anchor at Spithead, As I heard the Captain say he was going Ashore. We set sail from Spithead on Sunday 15th November, with a fine Easy wind. And on Monday the 16th, as we [were] sailing In the British Channel [a]t four o'Clock in the afterNoon, one of the hardest Gales of wind Sprung up that the Master of the vessel Ever experienced [in] Six Years, which only abated this Morning at five. And now we have hard squalls in Coming to this Harbour again. During the gale of wind, My Dear, The Seas [ran] Mountains High and Every poor Soul, Both Sailors and Soldiers on Board, thought of being swallowed In the Deep Every Moment.

But God has Brought us through this Danger, for which I Return thanks for it. As we were sailing this Morning a Light was seen which the Captain took to be from one of the Ships of the Fleet. But to our Surprise [it] proved to be a Lighthouse upon a rock. If we Had gone on ten minutes Longer the ship would have been Dashed to pieces.

My Dear, I hope you got my last [letter dated the 9th] to Hand ... Before we Sailed ... I gave it to a Boy on Board of a Sloop, which was Lying [to] the right of the Boddington, the Ship that Colonel Riddell is on board of. ... I had been on board for orderly. Coming back a gust of wind rose and the tide, Coming strong against me, I was obliged to Run the boat alongside of a Sloop which was fastened to one of the Transports, and there wait until I was fetched off By another Boat Belonging to the Julius with Some More Sailors... But of 200 Sail of Ships with troops on Board ... My Dear, I am afraid there is a great Many accidents happened During the Storm ... Again our Fleet is all dispersed. Some put into Plymouth and other seaports and Some, I am afraid, will never be Heard of More

---

1   Dryden, from D. Defoe, *An historical narrative of the great and tremendous storm which happened on Nov 1703* (London: W. Nicoll, 1769).

> …this Very Moment a Squall of wind has broke[n] the Yard Arm in Sunder & taking away our masts. Never was [k]nown such weather. I hope we shall not put to sea again for a while.[2]

The 44th had been on board transports in a storm before. Their return from Bremen earlier in the year was marred by storms, but nothing had prepared them for a storm of this magnitude. From his account as a man more familiar with solid ground, Roworth must have approached the duty of orderly with some trepidation. As the serjeant major it was his duty to ensure that 'all orderly men are properly dressed and accoutred, before they are inspected by the adjutant who [in normal circumstances], would parade them every morning in front of the main guard'.[3] That particular morning must have been excruciatingly difficult for any serjeant who found himself attending his duties when his orderlies were on different ships, his own obligatory sash for the occasion being the least of his worries. The soldiers were probably scattered throughout at least three to five transports, which had just returned from the experience of a hurricane in the Channel, the ships were unlikely to be rowed up neatly waiting for inspection. For Roworth, it would have required moving from ship to ship in a tender, which might have been a small boat with a sail or a large rowing boat, oared by sailors. Whichever it was and however competent the crew, it would have been a harrowing experience for any soldier out of his own element. Roworth would have had to direct the tender to search out each of the 44th's transports.

The storm took its toll on the mighty HMS *Commerce de Marseilles*, which had been taken by the British at Toulon in 1793. In spite of being praised as 'a very fine sailer' and 'notwithstanding her immense size she worked and sailed like a frigate', on this occasion it was not to be. She was loaded with stores and a crew of about 850 added to which she carried 900 rank and file of the 57th Foot.[4] The troops were all embarked by 4 October and it was not until three weeks later that Abercromby requested the *Commerce de Marseilles* and her convoy be moved from her current position to the Cowes Roads so that the troops might land on the Isle of Wight occasionally.[5]

When the fleet finally sailed on 15 November *Commerce de Marseilles* was very weak and she could not rise in the water and her fabric was almost shaken to bits by the storm. Commanded by Captain Smith Child she had the 57th taken onto HMS *Charon*, *Ulysses* and *Experiment* for their safety. She did not join the fleet again. 'Her structure was found to be very weak and she was reduced to harbour service by 1800'.[6] By great good fortune, the *Commerce de Marseilles* had not sailed when Christian had originally ordered, on 4 October 1795, but her captain missed the opportunity to sail, thereby saving the lives of approximately 1,700 soldiers and sailors and

---

2   NA: DDRW 16/25: Roworth to Mary, Julius at Sea, 19 November 1795.
3   James, *Dictionary*.
4   Lavery, *Nelson's Navy*, p.46.
5   TNA: ADM 1/317: Christian to Nepean, *Prince George*, Spithead, 5 October 1795.
6   Lavery, *Nelson's Navy*, p.46.

innumerable tons of stores.[7] Child may have taken her out on a kind sea only to have her shake to pieces once the winds became contrary. She was indeed a huge ship. When she was moved to Plymouth for fitting out in ordinary in January 1796 there was not a dock large enough to take her. Winfield records that she was broken up under admiralty orders in June 1802.[8]

Roworth wrote to his wife again from his berth on the *Julius*.

> O My Dear Mary, if You was But to hear of the Accidents that has happened to Some of our fleet and to See the wrecks along the Shore [with] Masts and Rigging cut away, and Some sunk with Troops on Board – it makes my blood go Cold to think [of] it … One Ship [*Piedmont*] went to the Bottom with one Company and a Half [of] the 63rd (139) on Board and Numbers more Besides.[9]

After such an experience, it was hardly surprising to hear from Roworth that the '44th's Drum Major deserted at Southampton'.[10] On the other hand, the Drum Major, James attests, 'must be an example to the Drummers', which may account for the desertions of Drummers Robert Fitch and William Darbyshire, who deserted on 1 and 5 January 1796 respectively.[11] The Drum Major had deserted from Southampton, however, before the latest series of storms, so his reasoning may have been due to knowledge of the destination rather than inclemency of the weather.

Of those soldiers who survived the Chesil Beach ordeal, 'Sergt Richardson of the 63rd and the soldiers who were unhurt, from the *Piedmont*, set out the following day by road for Portsmouth, disobeying orders [to] go by sea'.[12] Their reluctance could be understood, and it was to be wondered how many of that particular group actually arrived back in Portsmouth. They may have felt it was an opportunity not to be missed and at the very least would have empathised with Roworth, when he wrote from the constantly heaving *Julius*, that 'Very oft[en] I Look at the Shore and think how happy it would be for all us unhappy Souls to Disembark'.[13]

On 1 December, the *Julius* and the *Estridge* waited with all the other returned ships, repairing the sea damage and preparing yet again for their next attempt. The *Boddington*, which also carried some of the 25th Foot and their lieutenant colonel, William Dyott, was one of the 10 which had put into Torbay. On 1 December, *Estridge* was proclaimed 'Complete and fit to proceed to St Hellens [*sic*]'. 'Only eleven sail could fetch in; our ship was fortunately one of the number'.[14] Dyott returned to Portsmouth separately

---

7 Boult, *Christian's Fleet*, p.54.
8 Rif Winfield, *British Warships in the Age of Sail: Design, Construction, Careers and Fates* (London: Chatham Publishing, 2005), p.9.
9 NA: DDRW1/17: Roworth to Mary, On Board the Julius, 30 November 1795.
10 NA: DDRW 16/25: Roworth to Mary, on board the *Julius*, Spithead, 19 November 1795.
11 TNA: WO 12/5638: 25 June to 24 December 1795.
12 Boult, *Christian's Fleet*, p.84.
13 NA: DDRW 1/17, Roworth to Mary, on board the *Julius*, Spithead, 30 November 1795.
14 Reginald W. Jeffery (ed.), *Dyott's Diary 1781–1845: a selection from the journal of William Dyott, sometime general in the British Army and aide-de-camp to His Majesty King George III* (London: Archibald Constable and Company, 1907), vol.1, p.82.

ATTACKING THE ATLANTIC: IT MAKES MY BLOOD RUN COLD

where he joined with the *Boddington* again in time for embarking for the second attempt on 9 December. In the meantime, further repairs were made and stores were stowed. *Julius* 'wants some water and [is] employing her own boats to complete her'.[15] The *Boddington* was doing the same.

Roworth managed to get one last letter away to Mary on the very day of the second sailing of Rear Admiral Christian's Fleet.

> 9th Decr 1795. My Dear wife … we are just weighing Anchor to Sail on our intended Voyage as the wind is Quite fair for us, and I Embrace this opertunity of Sending these few lines on Shore By the Pilott, which takes us Round the Isle of [Wight], and I hope, My Dear Mary, youl Get them Safe to hand, and find you and your father and Mothar and Sister and My Dear Son In good Health, as these L[e]aves me in good Health at Present, for which I return god thanks for it Night and Day.[16]

Even after such a trial of strength and courage, that elusive pinnacle of ambition was still a constant thorn in both their lives, as Roworth found time to answer Mary.

> My Dear Mary, you mentioned in your Last about Me not Letting you know of Me Being Promoted to Adjutant in the 44th Regt. I do assure you I Did not know for certain at that time although it was wisperd about the Regt and I Expeckt My Commission Every Day as they are Some time in coming Down after Being Gazetted. Sergt Donaldson that Come from the West Indies is appointed Ser. Major in My Room … S[erjeant] Gardiner is Qr.Master and Mr Legge Ensign, but the adjutant answers me better, as there is More Income … My Dear, you spoke of Me not to keep bad Company. [H]ad I Done that I Should not have Been promoted to this Rank. My Dear & Loving wife I Conclude and Shall Evar Remain your Sincere and Loving Husband Wm.Roworth till Death. God Bless you, god bless you. My Dear, I nevar Shall keep anything from you, you May Depend on it, nor Shall I evar turn My Back from you wile breath remains in me, but Strive to do all I Can for our best.[17]

Due to the storm damage done to the *Prince George*, on 30 November Christian had hoisted his flag on HMS *Glory* (98), taking with him Captain James Bowen and most of the crew from the former. He finally weighed anchor, the majority of the convoy with him, on 9 December. Also on the ship, acting as a lieutenant was a young Francis Austen, brother of Jane.[18] Midshipman William Henry Dillon, who in the future would become an admiral of the red and a knight, kept a narrative and was to be a useful eyewitness. Elsewhere among the accompanying transports was the *Julius*,

---

15 TNA: CO 318/18: 1 December 1795, p.198.
16 NA: DDRW 19/25: Roworth to Mary, on board the *Julius*, Spithead, 9 December 1795.
17 NA: DDRW 19/25: Roworth to Mary, on board the *Julius*, Spithead, 9 December 1795.
18 'Sir Francis William Austen', <https://threedecks.org/index.php?display_type=show_crewman &id=2037>, accessed July 2023.

with Roworth on board and for the *Julius* this was to be second time lucky. Her captain was persistent in his struggle to cross the Atlantic and succeeded. Although no-one could fault Christian's persistence in his endeavours to reach the Windward Islands, it was not to be the same outcome for the *Glory* or the majority of the fleet, which was harassed yet again with terrific storms and winds. Christian in the *Glory* struggled with 'the storms for six and a half weeks' without, in effect, travelling no further in distance than 'four days' from England, only to finally turn back.[19]

Those six weeks were fraught with troubles. As early as 16 December, after just seven days at sea, Christian had written to Huskisson words which were filled with constant worry, that the:

> … storms were as violent as before … [that] two ships were seen sinking by one of the hospital ships … we are scattered considerably … I have but one Frigate [available] in chasing them … the *Alexander* has proved leaky … I am now withdrawing the detachment of the 27th Regt from her to the *Colossus*, *Impregnable* and *Invincible* … [one transport] was in tow of the *Impregnable* but broke her hawser in the night … the Transports have never been numbered with regularity …[20]

Christian's and Abercromby's relationship was never clearer than during this enormous test of endurance, also the anxieties experienced, 'I am worried. I am anxious, the General feels, and by his participation of my difficulty, the Burthen is lighter'. Christian describes them both as 'Companions in Misfortune' but that Abercromby's 'mind is a great one – his Heart the best … to look forward in Hope'.[21]

It was during this second attempt of the fleet to reach the West Indies, that the following heart-warming anecdote was recorded (demonstrating Abercromby's support for his counterpart) when his own confidential servant rushed into the cabin where he was with Christian and addressing him said '"We are going to be drowned." "Very well," replied Sir Ralph, "You go to bed."'[22] Apart from the general's unflappable coolness, the direness of the situation presents another of those 'what if?' moments. If both the commander of the army and the commander of the navy on that particular expedition had drowned together – what then?

Christian's anxieties in the current and very real danger surfaced as he exhorted, Huskisson 'to be helpful to Mrs Christian. I have left a large family, relating to whom I necessarily feel great anxiety … the weight of responsibility I feel [is] wretched.'[23]

---

19   Boult, *Christian's Fleet*, p.100.
20   TNA: CO 318/18: *Glory* at sea, Christian to Huskisson, 16 December 1795, p.207.
21   TNA: CO 318/18: *Glory* at sea, Christian to Huskisson, 16 December 1795, p.209.
22   James, Lord Dunfermline, *Lieutenant-General Sir Ralph Abercromby, 1793–1801. A Memoir* (London: Naval & Military Press, 2009), p.55.
23   TNA: CO 318/18: *Glory* at Sea. 26 December 1795, p.287.

ATTACKING THE ATLANTIC: IT MAKES MY BLOOD RUN COLD

The reasons for this can be seen in HMS *Glory*'s logbook, for Saturday 26 December alone, which provided a graphic description of the current state of the flagship's own precarious position:

> Strong gales and Squally with Rain at times. Foresail the Main Topsail split, endeavoured to take it in, but ineffectually; and it blew entirely to pieces. The gale increasing with every violence, a great Sea running, and thick weather with Rain, about 1 the Starboard lower quarter Gallery was stove by the Sea, and many of the Middle deck ports; by which such great quantities of water were shipped that the Ship became water logged, and Settling fast to Starboard, let fly the Storm Mizen Staysail [But] the Sail split, and went entirely to pieces I got the Ship before the Wind, scuttled the Lower deck in several parts to let the watr [sic] off, kept the pumps going, and at ½ past 3 got the Water under[control], and the Ship in condition for heaving to – Brought to at ½ past 3, observed the flash of several Guns, during the time we were employed in freeing the Ship, supposed them to be Signals of Distress, but unable to answer them, the whole of the People's Provisions &c., between decks was spoiled.[24]

If this voyage was a nightmare to the men of the navy, how much more must the fear have been multiplied for the redcoats, many recent volunteers may never have set foot on a ship before, though physical employment on the pumps may have exercised minds as well as bodies. Whether to be below decks or above must have held its own terrors for both land-based redcoats and cavalry horses. Dealing with a horse with a broken limb or worse, would present a different kind of logistics on an erratic and disorderly ocean.

Other ships were forced yet again to take shelter at multiple ports. Sir Chichester Fortescue, Principal Agent for Transports in Ireland, wrote on 28 December 1795:

> The following ships arrived here yesterday … His Majesty's ships *Fourtourelle* and *Laurel, Jane 2nd,* [with] Cavalry and Infantry on board, parted from Admiral Christian's Fleet the 19th instant; her false Stern loose, but will soon be repaired. The *Bellona*, John Noddins master, with Cavalry also, both these ships are in want of water and forage. The *George and Bridget,* ordnance ship, and the *Charlotte* with Foreign Troops, Both leaky, the former has carried away her Fore-Rigging … It is reported that three Ordnance Ships have arrived at Kinsale, but I have not yet learned their names.[25]

There were some vessels which never even left their berths at Portsmouth: two ordnance and store-ships, *Britannia* and *Prince of Piedmont*; another store ship, *Providence*; a bomb ship, *Somerset,* and a hospital ship, *Mary,* were left behind.

On this second attempt some transports were able to put into Plymouth, including *Superb*, carrying part of the 37th Foot; *Mentor* with the Royal Irish Artillery on board; *Kingston* with Löwenstein's Chasseurs; *Lord Hood* with

---

24 TNA: ADM 1/318: HMS *Glory*, log, 26 December 1795.
25 TNA: WO 1/799: Fortescue to Transport Board, 28 December 1795, pp.132–133.

NOT SO EASY, LADS

Major General David Stewart of Garth 1772–1829. By James Montgomery Scrymgeour (The Black Watch Museum)

ATTACKING THE ATLANTIC: IT MAKES MY BLOOD RUN COLD

part of the 28th Foot and the *Aid*, which disembarked Dragoons.[26] Seven store ships were scattered between the ports of Dartmouth, Falmouth, Cork, Bristol and Milford. The *Commerce*, 252 tons, carrying ordnance and stores was lost, but her crew was saved.

The *Bridgewater* and the *Horn*, hospital ships, had similar cargoes and were driven to take shelter, probably in Dublin. The *George and Bridget* lived to tell the tale, her hospital bedding was returned to Portsmouth as 'being rendered unserviceable by Sea Water'. She had carried '200 Sheets, 430 Blankets and 250 Coverlets, 50 Paliasses and Bolsters. 6 cwts of oatmeal, 5 cwts of barley, 1 cwt of currants, 1 ½ cwts Hard Soap, 3 Half Firkins of soft Soap and 1 Large Bathing Tub', little of which may have still been serviceable.[27]

The fleet from Cork had not left harbour and did not do so until 25 February 1796. David Stewart (an eyewitness to many of the events during the years 1793–1797 as a lieutenant in the 42nd Regiment (Black Watch) both in Flanders and the West Indies), reckoned the infantry embarking from England to be 16,479 and that from Cork 5,680, totalling 22,159. Cavalry from England was 460 and that of Cork, 2,600, totalling 3,060.[28] In the event and in such terrain 'the cavalry were found to be totally useless; and the horses died so fast' that there were insufficient numbers even to carry the general's orders.[29]

Information arrived with the Secretary of State informing him that some 5,000 of the men at Cork had already eaten their way through most of the provisions. They would soon require more, and the blame appeared to lie squarely on the lack of communication between the Victualling and Transport Boards.[30]

Despite the efforts of the whole fleet, the second attempt to sail was almost as ineffectual as the first, the storms blowing so hard as to send some of the fleet backwards and past the entrances to Portsmouth and Southampton. A few transports managed to make the crossing to the West Indies, but took many extra weeks in the doing of it. Many ships were forced to turn back: the *Adventure* limped into Plymouth, with barrack stores, she was leaky but deemed fit to get back to Portsmouth. The *Jane* put into Falmouth, with a cargo of forage and 70 Löwenstein troops. The *Neptune* was also in Falmouth with her cargo of forage.[31] *Neptune* escorted the *Jane* back to Portsmouth, with 'her Pumps so much choked …[and] with three feet of water in her hold'.[32] The *Lively* parted from the fleet on 16 December with her main yard gone. She carried some of the 38th, part of which were 'shifted into HMS *Lion*'. The *Alexander* which arrived back at Spithead with part of 27th

---

26 TNA: CO 18/18: Transports and ships put back into port, 22 & 24 December 1795, p215.
27 TNA: ADM 1/318: Letters from Commanders in Chief, Leeward Islands 1796, p.133.
28 David Stewart, *Sketches of the character, manners, and present state of the Highlanders of Scotland: with details of the Military Service of the Highland Regiments* (Edinburgh: Archibald Constable & Co. 1822), p.409.
29 Stewart, *Sketches*, p.410.
30 Julian Corbett (ed.), *Private papers of George, second Earl Spencer First Lord of the Admiralty 1794–1801* (Unknown: Elibron Classics, 2005), vol.1, p.166.
31 TNA: CO 318/18: Colonial Office, Naval Dispatches.
32 TNA: WO 1/789: Letters from Commanders in Chief.

on board, was 'torn to pieces'. The troops were moved into HMS *Colossus*, *Impregnable* and *Irresistible*, the redcoats far more secure, if still seasick.[33]

Others found themselves in foreign waters. The *Mary* transport, with 134 men of the 48th Foot on board, which had left with Christian on 9 December, put into Lisbon, sailing again from there for the West Indies on 25 February 1796. The *Prescott* transport, having 126 men of the 88th aboard, put into Gibraltar on 10 February in a very leaky condition. The prize for a lucky survival must surely be given to the ship, probably the *Prescott*, described by historian John Fortescue: 'One vessel, containing part of the Eighty-eighth, Connaught Rangers, actually blown through the Straits of Gibraltar, was frapped together at Carthagena and thence navigated once more to Gibraltar, where the men had hardly been landed before she fell to pieces'.[34]

There would be two more attempts to get the whole fleet across the Atlantic. The first of these left Spithead on 29 February 1796, commanded by Vice Admiral William Cornwallis. In sailing down the channel, with a fair wind, a disastrous accident occurred, not infrequent in large fleets. The *Belisarius* transport, full of troops, ran athwart the hawse of the Cornwallis's flagship, HMS *Royal Sovereign*. The former lost 100 of its troops, while the latter lost her coppering and 'the Stem laid bare Eight or Nine feet under *Water*' thus rendering the *Sovereign* unfit to proceed to the West Indies. Cornwallis took the decision to return for repairs, in spite of the Admiralty ordering him to move his flag onto the *Astraea* and proceed on his orders. Consequently, the vice admiral was the focus of a painful court-martial for not obeying Admiralty orders which, although he was acquitted, was of no use to the company of Löwensteins which had drowned.[35] The regiment had embarked early in October, and left Germany for England in November, the majority arriving at Portsmouth a fortnight later but one of its transports, the *Two Sisters* with 150 of all ranks, was wrecked off Calais, though the men were rescued.[36] While Cornwallis faced a court-martial much of the fleet sailed on to Barbados, arriving in April, escorted by indomitable Captain Drury of the *Alfred*.[37]

Christian finally sailed for his third personal attempt on 20 March 1796, on board HMS *Thunderer*. In company with him were 'six warships, forty-one transports and over five and a half thousand men'.[38] By the time Christian left Britain, Roworth with the 44th and John Simpson with the 42nd, had been in the West Indies for some five to six weeks. For Christian, it was third time lucky and he 'arrive[d] at Carlisle Bay on the 21st of April 1796', after a mere four-week voyage.[39] His relief must have been acute.

---

33 TNA: WO 1/789: Transport Office, War Department In-Letters.
34 Fortescue, *History of the Army*, vol.IV, Part 1, p.481.
35 James Carrick Moore, *The Life of Lieutenant General Sir John Moore* (London: Murray, 2011), vol.1, p.110.
36 C.T. Atkinson, 'Foreign Regiments in the British Army 1793–1802, Part 6', *Journal of the Society of Army Historical Research*, vol.XXII, p.248.
37 Boult, *Christian's Fleet*, p.102.
38 Boult, *Christian's Fleet*, p.102.
39 Boult, *Christian's Fleet*, p.102.

ATTACKING THE ATLANTIC: IT MAKES MY BLOOD RUN COLD

David Stewart, 42nd Foot, made a perceptive comment concerning the debacle of Christian's fleet in his book:

> … instead of dispatching the transports in detachments, as the troops embarked, it was unfortunately determined to detain the whole till the embarkation was complete. To this desire of making one great display, the subsequent misfortunes of the expedition may be chiefly attributed; for not only were the colonies thus endangered by the prolonged delay of reinforcements, but several intervals of fine weather and fair wind were lost.[40]

Stewart was not alone in this supposition and he pointed to the successful voyage of the *Stanley* transport to support his theory. Dundas and Fortescue were for once in agreement (however briefly) when the former wrote to Abercromby 'frantic with rage', demanding why the fleet has not already sailed. 'I shall be glad to know where the blame lies, for the public will hold me responsible if the wind is lost. Should you not sail with what is ready and let the rest follow?'[41] Much can be accomplished with hindsight. By Christian's third sailing the 'great display' syndrome (at least for this fleet) had finally been eradicated. The original decision must have been taken with safety in numbers in mind, together with the optimum number of naval ships to convoy vulnerable transports.

One wonders how the troops of the 44th were faring for the duration. The *Boddington*, which carried Lieutenant Colonel Robert Riddell and part of the 44th itself, plus part of the 25th Foot, was one of those ships which had seen the first storm out in Torbay. She continued her voyage at the second attempt on 9 December 1795, although returning first to St Helens, as all the ships were ordered, to start again.

The *Julius* arrived in Barbados on 9 February 1796. Before Christian's first attempt and while the fleet was still in preparation, 300 troops of the 44th were already embarked on the *Trelawney* and the *Estridge* (150 each) with the following noted: '… when removed to be ready to receive the Foreign Corps'.[42] In fact, only the *Estridge* took Löwenstein troops and the *Trelawney Planter* became a store ship.

The question remains, as to which other ship or ships were those 300 soldiers of the 44th removed, for the first aborted voyage? There is a possible clue given by Lieutenant Thomas Phipps Howard, York Hussars, in his *Haitian Journal*. Just two days before his transport, the *Elizabeth*, arrived in Carlyle Bay, she was approached and spoken to, by two of the convoy's ships of war. He wrote that 'The Ship we spoke [to] first had the 44 Regt. OnBoard'.[43] She was a 64-gun ship, so must have been HMS *Lion* as that was the only 64 with the original convoy. However, this occurrence happened on the third attempt when *Lion* was carrying part of the 38th Foot, whose facings were yellow. Did

---

40   Stewart, *Sketches*, p.410.
41   Fortescue, *History of the Army*, vol.IV, Part 1, p.479.
42   TNA: CO 318/18: Colonial Office, Naval Dispatches, p.309.
43   Roger Norman Buckley, *The Haitian Journal of Lieutenant Howard, York Hussars, 1796–1798* (Knoxville: University of Tennessee Press, 1985), p.22.

Howard mistake them for the 44th, whose facings were also yellow? Or was his identification correct? Within two days, Howard reported dining with officers of the 44th at Bridgetown, but as half the 44th were already there when he arrived, it might have been those.

The confusion about the uniform of the 44th would seem of little concern in the scheme of things, but they apparently had not received their 1795–1796 quota of clothing before sailing and their agent, Mr Bownas, had placed a query about the missing supply, receiving an answer on 10 February 1796. But by the end of the following November there was still a search for a 'proper conveyance' for eight tons of clothing for the 44th, to be sent to the West Indies 'discreatte[ly]' as there was already 'some other clothing … already shipped … to which this is an addition'.[44] By November 1796 so many of them were dead that the uniforms would no longer be of use and must have found their way back to Britain again in 1797 with what was left of the regiment.

After an exhausting voyage which most of the redcoats would, no doubt, rather not have endured, a whole new scenario was about to be introduced to them, in the guise of the West Indies and ultimately, for the 44th – St Lucia – which, as with so many of his brother soldiers, was to be Roworth's nemesis.

---

44   TNA: WO 4/338: Secretary at War, Out-letters, West Indies, pp.286–287.

12

Late Arrivals: The Waiting Game

I embrace this opportunity ... for night and Day you are both before my Eyes[1]

The *Boddington* and the *Julius* were some three weeks into their voyage at sea on 1 January 1796 when Major Rufane Shaw Donkin took the Monthly Return of the 44th Regiment of Foot and their whereabouts, which makes for interesting reading. 'Part of His Majesty's 44th Regiment of Foot, January 1st, 1796. Head Quarters. Lieut. Col: Riddell, commanding the Regiment, in the *Boddington* West Indiaman, Separated from the Fleet.'

The return provides the following information: the Colonel is Charles Rainsford, the Lieutenant Colonel Robert Riddell, and the Major Rufane Shaw Donkin. Two majors, two captains, four lieutenants and three ensigns are present. Only one member of the staff is present, the surgeon. Twenty serjeants are on board and six drummers or fifers, 252 rank and file are fit for duty, three are sick in quarters and six are in hospital, making a total of 261. The captaincy of one company was vacant as Edward Wilson had been promoted to major. The return was signed by Donkin, together with a note: 'The Column "wanting to compleat" not filled as it is not known what men are in the absent ships'.[2] The following return for 1 February 1796 was identical, even down to the three sick and six still in hospital.

Rear Admiral Christian's fleet was under orders to meet up at Bridgetown, in Carlisle Bay, Barbados. The first transport attributed to arrive was the *Stanley*, West Indiaman, with troops from the 48th on board. She sailed into Carlisle Bay on Christmas Day 1795. The *Stanley* was reputed to be the only transport in the fleet to have left Portsmouth on 11 November and to have succeeded at the first attempt. There is some discrepancy here, as it is mentioned elsewhere, that Dr James McGrigor claims to have arrived first in Carlisle Bay in the *Betsey*, also carrying soldiers of the 48th, though in the army records she was carrying the 38th. Surprisingly, McGrigor did not date his autobiography, so may not have made his notes until many years later,

---

1 NA: DDRW 20/25: Roworth to Mary, Barbados, 11 March 1796.
2 TNA: WO 17/155: Return 44th Foot, 1 January 1796.

in which case he might have misremembered, either the name of his vessel (unlikely) or the time of arrival (possibly).

Whichever ship they arrived on, the men on board, not least the captain, must have been increasingly disturbed by meeting with so few members of such a large convoy during the voyage. The entrance to the bay would have been watched with anxiety for many weeks before others appeared.

Private John Simpson and part of the 42nd (Black Watch) arrived on 9 February 1796, after a variable voyage. The *Middlesex* arrived 'with five companies of the Highlanders, in such good a state of health, that only two men, with slight bruises, were on the surgeon's list. So well navigated and appointed was this ship, that in all those gales, in which so many had suffered, the slipping of one block was the only accident sustained from Portsmouth to Barbadoes'.[3]

This was the second attempt of the *Middlesex* to get to the West Indies. Both she and the *Rose*, also carrying troops of the 42nd, had returned to St Helen's after the first attempt for repairs to bowsprit and mizzen respectively. When the *Middlesex* made it out of the Channel, Simpson recorded that:

> … the captain broke open our instructions and found [we] were bound for Barbadoes which caused us to make the best of our way to the place of our destination. There was then in company with us at this time the *Seaman Taylor* [*Simon Taylor*] West Indie trading ship and the *Britania* [*sic*] transport with British Artillery & ordnance stores on board … General McDonald with a part of the Royals were on board of the *Seaman Taylor*, William Watt, master, the other two ships followed our examples, and we Kept looking about in the Bay of Biscay with the wind against us, and blowing a severe storm for the space of 4 weeks, till we came in sight of the Medeira [*sic*] Islands, when the wind calmed and turned on our favour, after which we came into the trade winds, & had a very pleasant passage of it all the remainder of our voyage, and we came to anchor in Bridge Town Bay in the Island of Barbadoes on the 5th day of Feby 1796.[4]

Lieutenant David Stewart of the 42nd Foot says the *Middlesex* arrived on 9 February 1796. Boult tells us that both the *Simon Taylor,* carrying the 2nd, and *Boddington,* the latter carrying part of the 44th and the 25th Foot, were among the 10 ships which sheltered in Torbay during the first storm and were among the earliest of the next arrivals to make it into Bridge Town. Both Lieutenant Colonel Robert Riddell in *Boddington* and Serjeant Major Roworth in *Julius* would have been among the first half of the 44th to have set foot on St Lucia. As ill-luck would have it, in spite of her epic journey to the West Indies and back (or perhaps because of) the *Middlesex* sank in the Thames on 16 August 1796.[5]

Dr George Pinckard, who was fortunate in his voyage, sang the praises of his transport, the *Lord Sheffield,* and claimed it to be:

---

[3] Stewart, *Sketches,* p.413.
[4] Simpson, *Memorandums,* pp.1–3.
[5] Richard & Bridget Larn, *Shipwreck Index of the British Isles* (London: Lloyd's Register of Shipping, 1995), index to volumes 1–4.

> ... a very fine West India ship. She is thoroughly clean, has a general air of neatness, and, if we may judge from her appearance, seems likely to verify the commander's report of her sailing. She is conveniently fitted out for passengers, and is, expressly, calculated for the West Indies, having awnings, scuttles, portholes and all the necessary accommodations for the climate. The cabin is commodious, glasses, chairs, sofa, &c. due regard being paid to taste and ornament.[6]

The majority did not fare so well, but the *Lord Sheffield* arrived at Carlisle Bay, Barbados, on 9 February 1796, having sailed with the second convoy. Pinckard writes that the news greeting the newly-arrived transports was 'not very gratifying. Grenada, we were told, was, almost wholly, in possession of the brigands; ... and Guadeloupe, if not St Lucia, so strengthened by reinforcements from France as to bid us defiance'. Roworth in the transport *Julius*, with part of his regiment, arrived four days later, on Saturday 13 February, and wrote to his wife:

> I Embrace this opportunity of Letting you Know of our Safe arrival after a passage of Nine weeks and three Days of which we had Six weeks bad weather as ... our Captain of the Ship Ever Experienced ... there is only one Halfe of our Regiment arrived at presant and they [are] all in good Health and Spirits and [there is] no sickness among us but I am Sorry to Say othar Regiments Cannot Say the Same. Mary how happy Shall your Roworth be if it pleases God to Send me a Safe Return to you and My Son once more, which I trust He will and if I Evar put my foot on English soil once more I think I nevar Shall Leave it ...[7]

This first letter from Roworth, dated 8–11 March 1796, a month after his arrival in the West Indies, demonstrated the difficulties of being a married man whose wife and child had not accompanied him. His position as serjeant major involved him in constant duties with his regiment, from the time *Julius*'s anchor dropped in the sparkling waters of the bay, under (for many) a searing sun. He would have had to oversee the disembarkation of the troops for drill and exercise and the re-embarkation twice daily; these would probably have taken place in the cool of the early morning and evening, as the heat and humidity of the day would sap many soldiers' energy.

As the missing ships arrived in various disreputable states after some two to three months of appalling storms, they had still one more gauntlet to run, that of two French frigates and 'hordes of privateers' cruising voraciously outside the bay to pick off battered transports and merchantmen – and succeeding. The frigate HMS *Charon* (44), which was mentioned by Pinckard as 'one of the earliest arrivals of the Spithead fleet, had been sent out, with *Pique* frigate, in pursuit of them'. HMS *Charon* was not listed among Boult's naval vessels, but she sailed for the West Indies on 7 December 1795. Pinckard also records that HMS *Leda* (36), frigate, Captain John Woodley commanding, though nurse to a convoy of victuallers coming from Cork, was sunk with only seven of her crew picked up by one of the victuallers,

---

6   Pinckard, *Notes on the West Indies*, vol.1, p.143.
7   NA: DDRW 20/25: Roworth to Mary, 8–11 March 1796.

Captain Woodley included.[8] A fifth-rate frigate of 881 tons she would have been carrying a crew of approximately 225 men, so would have lost over 200 of them. Duly unprotected, several of the convoy were taken by the enemy. *Leda* was recorded as having hit a rock near Madeira with HMS *Bulldog* rescuing the surviving seven crew.[9]

While the 42nd and part of the 44th Foot lay at Bridge Town by early February, many transports and their cargoes (human or otherwise) had not yet left England. Brigadier General John Moore, who was to be a pivotal figure in the lives of all those destined for St Lucia as well as the inhabitants, received his orders from the Duke of York so late in the proceedings that they reached him on the evening of 27 February when the fleet was to sail [again] the next morning. He managed to find a berth on the transport *John and James* and caught up with the fleet at the Needles, on the western end of the Isle of Wight.

After the arrival of his transport on 9 February 1796, John Simpson and the 42nd were kept on board the *Middlesex*, for lack of room on shore, which was partly due to troop numbers having swelled with complements from the other Windward Islands. Troops drafted in from St Vincent, Grenada, Dominica and Martinique were there to boost those arriving for the intended reduction of St Lucia, as and when the rest of the troops arrived. Simpson was amused by the fact that his regiment had arrived in Bridge Town with 'one more soul' on board than embarked at Gosport. Whether a stowaway or a birth was not recorded but most likely the latter. Later the 42nd Foot was sent on shore, for daily exercise, returning to the ship afterwards every day, until the arrival of the rest of the fleet. David Stewart noted that 'Of the five companies of the 42nd regiment embarked in the *Middlesex*, East Indiaman, none died, and only four men, with trifling complaints, were left on board when the troops were disembarked at St Lucia in April'.[10] The troops who were kept on board from arrival to disembarkation other than for exercise, thus added another couple of months to their incarceration. Some regiments were kept longer on board at anchor in Bridge Town than it took some transports to sail across the Atlantic. Other than waiting for arrivals in Carlisle Bay, the main reasons for keeping the men cooped up for so long were to prevent desertion; to deter drunkenness on shore, thereby averting trouble and fighting; and to reduce the incidence of venereal diseases.

Looked on by his men as a bit of a martinet, Riddell most likely kept the 44th on board the *Boddington* to retain control. They must have prayed for the arrival of the rest of their regiment together with the rest of the troops, which were still to heave over the horizon. With fewer than half their regiment in Barbados, they expected the rest of the fleet daily unaware, of course, that Christian and Abercromby had not yet left England. Roworth wrote home on 10 March 1796 that:

---

8   Pinckard, *Notes on the West Indies*, vol.1, p.224.
9   *The Times*, 2 March 1796.
10 Stewart, *Sketches*, p.413.

[The men] are all in good Health and Spirits and [there is] no sickness among us but I am Sorry to Say other Regiments Cannot Say the Same … for My part My Dear I take the greatest of Care of my Selfe and avoid all kind of Liquor and fruit which Destroys numbers of British Soldiers in this Country. My Dear, [the] Climate is not So Hot as Represented, though it is a great Deal Hotter than England, but Very pleasant Morning and Evening. the Island is Very Beautyfull with the Differant plantations, [although] Every thing is so Very Dear …

The mention of fruit and liquor 'which destroys numbers of British soldiers' on St Lucia seemed to indicate that sickness might already be happening. If he was eating no fruit then it looks as if he was currently sticking with salt pork and biscuit! He asked her to direct her post:

… to the Island of Barbadoes … and Give me Every particular of the affairs in England … we have been waiting for the English packets but none has arrived. There [are] three Due … this [letter] Comes [to you] … by a Liverpool Ship and I hope you will get it Safe. Remember me to that Dear Boy, for night and Day you are both before my Eyes. So, My Dear Mary, I Conclude And Remain Your Evar Loving Husband, Wm Roworth, till Death.[11]

He signed off his farewell to her with one of the familiar codas, then popular with soldiers in foreign fields. Private Henry Willis of the Lifeguards used the same phrase to his sister, from Lisbon in 1812, viz 'I remain, dear sister, your affectionate brother, till death.'[12] Life in the military was so precarious.

Roworth caught the expected post. The envelope of the relevant letter has a partial stamp for Liverpool. This ship was not a packet boat but a merchant ship which had left Liverpool on 9 January and was returning that way. Mary would have paid for her letter upon receipt. For all redcoats, from the privates to the generals, post from home was as incredibly important to the men then, as it has been in every war since. It was about this time at home in England that the Duke of York was ensuring that the soldiers continued to receive a postal service at least twice weekly on the continent.

It was not so easy to keep to timed crossings across the Atlantic, as has been proved by the fleet fiasco and the English mail packet boats slow in arriving, too. Hardly surprising, considering the chaos the weather had brought upon all shipping from the other side of the Atlantic, literally for months. By the 1790s the postal system was quite advanced in its arrangements, with a regular timetable set up from various ports in Britain which served specific ports on the Continent and North America. The Post Office Packet Service boats were built for speed and their sole purpose was to deliver the mail, including state papers, sailing from A to B as quickly as possible, without being taken by enemy ships, privateers or pirates. Sailing east to west was always going to take longer than from west to east, because of the prevailing westerly winds. But if the weather was foul, maybe for

---

11   NA: DDRW1/20: Roworth to Mary, 10 March 1796.
12   Gareth Glover (ed.), *The Letters of Private Henry Willis* (Huntingdon: Ken Trotman Books, 2017), p.22.

months on end, sailing ships, whether naval, commercial or mail packet, would struggle to keep to any sort of schedule as they tacked across the ocean, often blown many miles from their destinations. As proof of the still appalling conditions at sea, the first of the two January packets that finally arrived had not left Falmouth until 9 January and arrived into Bridgetown on 16 March; over two months later.[13]

John Simpson, together with the 42nd at Bridgetown from the *Middlesex* and the *Rose*, continued to spend each day exercising and getting ready for the expedition to whichever island the commander-in-chief decided upon. The 44th and other regiments slowly trickled into port and joined their comrades, in what turned out to be a very extended waiting game. There were 36 serjeants in total, travelling with the 44th, spread out between the three or four transports and (possibly) one or maybe two ships of war carrying the 'missing soldiers' of the 44th. Whichever way they travelled, just under half their number would be dead within less than a year.

Lieutenant Colonel William Dyott, 25th Foot, had found another ship at Portsmouth, re-embarked and put to sea at Christian's second attempt on 9 December. His description of the journey sounded somewhat surreal and very isolated, though they occasionally saw or 'spoke a ship':

> On the 24th we could see only four sail, the weather … very foggy. A ship hoisted a signal of distress in the morning; we bore down to speak to her, but she fired a gun and bore away … we considered ourselves completely separated from the fleet … and found that in case of separation the rendezvous was Carlisle Bay, Barbadoes … Christmas Day … I allowed the men an allowance of porter in addition to their grog … The first [of] January … spoke a ship, the *Europa*, belonging to the fleet, a transport, but had no troops.[14]

Once on the island Roworth may have found the weather quite endurable and pleasant, but for William Dyott it was '… very warm, and for some days [I] had some fever and headache. I took calomel pills and rhubarb, which I found of great help'. Calomel was a mercury chloride mineral, used as a cure-all up to and into the early years of the twentieth century. In fact, it was toxic and of no medical benefit whatsoever. It was probably the rhubarb which was effective. At that time it was still early in the year and Bridgetown was experiencing the usual average temperatures in the low 70s°Fahrenheit (20s° Celsius), although humidity was always present at between 70 to 90 per cent, so difficult conditions for those not used to it.

Unlike the private men confined to ship, the officers could not only go ashore, but could leave the ship for days at a time. So, Dyott left his regiment to visit friends and acquaintances, leaving the 25th Regiment on board the *Boddington*, under the charge of his major, captains and lieutenants, or at the very least his serjeants if all the former had disembarked.

---

13   Pinckard, *Notes on the West Indies*, vol.1, p.400; Arthur Hamilton Norway, *History of the Post–Office Packet Service Between the Years 1793–1815: Compiled from Records, chiefly official* (London: Macmillan and Co, 1895).
14   Jeffery (ed.), *Dyott's Diary*, vol.1, p.84.

Usefully, Dyott provided impressions of Bridgetown as he saw it, which Simpson and Roworth did not:

> [It] is a large straggling town, with narrow sandy streets; many of the houses large and constructed for the climate with an open gallery in front and a shed over it to keep off the rays of the sun. The county [*sic*] round the town appears like an unenclosed common in England, excepting the cocoa and cabbage trees, which are very beautiful and grow in abundance immediately adjoining the place. The country round Sir Francis's house, and indeed every part of the island, is one open field, as there are no fences ... The principal things I saw growing were cotton, Indian and Guinea corn, and sugar.[15]

This is what all the redcoats would have seen as and when shore leave was allowed. After Dyott's visits and ramblings he was back in time for 1 March when he and the 25th Foot 'disembarked from the *Boddington*, and left Barbados for Grenada, on board three small schooners'. That was the last time we see him and the 25th. Dyott's diary moved on with him to record his experiences in Grenada.

While Brigadier General John Moore left England, with great haste, on the *John and James* transport on 28 February 1796, Dr George Pinckard was in Carlisle Bay enjoying the comfortable appointments of the *Lord Sheffield* and cogitating on the voracious habits of the press-gangs, which were at work in the bay, menacing the transports. Ironically, in the world of slavery into which he had recently sailed, he referred to the pressing of men as 'the exercise of that necessary custom, so repugnant to the feelings, and the freedom, of Englishmen'.[16]

Over the next two-and-a-half weary months, the fleet trickled into Carlisle Bay, in preparation for the retaking of the Sugar Islands. In the meantime, the troops waited on in the heat of Barbados, in their short wool jackets, round hats and flannel underwear, whiling away the hours, days and weeks waiting for a fleet which, for all they knew, might never come.

Abercromby, in HMS *Arethusa*, arrived safely on 17 March, having left Portsmouth on 14 February, just 31 days previously. The *General Cuyler* and the *Clarendon* entered Carlisle Bay simultaneously the same day. This arrival date highlighted the difficulties faced by the *General Cuyler* on her voyage, as she left England on 9 December, with the second fleet, while the *Clarendon* left two months later on 9 February – the latter taking only 30 days to the *General Cuyler*'s unhappy 99. That ship's miserable journey was made worse when she sprang a leak on 7 January and her crew and passengers spent three weeks pumping her out (in eight-hour shifts) day and night, until she made it to the Canary Islands for repairs. Nevertheless, there she was, safe in Carlisle Bay – and so (at last) was Abercromby. Pinckard wrote: 'Crowded with yards and masts the harbour resembled a thick forest ... Loud shouts of welcome resounded throughout the bay ... each ship repeated three cheers

---

15   Jeffery,(ed.), *Dyott's Diary*, vol.1, pp.91–92.
16   Pinckard, *Notes on the West Indies*, vol.1, p.403.

as he passed ... on reaching the government house ... [he] was received with a salute of 21guns ... the same was then repeated from the fort.'[17]

Pinckard painted the ecstatic relief felt by all, as the anxious wait for the Commander-in-Chief was finally over – which only left the long-awaited arrival of Rear Admiral Christian in the *Thunderer* (74), and the rest of the fleet. This was to add another month to the time before operations could commence in earnest. He eventually arrived in Carlisle Bay on 21 April. He had the time, while still on shore in England, to be knighted for all his efforts in both assembling the fleet and ensuring it reached its destination. In which most of the latter he had been successful, if at a somewhat retarded pace.

The arrival of the Commander-in-Chief was the signal for general animation and exertion. The disasters and dangers of the voyage were forgotten, although by the delay, much of the best of the season for action was lost. The Windward Islands were heading towards high summer and the hurricane season.

Unfortunately, when ships began arriving that had sailed from Cork, they brought sickness with them. A large number of men, plus several officers, died. They had suffered dysentery and typhus, while cramped in poor conditions on Spike Island in Cork Bay, waiting for their transports. Boult reported that 500 died and 3,000 were hospitalised. Stewart wrote of 'the sick ... so numerous as to fill the hospitals'.[18] These were not helped by the fact that two ships, stuffed with medicines and curatives, had not yet made an appearance. They may well have been lost, either to the sea or to the enemy, indicating yet again the conditions fraught with difficulty when dealing with such huge distances.

The following September, huge quantities of medical cases, casks, jars and packages were being sent out yet again to the Windward Islands – some 392 tons. A further 26 cases, 20 casks, two jars, 28 tons for each island of St Domingo, Jamaica, Barbados and Martinique and yet another eight tons each for Grenada, St Vincent's, St Lucia, St Kitt's, Antigua, Dominica and Tobago.[19] The costs were astronomical and medicines themselves, so greatly prized by the medical men, were to have little or no effect on the numbers of redcoats with fever. But that comes in the future. For the present, 'Christian's Fleet' had arrived. It was time to begin the assault on St Lucia.

---

17 Pinckard, *Notes on the West Indies*, vol.1, p.432.
18 Stewart, *Sketches*, p.414.
19 TNA: WO 4/388: Medical supplies to West Indies Islands, p.252.

13

St Lucie: La Fidèle

If there is no struggle, there is no progress.[1]

St Lucia, or St Lucie to the French, is one of the Windward Islands in the Caribbean, about 4,200 sea miles across the Atlantic from Britain. It is an island of lush forests, steep mountains cloaked with vegetation, magical beaches with the turquoise seas of a desert island. A thing of beauty and possibilities for the two European nations who constantly squabbled over it.

Both French and British disputed its ownership – the French in 1643, 1674, 1756, 1763, 1783 and 1802, and the British in 1664, 1722, 1762, 1778, 1796 and 1803, until St Lucia was finally left in British hands in 1814 and changed back to her English name permanently. Two of Europe's oldest enemies for some 200 years played voracious Caribbean football with the island of St Lucia and her peoples.[2] Mostly the island changed ownership through multiple treaties, with little reference to the indigenous inhabitants whatsoever. During those years of recurring disruption, the whole make-up of St Lucia changed. Admiral George Brydges Rodney was convinced that the principal harbour of St Lucia, the Carenage, was 'so secure and capable of being defended, which alone is of the utmost consequence to a maritime power'. He was persuaded that this single harbour was of infinitely more value to the British than all four harbours of Martinique. It was more secure, better placed, sheltered from hurricanes, and had more sea-room. It also boasted the Little Carenage where the largest of ships could be taken out of the water and turned on their sides for repairs and careening. It therefore needed to be secured by the British as their prime domain in the Sugar Islands.[3] This reasoning would be an advantage to the military as well. Rodney took St Lucia in 1762 only for it to be returned to the French the following year by the Treaty of Paris. The French occupied the island undisturbed for 14 years from 1763–1778, when war broke out between France and Britain once again.

---

1   Frederick Douglass, 'West India Emancipation' speech at Canandaigua, New York, 1857, quoted in *Two Speeches by Frederick Douglass* (Rochester: C.P. Dewey, 1857), p.22.
2   Gregor Williams, *The Biggest Battle over St Lucia*, unpublished paper, accessed December 2015. Dr Williams, is a St Lucian historian, educator, and conservationist.
3   Williams, *The Biggest Battle*.

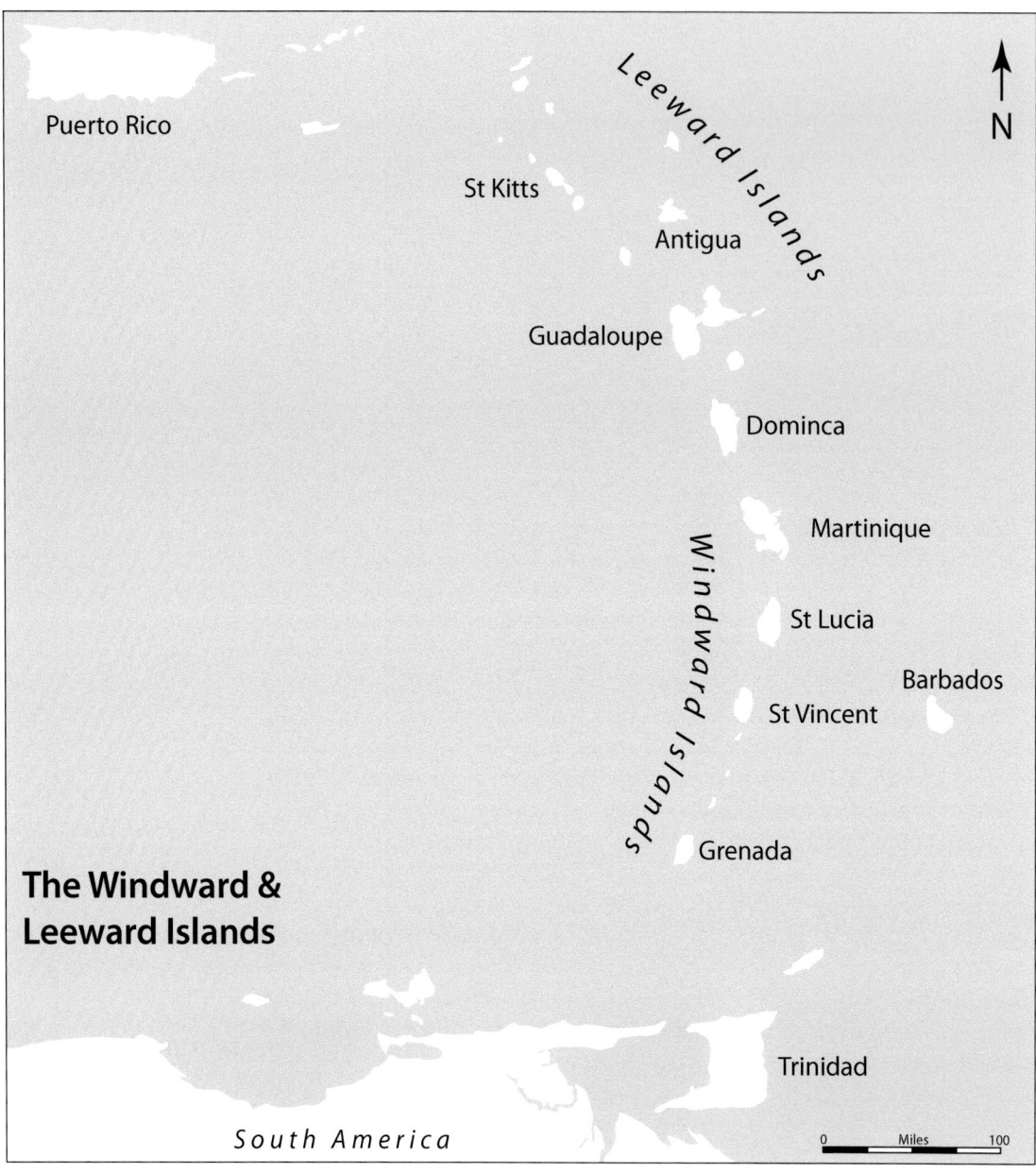

The Leeward and Windward Islands. St Lucia is in sight of Martinique. (© Rob Griffith)

Britain, as always, looked to her own advantage. Rodney had knocked it on the head when he married the excellent harbours of St Lucia to the results of the hard agricultural labours of the French, but a sugar island was, by default at that time, a slave island in view of the extensive labour required to grow, harvest, and process the sugar cane. By the following year, 1789, Harmsen gives the population of St Lucia as 18,218 slaves with 1,588 free people of colour and 2,181 Europeans.[4]

---

4   Jolien Harmsen, Guy Ellis, Robert Devaux, *A History of St Lucia* (St Lucia: Lighthouse Road Publications, 2014), p.58.

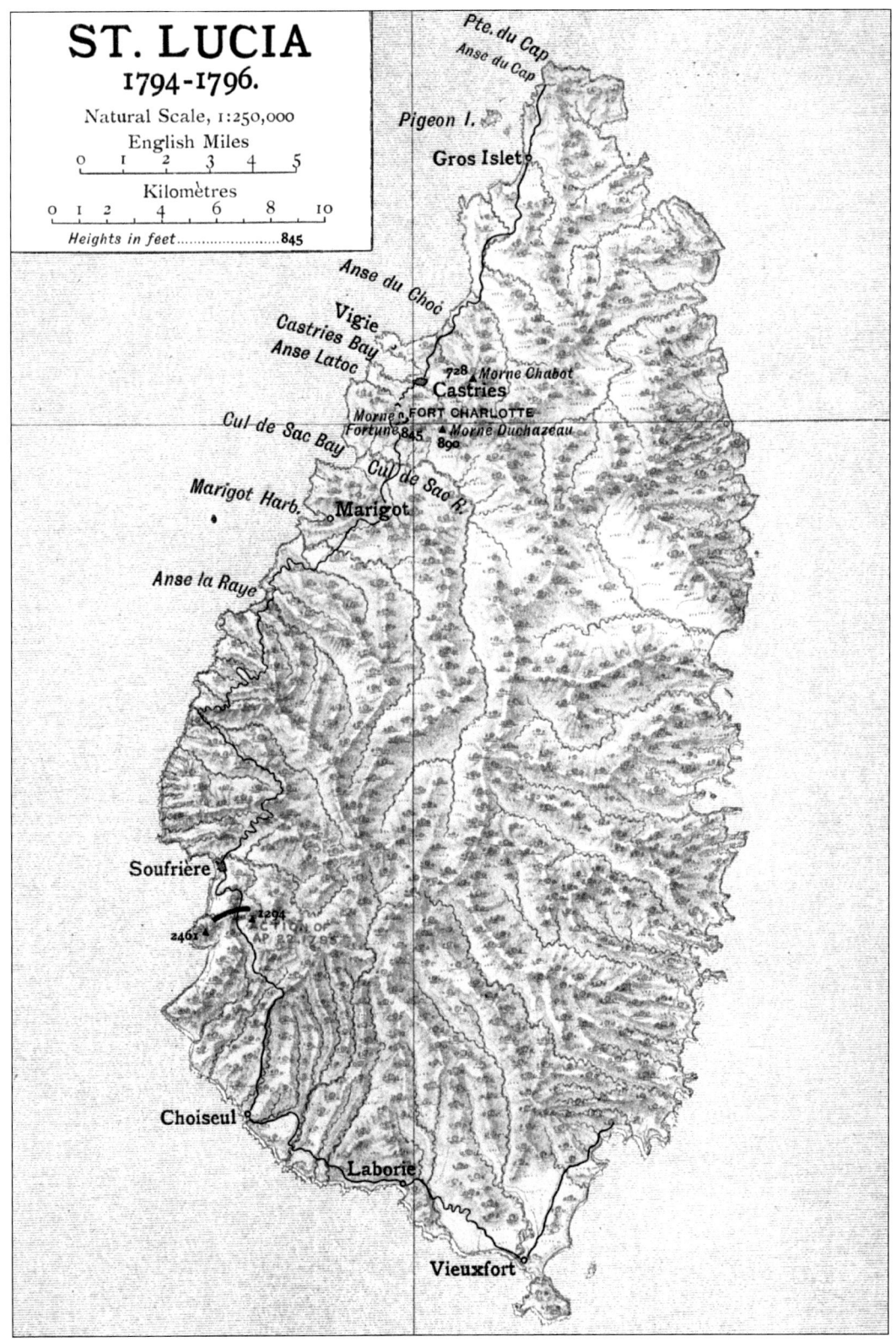

St Lucia, 1794–1796.

NOT SO EASY, LADS

The French Revolution of 1789 was to have a great effect upon the inhabitants of St Lucia who were essentially French in outlook and culture. Williams tells us that '... St Lucia became actively engaged in the events taking place. The people had been ardent supporters of the Revolution, Liberté, Egalité, Fraternité. By 1792 St Lucia earned for herself the soubriquet of 'St Lucie La Fidèle' (St Lucia the Faithful) 'in recognition of [the] support for the revolution.'[5]

A huge step for freedom was made on 4 February 1794 when the National Convention in Paris abolished slavery in all the French colonies. 'Henceforth, all inhabitants, without distinction of colour, were to be French citizens with full constitutional rights.'[6] Historian Jolien Harmsen tells us that this decree arrived around September 1794, too late for the St Lucians, as the British had already retaken the island. This had happened on 4 April 1794, when *Maréchal de camp* Nicolas Xavier de Ricard, French Administrator of St Lucia since 1793, relinquished the island into the hands of Colonel Sir Charles Gordon who, in turn, passed the reins to Brigadier General James Stewart.

Meanwhile a small force of about 1,500 soldiers under the charismatic leadership of Victor Hugues, sailed from France on 7 June 1794, to retake Guadeloupe, of which he has been declared governor by the *Comité de Salut Public*. He introduced himself before he even set foot on shore, when he brought a guillotine 'shrouded in the bows of his ship. As he approached the shore, he tore off the tarpaulin sheet and the sunlight glittered on the steel blade.'[7] On arrival he announced an end to slavery and subsequently swelled his numbers with slaves and people of colour (*gens de couleur*). Despite the revolutionary cry of *Liberté, Egalité and Fraternité*, he rid the islands of any who opposed him, with the help of the guillotine he had brought from France.

Victor Hugues – the 'terrible little man', Jacquin. (Illustrated by Jo Davies)

One of his first acts after he landed in Guadeloupe was to capture 1,200 royalists, all of whom were guillotined. At the battle of Morne Savon on Guadeloupe 865 royalists were shot and 27 saved for the guillotine. By October he had retaken Guadeloupe from the British. He continued to build up his revolutionary army as he moved through the islands and by February 1795, Hugues had sent men, arms, supplies and military uniforms to St Lucia. While he was building on his early successes the atmosphere of revolution continued contagious and mounting.

---

5   Harmsen, et al., *St Lucia*, p.63.
6   Harmsen, et al., *St Lucia*, p.64.
7   Harmsen, et al., *St Lucia*, p.60.

ST LUCIE: LA FIDÈLE

At the beginning of 1794, St Lucia had been under French control. But two months later on 1 April, Vice-Admiral Sir John Jervis and Major General Prince Edward, Duke of Kent landed 'troops at Ance du Cap, Choc beach and Roseau Bay'. British colours were raised within four days at La Toc Battery, Morne Fortuné and Castries, all of which had been taken with relatively little opposition. The British then made the mistake of believing they had control of the whole of St Lucia.[8] Sir Charles Gordon was appointed governor but he was to be court martialled for extortion and bribery in 1795. His successor was Brigadier General James Stewart, who did what he could with those troops which were available. But radical French politician Victor Hugues, recognising that St Lucia was one of the strengths in his armour, so to speak, had sent in fervent men ready and able to do what he ordered and others with the skills of politicians or administrators. He set up an influential black republican, Jean-Joseph Lambert 'as representative of the Republic, a commissioner for the leader of the insurgents, a free black called Marinier, to be commander-in-chief of French Forces on the island and a proclamation … ordering all inhabitants to join them on pain of death'.[9] Liberté? All this while St Lucia was officially in the hands of the British under the command of Brigadier General Stewart.

France sent more reinforcements and Victor Hugues was joined by a new Commissioner for St Lucia – Gaspard Goyrand. He left Brest in November 1794 in the *Hercule*, together with three frigates and 19 transports. The latter were carrying 2,000 men and the *Hercule* had 200,000 francs on board, for the continued requirements of the French islands.[10]

Goyrand finally arrived at Guadeloupe after a journey of 52 days. A man in his early 50s and a civil servant rather than a soldier, Goyrand stayed in Guadeloupe with Hugues for three months, after which he was invited to take over the governorship of the tinderbox that was St Lucia. Ironically, there were to be black troops fighting for both protagonists – France and Britain. When the news of the French Revolution arrived in 1789 and Thomas Paine's *Rights of Man* was published, the island had declared its solidarity with France and 'the 14th of July was declared a public holiday in St Lucia and the mood was generally expectant'.[11] Three years later, when there was news given out (mistakenly) in September of a reinstated monarchy in France, and the French and royalist islands of Guadeloupe and Martinique flew the white royal flag, St Lucia defiantly flew the tricolour, not only comfortable with being French, but French Republican, as well.

In the West Indies the responsibility for retaking the French islands, lay upon the shoulders of Vice Admiral Sir John Jervis, later Earl St Vincent, for

---

8   Harmsen, et al., *St Lucia*, p.65.
9   Michael Duffy, *Soldiers, Sugar and Seapower: The British Expeditions to the West Indies and the War against Revolutionary France* (Oxford: Clarendon Press, 1987), p.142.
10 J.A. Chymiste Le Rouge, *Compte Rendu Adresse a Bourdon, Ministre da la Marine et Des Colonies. Par Citoyen Le Rouge Chymiste, attaché au service de la Marine, dan les ports, de la République Francaise Procédés pour le conservation des Decrées de Premiere Necessité* (Brest: Audran, 1797), p.2.
11 Harmsen, et al., *St Lucia*, p.60.

the navy, and Lieutenant General Sir Charles Grey, for the army. By the end of 1794, Grey was replaced by Lieutenant General Sir John Vaughan whose intentions were 'to fight fire with fire' and 'sent the Black Carolina Corps to St Lucia' for the purpose of destroying the Brigands. In St Lucia, unsurprisingly, 'a rebellion was fomented against the British'.[12] All patriots, including whites, free blacks and free people of colour headed for the mountains to join the escaped slaves and a true guerrilla war began.

Goyrand embarked for St Lucia in April 1795, after receiving orders from Hugues, who 'hoped that my presence and my devotion would disconcert the plans of the enemy'. The French troops had been forced back to Morne Doudon (some three miles east of Castries and two miles from Morne Fortuné), by the British troops under Brigadier General James Stewart. Goyrand arrived at Soufriere on the west coast of the island and his efforts were unremitting and (temporarily) successful. In essence he took it upon himself to be solely responsible for forthcoming events.[13] Included in his new troops were soldiers of Rochambeau's black republican troops, who had previously been British prisoners of war. Goyrand wrote: 'I affected a great deal of self-possession and decided assurance; I declared that I was a stranger to all parties, that I had a horror of cruel and avaricious men; I did more; I caused a forgetfulness of the past to be proclaimed for all the colonists who would join me.'[14] Although an admirer of Hugues, he had talked of the latter's 'predilection for cruelty and bloodshed', while Goyrand's deputy, artillery officer Pierre Jacquin, called Hugues 'a terrible little man'.[15] There were many stories of Hugues' appalling inhumanity.

Goyrand defeated the British troops who attacked them in the Battle of Rabot, south-east of Soufriere, on 22 April 1795. This defeat persuaded Stewart to retreat to the garrison at Morne Fortuné. On the last night before the assault on the garrison, Stewart evacuated the island under the cover of darkness on the night of 18–19 June. Goyrand, who was not an unsympathetic man, was shocked to find that Brigadier General Stewart had left behind his wounded together with 36 wives of the 68th Foot and he organised their return to their regiment by ship. He was much lauded by the locals for his humanity. But he himself admitted that his 'beneficent act' was partly due to wanting rid 'of useless mouths'.[16] With Goyrand's governorship came St Lucia's first real year of liberty.

Gaspar Goyrand made his headquarters at the Devaux house in Soufriere and attempted to bring order out of disorder and in succeeding for the most part, became thereby a major player in the island's history. Under this administration, Goyrand and the authorities he set up, met every 10 days to discuss progress and 'public behaviour … the mayors exercised police duties and could summon the army'. Goyrand was tough on any who came under the umbrella of 'traitors' whether the sedition was in act, spoken or written

---

12 Harmsen, et al., *St Lucia*, p.66.
13 Le Rouge, *Adresse*, p.1.
14 Le Rouge, *Adresse*, p.5.
15 Harmsen, et al, *St Lucia*, p.67.
16 Le Rouge, *Adresse*, p.9.

word, but 'Civil rights would be respected and no unjust or arbitrary action would be tolerated.'[17]

He set to work at readying the island for a state of war. History had taught him that the British would return. They always did. The island was of great use to them, not only for its plantations but also for its harbour and for Britain's expanding empire. His work as commissioner was to stabilise the island communities in those first months of freedom from slavery, which included urging any unruly islanders to adhere to the law, by which he succeeded with the help of troops. He wrote: 'As soon as [the] Carenage fell into our hands, I began establishing a temporary administration. I [encouraged] all men to return to their places and resume their former occupations.'[18] He organised the island into six municipalities, making good use of all literate and able men of whatever colour. So, the next 12 months were spent preparing for the undoubted British invasion.

To ensure that St Lucia had a fighting chance Goyrand organised a battalion of Africans, under the command of Citizens Marinier and Marin Pèdre, who were known for their adherence to republicanism. He cleared and re-armed, where possible, the fort at Morne Fortuné, the Cizeron's redoubt and all other batteries near to the Morne. When this was done, he made a tour of the island to see what else needed to be achieved and to check on the smooth running of the municipalities. Thus, he restored all the coastal batteries; he built a new fort on the point at the Carenage, arming it with four 36-pounders from the Drouilhard battery; he repaired Fort Rodney and added an entrenchment to the Caules battery.[19] Goyrand wrote:

> I shall omit certain small details relating to my provisional organization; it had produced the desired effect; I often travelled in the cantons; I assembled the *decadi* African citizens [i.e. in groups of 10]; I defined to them, in a speech on their scope, civil liberty, political equality, the respect of property, of persons, willed by law; I told them that they would be treated as good citizens, if they redoubled their ardor for work, which would certainly consolidate their present existence.[20]

Over the following 10 months St Lucia virtually became the headquarters and wellspring for support of the revolutionaries for the nearest islands. From the British point of view, 'Not only were the Republicans left in the undisturbed possession of an important military post, but they were enabled to send reinforcements to their friends in the other Colonies, by means of which the [revolutionaries] in St Vincent, Grenada and Martinique opposed a successful ... resistance to the British arms.'[21]

Henry Breen, a much later administrator of St Lucia, recounted a whole series of incursions and sudden sorties throughout the months preceding

---

17 Le Rouge, *Adresse*, p.9.
18 Le Rouge, *Adresse*, pp.7–10.
19 Le Rouge, *Adresse*, pp.9–10.
20 Le Rouge, *Adresse*, pp.11–12.
21 Henry Hegart Breen, *St Lucia: Historical, Statistical, and Descriptive* (London: Longman, Brown, Green and Longmans, 1844), p.85.

Cannon at one of Rodney's batteries on Pigeon Island. (Donald Roworth)

the next attempt to retake St Lucia by the British in 1795. In September Victor Hugues sent another force of 500 men to St Vincent. The result of this incursion was the retreat of the British from their positions back to the capital of Kingstown. In October, more of the same, but this time in Grenada. In December it was the turn of Martinique. While Victor Hugues continued in his efforts to overthrow the British, Gaspard Goyrand worked hard to create order from chaos in St Lucia.

As Goyrand had predicted, St Lucia was the first island chosen by Sir Ralph Abercromby to be invested prior to setting up British rule again which, if achieved, would reintroduce slavery back to that island. This goal was not to be so easily achieved. By the end of 1795 the British were left with their main forts in St Vincent and Grenada only. Abercromby's army, on board Christian's fleet and bound for the West Indies, with orders to retake the British islands yet again, was struggling to beat westwards against those severe winter storms. Neither did the two British commanders know of the lengths to which the island of St Lucia had been preparing for such an onslaught.

During this period, Goyrand's Africans learned what it was to be free and walk away from the plantations, they remained in a halcyon state of euphoria until the British strove to re-impose pre-revolution conditions again. Not all Britons agreed with this policy, it needs to be said – and many were fighting in the British parliament with angry words, but the St Lucians were only too aware of what a return to British rule would mean at that time. The British placed many of the St Lucians under one umbrella term of brigands. St Lucian Historian Robert Devaux wrote, 'I see the Brigand as a true freedom fighter – a guerrilla warrior.'[22]

So, enter *L'Armée Francaise dans les Bois* ('French Army in the Woods'). A resistance army had been building up in the forests of St Lucia, since 1794. Two French soldiers, Kermené and Sabathier Saint-André, headed up the forces and began to forge them into a well-schooled and disciplined army of men, entirely intimate with their own terrain and its abundant cover. In Harmsen's opinion, 'In the densely forested mountains, a republican resistance army was emerging that would become one of England's worst nightmares.'[23] In fact, much of the fighting to come was what we now think of as guerrilla warfare. Because of the geography and topography of this mountainous and thickly forested island, it was ideally suited to that kind of combat, with huge opportunities for ambush. Weight of numbers certainly had their place, but in circumstances such as those on St Lucia, light infantry was invaluable.

Despite Britain's interaction with St Lucia since the seventeenth century, for those who had never seen it before, neither their experience of Britain, nor that on the Continent, had prepared the soldiers in any way for the lush vegetation of the West Indies, much of which grew on perilous inclines and mountains. The island was 'covered with forest trees of every form and endless variety'.[24] Henry Breen went on to list over 60 trees indigenous to the island and '… the woods are inhabited by wild ox, musk rat, wild hog, iguana and agouti'.[25] There followed innumerable birds, fish, and insect-life and Breen was lyrical with his descriptions, quoting (he said), from the *Edinburgh Review*:

> The bete-rouge [laid] the foundations of a tremendous ulcer. In a moment you [were] covered in ticks; flies enter[ed] your mouth, into your nose: you [ate] flies, [drank] flies, and breath[ed] flies. Lizards, cockroaches, and snakes [got] into your bed: ants [ate] up the books: scorpions [stung] you on the foot. Everything [bit], [stung], or [bruised]: every second of your life you [were] wounded by some

---

22 R. Devaux, *They Called Us Brigands: The Saga of St Lucia's Freedom Fighters* (St Lucia: Optimum, 1997), p.xiv.
23 Harmsen, et al., *St Lucia*, p.65.
24 Breen, *St Lucia*, p.152.
25 Breen, *St Lucia*, p.152.

piece of animal life. An insect with eleven legs [was] swimming in your teacup; a nondescript with nine wings [was] struggling in the small beer, or a caterpillar with several dozen eyes in its belly [was] hastening over the bread and butter.[26]

Somewhat tongue-in-cheek maybe, but his description showed the potential of St Lucia to bestow considerable pain and discomfort – and then there were snakes, which included the Cribo, the Fer-de-lance, the Worm Snake, and Boa Constrictor, all of which may have been a veritable Darwinian heaven, but not so easy to struggle through wearing full British army 'tropical' uniform, which included the ubiquitous flannel underwear and carrying a 10 and a half-pound Brown Bess musket, plus 17-inch bayonet. Not all the flannel in the world would stop the fangs of the Fer-de-lance inflicting its venom into the leg of the redcoat. It certainly would not ease the fear of that happening either.

So, this was the country to which the red-jacketed men from the fens of Huntingdonshire and flat fields of Essex came, the men from the mountains, valleys and lakes of Westmorland, the Highlands of Scotland and the loughs of Ireland. This was the country described by a Highlander, David Stewart, when he echoed Breen: 'No part of the Highlands of Scotland is more rugged and broken than the proposed scene of action in … St Lucia [in which] there are woods and ravines almost impassable to any four-footed animal, except to such as could scale rocks, or creep beneath the thick underwood.'[27] Not the easiest terrain for horses then.

Once on duty the redcoats would surely have felt they were physically and mentally wading through treacle. Not exactly the easiest of foreign fields, but St Lucia and her soldiers were ready to do their best. So were the British redcoats. Unfortunately, as with many line regiments, the 44th Foot had lost their flank companies to the West Indies and Sir Charles Grey in 1794 and a good many of those had already lost their lives to disease and battle.

Iguana and Fer De Lance – two of St Lucia's many unusual animals. (Illustrator Jo Davies)

---

26 Breen, *St Lucia*, pp.156–157. The description is also attributed to Sir Sidney Smith.
27 Stewart, *Sketches*, pp.409–410.

ST LUCIE: LA FIDÈLE

Brigand – St Lucia's foot-soldier and freedom-fighter. (Illustrator Jo Davies)

14

Brigands and Bushfighters: April 1796

> *The sergeant-major's shout frighten the mountains, and ... six-hundred boots Presented Arms.*[1]

Goyrand was now the effective commander-in-chief of some 2,000 well trained, regulated, disciplined and able black soldiers, who were enthused and ready for the battles to come. After a year of freedom from slavery, they were convinced of their right to remain free and were well aware that being back under British rule meant the loss of that right – but not if they could help it. If defeated, a return to slavery and the sugar fields would be their unremitting future.

Goyrand had spent the last year in much time and energy as he prepared his defences. Batteries and all forts between Pigeon Island and Grand Cul de Sac had been improved and restored wherever possible by erecting palisades. His troops now included two companies of cannoniers. Determined to fill any insufficiency, he solicited aid from his counterparts in Guadeloupe to provide for those all-important needs required by all soldiers – food and ammunition. With his general, Cottin, in charge of the forces, Goyrand was as ready as he ever would be, without having extra time to prepare or recruit larger trained forces. He made careful observations and watched ceaselessly 'with his telescope' all the coasts of the island, to prevent any surprise disembarkation of British troops.[2] All was ready.

While still at headquarters in Barbados, Abercromby, prepared his men by issuing each regiment with two horses, one for the surgeon's packsaddle and one for the quartermaster. A 'negro pioneer' accompanied each horse and for every 100 men there were four pioneers.[3] Three flints and 60 rounds of ammunition were provided for each soldier. Abercromby's concern for the troops was evident in the series of cautions given concerning the hazards of drinking dirty water, over-exertion in the heat (this was often ignored, primarily by the officers over their subordinates,

---

1 Derek Walcott, *The Arkansas Testament* (New York: HarperCollins, 1987), p.41.
2 Le Rouge, *Adresse*, p.19.
3 Duffy, *Seapower*, pp.222–223.

with often fatal consequences) and the all-important extra grog on wet days. No doubt remembering the depredations caused latterly by the soldiers on the continent, the Commander-in-Chief stressed the need for the personal self-discipline required of each man, together with the punishment involved should there be anything less than the expected good behaviour. Drunkenness and pillaging would not be tolerated, the latter receiving the death penalty. Further there was to be no unnecessary waste of ammunition.[4]

The protagonists were coming together slowly. Goyrand and his troops were waiting, and Abercromby could wait for Christian no longer and left Carlisle Bay on Friday 22 April 1796 with those troops earmarked for the reduction of St Lucia and sailed for Martinique, dropping anchor 'in St Anne's Bay on the evening of the 23rd, but not without incident; an ordnance sloop was lost and the *Minotaur*, 74, ran ashore; some ships, missing the bay, were carried to leeward'.[5] Christian finally caught up with the fleet in St Anne's Bay on Sunday 24 April and sailed for St Lucia with them the next day. James Carrick Moore took from his brother's descriptions of St Lucia, the following:

> ... mountainous, remarkably strong by nature, and ... fortified by skilful French engineers. There rises from the sea, near the harbour, a high hill called Morne Fortuné, on which a strong fortress had been constructed. And at the basis of the hill along the beach, and on an island called Pigeon Island, there was a range of batteries, rendering it dangerous for ships to approach the shore.[6]

The sight of the island's forest-covered hills and valleys must have given just cause for concern. The topography alone was to cause severe problems for the invading forces, both during the investment and its aftermath; but with the human element added, it was an entity like no other – an alien environment to the many who had not been there before and a probably a renewed threat to many of those who had, as the troops observed the shores from their slowly advancing transports. Then there would be the suffocating heat and humidity exerting its own influence, together with the sheer possibility of getting lost within yards of entry to this forest-covered land.

The exertions and difficulties experienced during this investment, were to build more understanding of the particular trials and modes of battle required in such an environment and with such an enemy. This was to add to the already expanding body of knowledge and enlightenment which would change (with a number of retrograde mistakes along the way) whole ingrained attitudes to warfare in the British army, which in turn released and promoted new methods of facing the foe.

The feared and inevitable invasion, for which Goyrand had spent so long preparing, began in earnest early on Tuesday morning 26 April. The Royal Navy ships Christian had at his command included *Thunderer*, *Vengeance*,

---

4   Duffy, *Seapower*, pp.222–223.
5   Maurice, *John Moore*, vol.I, p.197.
6   Carrick Moore, *Sir John Moore*, vol.1, p.112.

NOT SO EASY, LADS

Storming and Taking the Fort and Town of Fort Royal, in the Island of Martinico, by General Sir Charles Grey and Vice Admiral Sir John Jervis, March 24, 1794, by Dodd. (Author's Collection)

Ganges, Hebe, Madras, Pelican, Arethusa, Victorieuse, Alfred, Beaulieu, Astrea, Bull Dog, and *Fury*. Thousands of British soldiers were crushed together on board multiple wooden decks, experiencing feelings of anticipation, excitement and apprehension. With the support of these ships, their massive firepower and their experienced crews, surely a mere 2,000 defenders would not hold out long against 8,000 plus armed and disciplined redcoats? Just two years before, also in April, other redcoats under Lieutenant General Sir Charles Grey had taken St Lucia in just five days.

Abercromby could not hope for such a speedy result on this occasion. His plan was to land three forces at different parts of the island, much as Grey had two years previously. The first would be at Anse Le Cap Bay (close under and to the north of Pigeon Island), heading for Longueville House in the north, together with artillery where Major General Alexander Campbell would disembark with 1,900 men whom Christian would support with three ships. The second division was to disembark at Choc Bay, the next bay south and just north of Castries and the Vigie Peninsula, as soon as the head of Campbell's division appeared, supported by the *Madras* and the *Beaulieu*. The third was to take place at Anse la Ray, 18 miles further south of the Cul de Sac, under the command of Major General William Morshead, also with 1,800 or 1,900 men. Colonel Donald MacDonald, of the 55th Foot, was given command of the reserve.

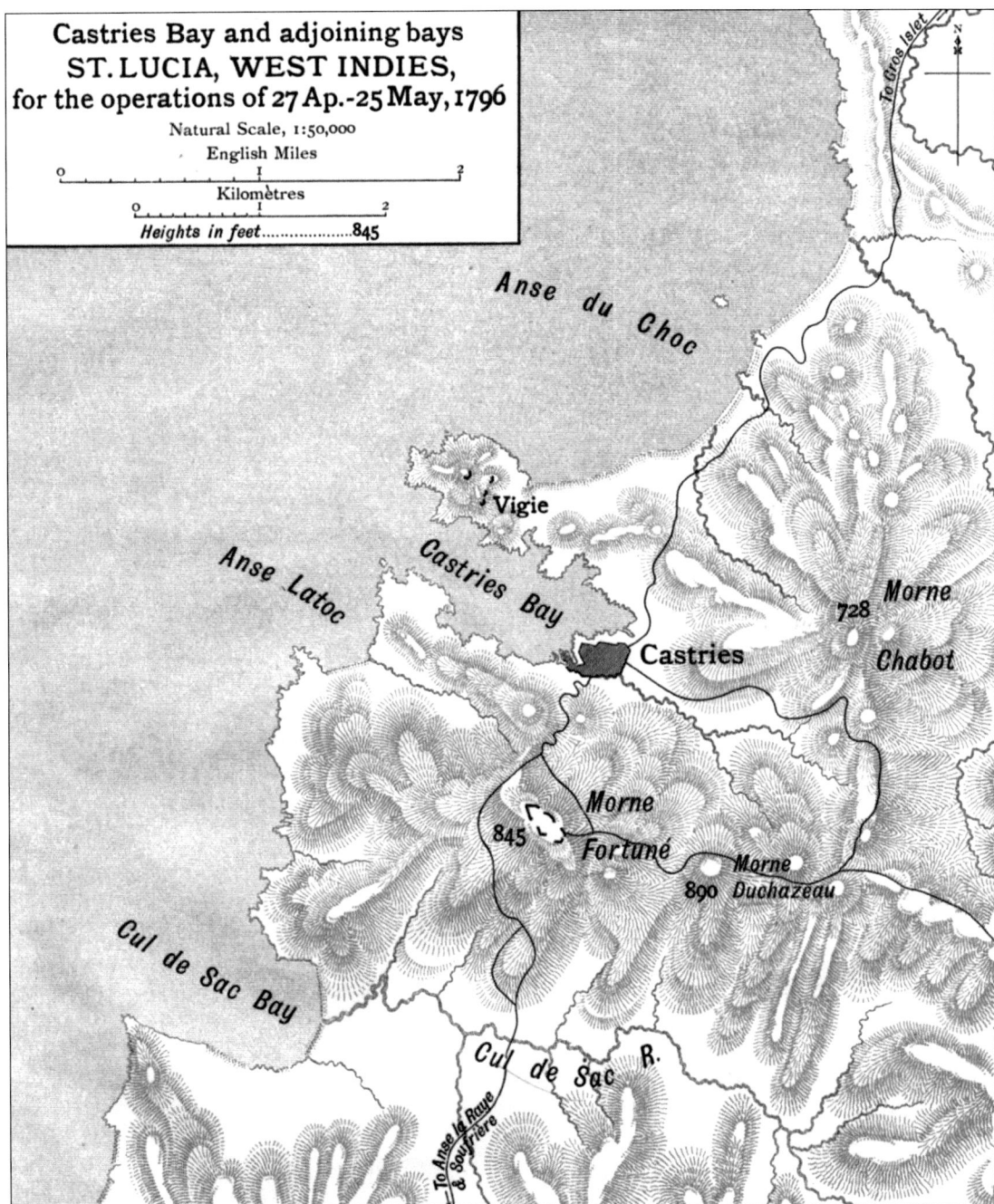

Castries, Choc and Cul de Sac. bays. Sites of the operations of 27 April–25 May 1796. (Author's Collection)

The 44th Regiment of Foot was in the third landing, at Anse la Ray, but as the wind and strong currents were taking the transports further and further south of their landing point their disembarkation could not take place until the ships had tacked their way back again.

Once HMS *Ganges* (74), arrived in Anse le Cap Bay, at about 4:00 a.m. on the 26th, her captain, Robert McDougall, anchored and offloaded the ships' launches and flat-bottomed boats. Moore claimed that only the transports carrying the 42nd and 14th Foot had arrived, with the other ships still some way off, so the decision was taken by Campbell to offload those troops already arrived into the boats and for Moore to lead them. As HMS *Hebe* came closer to the shore, the guns on Pigeon Island (Rodney's original fortified base) fired upon her, but the distance was too great for any effective damage. *Vengeance*, *Ganges* and *Hebe* returned fire with grape into the woods, damaged the fort, and engaged the five-gun batteries located on Pigeon Island with the result that one of the enemy guns was dismounted and the others silenced.[7]

Prior to this Goyrand had placed 200 volunteers across the Longueville/Anse le Cap Cove where his men had erected a camp. Acting on Major General Campbell's request, Moore, with some 1,900 men in all, reached the shore at about 8:00 a.m. They took with them a howitzer and two light guns. The plan was to split the men into two columns, clearing any resistance they might find as they moved towards the batteries of Trouillac and Brelotte, which overlooked Choc Bay, on the west side of the island. They would re-unite to attack and render the batteries useless against Sir Ralph's second and by far the larger landing of troops, disembarking on the beach at Choc.

Goyrand's 200 men were among the first defenders whom Moore said assailed him for some hours. Goyrand was not far out in gauging the British 1,900 men as 2,000 troops. Moore with the 42nd had ordered that, as they arrived the jäger of Löwenstein's Chasseurs were to take up a defensive position at Longueville House, about a quarter of a mile from the beach and they spent those succeeding hours exchanging fire with the French troops covering the remaining initial disembarkation, which was complete by 2:00 p.m. Moore ordered them to occupy and hold the house.[8] One jäger was killed and six or seven injured.

Goyrand reported that his French volunteers, who were commanded by Pelage, fought all day and did not yield until the next morning. Pelage was badly injured.[9] They retired to a small hill from where they could watch the enemy movements. Private John Simpson of the 42nd wrote that the landing had been remarkably easy as the French had only a small force in that part of the island. He observed that having ascended the heights, a halt was made to allow the field guns to arrive for support. The French posted themselves at a sugar plantation and took advantage of the cover that afforded, although still within musket shot. The Löwensteins were ordered to advance and drive the enemy from their post. Simpson watched the riflemen employ their usual tactics:

> … extending independent of one another, and attacking at the most advantageous points. A warm action took place in which there were a few wounded on both sides, and the French defended themselves with great bravery, contending for the place and seeing no more of our army advance, put our riflemen off the ground

---

7   Anon. (ed.), *Bulletins of the Campaign* (London: Clarke, 1796), Christian, *Thunderer*, Choc Bay, St Lucia, 4 May 1796, p.104.
8   Maurice, *John Moore*, vol.I, p.199.
9   Isidore Henry de Poyen-Bellisle, *Les Guerres des Antilles de 1793 a 1815* (Paris: Berger-Levrault et Cie, 1896) p.129.

after they had taken possession of it, but they soon found what kind of troops they had to contend with, for as often as one of them fired there was one of the French fell so sure were they of their aim. When the French found this, they took the retreat and posted themselves on a high hill, about two miles distant from us. The place they had left was a fine sugar plantation, with a good house and a number of negro huts, and sugar houses with great stores of sugars of all kinds.[10]

This action on the first day, according to Goyrand, killed 80 French, whereas just one of the jäger of the Löwensteins was killed that morning, with six or seven wounded.

The first real obstacle came when Campbell reported the Commander-in-Chief's orders, which were to cancel further action as Christian was not in a position to cooperate – due to contrary currents. However, Moore was convinced of the need to carry on with the action and to march as soon as the grenadiers, the 48th and the artillery had amassed. He pressured a very sick Campbell that a message should be sent to Abercromby requesting permission for a night march. The latter succumbed and in essence gave Moore *carte blanche* to continue whenever Campbell thought proper. The general was so ill that in reality he left the arrangements to Moore who, once the other corps were ready, marched at 3:00 a.m. In the lead was a company of grenadiers closely followed by a howitzer, while Moore kept to the rear with the Löwensteins and the 14th Foot.[11]

When nearing the heights at Choc, the leading grenadiers found themselves almost upon a small group of the enemy, who fired and retreated, probably aware of their being precious few against overwhelming British numbers. Mid-morning brought news that the two batteries, Trouillac and Brelotte, had been abandoned. The ships could be seen in the bay and by evening both Christian and Abercromby came ashore with more troops. Christian obligingly landed 300 of his seamen at the general's request. In his first report to the War Office he recognised 'the natural strength of this Country is Such that Time and great Exertion will be necessary for its reduction.'[12] He and Abercromby both realised that they were in for a long haul.

Historian Poyen de Bellisle wrote that the 200–300 French troops available and in position at Angiers House were too few to make any inroads into the landing of the British regiments, due to the accompanying fire from the ships. Abercromby ordered the advance of a gun and grenadiers to remove them. The French troops retired to Morne Fortuné to regroup, thus enabling the British to take over Angiers House as a temporary headquarters.

On the 28th, Goyrand found himself on the end of an ultimatum, delivered by Lieutenant Colonel John Sontag, sent to him jointly from Abercromby and Christian. The intention was to produce a quick end to hostilities:

> In the name of His Britannic Majesty, whose Land and Sea Forces we command. We summons you to surrender the Island of St Lucia.

---

10   Simpson, *Memorandums*, pp.6–8.
11   Maurice, *John Moore*, vol.I, p.199.
12   Anon. (ed.), *Bulletins, 1796*, Christian, *Thunderer*, Choc Bay, St Lucia, 4 May 1796, p.107.

> If the effusion of Blood is prevented by your immediate compliance, We offer protection to Persons and Property, but the armed Force to be Prisoners of War.
> If you persevere in resistance, you must expect to suffer the consequences.
> The officer bearing this has Orders to wait One hour for your answer.[13]

This elicited a very French response from Goyrand and Cottin, his military commander, 'We scorn your threats to us and we stand firm. Republicans Never Capitulate to Tyrants.'[14]

The tyrannical admiral and general surely could imagine the stamp of the Gallic foot. This response was not unexpected. All very serious stuff and so everyone knew exactly where they stood and what the coming days were likely to bring. This same day Goyrand tried to get a dispatch through to Guadeloupe with papers for Victor Hugues, but the fishing boat he entrusted it to was captured leaving the Carenage.[15]

In the meantime, Captain Thomas Drury, of HMS *Alfred*, (he who gathered his transports and led them to shelter during the hurricane in the Channel), was once more taking the lead to usher the second division into their landing place at Choc Bay. Captain John Dilkes of the *Madras* (56) had the responsibility for doing the same with the third division of transports. But the strong current swept the transports so far to leeward that neither landing was effected at the planned times. As 'the Minotaur 74 ran aground [and] an Ordnance sloop was lost', the troops were finally disembarked on the mornings of the 27th and the 28th respectively.[16]

At this point Brigadier General John Hope, Adjutant General, recorded at Angiers House, that numbers of men from individual regiments were to 'parade this night at twelve o'clock'.[17] This did not bode well for Moore who faced yet another sleepless night. He and Hope had orders from Abercromby to attack Morne Chabot to drive out the enemy. Moore's division was to march at midnight and Hope's half an hour later, the latter with instructions not to attack until the action had begun. Moore would command the 53rd Foot, 50 Löwensteins, and 100 of Lieutenant Colonel Malcolm's Royal Rangers. Hope was to command the 57th, 50 Löwensteins, and 200 of the Rangers, to leave half an hour after Moore. The latter was already exhausted and snatched an hour's sleep before leaving with his division at midnight.[18]

Abercromby sent two of his aides-de-camp, Lieutenant Colonel Andrew Ross (of the 21st) and Lieutenant Colonel John Abercromby (Abercromby's second son) to attend Moore on the march and to join him at the front of the grenadiers. It was a brilliantly moonlit night, but the path into the forest was narrow, broken, hazardous, and only wide enough for the men to negotiate in single file. After some four hours of difficult terrain the leading men were suddenly challenged by an advance enemy picquet, which fired on them. All

---

13 TNA: ADM 1/318: Ultimatum and response.
14 TNA: ADM 1/318: Ultimatum and response.
15 Poyen-Bellisle, *Les Guerres des Antilles*, p.130.
16 Duffy, *Seapower*, p.223.
17 Maurice, *John Moore*, vol.1, pp.200.
18 Maurice, *John Moore*, vol.1, p.200.

surprise lost, there was only one decision and that to stand and fight, but the result (in Moore's opinion) was a shambles. In spite of his orders, Moore 'could not prevent [his inexperienced men] from firing or induce them to advance with the bayonet'.[19] The enemy picquet fired, killing or wounding a number. Although continuing to move forward Moore's men were fired upon every few yards. On finally reaching the summit they used their bayonets on the few who had not already melted into the bushes. Moore was aware of his own good fortune when a grenadier had fallen against him, having taken the bullet which appeared to be for Moore himself.

The tally of killed and wounded was high: 70–80 men. Moore's own Brigade Major, Captain Paul Anderson, was shot in this engagement, but lived. Fewer than 20 of the enemy were dead, with the same numbers of wounded, about half the number of the British fallen. This action proved to Moore that the reduction of St Lucia was not going to be a walk-over. His assessment of his men allowed that they did not lack spirit but certainly lacked the necessary discipline for and trust of, their officers, due to their youth and insufficient training.[20] Hope reached the foot of the Morne, with his own division, but because of Moore's precipitate start they arrived as the action ended and on hearing the drum roll of the grenadiers' march, the men cheered.

As dawn came, Morne de Chasseur began to loom out of the gloom. Moore and Hope became aware of its commanding presence some three miles distant and its more salient position from which to attack the fort on Morne Fortuné, as well as to present a better and easier communications point with the 3rd Division under Brigadier General Morshead on Morne Petit, when he managed to disembark and reach that point. Morshead gained the beach later that day, the 28th.

Moore and Hope took the initiative and opportunity to reconnoitre immediately and started their march to Morne Chasseur together with their troops, leaving Lieutenant Colonel Abercromby in situ at Morne Chabot together with the 53rd supported by some men from Löwenstein's Chasseurs, Moore being well aware of the strengths of the latter. He ordered Ross to return to Sir Ralph Abercromby to report. The Commander-in-Chief appreciated his junior officer's efforts when he wrote his own assessment of the action just completed, sympathising with the loss of life and commending the troops for their conduct in the difficult circumstances. He returned to Angiers House later in the day and proposed to send forward the 55th and part of the 42nd to march to Morne Chabot that evening, followed by the remaining parts of the 53rd and 57th the following day, 29 April. He ordered Moore to submit a daily report.[21]

During the above actions the 44th were still on board the transports as part of the 1st Brigade. Historian Michael Duffy, using the General Orders for 15 April together with the Leeward Muster Returns for 1 May, states that the 1st Brigade consisted of the 14th, 27th, 28th, 44th and 48th Regiments of

---

19 Maurice, *John Moore*, vol.1, p.202.
20 Maurice, *John Moore*, vol.I, p.203.
21 Maurice, *John Moore*, p.205.

Foot. The 44th was the largest regiment in the brigade with 36 officers and a total of 915 men.[22] Not far off the thousand that Roworth gauged during the preparations back in Britain.

Christian describes the difficulties encountered by the Third Division, of which the 44th were a part. There was a 'strong Lee Current' which had already interfered with the landing of the troops in Choc Bay and was now doing the same to the proposed landing at Anse La Raye. The signal to land had been given by the Admiral to both divisions to effect in the morning of the 27th. The Second Division achieved this around 10:30 a.m., but despite the order to Captain Dilkes in the *Madras*, with the support of the *Beaulieu*, the men of the Third Division (including the 44th) were fated to spend another night at sea and to land on the 28th, to await orders from Major General Morshead for their part in the reduction of Morne Fortuné.[23]

Roworth reported, 'The troops Landed in two Different partys at the Island on [28] April and we have only one of our Grenadiers wounded on landing. I went in the Second Boat with troops and Landed them Safe without any harm'.[24] Unfortunately he does not state which transports brought the 44th into the bay, whether they were the same that had brought them safely across the Atlantic or whether they were squeezed onto others for the disembarkation onto flat boats. Anse La Raye (or the Bay of Rays) is on the west side of St Lucia, the leeward side, some 10 miles south-west of Castries and about 18 miles south-west of Pigeon Island. Vieux Fort is about 34 miles south of Anse La Raye. Finally, when all were ashore Morshead was able to follow the River Cul de Sac to Morne Petit which was to be the divison's camp.[25]

It was here that the 44th would feel the stultifying heat and humidity for the first time, on their march on narrow paths through the tangled forests of St Lucia. They would have set about camping and cooking, no doubt, until required for service.

Moore and Hope, after a march of some hours more fully appreciated the advantages that Morne de Chasseur offered, with a convenient ridge extending towards the main focus of Morne Fortuné. Malcolm and his Royal Rangers were ordered to take over Morne de Chasseur while Moore took advantage of the ridge to place the rest of his corps and establish his 'advanced posts to within 1,200 yards' of the fortified Morne Fortuné. This move was justified when the enemy set up their own posts within 600–700 yards of his own.

Simpson, 42nd Foot, was involved in the action of 28 April and left an account of the occasion:

> The five companies of the 42nd Regt to which I belonged received orders to advance with the utmost speed, and to take the near way by the hills. It being the heat of the day, & the men wanting water were very much fatigued. They were

---

22 Duffy, *Soldiers*, p.221.
23 Anon. (ed.), *Bulletins 1796*, Christian, *Thunderer*, Choc Bay, St Lucia, 4 May 1796, p.105.
24 NA: DDRW 22/25: Roworth to Mary, St Lucia, 15 August 1796.
25 Duffy, *Seapower*, p.226.

falling down in faints, with their tongues hanging out of their mouths, and their comrades were obliged to bring them to their senses by their own wine in place of water, there being none to be got. After we got to that post we reinforced it by sending out pickets and guards. We remained on this post till the 2nd of May.[26]

Simpson was not exaggerating the effects of the terrain and the heat upon the redcoats. Bearing in mind that the troops had been on the move since midnight, it appears that the provision of water was insufficient. Just two months later, Lieutenant Thomas Phipps Howard of the York Hussars was to experience very similar conditions on St Domingue:

> ... when our troops marched to take Bombard, so ill were Measures taken for supplying the Troops with Provisions & Water, that their Distress was beyond the power of words to express. Exposed from nine oClock in the Morn: until 4 in the Even: to a Meridian Sun, many having been under Arms all Night, no water in their Canteens or any to be met with on the Road, their misery was not to be conceived without having been an Eye witness to it. At every three or four hundred y[ar]ds you met Men lying on their backs, their tongues lolling out of their Mouths & in the agonies of Death for want of Water. Many were absolutely by way of moistening their Mouths obliged to drink their own Urine in this wretched manner; [and] upwards of 50 Men died in a March of 12 Miles.[27]

Known as 'coup de soleil' by the French and heatstroke by the British today these men would have felt incredibly hot as their core temperature climbed above 38°C in the excessive heat, causing dizziness and headache, nausea and cramps in the muscles, profuse sweating and above all an all-consuming thirst. Simpson's account highlighted precisely that situation which was visited on the redcoats of the 42nd when they were involved in the taking of Morne de Chasseur. They were fortunate to survive the experience. These acute trials speak for themselves of the appalling conditions endured.

Lieutenant Colonel Donald MacDonald added the first reports of dead, wounded and missing to the campaign bulletins for Secretary of State Dundas, on this occasion. The return for 28 April listed: one drummer, 12 rank and file, killed; one captain, two lieutenants, two serjeants, 44 rank and file, wounded; one drummer, eight rank and file, missing.[28]

That particular action over, yet again Moore went without sleep. It was he who woke the picquets, as the officers were 'so little to be depended upon'. He and Hope patrolled all night to prevent a sudden incursion by the enemy, just half a mile away. Throughout his time on St Lucia Moore was repeatedly despairing of the quality and effectiveness of the commissioned officers and the lack of direction they gave to their troops.

During daylight hours the men were camped in wigwams to shield them from the tropical sun and torrential downpours. Occasional firing and shelling from Morne Fortuné caused the death of two of the Löwensteins. On

---

26 Simpson, *Memorandums*, pp.14–16.
27 Buckley, *Haitian Journal*, p.42.
28 Anon. (ed.), *Bulletins 1796*, Macdonald, St Lucia, 2 May 1796, p.100.

1 May, the enemy troops attacked one of the outposts held by the grenadiers of the 55th. MacDonald recorded a total of 11 killed and 38 wounded.[29]

While decisions were made about earthworks to be undertaken by Brigadier General Knox, a report came in to Moore from Captain Hay, that Morshead was 'found wavering and uncertain', probably exacerbated by an unexpected skirmish between the grenadiers and the enemy at Grons.[30] He was already ill and possibly affected by the heat as well, but heat, terrain and vegetation notwithstanding, Moore drove his men on as the investment of Morne Fortuné continued.

The next major action taken was to drive the French from their sea batteries at the base of Morne Fortuné, thus opening up the way from the Grand Cul de Sac to facilitate the entry for the ships of war into the bay at Anse la Raye, which in turn would ease the movement of ordnance and men. The plan was to involve Moore's troops from Morne Chabot, under Hope's command; the 3rd, 42nd, the light company of the 57th, plus 200 Royal Rangers. Hope would approach the batteries from Morne Chabot. Morshead was to lead the 1,200 men from the camp at the Grand Cul de Sac, in two columns; the right column, to cross the river at Cools, to attack a battery on the right and the left to cross at the mouth of the river. Lieutenant Colonel Riddell of the 44th, with his men – including William Roworth – headed the left-hand column, crossed a ford on the river, took possession of the battery named Chapuis and held it 'for a considerable time'.[31]

Hope ordered Malcolm to take a battery with his Royal Rangers, but Malcolm was killed before he even reached it. This caused great distress among his men, who carried his body away from the place and refused to fight further on that occasion. Simpson observed that 'on Colonel Malcolm receiving a mortal wound his Regt. would not stand any longer, but took him up and retreated',[32] while Stewart noted that his men crowded round his body 'lamenting his loss'.[33] In later years Malcolm's obituaries varied from Fortescue's glowing and somewhat patronising 'an excellent officer who may be called the father of our African regiments … whose skill, courage and magic of leadership can turn the rawest of material into the most devoted and efficient of soldiers'[34] to Duffy's description of him as, '… one of the most energetic and experienced officers in Caribbean warfare, and the man who pioneered the use of negro units on the British side'.[35]

As part of the 44th, Roworth was involved in this action. Like Simpson, his words provide an immediate and evocative picture:

> On the 3d of May we attempted to Storm two of their Battrys with 400 Men of our Regiment. the one Battry on a High Hill which was well Defended by their Troops. … we had to Cross a River and to Scramble up the Woods which was

---

29 Anon., *Bulletins 1796*, p.100.
30 Maurice, *John Moore*, vol.I, p.206.
31 Anon. (ed.), *Bulletins 1796*, Abercromby Headquarters, St Lucia, p.101.
32 Simpson, *Memorandums*, p.21.
33 Stewart, *Sketches*, p.416
34 Fortescue, *History of the Army*, vol.IV, Part 1, pp.489–490.
35 Duffy, *Seapower*, p.228.

Very Steep, and a Little Rain falling that Night made it Verry Slippy. They poured Boath Grape and Rownd Shot upon us but we happily Got under their guns & Marched into the Lower Battry. The Enemy Lost Some few men Before they got out. A Party of men should have Come to our assistance Commanded By Genl Perryn, But he was too Late and [the Enemy] Being in Such a Strong Force at that Post [we] was obliged to [go] Back to our old Ground With the Small Loss of only Eight Rank & File Kill'd And about thirty wounded.[36]

In this Roworth was not too far out, as four of the 44th were killed and 37 wounded in total.[37] The other battery was taken by Hope and his troops, turning the gun on the enemy briefly. Hope and Riddell waited for support which never arrived, while being under fire from the Morne above. Morshead was seriously unwell with gout at the time, so he delegated the right-hand column to Brigadier General James Perryn, who failed to get his troops across the river at Cools. Perryn gave the reason as tiredness among the men. If 'tiredness', then possibly they were suffering from heat stroke and on the verge of collapse, as had Simpson's 42nd and Howard's York Hussars. Although historian Michael Duffy commented on another aspect of Perryn's outlook:

Perryn [was] lacking totally in Moore's spirit and enterprise. He had been impressed by the disciplined way that a small party of Negroes who contested his landing had held their fire until the boats were within half a musket-shot of the shore, also he was staggered by the terrain, which he compared with the Alps; the Morne Fortuné position was 'by far the stronger I ever saw'[38].

Simpson had a different take on this event, not previously mentioned, which involved an officer he referred to as 'Gen. Doil'. No General Doil, or more likely Doyle, seems to have been present, so Simpson probably misremembered the name. The 42nd acted with the troops who left Morne Chabot with Brigadier General John Hope:

… to form the communication, and on the way left the 55th Regt at an advantageous post, but on the march, there being no road through the woods, but foot paths, and the night being very dark, we lost the guid [guide], and all the rest of the troops, which hindered us very much, being by ourselves, and having Gen. Doil, who commanded the whole, along with us, he was very much afraid that we should fall into the enemies hands, we not knowing the place, nor where the enemy were posted. We however proceeded on to gain some part of the army posted on the other side of the garrison, but the black regt. which had parted from us with the guide, came upon the enemy & began the attack. We being by ourselves and it being dark, the General thought fit to post us as a corps of reserve … The action continued very hot on both sides for the space of an hour, by all the troops on that side of the garrison. The rest of the Army finding the enemy too

---

36 NA: DDRW 25/25: Roworth to parents, 4 November 1796.
37 Anon. (ed.), *Bulletins 1796*, Hope 4 May 1796, Headquarters, St Lucia, p.102.
38 Duffy, *Seapower*, p.227.

numerous, were obliged to retreat also, and it happened very well, that we were posted in the place that we were, as the army had to cross a small river, close to our rear, and the enemy was pursuing them very close. When they came up to us we opened in different places & let them pass through our ranks, and after they had got through, we closed again and kept a smart fire upon the enemy, which made them halt on purpose to form again.[39]

Simpson added that there was a field of very high sugar cane in front of them and intimates that they were able to use it as cover and also use the time to retreat over the river.

Poyen provided the French perspective as follows, the British: 'after having repelled a French post … had taken possession of the Dry [Seche] battery [they] even had [time] to turn a piece of 12 and to fire two blows at the fortress. Four men were killed [standing] beside Goyrand.' The fort returned fire. 'In two minutes the Dry Battery was completely swept and the English column dispersed'.[40] Whatever the cause, the action had to be called off.

The loss to the British during this action was considerable, as the Cul de Sac was kept under heavy fire from the French. Goyrand agreed that 'Immediately a well-fed file fire and 2 blows of cannon shot made the English retreat and strewed the vicinity of the fort with corpses'. Moore observed the action from his base. He could see the 'troops retreating through the valley of Cul de Sac, attacked on all sides'. After the action ceased, Moore commented that Abercromby was 'infinitely displeased'– code for livid. So livid, in fact, that Perryn had immediate orders to leave the island to 'escort the foreign cavalry to St Domingue'.[41] Morshead was also replaced with Brigadier General Charles Graham, Abercromby's second in command. In his report of 4 May Abercromby reported to Henry Dundas, Secretary at War, the news of the failed attempt on 2 and 3 May to knock out those batteries. The troops returned to their previous positions. The ships lost the opportunity and returned to their anchorage. Abercromby was greatly disappointed. On this occasion, 12 died, 52 were injured and 33 were missing. From the 42nd; Lieutenant Fraser, four rank file wounded and two rank and file missing. From the 44th; four rank and file were killed, Captains Johnstone and Tuffie, Lieutenant Gregory and 17 rank and file were wounded, Lieutenant David Ogilvie and 16 rank and file missing. All in all, much effort and loss of men for no return.

An alternative scheme was needed to invest Morne Fortuné, which would involve major earthworks, the expertise of the Royal Artillery and the muscle-power of Christian's sailors. Roads were to be made to bring up heavy armaments. This required 'large bodies of seamen and soldiers' employed in the making of them.[42] These exertions by both army and naval engineers and their men were continued until 16 May, when access from the sea to Morne Fortuné had been accomplished. Midshipman William Dillon wrote

---

39 Simpson, *Memorandums*, pp.17–22.
40 Poyen-Bellisle, *Les Guerres des Antilles*, p.31.
41 Maurice, *John Moore*, vol.I, pp.206–208.
42 Maurice, *John Moore*, vol.I, p.208.

of gun-boats and a bomb ship; of sloops of war constantly in motion; daily reinforcements; multiple reconnaissances; 'energies ... called into action, by land and sea'.[43] When accomplished, Abercromby and Moore had their battery on the top of Morne de Chasseur, placed to lay enough devastation to the fort at Morne Fortuné, to discourage the French garrison.

During this period of frenetic activity, yet another plan was made – an attack on the Vigie peninsula on 17 May. The Vigie stuck out from the land on the north side of the Carenage harbour. Where the land rose up three of Goyrand's batteries were placed, to cause maximum interference for the British fleet's unloading of ordnance and provisions, which they succeeded in doing. Because the Vigie, apparently, was 'held ... with a slender force', Abercromby thought it necessary to gain possession of it.[44] Another night attack was called for, in line with Abercromby's thinking that: 'in general in this Country, when you have to march to attack an Enemy's Post, who have Artillery, and where it is impossible for you to advance with any [artillery] on your Part, it is almost a matter of necessity to attack at Night'.[45]

The nights were cooler, of course. On the 17 May, as it was the nearest regiment, the 31st was ordered 'to march immediately after dark to take possession of the Vigie'. Historian Richard Cannon claimed that the regiment was based at Choc Bay, from which they marched at sunset. He describes the 'narrow isthmus' and position of the two batteries to be taken, 'the first placed midway upon the acclivity, and the second on the summit of the height. The approaches to both were by a circuitous path'.[46] It was believed to be held by not more than 200 men although Cannon disputed this, believing it 'remarkably strong'. The initial attack looked promising as the troops spiked a battery of three 18-pounders and man-handled them over a cliff. But during this action, the guide was wounded, and the troops became disorientated in the dark. Under heavy fire of grape Lieutenant Colonel Adam Hay ordered a retreat. Despite welcome covering fire by part of the grenadiers, under Lieutenant Colonel MacDonald, the 31st's losses were considerable: 'Captains Johnson and Walker, four serjeants, and eighty rank and file killed; Lieutenant Colonels Hay and Arbuthnot, Captains Murray and Sorrel, Lieutenants Sullivan and Hawkshaw, four serjeants and 121 rank and file wounded.'[47]

From his ship, HMS *Thunderer*, in Choc Bay, Midshipman William Dillon was an eye-witness – albeit to an attack that took place in darkness. Watching the cannon and musket fire made a lasting impression and it was he who wrote of subsequent firing of the town of Castries, calling it a conflagration.[48] Naval Surgeon Thomas Stewart wrote that 'the town ... was destroyed during the siege by our troops', while Goyrand claims that three fuses were set by

---

43 Michael Lewis, (ed.), *A Narrative of My Professional Adventures 1790–1839 by Sir William Dillon* (Abingdon: Routledge, 2019), vol.I, p.234.
44 Anon. (ed.), *Bulletins 1796*, Abercromby, St Lucia, 22 May 1796, p.126.
45 Anon. (ed.), *Bulletins 1796*, Abercromby, St Lucia, 22 May 1796, p.127.
46 Richard Cannon, *Historical Record of The Thirty-First or Huntingdonshire Regiment of Foot* (London: W. Clowes and Son, 1836), p.51.
47 Cannon, *Thirty-first*, p.52.
48 Lewis (ed.), *Dillon*, p.234.

NOT SO EASY, LADS

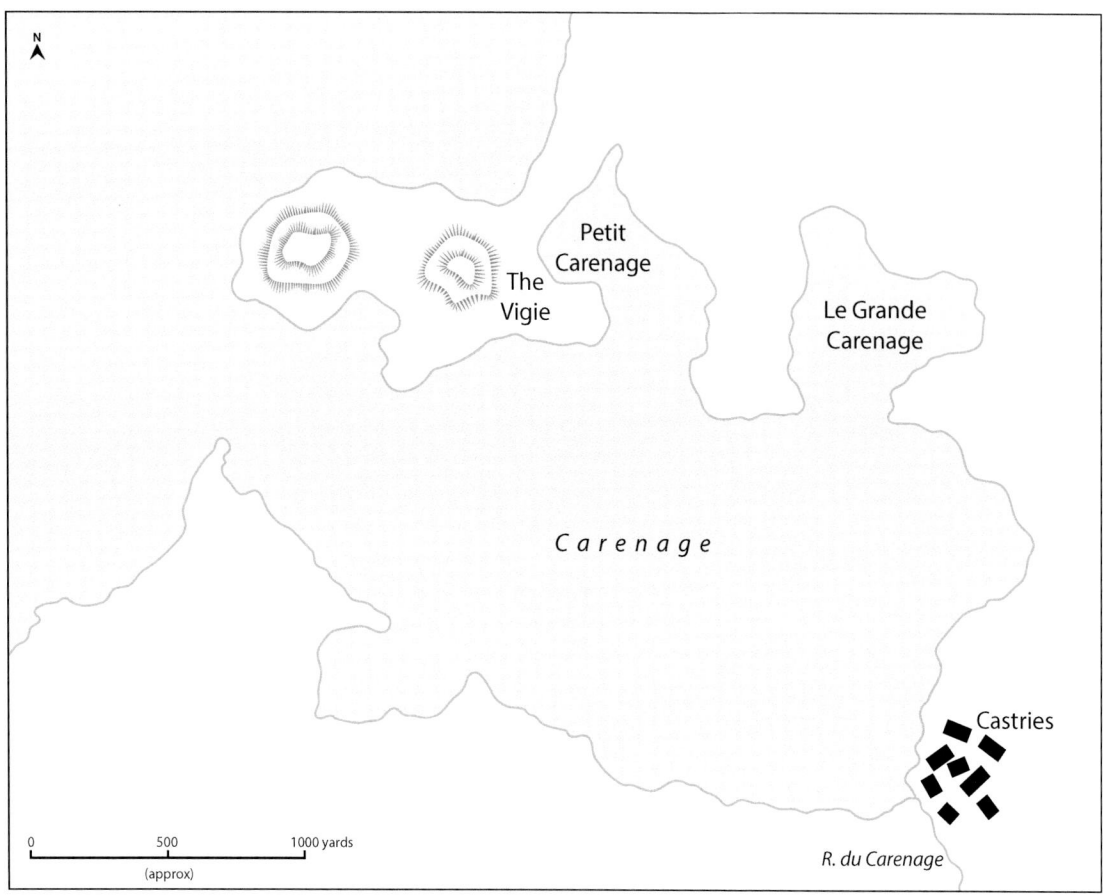

St Lucia's Carenage, site of the disastrous attack on the Vigie by the 31st Foot, 17 May 1796.

the British in three streets in the commune of the Carenage.[49] The British claimed that it was caused in error by ships' guns. However it started, the wind was blowing off-shore (as it does every night in the West Indies) and as the town was made of wood it burned completely, except for the prison, the general store and the house of the chief administrator. Goyrand intensely regretted the loss of the pharmacy, for obvious reasons, as well as the deaths of eight women and 10 children. Some 200 women and children, however, escaped and climbed to the fort on Morne Fortuné for shelter, making a further burden on the supplies of food and water.[50]

After the hours of darkness, daylight brought scenes of carnage on the Vigie. For Dillon it was 'covered with the dead bodies of our troops'.[51] Later, he watched the bodies being stripped of their red coats by St Lucian troops. This, however distressing to the onlooker, was nothing more than soldiers and camp followers round the world, including the British, had been guilty of in many wars. In fact, he was looking at (according to Moore) about 170

---

49   Poyen-Bellisle, *Les Guerres des Antilles*, p.137.
50   Poyen-Bellisle, *Les Guerres des Antilles*, p.137.
51   Lewis (ed), *Dillon*, p.234.

lost from the 31st alone.[52] The retreat was covered by MacDonald, in which only one of the 38th was killed – Lieutenant Robert Nuttall.

The constant assaults of the British on the island by land and sea were making severe inroads into Goyrand's ammunition supplies. Over the days his confident claims of firing 'vigorously' slowly regressed to 'in moderation' in order to conserve ammunition. There was never going to be a positive outcome for Goyrand and his brave freedom-fighters, but they were going to give of their best. Freedom was the key word in their thoughts.

Moore's account of the investment is the one which is most often quoted, for its detail and depth. Goyrand also leaves an account, in his address to Marc Antoine Bourdon de Vatry, Minister of the Marines and Colonies. This is a very interesting and informative stand-alone document, but the information within does not always correlate with Moore's. Allowing for discrepancies, and even hyperbole, as is often the case in military reporting (on all sides), it is sometimes difficult to recognise two versions of the same event, or to marry up the time-line of those events. Diaries and letters, by their nature, are more contemporary, even if selective, while memoirs often suffer from the ravages of time. Because Goyrand died in 1799, just three years after his service to his country ended, his account remains fresh and evocative. What is never in doubt is his conviction about the rights of his fellow men and his devotion to providing an environment for them to flourish.

---

52   Maurice, *John Moore*, p.213.

15

The Taking of Morne Fortuné: Thank God for the 27th!

The opportunity of defeating the enemy is provided by the enemy himself. Never give the enemy's soldier a target[1]

'You would Be Surprized how we Got our 24 Pounders, mortars, [and] Howitzers up those Steep and High Hills. The Enemy never thought we Could make Any Battrys on Such places …'[2] So Roworth wrote to his parents. Moore had great respect and faith in the Royal Artillery and their armaments, from his earlier experience in Corsica. He was familiar with the work achieved by sailors and garrison gunners, with the tackle used to haul very large guns over rough terrain and up steep and near vertical cliffs, in order to build batteries in positions selected by artillery officers, as the places from which to cause optimum damage and annoyance to the enemy. The more the 'annoyance' the more the enemy was likely to surrender.

The work went on with unremitting diligence from 8–16 May, with large numbers of soldiers and sailors employed on the earthworks, making the 10-mile road from the coast to the Morne and bringing up the armaments required. As Moore had decided upon Morne de Chasseur as his base from which to look down and attack the enemy fort on Morne Fortuné, he ordered batteries for 'ten pieces of ordnance' to be constructed at that post.[3] Other mortar batteries were being built where necessary and a chain of posts surrounded Morne Fortuné, to prevent the escape of any of the enemy into the woods. Moore's intentions were to keep up a regular fire on the enemy and irritate them, so that they would either surrender, run out of ammunition, or get so worn out that the British could attempt an assault. This was essentially siege warfare, where the enemy was blockaded and would come to terms when their provisions ran out. He hoped the strategy would work.

At 8:00 a.m. on 17 May 1796, the batteries opened fire, but to little effect and great disappointment – as they were too far away. It seems someone miscalculated there. The enemy with their three mortars and seven guns, in

---

1 T.E. Lawrence, *Guerilla Warfare*, p.15.
2 NA: DDRW 25/25: Roworth to parents, 4 November 1796.
3 Maurice, *John Moore*, vol.I, p.208.

THE TAKING OF MORNE FORTUNÉ: THANK GOD FOR THE 27TH!

particular a 9-pounder from their advanced post, began to 'plague' Moore again, though by the end of that day, they fired very little. But that single gun proved difficult to destroy, and so required a different approach, that of manoeuvre warfare, involving an unexpected strike and a determination, on Moore's part, to see that the manoeuvre succeeded. On 18 May 150 men under Captain Lewis Hay, Abercromby's chief engineer, made their way around the enemy by an unseen path, while Moore's soldiers continued to fire at the enemy gun as a distraction.[4] Captain Hay's detachment climbed the hill unseen and surprised the enemy who deserted the position and ran, but not before 'twelve or fourteen' were bayoneted.[5] Once the gun was spiked and thrown over the hill the detachment made its way back unharmed. They had neither fired a shot nor lost a man.

Moore then established a post of 200 men just 200 yards from the advanced batteries. The manoeuvre having worked once, he repeated it with Colonel Count Theodore Heillimer, of Löwenstein's Chasseurs, to remove another vexatious gun constantly firing at the Count's own post at Ferrands. This time the men used woods for cover and by drawing the enemy's attention by firing, the same ruse worked again. But the Morne was the position to defeat; to do so it would be necessary to haul up larger guns, but hauling them up the current positions would take more time and manpower. Rear Admiral Christian added some 1,000 more sailors for the execution of the project.

To Moore nothing mattered so much as the reduction of Morne Fortuné and he took the unusual step of asking Abercromby for the assistance of Brigadier General John Knox (Quartermaster General), Moore's senior, whom he considered a 'man of sense [and] a good officer'.[6] He stated his reasons in his diary:

> 21st May. Brigadier-General Knox appeared in yesterday's orders to command these advanced posts. This appeared singular to many, who cannot conceive that anybody could apply to have an officer put over them; but zeal and talent are now more than ever rare in the army. General Knox possesses both. I could not hesitate when the alternative was to lose his services or to serve under him.[7]

The two men worked well together and were of one mind. Only the weather was a hindrance. Tropical downpours washed out one of the roads and delayed the arrival of the 24-pounder guns by 48 hours. So, it was not until daylight on 25 May that all the batteries finally opened fire on Morne Fortuné. Roworth wrote: 'When Completed, We opened them all at once on them, on Each Quarter. Before we took the main Fort, We Battred [sic] Down their works [and] Buildings with our Shot and Shells, which was Verry well Directed from our Battrys from the Heights [Morne De Chasseur] opposite the Fort.'[8]

---

4   Maurice, *John Moore*, vol.I, p.211.
5   Maurice, *John Moore*, vol.I, p.211.
6   Maurice, *John Moore*, vol.I, p.214.
7   Maurice, *John Moore*, vol.I, p.215.
8   NA: DDRW 25/25. Roworth to his parents, St Lucia, 4 November 1796.

NOT SO EASY, LADS

The powder magazine on Morne Fortuné was built by the French between 1763–1765. (Donald Roworth)

At 6:00 a.m., guns fired on the advanced post and the flèche to the right. The light infantry and grenadier companies of the 27th Foot, advanced under Lieutenant Colonel James Drummond. Resistance was not expected after such a mauling with the guns, yet they were still fired on by some 30 or 40 enemy troops from the flèche. Moore ordered an immediate attack on the position and the enemy abandoned it. It appeared from the lie of the ground that further batteries would need to be made to keep this flèche secure. As Moore and Knox discussed the next move they were surprised by 'a body of men [who marched] out of the fort and [advanced] towards the post' Moore had just taken. They took the offensive and began to fire. The firing was 'brisk and well-directed … our men were falling fast'.[9] The 27th charged and beat them back, but the enemy charged again and brought down more officers and troops. Despite the spirit of the British troops Moore considered at that point that 'the enemy's force was superior to ours: that they could not stand the bayonet, but were superior in firing'. The French continued to fire grape from the fort, but it slowly slackened and this gave the British the opportunity to prepare the ground in front of the Morne for further attack. Surprisingly it was not to be required.

Goyrand was aware that the odds were stacked against them. He realised that at once, when he could see the enemy artillery on the level of the redoubt. Together with the depleted powder magazine, the empty water cisterns, the

---

9   Maurice, *John Moore*, vol.I, pp.215–217.

poor quality of the stagnant water to which they had had to resort, plus the cries of 200 starving women and children, and only one convoy of insufficient cassava flour which had evaded the British blockade, the situation was overwhelming. Despite the killing of 120 of the 27th – including two majors, two captains and four subalterns – Goyrand knew there was no other way out. A courageous stand had been made and they had done their utmost against an enemy of superior numbers, ordnance, and artillery. They had fought for their freedom, but this time it was a lost cause and the bitter surrender of capitulation signalled the return of the inhabitants of the island to slavery.

Men were observed leaving the fort to pick up their dead and wounded. As night fell, an officer with a white flag could be seen. The British held their fire, in accordance with the rules of battle, allowing communication between the two forces. The officer brought a letter from the National Commissioner and the troop commander requesting a halt to hostilities until midday the next day, 26 May. Abercromby gave them until 8:00 a.m. the following morning.

The capitulation document ran to 13 points and was signed by Cottin, Goyrand, Abercromby and Christian. All military men and men under arms (referred to as the Garrison) would be considered as prisoners of war. Moore himself was ordered to take possession of the fort on the 26th, after the French had left. The 27th, 14th, and the flank companies of the 53rd Foot, with detachments from the Royal Artillery, Löwenstein's and the navy formed a lane through which the French garrison marched. The defeated men laid down their arms in the place specified and the officers retained their swords. Moore referred to the garrison as 'chiefly of blacks and men of colour'.[10] They were then marched down to the Vigie, to be put onto transport ships and taken to Britain. Duffy puts the total numbers of prisoners of war as 2,066 with 261 women and 94 children.[11]

Abercromby ordered the colours of the 27th Foot to be hung at the flagstaff for an hour in recognition of the vital part that regiment played in the reduction. This was then followed by raising the union flag.

Roworth sounded euphoric as he recounted these moments to his parents: 'When [they] struck their National colours, which I had the Happiness To See Lowered, and the Streaming British Flag hoisted in its Room, … we gave three Cheers, And I took a good Hearty Swig of Grog out of My Canteen, [and] Drunk his Majesty's Health and all Friends at Home.'[12]

These would have been the feelings of all the redcoats that morning. Lieutenant William Dillon spoke for all the men left on board ship as they cheered … 'all was joy and cheerfulness … out of compliment to the Navy, a detachment of seamen led the van'.[13] Dillon was later involved in the surrender of Pigeon Island when the latter held out for another couple of days.

Abercromby had no time to waste and the very next day after the capitulation, John Simpson and the 42nd were marched down to the bay and embarked on the *Ulysses* (44). They anchored in Kingston Bay, St Vincent,

---

10   Maurice, *John Moore*, vol.I, p.219.
11   Duffy, *Seapower*, p.235.
12   NA: DDRW 25/25 Roworth to parents, 4 November 1796.
13   Lewis (ed), *Dillon*, p.238.

NOT SO EASY, LADS

Three prison cells built by the French on Morne Fortuné 1763–1765. (Donald Roworth)

The 27th (Inniskilling) Regiment of Foot at the reduction of Morne Fortuné, showing their colours. (The Inniskillings Museum)

THE TAKING OF MORNE FORTUNÉ: THANK GOD FOR THE 27TH!

White obelisk commemorating the 27th (Inniskilling) Regiment of Foot. (Donald Roworth)

Plaque commemorating the capitulation of Morne Fortuné 1796. (Donald Roworth)

on 4 June 1796, to rest and be ready for their first fire fight with the French six days later.[14]

It was the custom of both army and navy to send bulletins back to Britain as quickly as possible. Amongst the general congratulations and reports returning to Britain via packet boat from St Lucia, that of Assistant Adjutant General, Major Tomlinson Busby, stands out for his emphatic assessment of the four weeks in which the reduction of St Lucia took place:

> During the Services which have been carried on in the Island of St Lucia, all the Courage and every Exertion of the Army would have proved ineffectual, if Rear Admiral Sir H.C. Christian, and the Royal Navy, had not stepped forward with the Alacrity which has been so conspicuous in for-warding the most arduous Part of the Public Service. To their Skill and Unremitting Labour is in a great Measure owing the Success which has attended His Majesty's Arms.[15]

It was clear that neither service would have succeeded without the other. Within five days Abercromby was en route to St Vincent, anxious to carry out the next of his orders.

Against all the protestations which Moore could possibly make, it was he, Moore, who was left as Governor of St Lucia. He was an man of action through and through, so this order would have cost him dear. That must have felt more like a punishment as 'above all things I hated a garrison'.[16] Yet, after Moore's performance during the siege, Abercromby felt there was none better to take over the position. 'Genl Moore whom I leave commandant, is a splendid Man, and I think a Man of [re]source, he will do his utmost, and with upwards of 3000 [troops] he will certainly be the [one] to keep the Morne and Vieux Fort'.[17] Vieux Fort had yet to capitulate. Appointing a military officer to govern a conquered territory was standard practice but commanding a siege and an army was one thing, governing an island people with an undoubtedly complex past (and present), was a totally different animal. So Moore, despite his personal misgivings would just have to buckle down.

Sir Ralph, writing from St Lucia on 31 May 1796, referenced the return of all rank and file who were killed, wounded and missing on the 26 days from 28 April to 24 May; 62 were killed (of whom five were from the 44th), while 329 were wounded and 112 were missing. Four of the five from the 44th who were killed had died in the attack made on the enemy's batteries on 3 May, in which the 44th had been led by Riddell (as part of Morshead's wing) who, it may be remembered, together with his men held one of the batteries and waited in vain for Perryn's support. The four recorded on the relevant muster roll were John Evans, William Marr, Cornelius Wynstanley and John Wilkinson. The fifth man, who had died during an unspecified attack from Morne Petit, was Richard Blaze, whose death was recorded on 2 May.[18]

---

14 Simpson, *Memorandums*, pp.22–26.
15 Anon., *Bulletins 1796*, extract from General Orders, p.142.
16 Maurice, *John Moore*, vol.I, p.220.
17 TNA: WO 1/798: Abercromby to Dundas, 1 June 1796, p.176.
18 Anon, *Bulletins 1796*, pp.133–134; TNA: WO 12/5638: Muster roll, 44th Foot.

16

Governor and Guerrillas: The Reluctant Ruler June 1796 – July 1797

> *It is not my intention to expend any powder tonight. We'll do this business with cold iron.*[1]

Most of us have a bête noir and Moore's seems to have been the governorship of St Lucia. After a more than unmilitary tirade vented in his diary, of those aspects of his current situation which displayed unequivocally his revulsion for a governor's role, 'how disagreeable it would be to me', it would 'plague me', 'it is not my wish to remain after the war in the West Indies', 'of all things I dislike a garrison' – the reader gets the message.

Moore spent the first month of his duties weighing up the various factions of the island population. Physical mountains were not the only ones he had to climb; 'Party feeling has been so long rampant in the country, that it is impossible to believe the reports they spread of one another'.[2]

With the reduction of St Lucia over (but in actuality, only Morne Fortuné and the burned and empty town of Castries), in spite of many fine words and praises sung by Sir Ralph of him, Moore was only too aware that 'everything military or civil [was] in the greatest confusion'.[3] He yearned for structure and military command; to use his skills as a tactician; to be leaving St Lucia and sailing for the next big operation. But the post of governor was offered and Moore was virtually shoehorned into the position. Even a heartfelt plea via his friend, Brigadier General John Hope, could not turn Abercromby from his decision. Moore's feelings appeared to be a mixture of smouldering anger and resentment, together with the knowledge of being trapped in a position not of his choosing. 'I was infinitely disappointed at not seeing Sir Ralph, and I cannot but think him most inexcusable for not sending to

---

1 John, Lewis-Stempel, *The Autobiography of the British Soldier: From Agincourt to Basra, in His Own Words* (London, Headline Publishing Group, 2007), p.141.
2 Maurice, *John Moore*, vol.I, p.226.
3 Maurice, *John Moore*, vol.I, p.220.

Sir John Moore 1761–1809 by Sir Thomas Lawrence. (Anne S.K. Brown Military Collection)

me or waiting for my arrival.'[4] Moore was an ambitious military man, but he considered himself a fighting tactician, not a political animal, added to which his appointment left him without those senior officers on whom he could rely – Hope, Campbell and Knox – and if Moore found the taking of Morne Fortuné a tough job, then he would find the governance of the whole island a whole lot worse.

Sir Ralph Abercromby, in his report to the War Office dated St Lucia, 30 May 1796, stated that he had 'left Brigadier General Moore Commandant of the Island with a Garrison of upward of 3000 men'.[5] In fact, Moore was left with some 4,000–5,000 men, although still faced with the fact that many of the free blacks had melted away into the woods to join the maroons – potentially a whole island of revolutionaries. What was considered to be a full capitulation of the island was nothing of the sort. It was, as previously mentioned, only the capitulation of the Morne and the town of Castries (the latter of which there was very little left) in the north-west; the understanding of their circumstances by the indigenous population was that the surrender of Morne Fortuné certainly did not equate to the island as a whole, so fight for their homes and freedom they would, in whatever way possible. For the time under the benevolent governorship of Gaspar Goyrand, St Lucians lived as a population of free men and women. The freedom which the French had gifted them in 1794 had given them that all-important taste of being free from both physical and mental fetters. They could not know then that Napoleon himself would take back that gift.

Moore inherited his unwanted mission from Gaspard Goyrand, a civilian, who had not only been the French Commissary of the island for the previous 15 months and whose primary concern had been to reinforce the island's defences, but also he was intimate with the islanders and their aspirations – experience which Moore lacked on all possible counts. Even Moore appreciated Goyrand the man. After the capitulation Moore wrote in his journal of 1 June, that 'I have been frequently since then in company with the General Cottin and the Representant Goyrand.' He painted the former as a 'hot-headed infamous blackguard'. His opinion of the latter could hardly be higher, he being 'a plain honest man … a man of humility, did good, and is much liked by the Colony'.[6] But a new totally-inexperienced British governor foisted upon the recently freed St Lucian populace was no replacement for Goyrand. Nor was Goyrand any longer available to him, as he would be on his way to Britain as a prisoner of war in the not-too-distant future. Between them, both being men of good will, they might have enabled St Lucia to move forward with some sort of reasoned governance, but Moore was by himself from now on.

On the same day, 1 June, that Moore was confiding to his diary, the Commander-in-Chief was still on St Lucia writing to Henry Dundas, Secretary of State for War. Moore might well have been surprised at some of

---

4   Maurice, *John Moore*, vol.I, p.231.
5   TNA: WO 1/798: War Department In-Letters, pp.196–198.
6   Maurice, *John Moore*, vol.I, p.219.

the enlightened comments under scrutiny. Abercromby, to his colleagues at the War Department, admitted that the surrender of St Lucia,

> ... cost more time and labour than it ought ... there is little prospect of holding it in tranquillity ... the Negroes will scarcely be induced to return to their Plantations and to hard Labour ... it is a wretched place and should not have held out 24 hours ... General Perryn is a Mad Man and led Morshead wrong ... I beg you will send out somebody to command here, Graham, Morshead & Hunter are not by any means equal to it.[7]

He was well aware of the difficulties involved in the hot potato of governorship.

The new Governor, Moore, was left with four British regiments, 'the 31st, 44th, 48th, and 55th York Rangers, together with O'Meara's Black corps, 100 Royal Artillery, two engineers [and] assistants, making in all 4,000 or 5,000 rank and file fit for duty, besides officers, serjeants and drummers'.[8]

He was supported from the sea by the Royal Navy in the person of Captain McDowall, 'with two line-of-battle ships and some frigates'.[9] Irrespective of numbers and already an embittered man, he must have felt the loneliest of commanders as Abercromby and Christian sailed away to the north-west on their next venture and he was left with a calibre of officers for whom he had little respect.

He was not the only one; for all the men wearing the red coat, this particular service was going to be the hardest and, for many, the last service of all. Abercromby left on 3 June. Nine days later Moore wrote to his Commander-in-Chief to say that everything remained quiet on the island. But, in truth, as early as 4 June, less than 24 hours after Abercromby departed, he was confiding his anxieties to his diary: the need to transport provisions, stores, ammunition and ordnance (left for his use in the town of Castries), two miles away; Vieux Fort was not yet in his possession, due to those contrary winds and currents; there were unknown numbers of armed blacks in the woods; the rainy season was causing untold difficulties on the ground and to his irritation and chagrin his men were already starting to fall sick. Typically, the deaths, of the men of the 44th Foot alone, peaked in the September at 30, with another spike the following November at 25. This will be examined elsewhere below.

By 31 October 1796, Sir Ralph Abercromby had returned to London and had laid out in writing the numbers of troops, throughout the islands, who were returned fit for duty, together with the numbers of sick. He pointed out that many of the latter were in fact 'convalescents & very unequal to the discharge of it', viz, their duty. For our purposes we look only at St Lucia which recorded 1,191 fit for duty who, added to the 1,544 men recorded as sick, made a total of 2,735. Allowing that perhaps half of those marked 'fit for duty' were not effective (as Abercromby suggested), there might have been only about 750 men actually fit for duty. As early as 2 July 1796 Moore had

---

7   TNA: WO 1/798: War Department In-letters, 1 June 1796, Choc Bay, p.176.
8   Maurice, *John Moore*, vol.I, p.220.
9   Maurice, *John Moore*, vol.I, p.218.

been placing the number of effective men as low as 600 to 700 on the Morne from three regiments.[10]

Dissatisfaction with his superiors ate at him. In Moore's estimation, if Abercromby and Christian had remained an extra week or 10 days, employing the army and navy to sort all ordnance and provisions and remove those earthworks of which the rebels could make use, the island would have been left in such an improved condition that he could have commenced governance immediately. He felt caught on the wrong foot: 'The moment the fort had surrendered, large detachments under proper officers ought to have been detached to different parts of the island to encourage and support the proprietors and disarm the blacks.'[11] He was probably right, but Abercromby, as Commander-in-Chief, had to attend to his own orders, bearing in mind that, due to those severe contrary winds commencing the previous November in the English Channel, the expedition was already running some six or seven months behind. One could say that in that case an extra 10 days was a drop in the ocean, but for Abercromby another 10 days wait to get the job finished was 10 days too long.

For the previous six weeks Moore had been in battle mode (as had all the troops) and focussed on the assault upon the Morne. His entrapment by Abercromby notwithstanding and conscious of his responsibilities, Moore kept his anger confidentially focused in his diary or in the long-suffering ears of his friend, Paul Anderson, and set out to make his governorship work. It would be the diary which was to deliver up that anger and bitterness in years to come, for other eyes to see. To use his first week as Governor he spent the time travelling from town to town, plantation to plantation and from estate to estate. His excursions were always accompanied by a detachment of redcoats. He addressed public meetings and assured plantation and estate owners that he would provide troops to protect them. He encouraged kindness, moderation and toleration. But the brigands and maroons, the blacks, the white planters, and Republicans were having none of it. Many of the plantation proprietors headed for town and safety; royalist émigrés appeared to thirst for revenge and despite Moore's efforts, refused to change their attitudes. He could not possibly understand the embedded mindset of all the different factions in just a few days.

His early attempts to govern the island's inhabitants with a velvet glove were positive and admirable but at the very least, naive. Yet the actions were worthy and included an amnesty and pardon to men who would submit their arms and return to their previous habitations and work, thereby continuing to support the economy; there should be no ill-treatment of blacks; he had 'no object to serve but the prosperity and welfare of the colony.'[12] He was well aware that that strategy would involve men returning to slavery, but he hoped (again naively) for a return to the status quo (under military control, of course) until terms were settled by the victors of the colonies. He talked to the plantation owners, the émigrés, the country people, the town people,

---

10   Maurice, *John Moore*, vol 1, p.223.
11   Maurice, *John Moore*, vol.I, p.221.
12   Maurice, *John Moore*, vol.I, p.222.

people he met in the woods. A month later he still saw 'no reason why a man should be treated harshly because he was black or of colour. All men were entitled to justice, and they should not meet with it from me without distinction or partiality, whether white or black, republican or royalist'.[13] He wrote in his first diary entry on 4 July 1796 after the exodus of Abercromby and Christian:

> I have issued a proclamation offering pardon to the people of all colours and description who would come in with their arms. I give passes and encourage everybody to return to their habitations and remain quiet and attend to their private affairs. I have warned the *émigrés* not to cast any reflections upon those who have been republicans; if they did so they might expect to be punished.[14]

But that month, however good Moore's intentions, gave the brigands time to regroup. These were primarily people who had been freed from slavery in 1794 by Gaspar Goyrand, on the orders of Jean-Baptiste Victor Hugues, the Governor of Guadeloupe. Understandably, the slaves just walked away from their masters – leaving the plantation estates unattended, thereby in one stroke weakening the economy and providing a ready source of potential guerrillas. There were few circumstances in which they would give up a freedom which by June 1796 they had experienced for nearly two years. 'For the Brigands, it was the dreaded prospect of a return to bondage and for the royalist planters … a sense of terror mixed with a deep-seated resentment at having lost their control over 'their' slaves and free people of colour.'[15]

True, a small minority accepted Moore's offer and returned to their previous life of enslavement but with so few, there could be no successful plantations and estates, so the money no longer flowed freely in any direction and St Lucia's plantation days were both weakened and numbered. It was just never going to happen, but to obey Abercromby's orders Moore ended up doing many things he would much rather have not.

Before Abercromby and Christian had even left the island men of the 44th Foot were beginning to die from undisclosed causes. The muster roll covering the relevant dates is in very poor condition and spans a far wider period of time than is usual. Although dated from 25 December 1795 to 24 June 1796 it contains deaths from both arenas of war – Flanders and the West Indies – presumably, to make sure that the deaths were recorded whatever the difficulties. Aside from those that were killed in action and already mentioned, Serjeant Thomas Foxcroft, Privates John Baillie, John Barr, John Buckley(1st), Joseph White, James Wade, … Pollett, George Baillie (John's brother?) and John Verrity died on various days in May. Seventeen were wounded on 4 May, but none are recorded as dying of wounds. It is likely that these nine men died of some kind of fever.

For Moore the first month was made particularly difficult through the intransigence of the St Lucians and the inefficacy of Moore's own officers and

---
13 Maurice, *John Moore*, vol.I, p.224.
14 Maurice, *John Moore*, vol.I, p.222.
15 Harmsen, et al, *St Lucia*, p.76.

GOVERNOR AND GUERRILLAS: THE RELUCTANT RULER JUNE 1796 – JULY 1797

men. Add to that the rainy season and the unforgiving progress of disease – the mix became poisonous. The former arrived with its torrential and virtually constant tropical downpours and Moore found that almost nothing could be achieved. Huge landslides (often causing death) were common in the rainy season and the waters running from the land washed out or damaged much of the fragile road system. The swollen rivers flooded ravines and fields of crops – something else he was unable to control, plus, the season had brought with it the usual sickness and disease. He could not know it but 1796 was to be a bad year for fevers – yellow fever in particular. The soldiers were already succumbing and beginning to fill the hospitals. Moore's diary of 2 July, just a month after Abercromby's departure, recorded that the troops from 'the three regiments on the Morne could only furnish between 600 to 700 men … fit for duty'.[16] This he seemed unable to understand and placed the blame on a lack of discipline by the regiments' commanding officers; 'I wrote … a private letter to the Commander-in-chief giving him my opinion fully respecting my situation and the character of those under me, showing the necessity of a change in the departments … The troops, I observe, which have been most active are the most healthy a proof that the sun is not the cause of the sickness.'[17]

With hindsight, it was more likely to be the other way around, that those with good health were able to be active, rather than those heading for the hospital already infected with disease. It is possible that the three regiments kept on the Morne, mentioned by Moore, were the 44th, the 48th and 55th, as the 31st Foot, appears to have been split between Vieux Fort and Choc Bay, for much of the time that they were on the island. Cannon tells us that, at first, like all four regiments remaining from 1 June, the 31st were drawn on in the constant search for the enemy. They were 'employed on this harassing duty, and suffered much from fatigue, privation and continual exposure; on the service being concluded, the regiment went into quarters at Vieux Fort and other posts'.[18] Cannon claims that the 31st was losing 16 men daily at their lowest point. In comparison, the 44th's worst point was to be reached in September when the number of deaths reached was 25 for the month. It appears however that by the time of Roworth's third letter to Mary from St Lucia he says ' … we have Such a Sickness In this Island our Men are going of(f) [dying] Eighteen or twenty every week of a fev(e)r'.[19] By the end of August Moore wrote: 'the deaths upon the Morne Fortuné alone are from sixty to seventy a week'.[20] For the three regiments camped there this is equivalent to over 20 deaths per regiment per week.

With military deaths apparently a nuisance, the things that really provoked Moore to testy explosions were the conditions and attitudes of the officers under his command. He had already written to Abercromby of the difficulties he was working under and that his (unnamed) deputy was 'so

---

16   Maurice, *John Moore*, vol.I, p.223.
17   Maurice, *John Moore*, vol.I, p.239.
18   Cannon, *The Thirty-First*, p.53.
19   NA: DDRW 22/25: Roworth to Mary, St Lucia 15th August 1796.
20   Maurice, *John Moore*, vol.I, p.236.

completely absurd and wrong-headed' that he, Moore, dreaded leaving the garrison.[21] This subordinate officer remained unnamed (though obviously known to Abercromby), but it may have been Colonel Robert Riddell of the 44th, who seems to have been the next most senior officer present. His pedantry and treatment of his men was evidenced as recorded in the Campbell letters, could be a very difficult man.

Among the commissioned officers serving under Moore were Lieutenant Colonels Robert Arbuthnot and Adam Hay of the 31st and Brigade Major Paul Anderson, who had been promoted to captain the previous 25 May, to replace an officer who had died. The latter was promoted into the 31st by Sir Ralph. Others were Lieutenant Colonel David Ogilvie and Major Edward Wilson of the 44th; Lieutenant-Colonel Archibald Campbell of the 48th and from the 55th there were Colonel Donald MacDonald and Major the Honourable John Lindsay. Moore would lose five of these eight officers through disease before the year was out but, excepting Anderson, it was some of these men whom Moore found so lacking in spirit and understanding; 'the composition of the officers is horrid … with such instruments it is impossible to work'.[22]

His personal decision, taken very early on in his military life, was to lead by example and yet that spirit and drive did not communicate itself to his subordinates in St Lucia. He felt beset on all sides: 'The sickness among the troops is dreadful. The discipline … takes up but an hour or two a day … The military spirit is now, I think, gone. The officers wish to be advanced, to get more pay and have less duty, and otherwise discuss only promotion, interest or patronage and their hoped-for return home'.[23]

It appeared that Henry Bunbury had the measure of the man when he wrote: 'Everything in Moore was real, solid, and unbending. He was penetrating and reflective. His manner was singularly agreeable to those whom he liked, but to those he did not esteem his bearing was severe.'[24]

Moore never suffered fools gladly and thought his troops in St Lucia 'so infamous … it required every exertion in myself and the officers with me to get them to charge the brigands, who were already half beaten the moment they were faced'.[25] However, he complained that he had 'hardly an officer capable of taking care of his corps'; that their composition was 'horrid'; of his need of 'proper people' to command and direct the troops; that he had not a single officer whom he could rely upon 'to command a district'.[26]

> I have much to complain of the officers. I have few who execute my orders … the want of zeal for the service is dreadful … I really believe many of them wish their men to die that they may get home … the officers wish to be advanced, to

---

21 Maurice, *John Moore*, vol.I, p.223.
22 Maurice, *John Moore*, vol.I, p.232.
23 Maurice, *John Moore*, vol.I, p.236.
24 Charles J.F. Bunbury, *Memoir and Literary Remains of Lieutenant General Sir Henry Edward Bunbury, Bart* (London: Spottiswoode & Co, 1868), p.33.
25 Maurice, *John Moore*, vol.I, p.232.
26 Maurice, *John Moore*, vol.I, p.232.

get more pay and less duty ... Little can be expected from men formed and led by such officers.[27]

Yet he was the commander after all. So why could he not carry his men's hearts and minds with him? Did he hector them as he hectored his diary? Was the weight of governorship so hateful that it somehow permeated into the driving of his subordinates? Perhaps he had forgotten that it must have been incredibly hard for those who were fighting on two fronts, both war and disease simultaneously. Wellington was to comment on Moore that 'He was as brave as his own sword, but he did not know what men could do, or could not do'.[28] Yet, for all his alarm and apprehensions and decidedly unpleasant inferences about his officers, his personal desires recorded in his own diary, simply reflected those of his subordinates: 'I would give the world to get quit of mine, or even to get home ... I may lose my life and reputation'.[29]

For Moore's redcoats, disease was to be far more deadly an enemy than ever were the brigands; fever was beginning to make itself felt. Looking at the situation of Roworth's regiment from the muster rolls, his friend Serjeant Thomas Foxcroft, died on 27 May.[30] He does not mention what caused Foxcroft's death, but the reference is made in the same sentence to his own possible dysentery 'A fortnight ago I was took very ... ill with a Gripeing of the Bowels'. The sentence immediately following begins with news of Cornelius Bowring who 'Died of his wounds at Martinique on the 19th June'.[31] So it appears that if Foxcroft had died of wounds Roworth would have said so. Before his next letter home (20 July), nine more rank and file had died in the month of June with yet another nine (including three corporals) before the end of July. Two serjeants, John Burke and John Holmes, and the Quartermaster Thomas Gardiner on the 26th brought that total to 12. On 20 July Roworth wrote that Gardiner was waiting with his wife to sail for Martinique, to take the regimental mail for posting. From his next letter of 15 August, we learn that was the last he saw of Thomas Gardiner. The shock can be heard in his words to Mary as he tells her, 'he left so fat and jolly and after he landed [in Martinique] he was carried off [with fever] in only forty-eight hours'.[32] A friend and military brother gone, but not with military glory.

The scenes can only be imagined as the men took sick and died in the hospital or some in front of their comrades. Then would come the procession to bury the officers on the Morne Fortuné itself, or on the beach or in the sea, if the soldier died in proximity to either. There would probably have been burial pits for some of the farther flung areas of the island such as Vieux Fort in the south and Gros Islet to the north.

Morne Fortuné was a particular hotspot for yellow fever on the island and while the months wore on and men of all ranks were succumbing to illness

---

27 Maurice, *John Moore*, vol.I, p.235.
28 Christopher Hibbert, *Wellington: A Personal History* (London: HarperCollins, 1998), p.153.
29 Maurice, *John Moore*, vol.I, p.232.
30 NA: DDRW 21/25: Roworth to Mary, St Lucia, 20 July 1796.
31 NA: DDRW 21/25: Roworth to Mary, St Lucia, 20 July 1796
32 NA: DDRW 1/22: Roworth to Mary, St Lucia, 15 August 1796.

and death Moore had, at the commencement of his governorship, remarked that on the Morne, 'There is no cover on this hill for two-thirds of the troops … The men begin to fall sick, and we have no hospital room'.[33] Surgeon Thomas Stewart agreed, 'The Army on Shore were remarkably sickly … The Hospitals on Morne Fortuné were crowded and their average of deaths from 7 to 10 daily'.[34] By September Moore admitted that 'The sickness is so much greater upon Morne Fortuné and its immediate dependencies than at the other posts, that I detain upon it a number only sufficient for the daily duties'.[35]

In the meantime, the rank and file and their serjeants continued to die. In August, 14 rank and file of the 44th died of fever, plus two of their serjeants and two corporals. September would take three serjeants, five corporals and 33 privates. The three months until 31 December took another 48 men, plus Colonel Riddell (after five days sickness), Surgeon Faron, Captain Lieutenant James Cooke, Major Edward Wilson, Captain William Creagh, five serjeants and two corporals – a total of 105.

Moore himself, despite his continual grousing in his diary, was constantly on the move. His sense of duty and determination were paramount and while his men were still alive he drove them on. It had taken him less than a month to realise that peace was not to be fulfilled by benign rule. Reports were coming in of devastation caused by the 'negroes in the woods' who were laying waste to parts of Soufriere in the west and Vieux Fort in the south.[36] He ordered a division of the country by sending Major Lindsay and five companies of the 55th, to control the areas of Laborie and Vieux Fort, while Major Edward Wilson of the 44th, also with five companies of the 55th plus a detachment of the black corps, was to command in the Soufriere and Choiseul region, under specific orders. They were to act as guards for the plantations from brigand depredations and to prevent support and supplies (including arms) from being landed on the coast from St Vincent.[37] It was to be a continual game of hide and seek.

During the next five weeks Moore wrote of his lack of confidence in many of the officers. Major John Lindsay, 55th Foot, attracted his criticism a total of six times, including accusations of timidity, lack of forethought and intention and allowing his fears to influence others, both military and civilian. Lindsay's conduct was 'miserable' and his attitude 'nervous' and 'frightened and [he] does not know what he is about'.[38] At almost every order he gave to Lindsay, Moore perceived failure in its compliance and then recounted in both diary and letters, to his Commander-in-Chief and to his parents, what the apparently miscreant officer should have done. He blamed his officers repeatedly. 'Little can be expected from men formed and led by such officers. They neither look up to them as officers, nor do they respect

---

33 Maurice, *John Moore*, vol.I, p.221.
34 TNA: ADM 102/790: Thomas Stewart, surgeon at Vielle Ville Vigie, and *Vanguard* and *Orpheus* Hospital Ships.
35 Carrick Moore, *Sir John Moore*, p.154.
36 Maurice, *John Moore*, vol.I, p.223.
37 Maurice, *John Moore*, vol.I, p.226.
38 Maurice, *John Moore*, vol.I, p.229.

them as gentlemen, I see this so strongly, that I fear if the war continues much longer in this country we shall be beaten by equal numbers of the blacks'.[39]

Major Edward Wilson was initially commended for his 'judicious and active arrangements'. The difference between his actions and Lindsay's was pronounced as 'remarkable', but when Wilson did not respond to rebel firing, (for 36 hours) some 'short way away', Moore was livid at Wilson's lack of judgement.[40]

Few, if any, of the officers seemed to be made in his image. Howard calls Moore assertive, and unforgiving, which he undoubtedly was.[41] Abercromby admired his 'Good Conduct and Spirit'.[42] Buckley mentions that Moore's attitudes to his own subordinates remained conflicted and unequivocal, 'openly and harshly criticising the officers under his command'.[43] Moore's character appears to have been a composite of his military abilities and ambitions, his concerns for humanity in general but an inability to see his subordinates in the same light. His actions on the battlefield could be coloured by his personal concerns for his career and the governorship was something of a position too far. Opinions about John Moore appear divided, but there is always an opinion to be expressed.

News of further trouble reached Moore of areas in the north end of the island in Dauphin and Gros Islet, almost in sight of his base on the Morne. Moore's constant fear was the arrival of assistance for the brigands from the island of Guadeloupe. Reports were coming in of brigands marauding around Gros Islet and Dauphin. Moore's anger was exacerbated by a letter from Major Lindsay. Moore rushed '190 men from the light companies of the 31st and 44th and the grenadiers of the Black Corps, to Gros Islet', which is the area to the north of Pigeon Island where Rodney had built his fort. This was only about six to seven miles from Castries and Morne Fortuné. Rodney and Choc Bays were very accessible for offloading not just food but, more importantly, armaments and troops from Martinique, Moore shipped provisions to Dauphin and Denérie and then marched to join his troops at Gros Islet, arriving on 25 June. He exercised a night march with the flank companies of the above regiments towards the Acquarts plantation, near Dauphin, ordering Major Campagne, with 200 of his black corps, to take a shorter route and meet up with him at Acquarts. Though arriving at 7:00 a.m. the house had been burned down the day before. It seemed to be this particular action, together with news of Major Lindsay's current predicament, having been attacked by 300 brigands, that persuaded him that enough was enough. Moore hanged one of the brigands, *pour encourager les autres*. He saw no other alternative but to remove the brigands and revolutionaries by

---

39 Maurice, *John Moore*, vol.I, p.237.
40 Maurice, *John Moore*, vol.I, p.234.
41 Martin R. Howard, *Death Before Glory: The British Soldier in the West Indies in the French Revolutionary Army & Napoleonic Wars 1793–1815* (Barnsley: Pen and Sword Military, 1988), pp.97, 101.
42 Anon. (ed.), *Bulletins 1796*, Abercromby, St Lucia, 31 May 1796, p.127.
43 Roger N. Buckley, *Slaves in Red Coats: The British West India Regiments, 1795–1815* (New Haven: Yale University, 1979), p.34.

force. As obsessed as he had been with the rightness of his cause and painful as the change of direction might be, he dedicated himself to the latter.

Despite his personal frustrations and tendency to blame others, Moore was aware of the effect that the difficulties of terrain, heat and humidity were having on his European troops and their increasing inability to function in those conditions, fevers aside. From his observations of the black corps, he saw how much more easily they coped with the conditions. As trained troops they were eager to follow their orders and were proud of their positions. Moore became convinced of the need for black regiments to police the interior of the island, which would allow his European troops to be placed on the coastal fringes where the roles of defence could be more easily undertaken by them. This would allow the latter to repulse the frequent attempts by Victor Hugues, French governor of Guadeloupe, to send reinforcements, arms, ammunition and provisions for the 'L'Armée Francaise dans Les Bois' in St Lucia, for any landings could easily overturn the fragile balance of his command in the island.

Moore was far from the first to appreciate the superiority of black corps. According to Devaux, the St Lucian historian, as early as 1780 suggestions had been made for the raising of non-white regiments.[44] Dr George Pinckard, who travelled with Christian's fleet, recorded his experience of watching, in Barbados, some 1,500 young blacks being armed and trained up for service by the British and observed them to be 'a fine body of men'.[45] General Sir John Vaughan succeeded Sir Charles Grey in the Windward Islands in 1794. It was he who was convinced of the 'opinion that a corps of one thousand men, composed of blacks ... would render more essential service in the Country, than treble the number of Europeans who are unaccustomed to the Climate'.[46]

Major Gordon Forbes from San Domingo wrote to Henry Dundas, Secretary of State for War, 'the Corps of black Chasseurs ... are excellent Soldiers for the kind of war indispensably necessary to be carried on in such a country as this'.[47] To which he received the reply from Whitehall, dated, 7 February 1796: 'I am to inform You, that the Zeal, which has been, manifested by the Island of Martinico, and its Alacrity in granting the Contingent of Negroes, is highly pleasing to His Majesty'.[48] William Dyott, of the 25th Foot, was very specific in his opinion concerning the usefulness of the black soldier and extended his opinion further: 'I am therefore for employing negroes for every purpose, both civil and military, and I wish the British Government would garrison all the West India Islands with black soldiers only'.[49]

Moore continued travelling from town to town, from plantation to plantation, estate to estate and scoured the woods for brigands who, in their turn, continued their guerrilla tactics of surprise and strike from what was

---

44 Buckley, *Slaves in Red Coats*, p.6; Devaux, *Brigands*, p.14.
45 Pinckard, *Notes*, p.382.
46 Buckley, *Slaves in Red Coats*, p.12.
47 TNA: WO 1/65: Forbes to Dundas, War Department letters and papers, p.345.
48 TNA: WO 1/32: Dundas to Forbes, 7 February 1796, p.45.
49 Jeffery, (ed,), *Dyott*, p.94.

essentially jungle. After his initial reconnoitre of the southern plain, from Souffriere to Vieux Fort, Moore ordered Major Lindsay with about 80 men of his own regiment, the 55th, to deal with a known band of brigands near Praslin. The 'plain' was (as it is today), an area of ridges and ravines, ideal for insurgents to sally forth and cause mayhem amongst the inhabitants. Moore marked out suitable points to send small detachments 'into the woods [and] the plantations' to cover the southern area from coast to coast.[50] He ordered Major Wilson of the 44th to cover Souffriere and Choiseul. Wilson had lost his brother Knevitt, a major in the 27th, in the attack on the advanced posts at Morne Fortuné on 24 May, less than a month before. Major Wilson was to command the 'other five companies of the 55th Foot and a detachment of black corps', which would have been drawn from O'Meara's, as that was the only black corps on St Lucia at the time. Moore's orders to both these men were to guard the local plantations from the brigands and to prevent boats landing with enemy provisions. On the return to Fort Charlotte (the name the British had wished upon Morne Fortuné as a compliment to Queen Charlotte), he and his troops arrived at Souffriere in time for Moore to order the execution of four men landed from St Vincent. The reason for the landing was not known but must have been thought nefarious from the response applied.

Moore immediately employed the black corps again, by ordering Major Campagne, with 100 of his black troops, to leave a detachment at Dauphin and to protect the estate of Ostia's and its planters with the remainder, constantly patrolling the woods and attacking any brigands they might come across. The estates of Dauphin and Denérie abutted each other on the north-east coast but the village areas were several miles apart. Even today there is no direct road between the two and a car journey takes about 40 minutes. Moore had marched to Denérie with the troops from Gros Islet, the 31st and 44th, some 22 miles by road today. When he gained sight of the house from the hill-side the woods were set on fire by some men who ran off. After 22 miles of St Lucian heat and in their full gear the troops of the 31st and the 44th were too exhausted to follow them. In such territory they would be suffering from the heat and thirst if their canteens had run dry.

The locals had had their houses burned and the women came to Moore for protection. He sent Lieutenant Colonel Adam Hay of the 31st to collect the troops from Castries and return to Denérie Bay, where he was to establish the troops who were tasked with guarding the estate from armed supporters of French inclination.

Moore's faith in Major Lindsay was severely tested when news arrived that the major, together with his troops from the 55th, had been attacked by about 300 brigands, not once, but three times. Lindsay had been successful in killing 20 or 30. Although he had driven the others away, he had failed to follow them. A defensive rather than an offensive fighter, Lindsay had then retreated to Vieux Fort, leaving a detachment behind him at Praslin to defend the post. Information had arrived that the brigands were displaying

---

50 Maurice, *John Moore*, vol.I, p.226.

colours and were posted near Praslin itself. 'He [Lindsay] knows I am here, yet had neither made any combination nor sent me the least intelligence,' Moore commented angrily.[51]

Moore was met on the road by troops with information and letters from Captain L'Aureal with his detachment of black corps, who reported that he and his corps had attacked the brigands at Praslin, who had fled. Moore had further information about two brigand camps near Praslin which required acting upon, but the detachments he sent at 2:00 a.m. to clear the camps, returned having found nothing. Moore was concerned about Lindsay who, from the letters he had received the previous evening, manifested fear and confusion. Brigands had cut the lines of communication between Praslin and Vieux Fort and Lindsay's indecision had, like Chinese whispers, communicated itself to the inhabitants instead. Moore stayed 24 hours in the house at Micaud, where Lindsay's detachment was in situ, leaving the following evening to get to the Rigby estate before dark. They were followed part of the way by a band of brigands who fired on them and generally made a nuisance of themselves, while they were ignored by Moore and his men. Moore looked for an open area suitable for forming line, then he ordered the men 'to halt and front; we gave them a fire, and charged them with bayonets'.[52] Only a box of ammunition was left behind by the brigands, which was promptly emptied and no doubt put to good use another day. This must have been one of the few times that, apart from forming on the beaches, Moore's men were actually able to form line with ease, which demonstrated the unsuitability of the terrain for line fighting.

As often as Moore or his officers found a deserted camp the soldiers were ordered to burn and destroy it. When discovered in situ, brigands would often run away, only to emerge from the woods in large numbers, taunt with their presence and then disappear into the trees again. Moore had a grudging admiration for the brigands to the extent that he commented, 'their attachment and fidelity to their cause is great; they go to death with indifference.'[53] He also observed that both the blacks in the woods and the blacks still faithful to their plantation masters were 'equally attached to their cause', the difference cited about the brigands being that although 'the cause in which they fight is praiseworthy' the excessive acts of cruelty used upon the general population were so great and shameful, he felt 'less remorse in ordering them to be put to death'.[54] The brigands were merciless in their own retribution and treatment of their fellow blacks from the plantations, whom they considered traitors, so burned their houses and stole their livestock. Moore wrote, 'Their numbers by all accounts are inconsiderable; the burning of the negroes houses and the cruelties they have committed will, I think, make the negroes less attached to them.'[55]

---

51 Maurice, *John Moore*, vol.I, p.229.
52 Maurice, *John Moore*, vol.I, p.230.
53 Maurice, *John Moore*, vol.I, p.234.
54 Maurice, *John Moore*, vol.I, p.234.
55 Maurice, *John Moore*, vol.I, p.229.

GOVERNOR AND GUERRILLAS: THE RELUCTANT RULER JUNE 1796 – JULY 1797

The Brigands continued to lay waste to plantations or spring surprise attacks on the troops and then melt into the forest, as if they had never been. The village of Praslin was burned to the ground and the troops were attacked by a large number of brigands at a nearby ravine. Moore continued to experience extreme difficulty when exhorting his men to charge.

The fact that the brigands would retreat into their fastnesses was thought (at that stage) by Moore to be cowardice. He was rarely able to make them stand and fight, which is the reality of guerrilla warfare. Just a handful of guerrilla fighters could cause mayhem from the woods and still survive to fight another day. More than once Moore and his troops had advance information on the whereabouts of large brigand camps, such as those at La Sorciere and again, at Morne Forcieuse. After what can only be termed 'forced marches' taken at speed and within a short distance of their goals, a gun was discharged on both these occasions, either on purpose or by accident but with the same result – that of giving the brigands time to disperse.

If Moore was infuriated by the attitudes and guerrilla tactics used by the brigands, he was also surprised and appalled at the amount of destruction they appear to have been wreaking on their own people. He decided to use a scorched earth policy: 'I have ordered the negroes' houses in the woods and on the heights to be burned and the ground provisions to be destroyed.'[56] Wherever possible, he hung, shot or put the brigands to the bayonet. He reported some 300 to 400 'killed, wounded and hanged' during his time on the island.[57] Once found, the camps would be destroyed and it was in this way that the brigands were very slowly worn down, as their camps and provisions were constantly demolished. Moore continued to use the men of the light companies and the black corps to achieve this result. It was not an easy task. The brigands were highly organised and their camps and hide-outs for caches of provisions were secreted all over the island in the most difficult places to reach, in ravines (of which there were many), in caves in the cliffs and on beaches. In the middle of the island, where the vegetation was almost impenetrable, they built tunnels and signal stations. In fact they stored provisions and armaments anywhere convenient for themselves. Since the coastline of St Lucia is some 92 miles long and the highest of its many peaks stands 950 metres (3,116 feet) above dense jungle, there were myriad hiding places almost impossible to uncover.

Every step taken demanded the most from the redcoats, who were not only exhausted, but were dying in their hundreds from 1796's particularly virulent strain of yellow fever. The few remaining white soldiers, primarily guarding the coast while not actually lying down and dying, must have prevented at least some of the support boats from Martinique and elsewhere from landing and distributing provisions or additional matériel.

For the 44th and their brother regiments there was worse to come.

---

56 Maurice, *John Moore*, vol.I, p.234.
57 Maurice, *John Moore*, vol.I, p.238.

17

Yellow Jack: One Has Not a Man Fit for Duty

> *It is a Yellow fever that takes all of our men they are hearty and well to Day and gone tomorrow*[1]

Conditions in the camp on the Morne had worsened considerably, Moore wrote that one regiment, 'has not a man fit for duty. The want of zeal for the service is dreadful. I really believe many of [the officers] wish their men to die that they may get home.'[2]

On the plus side Abercromby had sent him 300 men of Druault's Black Corps. These men provided the impetus for more offensive expeditions, many of which Moore headed himself. He continued to harass the brigands wherever they could be found, actively searching for them, killing them or driving them away and destroying their camps, right down to the garden produce. As he had predicted the black corps kept up the momentum, their stamina far superior to the white constitution in the local conditions. Moore's positive exertions paid off; in just three months, by the end of August things had become much quieter; 'From every account the Brigands are disheartened'.[3]

Relatively speaking yellow fever was swift in its mode of killing, up to about five days, but to the suffering men, the manner of dying must have seemed unbearably endless. However, it appeared that the longer you lived, the more likely you were to survive. At the same time sickness in the form of disease, malaria, dysentery and yellow fever continued to take its toll of the British soldiers. This was, Moore allowed, due to the climate, but also stemmed from the lack of 'a total want of discipline and interior economy of the regiments … Little can be expected from men formed and led by such officers. They neither look up to them as officers, nor do they respect them as gentlemen.'[4]

---

1   NA: DDRW 25/25: Roworth to his parents, 4 November 1796.
2   Maurice, *John Moore*, vol.I, p.235.
3   Maurice, *John Moore*, vol.I, p.236.
4   Maurice, *John Moore*, vol.I, p.237.

YELLOW JACK: ONE HAS NOT A MAN FIT FOR DUTY

There were others on the island who were equally under pressure and taunted by their rapidly worsening situations, with no good outcomes in sight. Surgeon Stewart was struggling with the sick at one land hospital at the Vigie, plus two hospital ships, the *Vanguard* and the *Orpheus*. When the *Vanguard* arrived on 16 July 1796, he was faced not only with 10 men on board who had fever, but others with dysentery, consumption, ulcers and rheumatism. The following day the ship 'was warped into the Carenage and moored on the 18th' as far away from the swamps as possible, though the 'exhalations' and stench could be 'very offensive'. He recorded that 'the Army on shore were remarkably sickly'.[5]

Stewart described the weeks since, referring to 'adventurers' who had built houses for themselves in the ashes of Castries, but were taken sick with yellow fever in September and 40 of them had already died; not one survived, including some native to Barbados and Antigua. The windward side of Vieux Fort did not escape the fever and lost most of its inhabitants. Stewart recorded how the same malign fever worked its way through the hospital staff, surgeons and mates, who 'suffered greatly', and what is most telling is that neither 'the Negroes and people of colour [were] exempted from the disease'.[6] Apparently once in the hospital environs the sick were almost a lost cause – black, mixed-race or white. To their shame (though understandable) those medical men on the island who treated private patients only 'fled from the islands' which added to 'the general distress', including Stewart's.[7]

By the time the sick list on the *Vanguard* had increased to 132, Commodore Simon Miller took the unilateral decision to land the sick and have them transported to the hospital at Viele Ville on the Vigie, in an effort to free up the ship and (hopefully) check the infection. The better houses in the area had been taken over as hospital quarters and made as suitable as possible. Miller provided both 'Nurses and Washermen' as attendants and his regular daily visits kept the attendants about their duty.[8]

By the beginning of September, Stewart had already lost one of the nursing mates to fever and he himself was seized with fever, leaving only one mate in the impossible situation of attending to all those sick on the *Vanguard* and the hospital ship. Commodore Miller sent the *Orpheus* to Martinique, carrying 52 of the worst cases to leave at that place; with orders to return and to take on board as many of the remaining sick from *Vanguard* as possible.

> In consequence of the great mortality in the Hospital at Vielle Ville, and on board the *Vanguard*; and, from the increased violence and Malignancy of the Fever, and Dysentery, which are now raging on board, I now judge it absolutely necessary for the good of the Service to remove His Majesty's Ship under m[y] Command to Gros Islet Bay, for the benefit of the Air, in order to check the progress of the

---

5   TNA: ADM 102/790: Report by Thomas Stewart, surgeon of Vielle Ville, Vigie, *Vanguard* and *Orpheus* Ships.
6   TNA: ADM 102/790: Stewart, Surgeon of Vielle Ville.
7   TNA: ADM 102/790: Report by Thomas Stewart, Surgeon of Vielle Ville, Vigie, *Vanguard* and *Orpheus* Ships.
8   TNA: ADM 102/790: Commodore Simon Miller.

infection, and the remaining crew … where we had much to fear from a hurricane, but which was less dreaded than the disease which raged in the Carenage. A strong proof of our dreadful situation.[9]

This also showed some foresight on Miller's part, as Surgeon's Mate W.F. Bickerstons also had succumbed to the fever, although both he and Surgeon Stewart pulled through. Stewart recorded his determination never to put himself in the same position again: 'No consideration would again induce me to take so Arduous, painful, and so dangerous a task and, with so few assistants, only two mates; but who deserve well for their diligence and perseverance.'[10] It must have been his personal nightmare.

Nor did he, once he had left the army, which he did in 1803 having finished his time of service. The situation in St Lucia must have left him feeling totally impotent and unable to achieve the slightest benefit to his patients, who were dying around him in their tens per day.

Surgeon Andrew Johnston, of the 44th Foot, striving on Morne Fortuné to save his men, must have been wretched that so few of his own ministrations appeared to work. The position was dire for all the men and, the replacement for Surgeon Thomas Facon who had died on Christmas Day 1796, was reduced to providing what would now be termed palliative care. At a minimum 10 men died daily.

Those three optimistic young men who had married in the Isle of Man, had seen the same service as Roworth on the continent, survived that disastrous winter retreat, had embarked for St Lucia in November 1795, and who had taken part in the re-taking of Morne Fortuné in May 1796, were not destined to survive. That year saw Thomas Thorne promoted to corporal on 21 January and John Brown to corporal on 11 April. The third of the group, George Gibb died on 30 July 1796. Brown died on 16 September, probably from disease. Thorne must have managed at least one trip back to the Isle of Man to visit Isabella soon after arriving back from the Continent. Their baby daughter, Selah, was baptised on 3 February 1796. Thorne died on 6 September. With communications as poor as they were that year, he may never have known that he had become a father. These three men of the 44th would have died of one of the forms of fever, as witnessed Roworth's blanket comment that his men were dying of a fever which turned them yellow.

As an example of the swathe that disease was cutting through the regiment the muster rolls show the fate of some of the 44th's drummers and fifers. Alexander McKinzie and Thomas Smith were both sent to hospital sometime between 25 June and Christmas 1795, McKinzie died on 23 February 1796. As it is unknown which transport he was on, he may well have already arrived in Barbados or have died of natural causes and been buried at sea. Of the remaining 29 drummers, six would die: Thomas Barrow (21 August 1796); James Clarkson (26 June 1795); Robert Dooley (25 March 1797); Robert Liddle (21 August 1796); Zachariah Swindells (7 December 1796); and Joseph Dones (27 December 1796).

---

9   TNA: ADM 102/290: Miller, Viele Vigie Hospital Book.
10   TNA: ADM 102/290: Miller, Viele Vigie Hospital Book.

By the end of August 1796 and by his own admission, Moore was becoming inured to the presence of death and disease. He grew accustomed to taking the offensive personally at all times, together with those few able redcoats who were still available to him, but increasingly his dependency grew on the indomitable black corps. Meanwhile he sought out every opportunity to achieve Abercromby's aims for the island. As he intended, many of the brigands were so harassed and sent running that many gave up, albeit unreconciled to their position, returning to their hateful masters or escaping to Martinique. Moore's white soldiers continued to die, some without lifting a musket. In a letter to Abercromby dated 2 September Moore regretted the condition of his regiments, when he wrote:

> The officers and men under my command ... have suffered severely. The sickness is so much greater upon Morne Fortuné and its immediate dependencies than at the other posts, that I detain upon it a number only sufficient for the daily duties. There are local situations in these islands – Morne Fortuné unfortunately is one of them – which are so unhealthy, that perhaps no care and management could altogether counteract the evil effects; but in general the greater part of the sickness proceeds from the want of interior discipline and economy in the regiments.[11]

Moore's conclusions seem hard to swallow, if downright biased, but if he could have been presented with the facts known now by modern medicine, he would surely have acted completely differently. Even David Stewart, in his *Sketches*, published in 1822, laid the blame on the 'destructive climate' and 'so unwholesome the constant subsistence on salt provisions, that three fourths of the troops were carried off before the end of the first year'.[12] As one historian pointed out, 'Casualties from disease in the Caribbean were expected, but the magnitude of those of the 1790s campaigns staggered everyone. These may have been facilitated by an unfortunate coincidence of the arrival from Africa of a new and virulent strain of yellow fever and successive highly favourable breeding seasons for the mosquito vectors of the killer diseases'.[13]

Only the consequences of this disease were known to Moore, not the cause and he continued to believe his own theories, invoking an older Roman regime of constant cleanliness, discipline and agility, in letters to his superior and to his father, that with cleanliness, 'sea or river bathing, constant activity and movement' his army would function effectively. He accepted that he differed with the majority of 'people I meet with on this subject; but *I am sure I am right ... I have not time to be ill*'.[14] These last words would rise up to bite him – twice.

Shortly after this communication to Abercromby and as the result of intelligence transmitted from the Morne, Moore and Anderson had a very

---

11   Maurice, *John Moore*, vol.I, p.239.
12   Stewart, *Sketches*, p.418.
13   David Barry Gaspar and David Patrick Geggus (eds), *A Turbulent Time: The French Revolution and the Greater Caribbean* (Indiana: Indiana University Press, 1997), p.87.
14   Carrick Moore, *Sir John Moore*, p.149.

near miss. When news that supplies had been landed from Guadeloupe to support the brigands, they took advantage of shipping round to Vieux Fort, believing it to be a safer mode of travel than by foot and for some reason Moore had decided to take neither redcoat support in any form, nor firearms in the boat. Instead of invoking naval help, they preferred the local method of a six-oared canoe and had travelled some leagues when they were cut off by two fully-manned brigand canoes, putting out from the shore with obvious aggressive intent. The only way to escape the pursuers was to row for the next island of St Vincent, which the frightened rowers did, in full knowledge of what the result would be if they could not out-row their pursuers for all 41 nautical miles. Fear lent wings to their oars and by dark the pursuers had given up the chase. After resting, the men took a very wide sweep and made it back to Vieux Fort by the morning, where Moore (ignoring his near brush with death) and his redcoats continued to search, assail and harass.[15]

Adhering to his own regime of constant activity and movement, his complete trust in that regime and faith in his own self-beliefs, Moore may well have been surprised when attacked by an initial bout of fever during October and November, while at Vieux Fort. Once over the worst, he removed himself to Soufriere where he stayed until he had been free of fever for three weeks, then returned to Fort Charlotte 'where I relapsed the very day I arrived [and] I believe I was very near dying'.[16] It was while Moore was recuperating that a return was made on 13 November 1796 of the distribution of the forces throughout the Windward and Leeward Islands.

Return of the numbers of sick and dead in the Caribbean from March to October 1796.[17]

Dates of Monthly Returns	Sick in Quarters	Sick in Hospitals	Dead
1 April	660	1,517	248
1 May	852	2,224	177
1 June	1,347	2,972	365
1 July	2,032	2,342	341
1 August	2,145	2,241	465
1 September	2,069	2,187	832
1 October as far as the Returns are received	945	1,419	484
Total (dead)			2,912

Moore survived to continue his policy of harassment in which his black corps were constantly sent out to search and attack. Once found, the camps would be destroyed and it was in this way, that very slowly the brigands were worn down, as their camps and provisions were constantly demolished. It was not an easy task. The brigands were highly organised, and they knew their jungle. Their camps and hide-outs for caches of provisions were to be found all over the island, in the most difficult places to reach.

---

15   Carrick Moore, *Sir John Moore*, pp.158–159.
16   Maurice, *John Moore*, vol.I, pp.240–241.
17   TNA: WO 1/86.

YELLOW JACK: ONE HAS NOT A MAN FIT FOR DUTY

Distribution of the Forces in St Lucia with the corps doing duty, taken from the latest returns, 13 November 1796.[18]

Corps	Commissioned Officers						Serjeants		Drummers		Rank and File				Total
	Lt Cols	Majors	Captains	Lieuts	Ensigns	Staff	Fit for duty	Sick	Fit for duty	Sick	Fit for duty	Sick in quarters	Sick in hospital	On com'd	
Royal Artillery			2					1		2	7	47			54
Royal Engineers			1				1		1		5	2			7
31st Foot	1	1	8	11		2		48		13	16	261	67		344
44th Foot		1	7	13		5	37	15	6	7	151	193	95	15	454
48th Foot		1	7	9	1	3	52		22		69		212	58	339
55th Foot		1	5	14	1	4	24	28	22		253	258	44	9	564
York Fusiliers		2	1	8	3	3	6	10	4	12	27	104	55	12	198
O'Meara's Black Corps	1		4	8	3	3	39		8		361	121	3	2	487
Drualt's Black Corps		1	1	6	3	3	16		3		206	49	33		288
TOTAL	2	7	33	72	11	23	175	102	66	34	1,095	1,035	509	96	2,735

The return above highlights those numbers of men and officers sick and in hospital. The 44th Regiment alone shows that there are more men incapacitated at 288 than there are fit for duty at 151. In comparison, however, the 31st Foot had the appalling number of 328 incapacitated with just 16 fit for duty. The numbers were a real eye-opener, and it is more than understandable that Moore sent the 31st home in December.

As for Roworth – he had written his last letters home already and had just seven weeks to live.

Moore survived to continue his work on the island. Meanwhile attempts were made to alter the current situation by bringing on side one of the most influential men who held the brigands' trust, Marin Pèdre. In December, Moore promised the return of Marin's property if he could persuade the brigands to surrender themselves, as had happened on St Vincent.[19] Moore trusted Marin, but the weeks wore on with nothing to show from the constant bargaining. Eventually, Moore became frustrated and proceeded with the hostilities again, sending his black troops into the woods to continue their work.

On 10 January 1797, Moore sailed for Fort Royal, Martinique, in the *Pelican*, following a summons to a meeting with Abercromby. After many complimentary remarks and apologies for Moore's unwanted situation, Abercromby set out other possible posts which might appeal to Moore rather better: firstly, that of Governor of Grenada and secondly, the joint post of Quartermaster General and head of the Barrack Department. Moore politely refused both, qualifying his refusal of the second, saying that, 'The employment of Quarter-master General was one I did not understand, and had no turn for it.'[20] While still attendant on Abercromby, Moore received letters to the

---

18   TNA: WO 1/86.
19   Breen, *St Lucia*, p.105.
20   Maurice, *John Moore*, vol.I, p.244.

effect that the brigands has surprised the 70-strong post at Praslin and had killed most of the soldiers. He rushed back and discovered that the attack had occurred during an afternoon when Captain de Marchay had been asleep, most of the men were washing at the river and the guard itself was asleep or drunk. 'They were bayoneted without resistance.'[21] Although de Marchay was woken by the fracas and tried to retrieve the situation, he was unable to improve matters and consequently shot himself. Moore's take on this was that 'being an amiable man in society, and [having] a strong sense of honour … [he was] determined not to survive the disgrace he had brought on himself'.[22] This was to Moore's satisfaction and the current ideals of personal honour. Fifteen of the men were killed in the event and 20 left wounded. Moore's return revived the remaining dejected soldiers and Praslin was soon occupied again, the brigand camp discovered and the occupants either killed or dispersed.

A similar attack was made by brigands at Denérie on the east coast, but with a more positive outcome. French emigrant, Lieutenant le Brun, prevailed with only 50 men against 300 Brigands. The latter were repulsed and chased into the woods where Le Brun's men achieved 'a considerable slaughter'.[23] Many brigand bodies lay around the palisades when Moore arrived. Le Brun and his men had fought them off for three hours and emerged triumphant. Moore was effusive in his congratulations.[24]

Moore continued to focus on his *raison d'etre* during his stay in St Lucia, although Abercromby had given him the option to leave. He felt that his efforts were beginning to make further inroads into the diminishing courage of the brigands, who were losing heart after such long-held aspirations and exertions on their part, having been constantly chased and kept on the move. Moore had for so long kept himself and his black troops active, he was certain that they were the answer to conquering the brigands, in the Caribbean islands. In a letter to his father dated 18 January 1797 (after his first weeks of illness) he wrote that only the black regiments could act effectively in the woods, neither the British nor German regiments were equal to even effectively guard the coastline. The 'white troops were melting away' – and succumbing to disease. From an earlier letter to his father, dated 8 January 1797, he stated he was placing detachments of black troops along the coast between Morne Fortuné and 'Soufriere to prevent communication with Guadeloupe'.[25] This action indicates that he may no longer have had a sufficient nucleus of coastal artillery to do the job. James Carrick Moore, in his 1834 version of his brother's diary, wrote of John Moore's continuing endeavours: 'He rose usually at six in the morning, was occupied in business till mid-day; then marched frequently in that sultry clime often thirty miles a day, and slept in his clothes on the ground. He was thus in continual exercise, until again seized with the yellow fever.'[26]

---

21 Maurice, *John Moore*, vol.I, p.246.
22 Maurice, *John Moore*, vol.I, p.247.
23 Carrick Moore, *Sir John Moore*, pp.166–167.
24 Carrick Moore, *Sir John Moore*, pp.166–167.
25 Maurice, *John Moore*, vol.I, p.242.
26 Carrick Moore, *Sir John Moore*, p168.

It struck sometime after a visit from Abercromby, who arrived on 20 March 1797. Moore made an entry on 12 May, when he recounted the details of his illness. This time he nearly lost the contest. Together with Dr George Pinckard, Moore was one of the few who left accounts of their personal fight with the 'yellow devil'. The fever had been receding in the island for some months, as the number of recorded deaths in the 44th demonstrated. In the four weeks of September 1796, 33 privates died, together with eight non-commissioned officers; in January 1797, only one non-commissioned officer died and six rank and file. Moore, like so many, may have thought the fever would not strike twice, but when it struck him for the second time, he knew that he was very ill indeed and again faced the fact that he might not survive.

A few days into this second bout he became comatose and was left unattended except for his personal servant and his friend, Captain Paul Anderson. These two cared for him when even the doctors had given up. Anderson, seeing no movement and believing Moore may have breathed his last, checked for body-warmth, then realised that life was still in the body and 'poured down a little wine'.[27] This appeared to be the beginning of Moore's slow recovery though he also had to contend with a large abscess on the hip, 'the inflammation [of which is] violent and the pain excruciating'.[28] This he survived, too. From this time onwards until he was relieved of his duties he passed few further derogatory comments on his officers in his diary, perhaps because he had finally walked in their boots and was impelled to look death in the face or that there were so few of them left alive to harangue. As he recuperated, Abercromby sent Colonel James Drummond to help him with the military business and less than a month later, it was agreed with Moore that he should leave St Lucia for good and return home to his family, with Colonel Drummond taking over command on the island. This Drummond did effectively, continuing in Moore's 'scorched earth' policy of ridding St Lucia of its brigands. He remained as Lieutenant Governor until 1798, when Brigadier General George Prevost (60th Foot) took over. Prevost, of Swiss descent, was a very enlightened man and a fluent French speaker. He was to stay as Lieutenant Governor for four years, at the end of which time his conciliatory and sensitive approach had laid the ground for a much altered and receptive population.

Moore embarked on the sloop, *Beaver*, on 21 May 1797, for Martinique. He finally disembarked at Falmouth on 9 July after 31 days at sea and then took the direction which eventually led him on the path to Corunna and his death in battle in January 1809.

Considering the huge death toll of redcoats by endemic disease in 1796 and the sheer wastage of manpower from yellow fever in particular, it behoves us to reflect on the cause of the disease and its ravages on the physical and mental welfare of the men themselves who took part in Moore's endeavours – whether brigadier general or private man.

What was this 'yellow-fanged fever', described at length by Dr George Pinckard? In letters home he wrote graphically of his many encounters with

---

27 Carrick Moore, *Sir John Moore*, p169.
28 Maurice, *John Moore*, vol.I, p.251.

yellow fever, in his profession as a medical man. But what is important to our understanding of what those soldiers experienced is that Pinckard recorded his personal endurance in great detail, as a survivor, but with the observation of a professional. He left, therefore, one of the most objective contemporary accounts available. It must be remembered that every single one of those thousands of redcoats, from a private, of just 18 years, to serjeant, from ensign to lieutenant colonel, who were infected with yellow fever (whether they survived or died), shared in the miserable effects of the virus and all the accompanying horrors of its progress through the body. Those who did not succumb would have had the hell of watching their comrades die in agony, as did Roworth so many times, before falling ill with it himself. By the end he may well have been happy to join them.

Pinckard succumbed to yellow fever in Demerara. A month earlier while in Mahaica, Guyana, he had the rather dubious distinction of being the only medical officer who had not been taken ill with yellow fever. He lost that distinction on 17 September 1796. The symptoms that he described commenced with heavy limbs, 'a severe headache and pain of the eyes, with a great thirst and dryness of mouth' and his sleep was very disturbed. He felt languid and a general malaise was followed by another 'most wretched night'. He realised that he had the same fever that he had seen in so many others and determined to fight it. But as it set in, although the faculties of his mind were undisturbed, he declared his body unable to respond to his commands. On day three light was intolerable to him and the pain in his eyes 'conveying a sensation as if three or four hooks were fastened into the globe of each eye then pulled backwards into the cranium'. His descriptions were very graphic, his calves 'feeling as if dogs were gnawing down into the bones'. His skin was burning, his mouth excessively thirsty yet dry of lips, tongue and teeth. He was plagued by 'excruciating pain', 'insatiable thirst', and 'unappeasable restlessness'. Combined they brought him 'almost to phrensy'. He threw himself about in the bed continuously, but could find no rest. He had 'twelve to fourteen ounces of blood' taken from his arm. He drank constantly but passed a third and a fourth night of severe discomfort and no sleep taking only a saline and camphor solution. On the 21st 'the heat and pain had subsided' but he was soaked through by 'copious perspiration'. His thirst was even more distressing, his strength and voice both left him. This was followed by 'exhausting diarrhaea'. By the 22nd (day six) he felt as if his life 'only hung by a slender filament' and was conscious that he

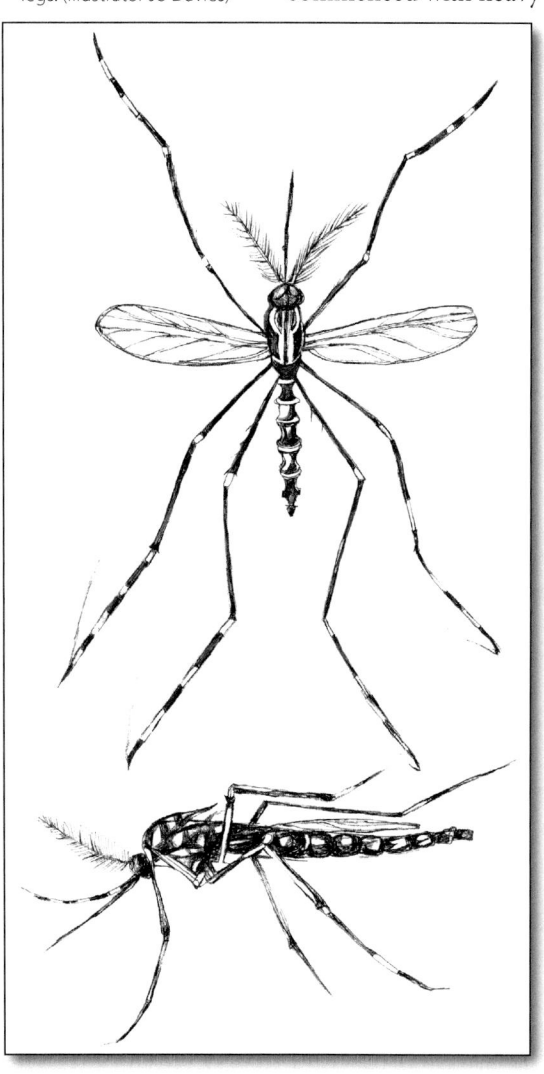

Aedes Agypti, the mosquito carrier of yellow fever, identified by the shape of a lyre on the top of its thorax and white markings on its legs. (Illustrator Jo Davies)

might be dying. He lay 'supine, and prostrate' – for when his head was raised he would faint. He was reconciled to the fact of dying and he waited patiently, thinking of home and saying his goodbyes to loved ones. This was also his worst day, when he was constantly aware of feelings of horror and at night 'all was horror, horror, restless deadly horror'.[29] These feelings continued for a day and a night before he was aware of his fever slowly receding.

He survived, with the help of fellow colleagues, six ounces of quinine, wine and cool baths as the pains began to fade, but was left enfeebled and barely able to 'lift a feather'. From what is known of yellow fever today, where modern medicine, by using the brick wall of a vaccine, can prevent a human from becoming infected, all those who survived in the 1790s would probably have survived without the quinine, wine and cool baths. It seems that all those thousands of men either died or survived – as simple as that – with or without a clinician.

Pinckard's account can be transferred many times over to those thousands of red-jacketed men who came to the West Indies to fight for king and country and who died as they would never have wished. Soldiers hoped to die in a welter of blood and glory, not in the clutches of a debilitating and particularly wretched disease.

Small wonder Moore did not harass his British regiments again. If not for Anderson's instinct, Moore may have been declared dead. Like George Pinckard he was most fortunate to live. In both cases the illness kept them prostrate for about 10 days, with considerably longer periods for recuperation. Moore experienced it twice, of course.

Whether they lived or died, the intolerable experience for the redcoats had been caused by an insect bite. The female mosquito *Aedes Aegypti* bit into the skin of a human and sucked blood after having previously fed on blood from another infected human and so on – mosquito to human, human to mosquito. It would be another 104 years until that fact was discovered, by which time hundreds of thousands of British and European military men and civilians had died, as well as many thousands in all those countries where yellow fever was endemic.

Returning to the dozens of regiments which served in the West Indies, between 1793 and 1801, some 69 line infantry regiments were sent there. Another 24 followed between 1803 and 1815. The death toll due to tropical diseases was very high for European troops. From 1793–1802, an estimated 45,000 British soldiers died in the West Indies, including about 1,500 officers, nearly all from fevers. In 1796 alone, some 41 per cent of the white soldiers died, most of them having arrived in the past year.[30]

This was a vicious year whichever way one looked at it and for each dead man, from officer to private, there was a family left to mourn, some who could rebuild a life, but many women and children who could not and who would enter the workhouse. The cost to lives lost, whether to death or the workhouse, was uncountable and obscene.

---

29   Pinckard, *Notes*, pp.134–150.
30   Chartrand, *British Forces*, p.3.

A peaceful corner of the cemetery for officers on Morne Fortuné (Donald Roworth)

The expenditure was also obscene, but at least countable. For example, the Transport Office laid out an 'Account of the Expense incurred … for the West India Expedition between the 4th September 1794 and 31st December 1795'. It totalled £654,473 3s 7d.[31] Ignoring the shillings and pence and using The National Archives converter for this sum to 2022's value works out at £50,238,081 for just 16 months.

---

31 TNA: WO 1/799: 3 May 1796, p.195.

18

Redcoats All: Resolution and Reckoning – The Regiments and the Men

Your Ever, Dear and Loving Husband, Wm Roworth till Death[1]

There must be few corners in foreign fields which cannot own to a smattering of red-coated soldiers claiming their little bit of England or Wales, or Scotland or Ireland in the earth. St Lucia not the least of them. Her soil holds so many thousands.

Fortescue gave an overview of the regiments on St Lucia, whose duty appeared to be to die for king and country, covered not with glory, but with ignominy. In the month of October, 'the garrison of St Lucia buried six hundred and thirty-three men'. By November, the remaining force, which on the first of June had been 4,000 strong, was reduced to 1,000 fit for duty and 1,500 sick, the remaining 1,500 having died.[2]

So, what happened to those much-depleted red-coated regiments, those officers and men left behind on St Lucia in the summer of 1797? On 1 May 1796, the 31st Foot had arrived at St Lucia, a healthy unit of 915 men. On 17 May, they were ordered to attack the Vigie, that peninsula of land to the north of the Carenage, which they did. After an initial success a retreat under fire was necessary. That retreat was a disaster for the 31st. From that regiment Captains Johnson and Walker, four serjeants, and 80 rank and file were killed on the night of 17 May, at the Vigie. At the same event Lieutenant Colonels Hay and Arbuthnot, Captains Murray and Sauvrell [Sorrel], Lieutenants Sullivan and Hawkshaw, four serjeants and 121 rank and file were wounded – an horrendous number for no positive outcome or return.

The continued hard service experienced under John Moore's governorship was to be the downfall of the 31st in St. Lucia. Cannon speaks of Moore's methods to 'eradicate [these] predatory bands' involving the commander taking to the 'wildest quarters of the mountains' with his troops, including the 31st, from whence they suffered much 'fatigue, privation and continual

---

1 NA: DDRW 24/25: Roworth to Mary, St Lucia, 19 October 1796.
2 Fortescue, *History*, vol.IV, Part 1, p.495.

NOT SO EASY, LADS

44th (East Essex) Regiment of Foot shoulder belt plate, as worn by the men fighting in St Lucia in the 1790s. (Essex Regiment Museum)

exposure'.[3] Moore must have realised that this particular regiment was experiencing major health problems and he sent them to Vieux Fort, to recuperate; which place became so unhealthy that he took the decision to remove the 31st from the island completely.

As previously mentioned Lieutenant Colonel Robert Arbuthnot had died in July 1796 from wounds received in the battle for the Vigie. Lieutenant Colonel Adam Hay, who overcame his injuries at the Vigie and was active during the ensuing months, then succumbed to fever and was carried out to the ship that was taking him home. He died on 22 December 1796, just as the ship docked in Barbados. George Fearon had been promoted major on 2 September 1795, before embarking for the West Indies, then made brevet lieutenant colonel, for the duration of his service in the West Indies only, on 22 September 1796. He was also given the post of Deputy Quartermaster General the same month, but died in October from yellow fever.

Before the 31st had left Nursling near Southampton on 25 October 1795, it had been reinforced by drafts from 'the 43rd, 88th, 92nd and 94th regiments' to bring it up to full strength to 'a thousand rank and file and with a second Lieutenant Colonel, a major and one additional lieutenant to each company, beside two recruiting companies'.[4] The deaths from yellow fever in that regiment alone were for a time 'sixteen each day'.[5] During the year 1796 the regiment had lost 17 officers, and 870 men, including those who fell in the attack of [the] Vigie, in St Lucia.[6]

The remainder embarked, probably from Castries, for Barbados on 22 December 1797, disembarking there six days later, where Colonel Morshead was handed a blank form as not one man was fit for duty and it was found necessary to hospitalise the whole regimental remnant. The men who were able, returned to England, where they disembarked at Gravesend the following July 1797, (together with the 44th) mustering 'only eighty-five … including serjeants, drummers and rank and file'.[7] The 1797 Army list recorded the deaths of commissioned officers as one lieutenant colonel, two majors, two captains, one lieutenant, one ensign and the quartermaster.[8]

---

3   Cannon, *31st Regiment*, pp.52–53.
4   Cannon, *31st Regiment*, p.49.
5   Cannon, *31st Regiment*, p.53.
6   Cannon, *31st Regiment*, p.53.
7   Cannon, *31st Regiment*, p.54.
8   TNA: WO 65/47: Army List 1796.

REDCOATS ALL: RESOLUTION AND RECKONING – THE REGIMENTS AND THE MEN

Shortly after disembarkation in England the regiment marched to Doncaster and alternated between barracks at Doncaster, Hull and York for the following two years. It was not until 1799 that the 31st recruited 853 volunteers from the militia and was at full strength once again, being re-deployed to the Low Countries.

The 44th Foot, 'greatly reduced in numbers, embarked for England, and landed at Gravesend … on the 31st of July'.[9] Carter remarks that 'the loss of the 44th Regiment from the 3rd to the 24th of May [1796] was only one man killed'.[10] In fact, on 3 May four rank and file were killed, two captains, Johnston and Tuffie, and Lieutenant Gregory were wounded, as were 17 rank and file missing during an attack on enemy batteries.[11] While the great reduction in numbers over the next year was due primarily to disease, which showed no favour to any redcoat, whatever his rank or status. There may have been some who died by the enemy's hand, but definitely they were in the minority. At one time the regiment could only muster 12 officers out of the full strength of 36 and 151 men out of 915.[12] Before leaving for England, those who were fit were drafted into the 55th Foot, together with any able men left from the 48th, to continue the fight. This ruling meant that those drafted still could not make it home, the opportunity to return having been taken from them. There were some rank and file who returned to England but, like many other regiments, they would have been unfit to serve. This was the second time that members of the 44th had served in the West Indies in fairly quick succession, with the flank companies in 1794 and the whole battalion in 1796.

Carter listed the officers who died in St Lucia from the 44th Foot in 1796–1797 and they were as follows: Colonel Riddell, Major Edward Wilson, Captain Lieutenant and Captain James Cooke, Captain William Creagh, Lieutenants John Charles Phipps, Samuel Tuffie, George Robert Stoney, William Waddell, John Wright, Donald McLeod, Robert Chambers, Jeffery Robinson and Adam Ogilvie, Quartermasters Thomas Gardiner and McCabe, and Surgeon Thomas Facon.[13] Carter mistakenly included Lieutenant Adam Ogilvie, as he later resigned – it was Lieutenant Ramsey Ogilvie who died.

The 44th Foot's relevant muster roll (where legible) marked as dead 136 privates from arrival on St Lucia to embarkation for England. Of those, only the five mentioned above were killed in action. The regiment also lost 13 serjeants, five drummers and 16 corporals.[14]

Colonel Robert Riddell died from fever 30 October 1796. Major Edward Wilson, so belittled by Moore, preceded Riddell by just nine days on 21 October. His parents would have lost two sons in six months, one in battle and one from disease. Captain Lieutenant James Cooke died on 10 December and Surgeon Thomas Facon died on Christmas Day 1796. The same muster roll shows that his Surgeon's Mate, Robert Constable, moved to another

---

9 Carter, *44th Foot*, p.33.
10 Carter, *44th Foot*, p.33.
11 Anon. (ed.), *Bulletins 1796*, pp.102–103.
12 Burrows, *Essex Regiment*, p.32.
13 Carter, *44th Foot*, pp.33–34.
14 TNA: WO 12/5638: Muster Roll 25 December 1797 to 24 June 1796.

NOT SO EASY, LADS

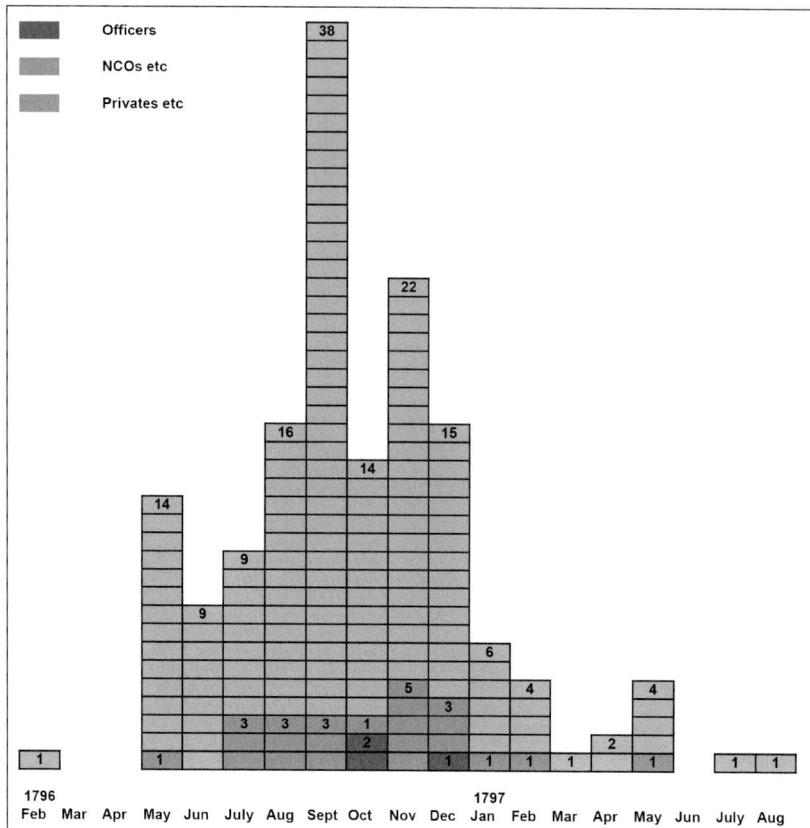

The 44th Foot in St Lucia: Deaths of Officers, NCOs and Private Men in 1796–1797. Extracted from TNA: WO 12/5638.

corps. Andrew Johnston was made Surgeon's Mate in the 44th and within six months was promoted surgeon. Quartermaster Thomas Gardiner had died of fever early on in his service on St Lucia, on 26 July 1796.[15]

Of the 16 serjeants who died of fever or other disease, the first was Serjeant Thomas Foxcroft on 27 May 1796, mentioned by William Roworth as a particular friend. Foxcroft and his wife were known to the Roworth family as a whole, and Roworth would regularly ask to be remembered to Mr and Mrs Foxcroft Senior at home. Serjeants John Burke and John Holmes died on 9 and 20 July respectively; likewise, Serjeants Robert Johnstone and Henry Ollett, on 6 and 24 August; Serjeants Thomas Page, James Chapman and Edward McGuiness, on 3, 14 and 28 September respectively; Serjeants Thomas Reily, Robert Beckwith and Ignatius O'Donald on 18, 24, and 27 October, all within 10 days; Serjeants Samuel Vincent and George Thompson on 14 and 22 December; Serjeant Major William Roworth died on 2 January 1797 followed by Serjeant James McDermott on 19 February.[16] It is interesting to note that the next serjeant major was Thomas Mackrell, who was appointed adjutant in September 1797 after Chaloner resigned. The promotion would have probably been Roworth's had he survived.

---

15 NA: DDRW 25/25: Roworth to his parents, 4 November 1796.
16 TNA: WO 12/5638: Muster rolls.

Record of the death of Serjeant Major William Roworth on 2 January 1797. Shown on the Muster Roll dated 25th Day of June to 24th Day of December 1796. TNA: WO 12/5638.

Unusually, on the relevant muster roll, there was a note dated 15 January 1798, a year after Roworth's death. 'By cash received for Dbt to Mrs Roworth £10.12s.2d' and marked in red 'Agent Jany.' This would have been paid by William Bownas, agent to the 44th Foot. There were no other payments to be found for other widows on that roll, although it was not an unknown occurrence and sometimes it would take years for the money to reach the next of kin.[17] The muster roll examined here covers the unusually long period, is in poor condition, and is very difficult to read, so it is more than likely there were considerably more deaths, with those names rendered illegible. However, the 1797 Army List records deaths of commissioned officers of the 44th Regiment as one lieutenant colonel, one major, two captains, four lieutenants, one ensign and the quartermaster.

After arriving back on British shores at Gravesend on 31 July 1797, time was taken to recuperate and build up the numbers again to fill the perpetual chasm. Carter reports that 'The Regiment did not remain long in England, as it embarked … on the 1st of October 1798 … for Gibraltar.' At least they were allowed 15 months respite, over twice as long as the six allowed between May and November 1795 on their return from the Continent. 'The numbers embarked were two field officers, seven captains, seventeen subalterns, forty-one serjeants, eighteen drummers, and three hundred and sixty-five rank and file.'[18] In 1800 they joined, once again, forces led by Sir Ralph Abercromby. Under his command they took part in the Battle for Alexandria, 21 March 1801, during which the old general received a mortal wound, from which he died on the 28th. On the 13th, when the British crossed swords with the

---

17 TNA: WO 12/5639: Muster Rolls.
18 Carter, *44th Foot*, p.34.

State of the 44th Regiment of Foot from Disembarkation Return on board the *Anna of Bengall* at Portsmouth, 31 July 1797.

Present					Rank & File				
Officers	Staff	QM	SJt	Drum	Present	Sick	On Com'd	Other	Total
19	2	-	45	6	-	8	[Note (a)]	-	84
Source TNA: WO 17/155/058									[Note (b)]

NOTE (a)
"NB Lieut Colon'l Ogilvy lost his passage at Antigua but expected to arrive with the first Packett. On command at Martinico 1 Cap't, 2 Lieut's, 1 Q'master and 1 Drummer not included in above."
[Noted at bottom of return]

NOTE (b)
To this total must be added the men identified in Note (a): viz. 90 in all.

French outside Mandora, two of the 44th's rank and file were killed, and on the 21st another was lost, together with Lieutenant Colonel David Ogilvie, who died of his wounds from that occasion, on 4 April. He had first appeared, already a captain, on the 44th's muster roll, on 11 November 1789, being taken on from half-pay in the stead of Captain Richard Timms who retired to half-pay on the 10th.[19]

In 1796 the 48th Foot, which left England with 847 men, was part of the army sent to recapture St Lucia. Barthorp, writer and historian, claims that in 18 months 'only 50 men remained', although casualties of war were only 30 men.[20] The remainder would have died from diseases like yellow fever, malaria and dysentery – a horrendous total of 767.

The 48th lost its Scottish commander, Lieutenant Colonel Archibald Campbell to fever on 23 October 1796. He had held that position for just 12 months and was 45 years old when he died. The copy of the 1797 Army List held in The National Archives records the deaths of commissioned officers as follows, two lieutenant colonels, one captain, five lieutenants, two ensigns and the quartermaster. Lieutenant General Sir Brian Horrocks, in his introduction to Barthorp's *The Northamptonshire Regiment* points out that 'The 48th had the misfortune to spend 14 years in these dreaded isles. Four times between 1760 and 1800 the 48th sailed to the West Indies; four times a pitiable remnant returned, their ranks decimated by disease.'[21]

Of the commissioned officers of the 55th Foot on St Lucia, the copy of the 1797 Army List held in The National Archives records the deaths of four captains, eight lieutenants and the quartermaster. As mentioned elsewhere, the 55th Foot was the recipient, while still in St Lucia, of the remnants of the fit men of the 44th and 48th, to replace many of its own depleted numbers. By December of 1797 the regiment was back in Chatham and in February 1798 it received men from the Kent Militia. During 1799, it received volunteers

---

19   TNA: WO 65/39: Army List 1789:
20   Michael Barthorp, *The Northamptonshire Regiment* (London: Leo Cooper Ltd, 1974), p.17.
21   Barthorp, *Northamptonshire Regiment*, p.14.

from a number of county militias, including the East Essex, to get back up to strength. Finally, in August of that year, the regiment embarked for the Continent again.

Lieutenant Colonel Donald MacDonald who survived was made major general 25 September 1803 and Colonel of the Cape Regiment on 9 August 1804. He was appointed Colonel of the 55th Foot on 20 March 1811. The much maligned and 'frightened' Major John Lindsay became a major general in 1812 after 12 years in the 5th (Northumberland) Regiment of Foot and died in 1820 in Brighton, aged 58.

After their considerable service in Flanders under the Duke of York 100 men of the Royal Artillery were also left in St Lucia, in June 1796, by Abercromby, to support Governor Moore. In fact, in 1793, there were nine companies of Royal Artillery in the West Indies. Five were stationed in Barbados where the headquarters was based, three in Jamaica and one in Grenada. The men were sent out in detachments to the various islands, whenever and wherever they were needed. There appear to be no numbers of deaths recorded specifically from St Lucia but records from other islands provide evidence of the likely numbers involved. For example, in San Domingo, referring specifically to the Royal Artillery, by 'the end of 1794, of the four officers and 60 O.R.s [other ranks] … one officer and 40 O.R.s were already dead'. By June 1795, on the same island, after drafts had arrived from Jamaica, with 'six officers and 200 O.R.s … these were dying at the rate of 40 a month'.[22] The numbers give an indication of what the 100 artillerymen might have expected in St Lucia in the malevolent year of 1796.

The black regiments, so appreciated by the beleaguered Moore, were men who could do virtually everything he asked – and then some, so to speak. He early realised that they were more than equal to the tasks required of them. The references he made to their skills, to their willingness to take orders, to their adaptability and their stamina, started as a trickle and became a flood. This was not the first time black soldiers had been used in the West Indies, but this was probably the first time that they virtually took the place of the white regiments and demonstrated their wide capabilities. The arrival of Drualt's Corps from Guadeloupe, sent by Abercromby, and composed of nearly 300 men, meant that Moore had about 600 men in total upon whose enthusiasm and stamina he could rely. Historian Tim Lockley states that by the end of 1796, Drualt's had 288 men and O'Meara's 487 men.[23] In 1798 the former was renamed the 9th West India Regiment and its colonel would be Major General John Moore himself. O'Meara's Corps became the 12th West India Regiment.

Without doubt, the men in these two corps were the men to whom Moore's successor, Drummond, owed the final reduction of St Lucia (not forgetting an injection from the 38th Foot).

---

22 K.W. Maurice-Jones, *The History of the Coast Artillery in the British Army* (Uckfield: Naval and Military Press, 2009), pp.108–110.

23 Tim Lockley, *Military Medicine and the Making of Race: Life and Death in the West India Regiments, 1795–1874* (Cambridge: Cambridge University Press, 2020), p.44.

The French soldiers who comprised the garrison on Morne Fortuné in April 1796 and who marched out from there with their arms, their colours and their self-respect definitely intact on 26 May, had eventually lost a hard month's siege. This was between only 2,000 French trained soldiers, (mostly black, some men of colour and some whites) and some 11,000 British soldiers and heavy ordnance. Some were of the group which had fled the burning town of Castries and taken refuge in Morne Fortuné (Fort Charlotte), just days before the capitulation. That is evident in the make-up of the passengers in the transports who disembarked in Britain, particularly those who reached Porchester Castle, Hampshire.[24]

What is known is that all those soldiers taken from the Morne were embarked on transports to Britain and travelled as prisoners of war – but not as slaves – this was an important distinction to the surrendering garrison and to Goyrand. This was agreed with Abercromby before the men laid down their arms on 26 May. This distinction made all the difference as to their treatment both on board ship and once they reached Britain.

There appear to have been three groups of POWs destined for the various prisons for prisoners of war in Britain. Historian John Penny tells us that there were approximately 2,000 from St Lucia, 700 from St Vincent and 180 from Grenada, taken on board the waiting transports. Before the POWs sailed in July, Rear Admiral Henry Harvey, who had taken over from Christian, gave instructions for all those from Martinique and St Lucia to be given appropriate clothing for a winter in Britain. The convoy of 103 vessels sailed on 16 July 1796, protected by HMS *Ganges* and HMS *Charon*. Storms and gales erupted again on the later part of the journey in the eastern Atlantic and the Channel. Seven weeks after embarkation, on Friday 7 October, the transport *London* was wrecked near Ilfracombe, on the coast of north Devon. In spite of the efforts of the local seamen, some 50 prisoners were drowned. The survivors were taken to the prison at Stapleton, in Bristol. Their details were recorded in the General Entry Book on 4 December.[25] The survivors were a Colonel Heaurmaux and his wife, from St Vincent, four French and 25 black soldiers. Four days later, once they had given their parole, the French colonel and his wife left for Cheltenham, to join their French compatriots and their families who were already on parole and able to lead a life somewhat nearer to normal, albeit in a foreign land. Two of the prisoners, Victor and Pierre, died within five weeks and two, Dumat and Biradelle, died in the April and February respectively. The cartel arranged between Britain and France allowed for the repatriation of prisoners. The last remaining prisoners were sent on board the 160-ton *Smallbridge* and were disembarked at Brest, towards the end of January 1798.

All captives and captors from St Lucia had had a very sickly journey across the Atlantic, with deaths, through disease, of some 268 prisoners of

---

24 'Black Prisoners of War at Portchester Castle', *English Heritage*, <https://www.english-heritage.org.uk/visit/places/portchester-castle/history-and-stories/black-prisoners-at-portchester/>, accessed July 2023.

25 John Penny, 'Shipwrecked West Indians in Stapleton Prison, Bristol 1796–1798', *The Regional Historian*, Spring 2004, pp.11–20.

The Wreck of the *London*. (Courtesy of Ilfracombe Museum collection)

war and 100 British soldiers. In spite of the deaths, 2,512 prisoners survived, which comprised 2,413 men and 99 women and children, when they disembarked at Portsmouth.[26] Once there, they were taken to Portchester Castle and separated into groups; white European officers were allowed out on parole, black and coloured officers and men were moved into the main prison buildings; the sick to the prison hospital; the women and children to a large ward at Forton prison hospital in Gosport.

Coming from the heat of the Caribbean many suffered from the shock of the British weather, in spite of Rear Admiral Harvey's gift of clothing. The prison doctor, James Johnston, cared much for those who were genuinely suffering and under his remit provided extra warm clothing, in the shape of thick woollen vests and socks to supplement the yellow prison clothing and blankets. Shoes came later because the Afro-Caribbean prisoners had larger feet (possibly wider from never having worn shoes) than the British, so they had to be made up specially for them. Also 'a special diet was arranged which included extra potatoes and soup before bedtime'.[27] Their beer had added ginger which was thought to aid warmth. Unfortunately, the new clothing was filched by European prisoners, so arrangements were made to transfer the Caribbean prisoners into two new hulks, the *Captivity* and the *Vigilant*, moored in the harbour just outside the castle. The doctor was delighted, professing the hulks to be 'more comfortable and warm',

---

26 'Black Prisoners of War at Portchester Castle', *English Heritage*.
27 'Black Prisoners of War at Portchester Castle', *English Heritage*.

NOT SO EASY, LADS

Napoleonic prisoners crowded into Portchester Castle Keep. (Modern reconstruction drawing by Peter Dunn)

presumably because wood holds warmth better then stone in the short run.[28] The prisoners were not kept for longer than necessary as the costs of keeping them were considerable and they were also, as with all prisoners of war, used as bargaining chips to exchange with British soldiers who were imprisoned by the French. So, by the end of 1797 most were exchanged and the hulks returned to housing other French prisoners and British felons.

To return briefly to St Lucia, after the capitulation was signed Gaspard Goyrand together with Cottin and a number of other officers, were taken to Barbados, where Goyrand was kept in detention for three months. He was then taken to England by Brigadier General Knox. After a crossing of 42 days, they arrived in Liverpool on 7 September 1796. The two then travelled on to London, where Knox obtained for Goyrand authorisation to return to France, whenever he was ready. 'Goyrand returned in November to Paris and after a two month leave of absence at Aix, gave in his resignation as agent, on the grounds that an inactive Republican should not receive emoluments. This scrupulous delicacy complete[d] the contrast between this honest citizen and his colleague Victor Hugues'.[29] Goyrand endeavoured to gain a position as a vice-consul but did not succeed and died just two years later in 1799, aged about 53.

'*They called us Brigands*' was the title St Lucian, Robert Devaux, gave to his second book about the freedom-fighters of St Lucia in the eighteenth century. In time, many of these men too wore red coats. 'Brigand' was a catch-all term used by the British, specifically for certain people in the West Indies. The word is middle English, derived from the Old French – brigand – derived from the Italian, brigante. It is given two meanings: one who lives by pillage and robbery or (interestingly), dating from 1795, a light-armed irregular foot-soldier. So there has to have been some acknowledgement, in that entry, of the emergence of a change in perception of the St Lucian Brigand. It appears that by their own actions the cognizance of them had altered from ruffians to foot-soldiers. In St Lucia and the other islands at that time, the brigands were runaway slaves but the British army looked on them as felons while, to Robert Devaux, they were foot soldiers. In fact he went one step further and stated categorically, that the St Lucian brigands were freedom fighters, people who believed their native ethnic group were not free and were willing to give their lives in their fight to rule themselves.

For the British it was these people, these brigands, whom they faced in the forests and woods of St Lucia in the months following the reduction of Morne Fortuné. Drummond continued with Moore's scorched earth policy of 1797–1798 'executing guerilla style attacks on Brigand camps in much the same way as the Brigands attacked military posts'.[30] Proof of a hard lesson learned by the British.

Once Moore had left St Lucia in May, the British written record of the brigands was no longer continued. In October 1797 a detachment of Druault's shot a brigand chief and from then on they appear to have lost heart and the

---

28 'Black Prisoners of War at Portchester Castle', *English Heritage*.
29 Poyen–Bellisle, *La guerres des Antilles*, pp.145–146.
30 Harmsen, et al., *St Lucia*, p.85.

troubles slowly came to a stop. Although Devaux added that, 'The Brigand War had ended but … runaways continued to escape into St Lucia's interior'[31]. Harmsen et al write that in the following November 'most of the remaining Brigands surrendered to a conditional cessation of hostilities', on the terms that they would not be reduced to slavery again.[32] Devaux expanded that to claim that the 'Brigands of St Lucia were placed in the West India Regiment and sent to the West Coast of Africa in accordance with their modest demands'.[33] This, however seems unlikely as it appears that the first contact between the West India regiments and the country of Sierra Leone was not until 1812. The raising of the first eight West India Regiments had already commenced in earnest in 1795, although not all with great success to begin with.[34] Nevertheless it is possible that some of these men were assimilated into the early West India Regiments where they saw service in the Caribbean Islands. Others were able to leave St Lucia on a voluntary basis, to enlist in the French service, thereby continuing as valued fighting units in the same fashion as the British.

In May 1798, George Prevost took over from Governor James Drummond. By this time the island of St Lucia was not the same animal that it had been when Moore was there in 1796. The conditions allowed Prevost to apply his mind to governing as opposed to ruling by force. He submitted to King George III a plan for re-establishing the administration of justice as it prevailed before 1789, and subject to the French laws in force at that period'. He commented on the remaining few 'Brigands who remained in the woods [were] so much reduced [as] to render them no longer to be dreaded'[35]. Those who had fought so hard to achieve the freedom to live on their own islands on their own terms, left a legacy behind them in the shape of the West India Regiments which from their raising in 1795 continued almost uninterrupted until 1927, over 130 years later. Their descendants would fight as St Lucians in the two world wars of the twentieth century.

---

31 Devaux, *Brigands*, p.38.
32 Harmsen, et al, *St Lucia*, p.85.
33 Devaux, *Brigands*, p.39.
34 Buckley, *Slaves*, p.30.
35 Harmsen, *St Lucia*, p.112.

19

Those Who Remained: The Long View

The Military

Frederick, Duke of York, 16 August 1763–5 January 1827
Taking the long view, Frederick, Duke of York, was probably the most important man of influence on the British military scene in the early nineteenth century. From the time that his father, George III, made him Commander-in-Chief of the British Army in April 1795, Frederick was assured of his place in history as an important reformer. Winterbottom quotes Thackeray in his assessment of York as 'big, burly, loud, jolly, cursing, courageous; he had a most affectionate and lovable disposition, was noble and generous to a fault and was never known to break a promise'.[1]

It was this larger-than-life character that was to pressure for changes to outmoded and unfair, in fact, almost mediaeval practices, in order to move the army towards that which we recognise today, from welfare and justice, toward a military meritocracy. His foresightedness brought reforms which improved the life of soldiers at every level. Aware of the woeful lack of many commissioned officers' personal integrity, ignorance and sheer neglect of the men under their command, York was party to and supportive of Lieutenant Colonel John Gaspard Le Marchant's vision for establishments for the education of officers at Great Marlow and High Wycombe, which became the foundation of the more familiar Royal Military College at Sandhurst we know today. Indeed, he cast his net further when he provided schools for soldiers' children, an asylum for the children of dead soldiers (based at Chelsea), and yet another for soldiers themselves to advance in literacy.

He was certainly popular with steady soldiers as the memoirs of many bore witness. He shared some of these traits with his own father who also shared the 'common touch' with his son. York was to be involved either as an instigator, supporter or facilitator personally or on the periphery of many necessary reforms to improve what was truly a blighted life for many soldiers and their families. An anonymous writer from the 43rd Foot probably spoke

---

1 Winterbottom, *Grand Old Duke*, p.77.

for much of the army when he left a heartfelt comment about Frederick, Duke of York. He wrote: 'No person ever understood and maintained the rights and reasonable solaces of a soldier better than the then Commander-in-Chief.'[2]

Lieutenant General Sir Ralph Abercromby, 7 October 1734–28 March 1801

Abercromby returned to England from the West Indies in the summer of 1797, to be appointed Commander-in-Chief of the Forces in Ireland, followed by a similar position in Scotland. He was later involved in the Helder Expedition of 1799 under the Duke of York. Abercromby refused both a peerage and the possibility of being presented with a parcel of lands in the Caribbean by King George.

His words to Dundas reveal a man of honour and integrity: 'If it is thought that I am deserving of any mark of public favour, it is from the public alone that I can receive it. I am not a beggar or a covetous person to ask private honours or private grants.'[3]

Abercromby remained in Scotland until his military services were required again, in 1800, first in Cadiz and then in Egypt in 1801. He was to receive a mortal wound at the successful Battle of Alexandria on 21 March. He died a week later on 28 March 1801, aged 66. His body was taken to Malta and buried at Fort St Elmo, where a simple monument is to be found.

Lieutenant General Sir John Moore, 13 November 1761–16 January 1809

Sir John Moore returned to England. After recuperation he was sent to Ireland and helped to contain the rebellion of 1798. He served in the Dutch Expedition, (1799); in Egypt (1801); in England, where he was concerned with preparations for a possible French invasion, part of which was the building of Martello Towers and the excavating the Royal Military Canal in Kent; in 1803 he was charged with the establishment of the training camp for light infantry at Shorncliffe, in Kent; In 1804 he was knighted and promoted to a lieutenant general. He died at the Battle of Corunna in Spain in 1809. A driven and able man, but one of considerable controversy.

Lieutenant General Colin Campbell, 1754–1814

Lieutenant Colonel Colin Campbell parted ways with the 44th in April 1795. He transferred to the 81st very briefly and was gazetted from there as lieutenant colonel to the 6th Foot, 29 April 1795. He did not go to the West Indies, fulfilling that promise to his wife. He commanded the 6th Foot from 1795 to 1798, when he became a brevet colonel in the same regiment on 1 January 1798 and served during the Irish Rebellion. Subsequently, still serving in Ireland, he became major general on 1 January 1805; lieutenant general on 4 June 1811; and finally served as acting Lieutenant Governor of Gibraltar from 1809 (for the Duke of Kent) until his death on 2 April 1814. Strangely, he died of fever, purportedly that yellow fever he had done so much to avoid. He is buried in the convent on Gibraltar.

---

2   Anon., *Memoirs of a Sergeant: The 43rd Light Infantry During the Peninsular War* (Stroud: Nonsuch Publishing, 2005), p.25.

3   Dunfermline, *A Memoir*, p.215.

THOSE WHO REMAINED: THE LONG VIEW

Bryan Blundell, 1757–1799

Bryan Blundell was sent to the West Indies with the flank companies of the 44th as a brevet lieutenant colonel; promoted to lieutenant colonel, without purchase, into the 45th Foot 28 May 1795; he was colonel in the army from August 1795; appointed on 4 November 1796 to be brigadier general in the West Indies only; promoted major general 18 June 1798. He died at Exeter, in Devon, aged 42 years, on 23 September 1799 and lies in Exeter Cathedral. His memorial includes the words 'His private Virtues and Military talents were alike conspicuous, the one bespoke the Man, the other the Soldier … A Grief to his friends and a Loss to his Country'.[4]

> Underneath lies the Body of BRYAN BLUNDELL *Esquire*, (Second Son of Jonathan Blundell Esq.' of *Liverpool* in the County of *Lancaster*) and Major General in the Army, and L.' Col.' of the 45.'ʰ Reg.' of Foot.
>
> He particularly distinguished himself in the Command of the Second Battalion of Light Infantry in 1794, under L.' Gen.' Sir Charles Grey *Bart*, at the taking of the Islands of *Martinique, Guadaloupe*, and S.' *Luciæ*.
>
> His private Virtues and his military Talents were alike conspicuous, the one bespoke the Man, the other the Soldier.
>
> He died in this City 23.ʳᵈ Sep.' 1799, at the early Age of 42.
>
> A Grief to his Friends, and a Loss to his Country.

Memorial tablet to Colonel Bryan Blundell. (Courtesy of Exeter Cathedral)

General Rufane Shaw Donkin, 1773–1841

Also from Exeter – Donkin, like Bryan Blundell, left for the West Indies with the 44th flank companies in 1794, under Sir Charles Grey. He was promoted to major 1 September 1795, then lieutenant colonel in 1796. He made an impression in 1798 in Ostend when leading a light company on Popham's raid, being wounded and then taken prisoner; he was in Copenhagen in 1807 and was promoted colonel on 25 April 1808; he commanded a brigade in Portugal under Wellington in 1809 and was promoted major general in 1811. From July 1812 to September 1813 he served in Spain, then in the Mahratta War from 1817–1818. He had married Elizabeth Markham in 1815 and she went with Donkin to India but died of fever in 1818, leaving their eight-month-old son, George David. The baby was sent home to be looked after by his maternal grandfather, the Dean of York. Donkin was almost prostrated by Elizabeth's death though still accomplishing much; from 1820 to 1821 he was Acting Governor of Cape of Good Hope. He took the opportunity to build a memorial to his wife and he named a developing town after her, Port Elizabeth. In spite of spending only two years in the colony Donkin was much respected and many years later (1861) the people of Port Elizabeth adopted his coat of arms. He spent his later years producing erudite papers and after he became a Fellow of the Royal Society he was a founding father of the Royal Geographical Society. He married again, to Anna Maria Eliot, the

---

4   Memorial to Lt Colonel Bryan Blundell of the 45th Regiment of Foot, Exeter Cathedral, Devon.

daughter of Sir Gilbert Eliot, Lord Minto, who had sacked Moore in Corsica. In 1837 he became Colonel of the 11th Foot (his old regiment) and was promoted to general in 1838. Donkin committed suicide on 1 May 1841 by hanging himself at his home in Portland Street, Southampton. He was buried in the family vault in Old St Pancras churchyard in the parish of Somers Town in London, together with an urn containing the heart of his first wife.

Sadly, that was not the last we hear of Rufane Shaw Donkin. He was indeed buried, but not to be left in peace. In 1868 the new St Pancras station was opened, and this occasioned the removal of the contents of many graves in the churchyard, including the Donkin family tomb. There were reports of bones left lying about and coffins uncovered. These were eventually gathered up and reburied in a mass grave elsewhere. Rufane Shaw Donkin's name can be seen on an obelisk raised by Baroness Burdett-Coutts, just one of 70 names of contemporary importance. It stands in what is now called St Pancras Gardens. The Donkin tomb itself has since been repaired but the whereabouts of his remains appears still to be unknown, like so many of those soldiers he fought beside.

General Charles Alexander Rainsford, 1728–1809

Charles Rainsford was Colonel of the 44th from 1781 until his death in 1809. He was a man of many parts, his military service being only one of them. Chronologically he served with Colonel Bland's Dragoons, the Coldstream Guards and the Grenadier Guards. He was aide de camp for the king, equerry to the Duke of Gloucester while Colonel of the 44th Foot, and in 1793 second in command in Gibraltar. In 1795 he was appointed General and Governor of the Cliff Fort in Tynemouth. In and amongst his busy military life Rainsford's political life included time as MP for Maldon, Essex, Bere Alston in Devon, and Newport in Cornwall. His other interests ranged from the Society for Antiquaries of whom he was a member; freemasonry; magnetism; alchemy and the occult. The British Museum holds his archive of nearly 40 manuscripts. He found time for two marriages, with three children from his first, one son and two daughters, one of whom died in infancy. A very busy man, to say the least but, from the 44th's point of view, a caring and steady colonel.

Captain William Tuffie, 1764–1799

Captain William Tuffie, the last member of the 44th Foot's regimental Tuffie family, who had survived his wounding at the reduction of St Lucia in April 1796, lost his wife Grace in 1797, while still on St Lucia. The cause was not given, so she may have died in childbirth, or of one of the many unsavoury diseases for which the West Indies was famed. Her name was not recorded on the memorial inscriptions available from the Morne Fortuné list of burials, but she would be there amongst the many who died of yellow fever.

In less than 12 months Tuffie remarried. The *Ipswich Journal* for 3 February 1798 reported the wedding as taking place on Sunday, 28 January 1798 at St Matthew's Church in Ipswich, where he married Miss Mary Hall, who was the daughter of Captain Hall, adjutant to the East Essex Militia. Unfortunately, their marriage was relatively short lived. Tuffie had signed his will on 19 August 1799, in Gibraltar, where the regiment was then on duty. He must have known that he was dying, as his death was recorded just five days later, on 24 August. One of the witnesses to his will was Andrew Johnston, he who became surgeon to the regiment and who had accompanied them to the West Indies. The other was Captain Henry Holland, also of the 44th Foot. Tuffie, born about 1764 (like Roworth), was about 36 when he died, having bequeathed his worldly goods to his then wife, Mary Tuffie. She remarried in 1802 having left a decent interval after Tuffie's death, so she was not the 'galloping widow' that William Roworth called Mrs Foxcroft – but then as widow of a captain, Mary Tuffie had no need to be.

George Pinckard, 1768–1835
Pinckard was a licentiate of the College of Physicians of London, who had been appointed as a physician to the forces. On his return from the West Indies he accompanied the forces to Ireland for the Irish Rebellion. He was promoted Deputy Inspector General of Hospitals and accompanied the Duke of York on the Den Helder expedition in 1799. He returned to live in London and established the Bloomsbury Dispensary where he was a physician for 30 years. In 1824 he started the basis of what would later become the Clerical Medical Assurance Society, which is still with us today. He also left behind a series of books concerning his experiences in the army, based on letters to a friend while he was in the West Indies, including that vivid description of those gruelling days as a sufferer of yellow fever.

Andrew Johnston, 1770–1833
Surgeon Andrew Johnston of the 44th, left the army in 1803, after serving in the West Indies and Egypt, and returned to Ireland to join the staff of the Royal College of Surgeons in Ireland. In 1813 he was made Professor of Surgical Pharmacy and six years later Professor of Midwifery. He died in 1833, a well-respected surgeon.

The Family

Wherever there are soldiers there are extended families left to celebrate or to mourn. So it was with the families of some 45,000 redcoats who had never made it back to Britain from the West Indies. Nor was it any different for William Roworth's parents, William and Elizabeth Roworth, who survived their eldest son. They moved to Knutsford in Cheshire from the family home in Dunham, sometime after the death of their employer, the Honourable Booth Grey, in 1802. It is likely that they moved with his widow, Elizabeth Grey, to live in the village of Nether Knutsford, at Heath House, where she was from 1803 until her death in 1823. Elizabeth Roworth died in 1804 and William in 1807. Both were 72 at death and today lie peacefully in the churchyard at Knutsford. Their headstone can be found now lying flat on the north-east side of the churchyard.

Mary Osborn Roworth appears to have educated Little Billy as his father had requested. He excelled in the world of corn factors. He did several terms as a sheriff of Nottingham, one year as the mayor and lived in a select area of the town, just as his father had wished, when he asked Mary to 'choose somewhere more genteel'. In 1839, the year of William Roworth Junior's tenure as Mayor of Nottingham, during and because of the Chartist Riots, he met with Major General Sir Charles James Napier who, at that time, was General Officer Commanding of the Northern District of England, dealing with the unrest. The fact that Roworth's father had been a military man might have made their meetings easier to conduct.

The following passage comes from Napier's '*Life*'. They were his own words to his brother, William Napier:

> … the misery is so horrid, the poor law rules are necessarily broken and put aside, and relief out of door is given perforce. We have 800 men paid by the private subscription; and, horror of horrors! 200 of them rank Chartists, employed by the mayor's order, at which some people here cannot sleep in their beds: they would ere this have slept less if they had a 'vigorous mayor', for the town would have been burned. My firm belief is that it has been saved by the good heart and good sense of Roworth the mayor, more than by anything else …

That Mayor Roworth was a man recognised as of 'good heart and good sense' by a person of the character and experience of Napier, speaks much for his own father's character and beliefs. Mary Osborn Roworth remarried when William Junior was 22 and became Mrs Joseph Dolman. Billy himself married and had two sons, the first another William. Billy's four grandsons William Selwyn, Lawrence, George and Alfred all went to Oxford University as young men, in the middle 1800s, the first three becoming clergymen, the fourth a doctor – not one of them 'went for a soldier'. That was left to their descendants in the First and Second World Wars of the twentieth century. Their great-grandfather the serjeant major, would have been so proud of them, but perhaps the three women memorialised at the beginning of this book should go to the top of the class, for it was they who kept and passed the serjeant major's letters down through his family. Those letters have helped to shed just a little more light on the lives of British redcoats, on that particular journey and that particular service to 'King and Country', in the late 1700s.

William Roworth, 1789–1886, the Mayor of Nottingham, 1839. Possibly similar in appearance to his father, Serjeant Major William Roworth. (Illustrated by Jo Davies)

THOSE WHO REMAINED: THE LONG VIEW

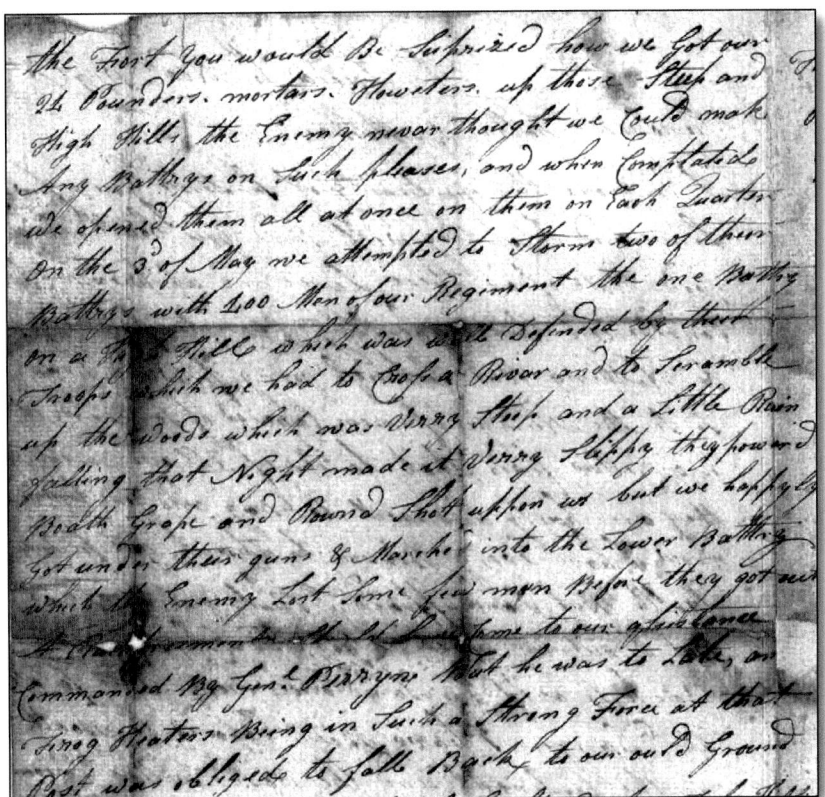

Part of Letter 25, dated 4 November 1796, that William Roworth wrote to his parents – his last letter home. (Nottinghamshire Archives)

Bibliography

Archival Sources

The National Archives (TNA)
ADM 1 Letters from Commanders in Chief
ADM 102/790 Hospital Muster Books, Vielle Viele, Vigie, St Lucia
CO 318/18 Naval Despatches
HO 42/29 Domestic Correspondence George III
HO 47/19/39 State Papers Domestic
PRO 30/8/135 Letters to William Pitt
PRO 30/8/157/1 Letters to Henry Dundas
PRO 30/8/160/1 Letters of Frederick Duke of York
PRO 30/8/171 Letters to William Pitt
PRO 30/8/190 Letters to William Pitt
WO 1/32 West Indies and South America
WO 1/65 Santo Domingo, Governor's Dispatches.
WO 1/798 Transport Office
WO 1/799 Transport Office
WO 4/338 West Indies
WO 6/147 Admiralty
WO 6/156 Commissioners of Transport
WO 12 General Musters and Pay Lists
WO 17 Regimental Returns
WO 97/595/124 Royal Hospital Chelsea, Soldiers Service Documents
WO 121/13/305 Royal Hospital Chelsea, Pensions

Manx Archives (MNH)
09073/3/2 Marriage Registers
09769/4/3 Marriage Registers

The National Army Museum (NAM)
1997-10-131 Digest of Services, Royal Highland Regiment the Black Watch
2016-10-23-4-11 Book No: G 152, Grenadiers General Orders.
85-12-9 Orderly book Earl of Moira's Army
1997-10-131 Atherley Letters
2002-08-144 Campbell, Letters and Notebook

Nottingham University Library (NUL)
CU R3/1 Castle Gate Meeting House Baptismal Register

Nottinghamshire Archives (NA)
NA: DDRW1–25 Roworth Letters

Newspapers

Caledonian Mercury
Chester Courant
Cumberland Pacquet and Ware's Whitehaven Advertiser
Derby Mercury
Finns Leinster Journal
Hampshire Chronicle
Illustrated London News
Ipswich Journal
Leeds Intelligencer
London Gazette
Newcastle Courant
Salisbury & Winchester Journal
Saunders Newsletter
Sheffield Register, Yorkshire, Derbyshire and Nottinghamshire Universal Advertiser
The Times

Online Sources

www.welcometoportsmouth.co.uk
www.britishbattles.com
www.westminster-abbey.org
www.findmypast.co.uk
www.battlefields.org
www.napoleon-series.org
www.parliament.uk
www.gov.uk
www.biographi.ca
www.english-heritage.org.uk
www.ancestry.co.uk
www.qdg.org.uk

Printed Primary Sources

Anglesey, Marquess of, *One Leg: The Life and Letters of Henry William Paget First Marquess of Anglesey. K.G. 1768–1854* (London: Leo Cooper, 1996)
Anon., *A Journal kept in the British Army, from the landing of the troops under the command of Earl Moira, at Ostend, in June 1794, to their return to England the following year* (Liverpool: Merritt and Wright, 1796)
Anon., *A soldier's journal, containing a particular description of the several descents on the coast of France last war; with an entertaining account of the islands of Guadeloupe, Dominique and also the isles of Wight and Jersey* (London: E. and C. Dilley, 1770)
Anon., *An accurate and impartial narrative of the war, by an officer of the Guards* (London: Cadell and Davies, 1796)
Anon. (ed.), *Bulletins of the Campaign* (London: Clarke, 1794–1797)

Anon., *Memoirs of a Sergeant: The 43rd Light Infantry During the Peninsular War* (Stroud: Nonsuch Publishing, 2005)

Anon., *Narrative of a Private Soldier in His Majesty's 92nd Regiment of Foot* (London: n.p., 1820)

Anon., *Regulations to be observed by troops in transports for service abroad, particularly by those designed for the West Indies* (London: War Office, 1795)

Anton, James, *Royal Highlander, A Soldier of H.M 42nd (Royal) Highlanders during the Peninsular, South of France & Waterloo Campaigns of the Napoleonic Wars* (Driffield: Leonaur, 2007)

Bankes, George Nugent (ed.), *The Autobiography of Sergeant William Lawrence: a Hero of the Peninsular and Waterloo Campaigns* (London: Sampson Low, Marston, Searle, & Rivington, 1886)

Bell, George, *Ensign George Bell in the Peninsular War: The Experiences of a Young British Soldier of the 34th Regiment 'The Cumberland Gentlemen' in the Napoleonic Wars* (Driffield: Leonaur, 2006)

Brown, Robert, *An Impartial Journal of a Detachment from The Brigade Of Foot Guards, Commencing 25th February, 1793, and Ending 9th May, 1795* (London: John Stockdale, 1795)

Brown, William, *The Autobiography, or Narrative of a Soldier, The Peninsular War Memoirs of William Brown of the 45th Foot* (Solihull: Helion, 2017)

Buckley, Roger Norman (ed.), *The Haitian Journal of Lieutenant Howard, York Hussars, 1796-1798* (Knoxville: University of Tennessee Press, 1985)

Bunbury, Charles J.F., *Memoir and Literary Remains of Lieutenant General Sir Henry Edward Bunbury, Bart* (London: Spottiswoode & Co, 1868)

Butler, Robert, *Narrative of the Life and Travels of Sergeant B–* (London: Knight & Lacey, 1823)

Cooper, John S., *Fusilier Cooper Experiences in the 7th (Royal) Fusiliers during the Peninsular Campaign of the Napoleonic Wars and the American Campaign to New Orleans* (Driffield: Leonaur, 2007)

Corbett, Julian. S. (ed.), *Private Papers of George, second Earl Spencer First Lord of the Admiralty 1794-1801* (Unknown: Elibron Classics, 2005)

Costello, Edward, *Rifleman Costello, 95th Rifles: The Adventures of a Soldier of the 95th (Rifles) in the Peninsular & Waterloo Campaigns of the Napoleonic Wars* (Driffield: Leonaur, 2005)

Crook, Jonathan (ed.), *The Very Thing, The Memoirs of Drummer Richard Bentinck, Royal Welsh Fusiliers, 1803–1823* (Barnsley: Frontline, 2011)

Dalrymple, Campbell, *A Military Essay. Containing reflections on the raising, arming, cloathing, and discipline of the British infantry and cavalry; with proposals for the improvement of the same* (London: D. Wilson, 1761)

Donaldson, Joseph, *Recollections of the Eventful Life of a Soldier* (Staplehurst: Spellmount, 2000)

Duncan-Jones, Caroline (ed.), *Trusty and Well-Beloved: The Letters Home of William Harness, an Officer of George the Third* (London: SPCK, 1957)

Dumouriez, Charles Francois Du Perier, John Fenwick (trans.), *Memoirs of General Dumourier* (London: Johnson, 1796)

Durey, Michael (ed.), *Andrew Bryson's Ordeal* (Cork: Cork University Press, 1998)

Glover, Gareth, (ed.), *A Short Account of the Life and Adventures of Private Thomas Jeremiah, 23rd or Royal Welch Fusiliers 1812–1837, including his Experiences at the Battle of Waterloo* (Huntingdon: Ken Trotman, 2008)

Glover, Gareth, (ed.), *John Westcott's Journal of the Campaign in Portugal: Late Bandmaster of the Band 1/26th (Cameronian) Regt* (Huntingdon: Ken Trotman, 2018)

Glover, Gareth (ed.), *Memoir of the Military Career of John Dayes, later Paymaster Sergeant of the 5th Regiment of Foot* (Huntingdon: Ken Trotman, 2004)

Glover, Gareth (ed.), *Seven Years on the Peninsula: The Memoirs of Private Adam Reed, 47th (Lancashire) Foot 1806–1817* (Huntingdon: Ken Trotman, 2012)

Glover, Gareth (ed.), *The Diary of a Veteran: The Diary of Sergeant Peter Facey, 28th (North Gloucester) Regiment of Foot 1803–1819* (Huntingdon: Ken Trotman, 2007)

Glover, Gareth (ed.), *The Journal of Sergeant David Robertson: 92nd Highlanders in Egypt, Denmark, the Peninsula and Belgium, 1795–1818* (Huntingdon: Ken Trotman, 2018)

Glover, Gareth (ed.), *The Letters of Private Henry Willis: 1st Regiment of Life Guards, 1807– 1814* (Huntingdon: Ken Trotman, 2017)

Glover, Gareth (ed.), *The Military Adventures of Private Samuel Wray 61st Foot 1796-1815* (Huntingdon: Ken Trotman, 2009)

Glover, Gareth (ed.), *The Peninsular War Journal of Sergeant Samuel Harrison of the 43rd (Monmouthshire) Regiment of Foot, 1796–1812* (Huntingdon: Ken Trotman, 2017)

Glover, Gareth (ed.), *The 3rd (Scots) Guards in Time of War: The Memoirs of Sergeant John Stevenson, 1793–1814* (Huntingdon: Ken Trotman, 2019)

Green, John, *The Vicissitudes of a Soldier's Life or, a Series of Occurrences from 1806 to 1815* (Louth: Jackson, 1827)

Green, William, & Smith, Harry, *Bugler and Officer of the Rifles: With the 95th (Rifles) During the Peninsular & Napoleonic Waterloo Campaign of the Napoleonic Wars* (Driffield: Leonaur, 2005)

Hagist, Don. N. (ed.), *A British Soldier's Story: Roger Lamb's Narrative of the American Revolution* (Baraboo: Ballindalloch Press, 2004)

Hale, James, *Journal of James Hale, Late Sergeant of the Ninth Regiment of Foot 1826* (London: Naval and Military Press, 2009)

Harrington, Peter (ed.), *With the Guards in Flanders: The Diary of Captain Roger Morris 1793–1795* (Warwick: Helion, 2018)

Hathaway, Eileen (ed.), *A Dorset Rifleman: The Recollections of Benjamin Harris* (Swanage: Swinglepicker, 1995)

Houlding, J.A., and Yates, G., 'Corporal Fox's Memoir of Service, 1766–1783: Quebec, Saratoga, and the Convention Army', *Journal of the Society for Army Historical Research*, vol.68, no.275. Autumn (1990), pp.146–168

Jackson, Thomas, *Narrative of the Eventful Life of Thomas Jackson, Militiaman and Coldstream Sergeant, 1803-15* (Solihull: Helion, 2018)

Jeffery, Reginald. W. (ed.), *Dyott's Diary 1781–1845: a selection from the journal of William Dyott, sometime general in the British Army and aide-de-camp to His Majesty King George III* (London: Archibald Constable, 1907)

Jones, Lewis Tobias, *An Historical Journal of the British Campaign on the Continent, in the year 1794; with the retreat through Holland, in the year 1795* (Birmingham: Swinsey & Hawkins, 1797)

Leach, Jonathan, *Captain of the 95th Rifles: An Officer of Wellington's Sharpshooters during the Peninsular, South of France and Waterloo Campaigns of the Napoleonic Wars* (Driffiled: Leonaur, 2005)

Le Rouge, J.A. Chymiste, *Compte Rendu Adresse a Bourdon, Ministre da la Marine et Des Colonies. Par Citoyen Le Rouge Chymiste, attaché au service de la Marine, dan les ports, de la République Francaise Procédés pour le conservation des Decrées de Premiere Nécessité* (Brest: Audran, 1797)

Le Marchant, Denis, *Memoirs of The Late General Le Marchant, 1766–1812* (London: Samuel Bentley, 1841)

Liddell Hart, B.H. (ed.), *The Letters of Private Wheeler 1809-1828* (Moreton-in-Marsh: The Windrush Press, 2000)

Macdonald, John, *Autobiographical Journal of John Macdonald, Schoolmaster and Soldier, 1770–1830* (Edinburgh: Norman Macleod, 1906)

MacMullen, John Mercier, *Camp and Barrack Room or the British Army As It Is* (London: Chapman and Hall, 1846)

McGrigor, James, *The Autobiography and Services of Sir James Mcgrigor, Bart* (London: Longman Green, 1861)

Maurice, J.F. (ed.), *The Diary of Sir John Moore* (London: Edward Arnold, 1904)

Miller, Benjamin, *The Adventures of Serjeant Benjamin Miller whilst Serving in the 4th Battalion of the Royal Regiment of Artillery 1796 to 1815* (Uckfield: Naval & Military Press, 2017)

Nicol, Daniel, *Sergeant Nicol: The Experiences of a Gordon Highlander during the Napoleonic wars in Egypt, the Peninsula & France* (Driffield: Leonaur, 2007)

O'Neil, Charles, *The Military Adventures of Charles O'Neil* (Worcester: Edward Livermore, 1851)

Parker, Joseph, *A Soldier's Retrospect: being a Narrative of Events in the Life of William Nightingale, of Banbury, a Private in the Eighty-Fourth Regiment* (London: Thomas Nelson and Sons, 1854)

Patterson, John, *Camp and Quarters, Scenes and Impressions of Military Life* (London: Saunders and Ottley, 1840)

Pinckard, George, *Notes on the West Indies: Written During the Expedition Under the Command of the Late Sir Ralph Abercromby* (London: Longman, Hurst, Rees, and Orme, 1806)

Pococke, Thomas, *Journal of a Soldier of the 71st, or Glasgow Regiment, Highland Light Infantry, from 1806 to 1815* (Edinburgh: William & Charles Tait, 1819)

Raeff, Marc (ed.), *The Diary of a Napoleonic Foot Soldier* (Moreton-in-Marsh: The Windrush Press, 1991)

Shaw, John Robert, *A Narrative of the Life and Travels of John Robert Shaw, the Well-Digger, Now Resident in Lexington, Kentucky* (Lexington: Daniel Bradford, 1807)

Shipp, John, *Memoirs of the Extraordinary Career of John Shipp – Late a Lieut. in His Majesty's 87th Regiment* (London: T. Fisher Unwin, 1840).

Simes, Thomas, *The Military Guide for Young Officers* (Philadelphia: Humphreys, Bell & Aitken, 1776)

Surtees, William, *Surtees of the 95th (Rifles): a Soldier of the 95th (RIFLES) in the Peninsular Campaign of the Napoleonic Wars* (Driffield: Leonaur, 2006)

Verney, H. (ed.), *The Journals and Correspondence of General Sir Harry Calvert* (London: Hurst & Blackett, 1853)

Secondary Sources

Barthorp, Michael, *The Northamptonshire Regiment* (London: Leo Cooper, 1974)

Boult, Edwina, *Christian's Fleet: A Dorset Shipping Tragedy* (Stroud: Tempus Publishing, 2003)

Breen, Henry Hegart, *St Lucia; Historical, Statistical, and Descriptive* (London: Longman, Brown, Green, and Longman, 1844)

Brereton, J.M. & Savory, A.C.S., *The History of The Duke of Wellington's Regiment (West Riding) 1702–1992* (Halifax: Duke of Wellington's Regiment, 1993)

Brown, Steve, *The Duke of York's Flanders Campaign: Fighting the French Revolution 1793–1795* (Barnsley: Frontline Books, 2018),

Brumwell, Stephen, *Redcoats: The British Soldier and War in the Americas, 1755–1763* (Cambridge: Cambridge University Press, 2002)

Buckley, Roger Norman, *Slaves in Red Coats: The British West India Regiments,1795–1815* (New Haven: Yale University, 1979)

Burne, Alfred. H., *The Noble Duke of York: The Military Life of Frederick Duke of York and Albany* (London: Staples Press, 1949)

Burrows, John, *The Essex Regiment: 1st Battalion 44th* (Southend-on-Sea: John H. Burrows & Sons, Ltd, 1931)

Cannon, Richard, *Historical Record of The Thirty-First or The Huntingdonshire Regiment of Foot* (London: Parker, Furnivall and Parker, 1850)

Carman, W.Y., *British Military Uniforms from Contemporary Pictures* (Feltham: Hamlyn, 1957)

Carter, Thomas, *Historical Record of the Forty-Fourth, or the East Essex Regiment* (Chatham: Gale and Polden, 1887)

Caulfield, J.E., *100 Years' History of the 2nd West India Regiment 1795 to 1898* (Uckfield: Naval and Military Press, 2006)

Chartrand, René, *British Forces in the West Indies 1793 to 1815* (Oxford: Osprey, 1996)

Clammer, David, 'A Disposition to Wander: Reasons for Enlisting in the British Army during the Napoleonic Wars', *Journal of the Society for Army Historical Research*, vol.100, Summer 2022, pp.98–106

Clark, William Mark (ed.), *Chronicles of the Sea VI: Or Faithful Narratives of Shipwrecks, Fires, Famines, And Disasters Incidental To A Life Of Maritime Enterprise* (London: William Mark Clark, 1838)

Clarke, Francis. L., *The Life of the Most Noble Arthur Marquis and Earl of Wellington, Viscount Wellington of Talavera and of Wellington, and Baron Douro of Wellesley, All in the County of Somerset* (New York: Van Winkle and Wiley, 1814)

Collins, Irene, *Jane Austen, The Parson's Daughter* (London: Hambledon Press, 1998)

Condon, Mary, *The Administration of the Transport Service During the War against Revolutionary France, 1793–1802* (PhD Thesis, University of London, 1968)

Conway, Stephen, 'The Recruitment of Criminals into the British Army, 1775–81', *Bulletin of the Institute of Historical Research*, vol.58, no.137, May 1985, pp.46–57

Cooper, Thomas Henry, *A Practical Guide for the Light Infantry Officer: Comprising Valuable Extracts from All the most Popular Works on the Subject; With Further Original Information* (London: Robert Wilkes, 1806)

Coss, Edward. J., *All For The King's Shilling: The British Soldier Under Wellington, 1808–1814* (Norman: University of Oklahoma Press, 2015)

Cust, Edward, *Annals of the Wars of the Eighteenth Century* (London: Murray, 1862)

Curtis, Edward E., *The British Army in the American Revolution* (Wakefield: E P Publishing, 1972)

Devaux, Robert, *They Called Us Brigands: The Saga of St Lucia's Freedom Fighters* (St Lucia: Optimum, 1997)

Divall, Carole, *Inside the Regiment: The Officers and Men of the 30th Regiment During the Revolutionary and Napoleonic Wars* (Barnsley: Pen & Sword, 2011)

Divall, Carole, *Napoleonic Lives: Researching the British Soldiers of the Napoleonic Wars* (Barnsley: Pen and Sword Military, 2012)

Duffy, Michael, *Soldiers, Sugar and Seapower* (Oxford: Clarendon Press, 1987)

Duncan, Jonathan, *The History of Guernsey with Occasional Notices of Jersey, Alderney, and Sark, and Biographical Sketches* (London: Longman, Brown, Green, and Longman, 1841)

Dunfermline, James Lord, *Lieutenant-General Sir Ralph Abercromby. K.B. 1793-1801, A Memoir* (Edinburgh: Edmonston and Douglas, 1861)

Ellis, A. B., *The History of the First West India Regiment* (Unknown: Createspace, 2021).

Fortescue, J.W., *British Campaigns in Flanders: 1690–1794 Being Extracts From 'A History of the British Army'* (Uckfield: The Naval and Military Press, 2014)

Fortescue, J.W., *A History of the British Army* (Uckfield: The Naval & Military Press Ltd, 2004)

Gaspar, David Barry, & David Patrick Geggus, *A Turbulent Time: The French Revolution and the Greater Caribbean* (Bloomington: Indiana University Press, 1997)

Glover, Richard, *Peninsular Preparation: The Reform of the British Army 1795–1809* (Cambridge: Cambridge University Press, 1963)

Grehan, John, and Mace, Martin, *British Battles of the Napoleonic Wars. 1793–1806* (Barnsley: Pen & Sword, 2013)

Grocott, Terence, *Shipwrecks of the Revolutionary and Napoleonic Eras* (London: Caxton, 2002)

Hagist, Don, N., *Noble Volunteers: The British Soldiers Who Fought the American Revolution* (Pennsylvania, Westholme, 2020)

Hamilton Smith, C., 'Experiments on the Comparative Effect of Rifle and Musketry Fire on Different Colours', *Aide-Mémoire to the Military Sciences*, 1853, pp.257–259.

Harmsen, Joliet, Guy Ellis & Robert Devaux, *A History of St Lucia* (Vieux Fort: Lighthouse Road Publications, 2012)

Haythornthwaite, Philip, *Redcoats: The British Soldiers of the Napoleonic Wars* (Barnsley: Pen & Sword Military, 2012)

Holmes, R., *Redcoat: The British Soldier in the Age of Horse and Musket* (London: Harper-Collins, 2001)

Howard, Martin R., *Death Before Glory: The British Soldier in the West Indies in the French Revolutionary Army & Napoleonic Wars 1793–1815* (Barnsley: Pen and Sword Military, 1988)

Hurl-Eamon, Jennine, *Marriage & the British Army in the Long Eighteenth Century: 'The Girl I Left Behind Me'* (Oxford: Oxford University Press, 2014)

James, Charles, *A New and Enlarged Military Dictionary* (London: Egerton, 1810)

James, Charles, *James's Regimental Companion* (London: Roworth, 1811)

Kelly, Catherine, *War and the Militarization of British Army Medicine, 1793–1830* (London: Pickering & Chatto, 2011)

Kipling, Rudyard, *Departmental Ditties & Barrack Room Ballads* (New York: Macmillan, 1892)

Knight, Paul, *A Very Fine Regiment: The 47th Foot during the American War of Independence, 1773–1783* (Warwick: Helion, 2022)

Larn, Richard and Bridget, *Shipwreck Index of the British Isles*, (London: Lloyd's Register of Shipping, 1998)

Lavery, Brian, *Nelson's Navy. The Ships, Men and Organisation 1793–1815* (London: Conway Maritime Press, 1989)

Lockley, Tim, *Military Medicine and the Making of Race: Life and Death in the West India Regiments, 1795–1874* (Cambridge: University Printing House, 2021)

McGrigor, Mary (ed.), *The Scalpel and the Sword: The Autobiography of the Father of Army Medicine* (Dalkeith: Scottish Cultural Press, 2000)

McGuire, Thomas J., *The Philadelphia Campaign, Vol 1. Brandywine and the fall of Philadelphia.* (Philadelphia: Stackpole Books, 2006)

McNeill, J.R., *Mosquito Empires: Ecology and War in the Greater Caribbean, 1620–1914* (New York: Cambridge University Press, 2010)

Marshall, Henry, *On the Enlisting, Discharging and Pensioning of Soldiers: With the Official Documents on These Branches of Military Duty; With the Regulations for the Recruiting Service in the Army and Navy of the United States, and a Preface* (Philadelphia: A. Waldie, 1840)

Maurice-Jones, K. W., *The History of the Coast Artillery in the British Army* (Uckfield: Naval and Military Press, 1956)

Minchinton, W.E. *Agricultural Returns and the Government during the Napoleonic Wars* (Newton Abbot: David and Charles, 1968)

Miller, David (ed.), *Lady De Lancey at Waterloo* (Staplehurst: Spellmount, 2008)

Moore, A.W., *A History of the Isle of Man* (London: T. F. Unwin, 2010)

Moore, James Carrick, *The Life of Lieutenant General Sir John Moore* (London: John Murray, 1834)
Napier, Sir William, *The Life and Opinions of General Sir Charles James Napier* (London: John Murray, 1857)
Norman, C.B., *Battle Honours of the British Army: From Tangier, 1662, to the Commencement of the Reign of King Edward VII* (London: John Murray, 1911)
Oldfield, John, 'From Spa to Garrison Town', in Miles Taylor (ed.), *Southampton, Gateway to the British Empire* (London: I.B. Tauris, Bloomsbury, 2007)
O'Neil, B. H. St. J., 'Castle Rushen, Isle of Man', *Archaeologia*, vol.94, 1951, pp.1–26
Poyen-Belleisle, Isidore Henry, *Les guerres des Antilles de 1793 a 1815* (Paris: Berger-Levrault et Cie, 1896)
Probert, Rebecca (ed.), *Catherine Exley's Diary: the Life and Times of an Army Wife in the Peninsular War* (Kenilworth: Brandram, 2014)
Rees, John U., *They were Good Soldiers: African–Americans Serving in the Continental Army, 1775–1783* (Warwick: Helion, 2019)
Reid, Stuart, *Redcoat Officer 1740–1815* (Oxford: Osprey, 2002)
Reid, Stuart, *The British Redcoat 1740–93* (Oxford: Osprey, 1996)
Rickword, G.O., 'Billeting in Inns in the Eighteenth Century', *Journal of the Society for Army Historical Research*, vol.XXXIV, no.138, June 1956, pp.86–89
Scotland, Tom, *Sir James McGrigor: The Adventurous Life of Wellington's Chief Medical Officer* (Warwick: Helion, 2021)
Snape, Michael, *The Redcoat and Religion: The Forgotten History of the British Soldier from the Age of Marlborough to the Eve of the First World War* (Abingdon: Routledge, 2005)
Stewart, David, *Sketches of the character, manners, and present state of the Highlanders of Scotland: with details of the Military Service of the Highland Regiments* (Edinburgh: Archibald Constable & Co., 1822)
Summerfield, Stephen, & Law, Susan, *Sir John Moore and the Universal Soldier: Volume 1: The Man, the Commander and the Shorncliffe System of Training* (Huntingdon: Ken Trotman Publishing, 2016)
Thomas, R.N.W., *No Want of Courage: The British Army in Flanders, 1793–1795* (Warwick: Helion, 2022)
Trimble, W. Copeland, *The Historical Record of the 27th Inninkilling Regiment* (London: Clowes and Sons, 1876)
Venning, Annabel, *Following the Drum: The Lives of Army Wives and Daughters Past and Present* (London: Headline, 2005)
Walcott, Derek, *The Arkansas Testament* (New York: HarperCollins, 1987)
Winterbottom, Derek, *The Grand Old Duke of York: A Life of Prince Frederick, Duke of York and Albany 1763–1827* (Barnsley: Pen and Sword Military, 2016)
Willyams, Cooper, *An Account of the Campaign of the West Indies, in the Year 1794, under the Command of Lieutenant General Sir Charles Grey, KB, and Vice Admiral Sir John Jervis, KB, with the Reduction of the Islands of Martinique, St Lucia, Guadeloupe, Marigalante, Desiada, etc.*, (London: Nicol, 1796)

Unpublished Works

Walton, Julian, *Geneva in Waterford* (2008)
Williams, Gregor, Dr, unpublished research concerning the history of St Lucia, undated

From Reason to Revolution – Warfare 1721-1815

http://www.helion.co.uk/series/from-reason-to-revolution-1721-1815.php

The 'From Reason to Revolution' series covers the period of military history 1721–1815, an era in which fortress-based strategy and linear battles gave way to the nation-in-arms and the beginnings of total war.

This era saw the evolution and growth of light troops of all arms, and of increasingly flexible command systems to cope with the growing armies fielded by nations able to mobilise far greater proportions of their manpower than ever before. Many of these developments were fired by the great political upheavals of the era, with revolutions in America and France bringing about social change which in turn fed back into the military sphere as whole nations readied themselves for war. Only in the closing years of the period, as the reactionary powers began to regain the upper hand, did a military synthesis of the best of the old and the new become possible.

The series will examine the military and naval history of the period in a greater degree of detail than has hitherto been attempted, and has a very wide brief, with the intention of covering all aspects from the battles, campaigns, logistics, and tactics, to the personalities, armies, uniforms, and equipment.

Submissions

The publishers would be pleased to receive submissions for this series. Please contact series editor Andrew Bamford via email (andrewbamford@helion.co.uk), or in writing to Helion & Company Limited, Unit 8 Amherst Business Centre, Budbrooke Road, Warwick, CV34 5WE

Titles

1. *Lobositz to Leuthen: Horace St Paul and the Campaigns of the Austrian Army in the Seven Years War 1756-57* (Neil Cogswell)
2. *Glories to Useless Heroism: The Seven Years War in North America from the French journals of Comte Maurés de Malartic, 1755-1760* (William Raffle (ed.))
3. *Reminiscences 1808-1815 Under Wellington: The Peninsular and Waterloo Memoirs of William Hay* (Andrew Bamford (ed.))
4. *Far Distant Ships: The Royal Navy and the Blockade of Brest 1793-1815* (Quintin Barry)
5. *Godoy's Army: Spanish Regiments and Uniforms from the Estado Militar of 1800* (Charles Esdaile and Alan Perry)
6. *On Gladsmuir Shall the Battle Be! The Battle of Prestonpans 1745* (Arran Johnston)
7. *The French Army of the Orient 1798-1801: Napoleon's Beloved 'Egyptians'* (Yves Martin)
8. *The Autobiography, or Narrative of a Soldier: The Peninsular War Memoirs of William Brown of the 45th Foot* (Steve Brown (ed.))
9. *Recollections from the Ranks: Three Russian Soldiers' Autobiographies from the Napoleonic Wars* (Darrin Boland)
10. *By Fire and Bayonet: Grey's West Indies Campaign of 1794* (Steve Brown)
11. *Olmütz to Torgau: Horace St Paul and the Campaigns of the Austrian Army in the Seven Years War 1758-60* (Neil Cogswell)
12. *Murat's Army: The Army of the Kingdom of Naples 1806-1815* (Digby Smith)
13. *The Veteran or 40 Years' Service in the British Army: The Scurrilous Recollections of Paymaster John Harley 47th Foot – 1798-1838* (Gareth Glover (ed.))

14	*Narrative of the Eventful Life of Thomas Jackson: Militiaman and Coldstream Sergeant, 1803-15* (Eamonn O'Keeffe (ed.))
15	*For Orange and the States: The Army of the Dutch Republic 1713-1772 Part I: Infantry* (Marc Geerdinck-Schaftenaar)
16	*Men Who Are Determined to be Free: The American Assault on Stony Point, 15 July 1779* (David C. Bonk)
17	*Next to Wellington: General Sir George Murray: The Story of a Scottish Soldier and Statesman, Wellington's Quartermaster General* (John Harding-Edgar)
18	*Between Scylla and Charybdis: The Army of Elector Friedrich August of Saxony 1733-1763 Part I: Staff and Cavalry* (Marco Pagan)
19	*The Secret Expedition: The Anglo-Russian Invasion of Holland 1799* (Geert van Uythoven)
20	*'We Are Accustomed to do our Duty': German Auxiliaries with the British Army 1793-95* (Paul Demet)
21	*With the Guards in Flanders: The Diary of Captain Roger Morris 1793-95* (Peter Harington (ed.))
22	*The British Army in Egypt 1801: An Underrated Army Comes of Age* (Carole Divall)
23	*Better is the Proud Plaid: The Clothing, Weapons, and Accoutrements of the Jacobites in the '45* (Jenn Scott)
24	*The Lilies and the Thistle: French Troops in the Jacobite '45* (Andrew Bamford)
25	*A Light Infantryman With Wellington: The Letters of Captain George Ulrich Barlow 52nd and 69th Foot 1808-15* (Gareth Glover (ed.))
26	*Swiss Regiments in the Service of France 1798-1815: Uniforms, Organisation, Campaigns* (Stephen Ede-Borrett)
27	*For Orange and the States! The Army of the Dutch Republic 1713-1772: Part II: Cavalry and Specialist Troops* (Marc Geerdinck-Schaftenaar)
28	*Fashioning Regulation, Regulating Fashion: Uniforms and Dress of the British Army 1800-1815 Volume I* (Ben Townsend)
29	*Riflemen: The History of the 5th Battalion 60th (Royal American) Regiment, 1797-1818* (Robert Griffith)
30	*The Key to Lisbon: The Third French Invasion of Portugal, 1810-11* (Kenton White)
31	*Command and Leadership: Proceedings of the 2018 Helion & Company 'From Reason to Revolution' Conference* (Andrew Bamford (ed.))
32	*Waterloo After the Glory: Hospital Sketches and Reports on the Wounded After the Battle* (Michael Crumplin and Gareth Glover)
33	*Fluxes, Fevers, and Fighting Men: War and Disease in Ancien Regime Europe 1648-1789* (Pádraig Lenihan)
34	*'They Were Good Soldiers': African-Americans Serving in the Continental Army, 1775-1783* (John U. Rees)
35	*A Redcoat in America: The Diaries of Lieutenant William Bamford, 1757-1765 and 1776* (John B. Hattendorf (ed.))
36	*Between Scylla and Charybdis: The Army of Friedrich August II of Saxony, 1733-1763: Part II: Infantry and Artillery* (Marco Pagan)
37	*Québec Under Siege: French Eye-Witness Accounts from the Campaign of 1759* (Charles A. Mayhood (ed.))
38	*King George's Hangman: Henry Hawley and the Battle of Falkirk 1746* (Jonathan D. Oates)
39	*Zweybrücken in Command: The Reichsarmee in the Campaign of 1758* (Neil Cogswell)
40	*So Bloody a Day: The 16th Light Dragoons in the Waterloo Campaign* (David J. Blackmore)
41	*Northern Tars in Southern Waters: The Russian Fleet in the Mediterranean 1806-1810*

(Vladimir Bogdanovich Bronevskiy / Darrin Boland)

42 *Royal Navy Officers of the Seven Years War: A Biographical Dictionary of Commissioned Officers 1748-1763* (Cy Harrison)

43 *All at Sea: Naval Support for the British Army During the American Revolutionary War* (John Dillon)

44 *Glory is Fleeting: New Scholarship on the Napoleonic Wars* (Andrew Bamford (ed.))

45 *Fashioning Regulation, Regulating Fashion: Uniforms and Dress of the British Army 1800-1815 Vol. II* (Ben Townsend)

46 *Revenge in the Name of Honour: The Royal Navy's Quest for Vengeance in the Single Ship Actions of the War of 1812* (Nicholas James Kaizer)

47 *They Fought With Extraordinary Bravery: The III German (Saxon) Army Corps in the Southern Netherlands 1814* (Geert van Uythoven)

48 *The Danish Army of the Napoleonic Wars 1801-1814, Organisation, Uniforms & Equipment: Volume 1: High Command, Line and Light Infantry* (David Wilson)

49 *Neither Up Nor Down: The British Army and the Flanders Campaign 1793-1895* (Phillip Ball)

50 *Guerra Fantástica: The Portuguese Army and the Seven Years War* (António Barrento)

51 *From Across the Sea: North Americans in Nelson's Navy* (Sean M. Heuvel and John A. Rodgaard)

52 *Rebellious Scots to Crush: The Military Response to the Jacobite '45* (Andrew Bamford (ed.))

53 *The Army of George II 1727-1760: The Soldiers who Forged an Empire* (Peter Brown)

54 *Wellington at Bay: The Battle of Villamuriel, 25 October 1812* (Garry David Wills)

55 *Life in the Red Coat: The British Soldier 1721-1815* (Andrew Bamford (ed.))

56 *Wellington's Favourite Engineer. John Burgoyne: Operations, Engineering, and the Making of a Field Marshal* (Mark S. Thompson)

57 *Scharnhorst: The Formative Years, 1755-1801* (Charles Edward White)

58 *At the Point of the Bayonet: The Peninsular War Battles of Arroyomolinos and Almaraz 1811-1812* (Robert Griffith)

59 *Sieges of the '45: Siege Warfare during the Jacobite Rebellion of 1745-1746* (Jonathan D. Oates)

60 *Austrian Cavalry of the Revolutionary and Napoleonic Wars, 1792–1815* (Enrico Acerbi, András K. Molnár)

61 *The Danish Army of the Napoleonic Wars 1801-1814, Organisation, Uniforms & Equipment: Volume 2: Cavalry and Artillery* (David Wilson)

62 *Napoleon's Stolen Army: How the Royal Navy Rescued a Spanish Army in the Baltic* (John Marsden)

63 *Crisis at the Chesapeake: The Royal Navy and the Struggle for America 1775-1783* (Quintin Barry)

64 *Bullocks, Grain, and Good Madeira: The Maratha and Jat Campaigns 1803-1806 and the emergence of the Indian Army* (Joshua Provan)

65 *Sir James McGrigor: The Adventurous Life of Wellington's Chief Medical Officer* (Tom Scotland)

66 *Fashioning Regulation, Regulating Fashion: Uniforms and Dress of the British Army 1800-1815 Volume I* (Ben Townsend) (paperback edition)

67 *Fashioning Regulation, Regulating Fashion: Uniforms and Dress of the British Army 1800-1815 Volume II* (Ben Townsend) (paperback edition)

68 *The Secret Expedition: The Anglo-Russian Invasion of Holland 1799* (Geert van Uythoven) (paperback edition)

69 *The Sea is My Element: The Eventful Life of Admiral Sir Pulteney Malcolm 1768-1838* (Paul Martinovich)

70	*The Sword and the Spirit: Proceedings of the first 'War & Peace in the Age of Napoleon' Conference* (Zack White (ed.))
71	*Lobositz to Leuthen: Horace St Paul and the Campaigns of the Austrian Army in the Seven Years War 1756-57* (Neil Cogswell) (paperback edition)
72	*For God and King. A History of the Damas Legion 1793-1798: A Case Study of the Military Emigration during the French Revolution* (Hughes de Bazouges and Alistair Nichols)
73	*'Their Infantry and Guns Will Astonish You': The Army of Hindustan and European Mercenaries in Maratha service 1780-1803* (Andy Copestake)
74	*Like A Brazen Wall: The Battle of Minden, 1759, and its Place in the Seven Years War* (Ewan Carmichael)
75	*Wellington and the Lines of Torres Vedras: The Defence of Lisbon during the Peninsular War* (Mark Thompson)
76	*French Light Infantry 1784-1815: From the Chasseurs of Louis XVI to Napoleon's Grande Armée* (Terry Crowdy)
77	*Riflemen: The History of the 5th Battalion 60th (Royal American) Regiment, 1797-1818* (Robert Griffith) (paperback edition)
78	*Hastenbeck 1757: The French Army and the Opening Campaign of the Seven Years War* (Olivier Lapray)
79	*Napoleonic French Military Uniforms: As Depicted by Horace and Carle Vernet and Eugène Lami* (Guy Dempsey (trans. and ed.))
80	*These Distinguished Corps: British Grenadier and Light Infantry Battalions in the American Revolution* (Don N. Hagist)
81	*Rebellion, Invasion, and Occupation: The British Army in Ireland, 1793 -1815* (Wayne Stack)
82	*You Have to Die in Piedmont! The Battle of Assietta, 19 July 1747. The War of the Austrian Succession in the Alps* (Giovanni Cerino Badone)
83	*A Very Fine Regiment: the 47th Foot in the American War of Independence, 1773–1783* (Paul Knight)
84	*By Fire and Bayonet: Grey's West Indies Campaign of 1794* (Steve Brown) (paperback edition)
85	*No Want of Courage: The British Army in Flanders, 1793-1795* (R.N.W. Thomas)
86	*Far Distant Ships: The Royal Navy and the Blockade of Brest 1793-1815* (Quintin Barry) (paperback edition)
87	*Armies and Enemies of Napoleon 1789-1815: Proceedings of the 2021 Helion and Company 'From Reason to Revolution' Conference* (Robert Griffith (ed.))
88	*The Battle of Rossbach 1757: New Perspectives on the Battle and Campaign* (Alexander Querengässer (ed.))
89	*Waterloo After the Glory: Hospital Sketches and Reports on the Wounded After the Battle* (Michael Crumplin and Gareth Glover) (paperback edition)
90	*From Ushant to Gibraltar: The Channel Fleet 1778-1783* (Quintin Barry)
91	*'The Soldiers are Dressed in Red': The Quiberon Expedition of 1795 and the Counter-Revolution in Brittany* (Alistair Nichols)
92	*The Army of the Kingdom of Italy 1805-1814: Uniforms, Organisation, Campaigns* (Stephen Ede-Borrett)
93	*The Ottoman Army of the Napoleonic Wars 1798-1815: A Struggle for Survival from Egypt to the Balkans* (Bruno Mugnai)
94	*The Changing Face of Old Regime Warfare: Essays in Honour of Christopher Duffy* (Alexander S. Burns (ed.))
94	*The Changing Face of Old Regime Warfare: Essays in Honour of Christopher Duffy* (Alexander S. Burns (ed.)
95	*The Danish Army of the Napoleonic Wars 1801-1814, Organisation, Uniforms & Equipment: Volume 3: Norwegian Troops and Militia* (David Wilson)
96	*1805 – Tsar Alexander's First War with Napoleon* (Alexander Ivanovich Mikhailovsky-Danilevsky, trans. Peter G.A. Phillips)

97	*'More Furies then Men': The Irish Brigade in the service of France 1690-1792* (Pierre-Louis Coudray)
98	*'We Are Accustomed to do our Duty': German Auxiliaries with the British Army 1793-95* (Paul Demet) (paperback edition)
99	*Ladies, Wives and Women: British Army Wives in the Revolutionary and Napoleonic Wars 1793-1815* (David Clammer)
100	*The Garde Nationale 1789-1815: France's Forgotten Armed Forces* (Pierre-Baptiste Guillemot)
101	*Confronting Napoleon: Levin von Bennigsen's Memoir of the Campaign in Poland, 1806-1807, Volume I Pultusk to Eylau* (Alexander Mikaberidze and Paul Strietelmeier (trans. and ed.))
102	*Olmütz to Torgau: Horace St Paul and the Campaigns of the Austrian Army in the Seven Years War 1758-60* (Neil Cogswell) (paperback edition)
103	*Fit to Command: British Regimental Leadership in the Revolutionary & Napoleonic Wars* (Steve Brown)
104	*Wellington's Unsung Heroes: The Fifth Division in the Peninsular War, 1810-1814* (Carole Divall)
105	*1806-1807 – Tsar Alexander's Second War with Napoleon* (Alexander Ivanovich Mikhailovsky-Danilevsky, trans. Peter G.A. Phillips)
106	*The Pattern: The 33rd Regiment in the American Revolution, 1770-1783* (Robbie MacNiven)
107	*To Conquer and to Keep: Suchet and the War for Eastern Spain, 1809-1814, Volume 1 1809-1811* (Yuhan Kim)
108	*To Conquer and to Keep: Suchet and the War for Eastern Spain, 1809-1814, Volume 2 1811-1814* (Yuhan Kim)
109	*The Tagus Campaign of 1809: An Alliance in Jeopardy* (John Marsden)
110	*The War of the Bavarian Succession, 1778-1779: Prussian Military Power in Decline?* (Alexander Querengässer)
111	*Anson: Naval Commander and Statesman* (Anthony Bruce)
112	*Atlas of the Battles and Campaigns of the American Revolution, 1775-1783* (David Bonk and George Anderson)
113	*A Fine Corps and will Serve Faithfully: The Swiss Regiment de Roll in the British Army 1794-1816* (Alistair Nichols)
114	*Next to Wellington: General Sir George Murray: The Story of a Scottish Soldier and Statesman, Wellington's Quartermaster General* (John Harding-Edgar) (paperback edition)
115	*King George's Army: British Regiments and the Men who Led Them 1793-1815, Volume 1* (Steve Brown)
116	*Great Britain and the Defence of the Low Countries, 1744-1748: Armies, Politics and Diplomacy* (Alastair Massie)
117	*Kesselsdorf 1745: Decision in the Fight for Silesia* (Alexander Querengässer)
118	*The Key to Lisbon: The Third French Invasion of Portugal, 1810-11* (Kenton White) (paperback edition)
119	*Not So Easy, Lads: Wearing the Red Coat 1786–1797* (Vivien Roworth)